ALSO BY SEAMUS HEANEY

POETRY

Death of a Naturalist
Door into the Dark
Wintering Out
North
Field Work
Poems 1965–1975
Sweeney Astray: A Version from the Irish
Station Island
The Haw Lantern
Selected Poems 1966–1987
Seeing Things
Sweeney's Flight (*with photographs by Rachel Giese*)
The Spirit Level
Opened Ground: Selected Poems 1966–1996
Beowulf
Diary of One Who Vanished
Electric Light

CRITICISM

Preoccupations: Selected Prose 1968–1978
The Government of the Tongue
The Redress of Poetry

PLAY

The Cure at Troy: A Version of
Sophocles' *Philoctetes*

FINDERS KEEPERS

SELECTED PROSE 1971–2001

FINDERS

KEEPERS

SELECTED

PROSE

1971-2001

SEAMUS

HEANEY

FARRAR STRAUS GIROUX

Farrar, Straus and Giroux

19 Union Square West, New York 10003

Copyright © 2002 by Seamus Heaney

Printed in the United States of America

Originally published in 2002 by Faber and Faber Ltd., Great Britain

Published in the United States by Farrar, Straus and Giroux

First American edition, 2002

Acknowledgements appear on pages 451–52.

ISBN: 0-374-15496-1

Library of Congress Control Number: 2002101044

Designed by Dorothy Schmiderer Baker

www.fsgbooks.com

1   3   5   7   9   10   8   6   4   2

for Dennis O'Driscoll and Julie O'Callaghan

CONTENTS

Foreword   ix

I

Mossbawn   3
from Feeling into Words   15
Learning from Eliot   28
Belfast   42
Cessation 1994   48
Something to Write Home About   51
Earning a Rhyme   63
On Poetry and Professing   71

II

Englands of the Mind   81
Yeats as an Example?   103
Place and Displacement: Recent Poetry
    from Northern Ireland   122
The Placeless Heaven: Another Look at Kavanagh   146
The Main of Light   158
Atlas of Civilization   167
from Envies and Identifications: Dante and
    the Modern Poet   184
from The Government of the Tongue   197

from Sounding Auden   209

Lowell's Command   220

from The Indefatigable Hoof-Taps: Sylvia Plath   238

The Place of Writing   253

    1. On W. B. Yeats and Thoor Ballylee 253

    2. On Thomas Kinsella   262

Edwin Muir   269

from The Redress of Poetry   281

from Extending the Alphabet: Christopher Marlowe   286

John Clare's Prog   300

A Torchlight Procession of One: Hugh MacDiarmid   319

from Dylan the Durable? On Dylan Thomas   339

Joy or Night: Last Things in the Poetry of W. B. Yeats
    and Philip Larkin   343

from Counting to a Hundred: Elizabeth Bishop   361

Burns's Art Speech   378

Through-Other Places, Through-Other Times:
    The Irish Poet and Britain   396

III

Stevie Smith's *Collected Poems*   419

Joyce's Poetry   422

Italo Calvino's *Mr Palomar*   425

Paul Muldoon's *The Annals of Chile*   429

Norman MacCaig, 1910–1996   433

Joseph Brodsky, 1940–1996   437

On Ted Hughes's 'Littleblood'   441

Secular and Millennial Milosz   444

Acknowledgements   451

FOREWORD

This book reprints work extracted from *Preoccupations* (1980), *The Government of the Tongue* (1988), *The Redress of Poetry* (1995) and *The Place of Writing* (Scholars Press, 1989), a volume containing the Richard Ellmann Lectures in Modern Literature given at Emory University in 1988. Also included are several pieces not previously collected in volume form, ranging from short newspaper articles to more extended lectures and contributions to books. A number of these were done since 1995, but I have also taken the opportunity to include material that might have appeared, had the circumstances been different, in earlier collections. 'Learning from Eliot' and 'Edwin Muir', for example, date from 1988–1989, the year *The Government of the Tongue* was published, but they still did not appear in *The Redress of Poetry*, because that book was made up solely of lectures given when I was Professor of Poetry at Oxford. On the other hand, 'Place and Displacement' (1984) has for years enjoyed a separate life as a pamphlet, but now seems to belong in this more general reckoning. Revisions have been made in almost all of the previously uncollected work; in pieces reprinted from the earlier collections, abridgements and a few revisions have also been made.

On the playground the phrase 'finders keepers' probably still expresses glee and stakes a claim, so in that sense it can apply as well to the experience of a reader of poetry: the first encounter with work that excites and connects will induce in the reader a similar urge to celebrate and take possession of it. My title is therefore an acknowledgement that many of these essays have their origins in such moments. Mostly they are appreciations, reports on the good of poetry itself, attempts to 'keep' it and to say why it is worth keeping. They are also, of course, testimonies to the fact that poets themselves are finders and keepers, that their vocation is to look after art and life by being discoverers and custodians of the unlooked for.

The book has the same shape as *Preoccupations*. There is an autobiographical or topical slant to the first section; in the second, the work has a more specifically literary focus and deals mostly with the achievement of individual authors; and the third section is a kind of kite-tail, a stringing out of miscellaneous pieces that for all their brevity retain, I hope, a certain interest.

Some words I wrote in the Foreword to *Preoccupations* still apply to what is going on in the following pages: 'The essays selected here are held together by searches for answers to central preoccupying questions: How should a poet properly live and write? What is his relationship to be to his own voice, his own place, his literary heritage and his contemporary world?'

I have to thank my editor at Faber, Paul Keegan, for proposing the idea of the book and for his informed interest in what it might contain. Obviously, the non-appearance here of previously collected work doesn't mean that it has been repudiated. I found it difficult, for example, to decide between the early, comparatively relaxed 'Yeats as an Example?' and a later, more soberly considered 'Introduction' that appeared first in *The Field Day Anthology of Irish Writing* (1991) and was reprinted in Faber's paperback selection of Yeats (2000). The contents list could have been longer, could have been shorter. As it stands, the book records some of the ways one poet answered poetry's call to seek beyond yet stay on course, to open up yet hold the line.

S.H., January 2002

I

Mossbawn

I would begin with the Greek word *omphalos*, meaning the navel, and hence the stone that marked the centre of the world, and repeat it, *omphalos, omphalos, omphalos*, until its blunt and falling music becomes the music of somebody pumping water at the pump outside our back door. It is County Derry in the early 1940s. The American bombers groan towards the aerodrome at Toomebridge, the American troops manoeuvre in the fields along the road, but all of that great historical action does not disturb the rhythms of the yard. There the pump stands, a slender, iron idol, snouted, helmeted, dressed down with a sweeping handle, painted a dark green and set on a concrete plinth, marking the centre of another world. Five households drew water from it. Women came and went, came rattling between empty enamel buckets, went evenly away, weighed down by silent water. The horses came home to it in those first lengthening evenings of spring, and in a single draught emptied one bucket and then another as the man pumped and pumped, the plunger slugging up and down, *omphalos, omphalos, omphalos*.

I do not know what age I was when I got lost in the pea-drills in a field behind the house, but it is a half-dream to me, and I've heard about it so often that I may even be imagining it. Yet, by now, I have imagined it so long and so often that I know what it was like: a green web, a caul of veined light, a tangle of rods and pods, stalks and tendrils, full of assuaging earth and leaf smell, a sunlit lair. I'm sitting as if just wakened from a winter sleep and gradually become aware of voices, coming closer, calling my name, and for no reason at all I have begun to weep.

All children want to crouch in their secret nests. I loved the fork of a beech tree at the head of our lane, the close thicket of a boxwood hedge in the front of the house, the soft, collapsing pile of hay in a back corner of the byre; but especially I spent time in the throat of an old willow tree at the end of the farmyard. It was a hollow tree, with gnarled, spreading roots, a soft, perishing bark and a pithy inside. Its mouth was like the fat and solid opening in a horse's collar, and, once you squeezed in through it, you were at the heart of a different life, looking out on the familiar yard as if it were suddenly behind a pane of strangeness. Above your head, the living tree flourished and breathed, you shouldered the slightly vibrant bole, and if you put your forehead to the rough pith you felt the whole lithe and whispering crown of willow moving in the sky above you. In that tight cleft, you sensed the embrace of light and branches, you were a little Atlas shouldering it all, a little Cerunnos pivoting a world of antlers.

The world grew. Mossbawn, the first place, widened. There was what we called the Sandy Loaning, a sanded pathway between old hedges leading in off the road, first among fields and then through a small bog, to a remote farmhouse. It was a silky, fragrant world there, and for the first few hundred yards you were safe enough. The sides of the lane were banks of earth topped with broom and ferns, quilted with moss and primroses. Behind the broom, in the rich grass, cattle munched reassuringly. Rabbits occasionally broke cover and ran ahead of you in a flurry of dry sand. There were wrens and goldfinches. But gradually those lush and definite fields gave way to scraggy marshland. Birch trees stood up to their pale shins in swamps. The ferns thickened above you. Scuffles in old leaves made you nervous and always you dared yourself to pass the badger's sett, a wound of fresh mould in an overgrown ditch where the old brock had gone to earth. Around that badger's hole there hung a field of dangerous force. This was the realm of bogeys. We'd heard about a mystery man who haunted the fringes of the bog here, we talked about mankeepers and mosscheepers, creatures uncatalogued by any naturalist, but none the less real for that. What was a mosscheeper, anyway, if not the soft, malicious sound the word itself made, a siren of collapsing sibilants coaxing you out towards bog pools lidded with innocent grass, quicksands and quagmires? They were all there and spreading

out over a low, birch-screened apron of land towards the shores of
Lough Beg.

That was the moss, forbidden ground. Two families lived at the
heart of it, and a recluse, called Tom Tipping, whom we never saw,
but in the morning on the road to school we watched his smoke
rising from a clump of trees, and spoke his name between us until
it was synonymous with mystery man, with unexpected scuttlings
in the hedge, with footsteps slushing through long grass.

To this day, green wet corners, flooded wastes, soft rushy bot-
toms, any place with the invitation of watery ground and tundra
vegetation, even glimpsed from a car or a train, possess an immediate and deeply peaceful attraction. It is as if I am betrothed to
them, and I believe my betrothal happened one summer evening,
thirty years ago, when another boy and myself stripped to the
white country skin and bathed in a moss-hole, treading the liver-
thick mud, unsettling a smoky muck off the bottom and coming
out smeared and weedy and darkened. We dressed again and went
home in our wet clothes, smelling of the ground and the standing
pool, somehow initiated.

Beyond the moss spread the narrow reaches of Lough Beg, and
in the centre of Lough Beg lay Church Island, a spire rising out of
its yew trees, a local mecca. St Patrick, they said, had fasted and
prayed there fifteen hundred years before. The old graveyard was
shoulder-high with meadowsweet and cow parsley, overhung with
thick, unmolested yew trees, and, somehow, those yews fetched me
away to Agincourt and Crécy, where the English archers' bows, I
knew, had been made of yew also. All I could ever manage for my
bows were tapering shoots of ash or willow from a hedge along the
stackyard, but even so, to have cut a bough from that silent compound on Church Island would have been a violation too treacherous to contemplate.

If Lough Beg marked one limit of the imagination's nesting
ground, Slieve Gallon marked another. Slieve Gallon is a small
mountain that lies in the opposite direction, taking the eye out
over grazing and ploughed ground and the distant woods of Moyola Park, out over Grove Hill and Back Park and Castledawson.
This side of the country was the peopled, communal side, the land

of haycock and corn-stook, of fence and gate, milk-cans at the end of lanes and auction notices on gate pillars. Dogs barked from farm to farm. Sheds gaped at the roadside, bulging with fodder. Behind and across it went the railway, and the noise that hangs over it constantly is the heavy shunting of an engine at Castledawson station.

I have a sense of air, of lift and light, when this comes back to me. Light dancing off the shallows of the River Moyola, shifting in eddies on the glaucous whirlpool. Light changing on the mountain itself, that stood like a barometer of moods, now blue and hazy, now green and close up. Light above the spires, away at Magherafelt. Light frothing among the bluebells on Grove Hill. And the lift of the air is resonant, too, with vigorous musics. A summer evening carries the fervent and melancholy strain of hymn-singing from a gospel hall among the fields, and the hawthorn blooms and the soft white patens of the elderflower hang dolorous in the hedges. Or the rattle of Orange drums from Aughrim Hill sets the heart alert and watchful as a hare.

For if this was the country of community, it was also the realm of division. Like the rabbit pads that loop across grazing, and tunnel the soft growths under ripening corn, the lines of sectarian antagonism and affiliation followed the boundaries of the land. In the names of its fields and townlands, in their mixture of Scots and Irish and English etymologies, this side of the country was redolent of the histories of its owners. Broagh, the Long Rigs, Bell's Hill; Brian's Field, the Round Meadow, the Demesne; each name was a kind of love made to each acre. And saying the names like this distances the places, turns them into what Wordsworth once called a prospect of the mind. They lie deep, like some script indelibly written into the nervous system.

I always remember the pleasure I had in digging the black earth in our garden and finding, a foot below the surface, a pale seam of sand. I remember, too, men coming to sink the shaft of the pump and digging through that seam of sand down into the bronze riches of the gravel that soon began to puddle with the spring water. That pump marked an original descent into earth, sand, gravel, water. It centred and staked the imagination, made its foundation the foundation of the *omphalos* itself. So I find it alto-

gether appropriate that an old superstition ratifies this hankering
for the underground side of things. It is a superstition associated
with the Heaney name. In Gaelic times, the family were involved
with ecclesiastical affairs in the diocese of Derry, and had some
kind of rights to the stewardship of a monastic site at Banagher in
the north of the county. There is a St Muredach O'Heney associated with the old church at Banagher; and there is also a belief
that sand lifted from the ground at Banagher has beneficent, even
magical, properties—if it is lifted from the site by one of the
Heaney family name. Throw sand that a Heaney has lifted after a
man going into court, and he will win his case. Throw it after your
team as they go out on the pitch, and they will win the game.

READING

When I was learning to read, towards the end of 1945, the most
important books in the house were the ration books—the pink
clothes coupons and the green 'points' for sweets and groceries.
There wasn't much reading done apart from the deaths column of
the *Irish Weekly* and the auctions page of the *Northern Constitu-
tion*. 'I am instructed by the representatives of the late John James
Halferty, Drumanee . . .' My father lay on the sofa and rehearsed
the acres, roods and perches of arable and meadow land in a formal tone and with a certain enlargement of the spirit.

On a shelf, behind a screen and too high to be reached anyhow,
there were four or five mouldering volumes that may have belonged to my Aunt Susan from her days in Orange's Academy, but
they remained closed books to me. The first glimpse I have of myself reading on my own is one of those orphaned memories, a moment without context that will always stay with me. It is a book
from the school library—a padlocked box that was opened more or
less as a favour—involving explorers in cork helmets and 'savages',
with illustrations of war canoes on a jungle river. The oil lamp is
lit and a neighbour called Hugh Bates is interrupting me. 'Boys,
oh, boys! This Seamus fellow is a great scholar. What book are you
in now, son?' And my father is likely wringing what he can from

the moment with 'He's as bad as Pat McGuckin this minute.' Pat McGuckin was a notorious bachelor farmer—a cousin of ours— who was said to burn his scone like King Alfred every time he lifted a book. Years later, when *Death of a Naturalist* was published, the greatest commendation at home was 'Lord knows Pat would fairly have enjoyed this.'

Of course, there were always religious magazines like *The Far East* and the *Messenger*—Pudsy Ryan in the children's corner of the former was the grown-ups' idea of a side-splitting turn, but even then I found his misspellings a bit heavy-handed. Far better were the technicolor splendours of Korky the Cat and Big Eggo in *The Dandy* and *The Beano*. The front pages of these comics opened like magic casements on Desperate Dan, Lord Snooty, Hungry Horace, Keyhole Kate, Julius Sneezer and Jimmy and his Magic Patch and probably constituted my first sense of the invitations of fiction. They were passed round at school, usually fairly tattered, but every now and again my mother brought a new one from Castledawson, without a fold in it, its primary colours blazing with excitements to come. Occasionally, also, an American comic— all colour from beginning to end—arrived from the American airbase nearby, with Li'l Abner, Ferdinand and Blondie speaking a language that even Pat McGuckin did not know.

There was a resistance to buying new comics in our house, not out of any educational nicety, but because of a combination of two attitudes: that they were a catch-penny and that somehow they were the thin end of the wedge, that if you let them into the house the next step was *The Empire News*, *Thompson's Weekly*, *Tit-Bits* and *The News of the World*. Nevertheless, I ended up persuading my mother to place a regular order for *The Champion*, a higher-class comic altogether, featuring a Biggles-rides-again figure called Rockfist Rogan and Ginger Nutt ('the boy who takes the *bis-cake*', in South Derry parlance) and Colwyn Dane, the sleuth. With *The Champion* I entered the barter market for *The Rover*, *The Hotspur*, *The Wizard* and any other pulp the presses of old England could deliver. I skimmed through all those 'ain'ts' and 'cors' and 'yoicks' and 'blimeys', and skimmed away contented.

So what chance had Kitty the Hare against all that? *Our Boys* appeared regularly, a cultural antidote with official home backing, healthy as a Christian Brother on a winter morning, the first step towards *Ireland's Own*. Cultural debilitations! I preferred the japes of Ginger Nutt, the wheezes of Smith of the Lower Fourth, the swish of gowns, the mortarboard and the head's study to the homely toils of Murphy among the birettas. It would take Joyce's *Portrait of the Artist as a Young Man* and Kavanagh's *The Great Hunger* to get over that surrender.

My first literary *frisson*, however, came on home ground. There was an Irish history lesson at school which was in reality a reading of myths and legends. A textbook with large type and heavy Celticized illustrations dealt with the matter of Ireland from the Tuatha Dé Danaan to the Norman Invasion. I can still see Brian Boru with his sword held like a cross reviewing the troops at Clontarf. But the real imaginative mark was made with a story of the Dagda, a dream of harp music and light, confronting and defeating Balor of the Evil Eye on the dark fortress of Tory Island. Cuchulain and Ferdia also sank deep, those images of wounds bathed on the green rushes and armour clattering in the ford.

Yet all of that yielded to the melodrama of Blind Pew and Billy Bones, Long John and Ben Gunn. *Treasure Island* we read at school also, and it was a prelude to the first book I remember owning and cherishing: there it was on the table one Christmas morning, Robert Louis Stevenson's *Kidnapped*. I was a Jacobite for life after that day. Instinctively I knew that the world of the penal rock and the redcoats—that oleograph to the faith of our fathers—was implicit in the scenery of that story. To this day, my heart lifts to the first sentence of it: 'I will begin the story of my adventures with a certain morning in the month of June, the year of grace 1751, when I took the key for the last time out of the door of my father's house . . .'

As a boarder at St Columb's College, I did the Maurice Walsh circuit—*Blackcock's Feather* remains with me as an atmosphere, a sense of bogs and woods—but again it was a course book that stuck its imagery deepest. When I read in *Lorna Doone* how John Ridd stripped the muscle off Carver Doone's arm like a string of pith off an orange, I was well on the road to epiphanies. Not that I didn't stray into the imperial realms of Biggles or the baloney of the William stories. But it is only those books with a touch of poetry in them that I can remember—all coming to a head when, in my last summer holiday from school, I sat up all night to finish Thomas Hardy's *Return of the Native.*

I missed Pooh Bear. I can't remember owning a selection of Grimm or Andersen. I read *Alice in Wonderland* at the university. But what odds? Didn't Vinny Hunter keep me in wonderland with his stories of Tarzan:

'When he jumps down off a tree
Tarzan shakes the world.'
So Vinny Hunter would tell me
On the road to the school.

I had forgotten for years
Words so seismic and plain
That come back like rocked waters,
Possible again.

RHYMES

A few months ago I remembered a rhyme that we used to chant on the way to school. I know now that it is about initiation, but as I trailed along the Lagan's Road on my way to Anahorish School it was something that was good for a laugh:

'Are your praties dry
And are they fit for digging?'
'Put in your spade and try,'
Says Dirty-Faced McGuigan.

I suppose I must have been about eight or nine years old when those lines stuck in my memory. They constitute a kind of poetry, not very respectable perhaps, but very much alive on the lips of

that group of schoolboys, or 'scholars', as the older people were inclined to call us. McGuigan was probably related to a stern old
character called Ned McGuigan who travelled the roads with a
menacing blackthorn stick. He came from a district called Bally-
macquigan—the Quigan, for short—and he turned up in another
rhyme:

> Neddy McGuigan,
> He pissed in the Quigan;
> The Quigan was hot
> So he pissed in the pot;
> The pot was too high
> So he pissed in the sky;
> Hell to your soul, Neddy McGuigan,
> For pissing so high.

And there were other chants, scurrilous and sectarian, that we
used to fling at one another:

> Up the long ladder and down the short rope
> To hell with King Billy and God bless the Pope.

To which the answer was:

> Splitter splatter holy water
> Scatter the Paypishes every one
> If that won't do
> We'll cut them in two
> And give them a touch of the
> Red, white and blue.

To which the answer was:

> Red, white and blue
> Should be torn up in two
> And sent to the devil
> At half-past two.

> Green, white and yellow
> Is a decent fellow.

Another one which was completely nonsensical still pleases me:

One fine October's morning September last July
The moon lay thick upon the ground, the mud shone in the sky.
I stepped into a tramcar to take me across the sea,
I asked the conductor to punch my ticket and he punched my
    eye for me.

I fell in love with an Irish girl, she sang me an Irish dance,
She lived in Tipperary, just a few miles out of France.
Her house it was a round one, the front was at the back,
It stood alone between two more and it was whitewashed black.

We weren't forced to get these lines by heart. They just seemed to spring in our mind and trip off the tongue spontaneously so that our parents would say, 'If it was your prayers, you wouldn't learn them as fast.'

There were other poems, of course, that we were forced to learn by heart. I am amazed to realize that at the age of eleven I was spouting great passages of Byron and Keats by rote until the zinc roof of the Nissen hut that served for our schoolhouse (the previous school had been cleared during the war to make room for an aerodrome) rang to the half-understood magnificence of:

> There was a sound of revelry by night
> And Belgium's capital had gathered then
> Her beauty and her chivalry, and bright
> The lamps shone o'er fair women and brave men.
> A thousand hearts beat happily; and when
> The music rose with its voluptuous swell . . .

I also knew the whole of Keats's ode 'To Autumn', but the only line that was luminous then was 'To bend with apples the mossed cottage trees', because my uncle had a small orchard where the old apple trees were sleeved in a soft green moss. And I had a vague satisfaction from 'the small gnats mourn/Among the river sallows', which would have been complete if it had been 'midges' mourning among the 'sallies'.

The literary language, the civilized utterance from the classic canon of English poetry, was a kind of force-feeding. It did not delight us by reflecting our experience; it did not re-echo our own speech in formal and surprising arrangements. Poetry lessons, in fact, were rather like catechism lessons: official inculcations of hallowed formulae that were somehow expected to stand us in good stead in the adult life that stretched out ahead. Both lessons did indeed introduce us to the gorgeousness of the polysyllable, and as far as we were concerned there was little to choose between the music with 'its voluptuous swell' and the 'solemnization of marriage within forbidden degrees of consanguinity'. In each case we were overawed by the dimensions of the sound.

There was a third category of verse which I encountered at this time, halfway between the roadside rhymes and the school poetry (or 'poertry'): a form known to us as 'the recitation'. When relations visited or a children's party was held at home, I would be called upon to recite. Sometimes it would be an Irish patriotic ballad:

At length, brave Michael Dwyer, you and your trusty men
Were hunted o'er the mountain and tracked into the glen.
Sleep not, but watch and listen, keep ready blade and ball,
For the soldiers know you hide this night in the Glen of Wild
    Imall.

Sometimes, a western narrative by Robert Service:

A bunch of the boys were whooping it up in the Malamute
    Saloon.
The kid that handles the music-box was hitting a ragtime tune.
Back of the bar at a solo game sat Dangerous Dan McGrew
And watching his luck was his light o' love, the lady that's
    known as Lou.

While this kind of stuff did not possess the lure of forbidden words like 'piss' and 'hell to your soul', it was not encumbered by the solemn incomprehensibility of Byron and Keats. It gave verse, however humble, a place in the life of the home, made it one of the ordinary rituals of life.

from Feeling into Words

I intend to retrace some paths into what William Wordsworth called in *The Prelude* 'the hiding places':

> The hiding places of my power
> Seem open; I approach, and then they close;
> I see by glimpses now; when age comes on,
> May scarcely see at all, and I would give,
> While yet we may, as far as words can give,
> A substance and a life to what I feel:
> I would enshrine the spirit of the past
> For future restoration.

Implicit in these lines is a view of poetry which I think is implicit in the few poems I have written that give me any right to speak: poetry as divination, poetry as revelation of the self to the self, as restoration of the culture to itself; poems as elements of continuity, with the aura and authenticity of archaeological finds, where the buried shard has an importance that is not diminished by the importance of the buried city; poetry as a dig, a dig for finds that end up being plants.

'Digging', in fact, was the name of the first poem I wrote where I thought my feelings had got into words, or to put it more accurately, where I thought my *feel* had got into words. Its rhythms and noises still please me, although there are a couple of lines in it that have more of the theatricality of the gunslinger than the self-absorption of the digger. I wrote it in the summer of 1964, almost two years after I had begun to 'dabble in verses'. This was the first place where I felt I had done more than make an arrangement of words: I felt that I had let down a shaft into real life. The facts and surfaces of the thing were true, but more important, the excitement that came from naming them gave me a kind of insouciance and a kind of confidence. I didn't care who thought what about it: somehow, it had surprised me by coming out with a stance and an idea that I would stand over:

> The cold smell of potato mould, the squelch and slap
> Of soggy peat, the curt cuts of an edge
> Through living roots awaken in my head.
> But I've no spade to follow men like them.
>
> Between my finger and my thumb
> The squat pen rests.
> I'll dig with it.

As I say, I wrote it down years ago; yet perhaps I should say that I dug it up, because I have come to realize that it was laid down in me years before that even. The pen/spade analogy was the simple heart of the matter and *that* was simply a matter of almost proverbial common sense. On the road to and from school, people used to ask you what class you were in and how many slaps you'd got that day and invariably they ended up with an exhortation to keep studying because 'learning's easy carried' and 'the pen's lighter than the spade.' And the poem does no more than allow that bud of wisdom to exfoliate, although the significant point in this context is that at the time of writing I was not aware of the proverbial structure at the back of my mind. Nor was I aware that the poem was an enactment of yet another digging metaphor that came back to me years later. This was the rhyme we used to chant on the road to school, though, as I have said before, we were not fully aware of what we were dealing with:

> 'Are your praties dry
> And are they fit for digging?'
> 'Put in your spade and try,'
> Says Dirty-Faced McGuigan.

Here digging becomes a sexual metaphor, an emblem of initiation, like putting your hand into the bush or robbing the nest, one of the various natural analogies for uncovering and touching the hidden thing. I now believe that the 'Digging' poem had for me the force of an initiation: the confidence I mentioned arose from a sense that perhaps I could do this poetry thing too, and having experienced the excitement and release of it once, I was doomed to look for it again and again.

I don't want to overload 'Digging' with too much significance. It is a big coarse-grained navvy of a poem, but it is interesting as an example—and not just as an example of what one reviewer called 'mud-caked fingers in Russell Square', for I don't think that the subject-matter has any particular virtue in itself—it is interesting as an example of what we call 'finding a voice'.

Finding a voice means that you can get your own feeling into your own words and that your words have the feel of you about them; and I believe that it may not even be a metaphor, for a poetic voice is probably very intimately connected with the poet's natural voice, the voice that he hears as the ideal speaker of the lines he is making up.

How, then, do you find it? In practice, you hear it coming from somebody else; you hear something in another writer's sounds that flows in through your ear and enters the echo chamber of your head and delights your whole nervous system in such a way that your reaction will be, 'Ah, I wish I had said that, in that particular way.' This other writer, in fact, has spoken something essential to you, something you recognize instinctively as a true sounding of aspects of yourself and your experience. And your first steps as a writer will be to imitate, consciously or unconsciously, those sounds that flowed in, that in-fluence.

One of the writers who influenced me in this way was Gerard Manley Hopkins. The result of reading Hopkins at school was the desire to write, and when I first put pen to paper at university, what flowed out was what had flowed in, the bumpy alliterating music, the reporting sounds and ricocheting consonants typical of Hopkins's verse. I remember lines from a piece called 'October Thought' in which some frail bucolic images foundered under the chain-mail of the pastiche:

Starling thatch-watches, and sudden swallow
Straight breaks to mud-nest, home-rest rafter
Up past dry dust-drunk cobwebs, like laughter
Ghosting the roof of bog-oak, turf-sod and rods of willow . . .

and then there was 'heaven-hue, plum-blue and gorse-pricked with gold' and 'a trickling tinkle of bells well in the fold'.

Looking back on it, I believe there was a connection, not obvious at the time but, on reflection, real enough, between the heavily accented consonantal noise of Hopkins's poetic voice and the peculiar regional characteristics of a Northern Ireland accent. The late W. R. Rodgers, another poet much lured by alliteration, said in his poem 'The Character of Ireland' that the people from his (and my) part of the world were

> an abrupt people
> Who like the spiky consonants in speech
> And think the soft ones cissy; who dig
> The *k* and *t* in orchestra, detect sin
> In sinfonia, get a kick out of
> Tin-cans, fricatives, fornication, staccato talk,
> Anything that gives or takes attack
> Like Micks, Tagues, tinkers' gets, Vatican.

It is true that the Ulster accent is generally a staccato consonantal one. Our tongue strikes the tangent of the consonant rather more than it rolls the circle of the vowel—Rodgers also spoke of 'the round gift of the gab in southern mouths'. It is energetic, angular, hard-edged, and it may be because of this affinity between my first accent and Hopkins's oddity that those first verses turned out as they did.

I couldn't say, of course, that I had found a voice but I had found a game. I knew the thing was only wordplay, and I hadn't even the guts to put my name to it. I called myself *Incertus*, uncertain, a shy soul fretting and all that. I was in love with words themselves, but had no sense of a poem as a whole structure and no experience of how the successful achievement of a poem could be a stepping-stone in your life. Those verses were what we might call 'trial-pieces', little stiff inept designs in imitation of the master's fluent interlacing patterns, heavy-handed clues to the whole craft.

I was getting my first sense of crafting words, and for one reason or another words as bearers of history and mystery began to invite me. Maybe it began very early when my mother used to recite lists of affixes and suffixes, and Latin roots, with their English meanings, rhymes that formed part of her schooling in the early part of the century. Maybe it began with the exotic listing on the wireless dial: Stuttgart, Leipzig, Oslo, Hilversum. Maybe it was stirred by the beautiful sprung rhythms of the old BBC weather forecast: Dogger, Rockall, Malin, Shetland, Faroes, Finisterre; or by the gorgeous and inane phraseology of the catechism; or by the litany of the Blessed Virgin that was part of the enforced poetry in our household: Tower of Gold, Ark of the Covenant, Gate of Heaven, Morning Star, Health of the Sick, Refuge of Sinners, Comforter of the Afflicted. None of these things was consciously savoured at the time, but I think the fact that I still recall them with ease, and can delight in them as verbal music, means that they were bedding the ear with a kind of linguistic hardcore that could be built on someday.

That was the unconscious bedding, but poetry involves a conscious savouring of words also. This came by way of reading poetry itself, and being required to learn pieces by heart, phrases even, like Keats's, from 'Lamia':

> and his vessel now
> Grated the quaystone with her brazen prow,

or Wordsworth's:

> All shod with steel,
> We hiss'd along the polished ice,

or Tennyson's:

> Old yew, which graspest at the stones
> That name the underlying dead,

> Thy fibres net the dreamless head,
> Thy roots are wrapped about the bones.

These were picked up in my last years at school, touchstones of sorts, where the language could give you a kind of aural goose-flesh. At university I was delighted in the first weeks to meet the moody energies of John Webster—'I'll make Italian cut-works in their guts / If ever I return'—and later on to encounter the pointed masonry of Anglo-Saxon verse and to learn about the rich stratifications of the English language itself. Words alone were certain good. I even went so far as to write these 'Lines to Myself':

> In poetry I wish you would
> Avoid the lilting platitude.
> Give us poems humped and strong,
> Laced tight with thongs of song,
> Poems that explode in silence
> Without forcing, without violence.
> Whose music is strong and clear and good
> Like a saw zooming in seasoned wood.
> You should attempt concrete expression,
> Half-guessing, half-expression.

Ah well. Behind that was 'Ars Poetica', MacLeish's and Verlaine's, Eliot's 'objective correlative' (half understood) and several critical essays (by myself and others) about 'concrete realization'. At university I kept the whole thing at arm's length, read poetry for the noise and wrote about half a dozen pieces for the literary magazine. But nothing happened inside me. No experience. No epiphany. All craft—and not much of that—and no technique.

I think technique is different from craft. Craft is what you can learn from other verse. Craft is the skill of making. It wins competitions in *The Irish Times* or the *New Statesman*. It can be deployed without reference to the feelings or the self. It knows how to keep up a capable verbal athletic display; it can be content to be *vox et praeterea nihil*—all voice and nothing else—but not voice as in 'finding a voice'. Learning the craft is learning to turn the windlass at the well of poetry. Usually you begin by dropping the bucket halfway down the shaft and winding up a taking of air. You are miming the real thing until one day the chain draws unexpectedly tight and you have dipped into waters that will continue to entice you back. You'll have broken the skin on the pool of yourself. Your praties will be 'fit for digging'.

At that point it becomes appropriate to speak of technique rather than craft. Technique, as I would define it, involves not only a poet's way with words, his management of metre, rhythm and verbal texture; it involves also a definition of his stance towards life, a definition of his own reality. It involves the discovery of ways to go out of his normal cognitive bounds and raid the inarticulate: a dynamic alertness that mediates between the origins of feeling in memory and experience and the formal ploys that express these in a work of art. Technique entails the watermarking of your essential patterns of perception, voice and thought into the touch and texture of your lines; it is that whole creative effort of the mind's and body's resources to bring the meaning of experience within the jurisdiction of form. Technique is what turns, in Yeats's phrase, 'the bundle of accident and incoherence that sits down to breakfast' into 'an idea, something intended, complete'.

It is indeed conceivable that a poet could have a real technique and a wobbly craft—I think this was true of Alun Lewis and Patrick Kavanagh—but more often it is a case of a sure enough craft and a failure of technique. And if I were asked for a figure who represents pure technique, I would say a water diviner. You can't learn the craft of dowsing or divining—it is a gift for being in touch with what is there, hidden and real, a gift for mediating between the latent resource and the community that wants it current and released. As Sir Philip Sidney notes in his *Defence of Poesy*: 'Among the Romans a Poet was called *Vates*, which is as much as a Diviner . . .'

The poem was written simply to allay an excitement and to name an experience, and at the same time to give the excitement and the experience a small *perpetuum mobile* in language itself. I quote it here, not for its own technique but for the image of technique contained in it. The diviner resembles the poet in his function of making contact with what lies hidden, and in his ability to make palpable what was sensed or raised.

THE DIVINER

Cut from the green hedge a forked hazel stick
That he held tight by the arms of the V:
Circling the terrain, hunting the pluck
Of water, nervous, but professionally

Unfussed. The pluck came sharp as a sting.
The rod jerked with precise convulsions,
Spring water suddenly broadcasting
Through a green hazel its secret stations.

The bystanders would ask to have a try.
He handed them the rod without a word.
It lay dead in their grasp till nonchalantly
He gripped expectant wrists. The hazel stirred.

What I had taken as matter of fact as a youngster became a matter of wonder in memory. When I look at the thing now I am pleased that it ends with a verb, 'stirred', the heart of the mystery; and I am glad that 'stirred' chimes with 'word', bringing the two functions of *vates* into the one sound.

Technique is what allows that first stirring of the mind round a word or an image or a memory to grow towards articulation: articulation not necessarily in terms of argument or explication but in terms of its own potential for harmonious self-reproduction. The seminal excitement has to be granted conditions in which, in Hopkins's words, it 'selves, goes itself . . . crying / What I do is me, for that I came'. Technique ensures that the first gleam attains its proper effulgence. And I don't just mean a felicity in the choice of words to flesh the theme—that is a problem also but it is not so critical. A poem can survive stylistic blemishes but it cannot survive a stillbirth. The crucial action is pre-verbal, to be able to allow the first alertness or come-hither, sensed in a blurred or incomplete way, to dilate and approach as a thought or a theme or a phrase. Robert Frost put it this way: 'A poem begins as a lump in the throat, a homesickness, a lovesickness. It finds the thought and the thought finds the words.' As far as I am concerned, technique is more vitally and sensitively connected with that first activity where the 'lump in the throat' finds 'the thought' than with 'the thought' finding 'the words'. That first emergence involves the divining, vatic, oracular function; the second, the making function. To say, as Auden did, that a poem is a 'verbal contraption' is to keep one or two tricks up your sleeve.

In practice, you proceed by your own experience of what it is to write what you consider a successful poem. You survive in your own esteem not by the corroboration of theory but by the trust in certain moments of satisfaction which you know intuitively to be moments of extension. You are confirmed by the visitation of the last poem and threatened by the elusiveness of the next one, and the best moments are those when your mind seems to implode and words and images rush of their own accord into the vortex. Which happened to me once when the line 'We have no prairies' drifted into my head at bedtime and loosened a fall of images that constitute the poem 'Bogland', the last one in *Door into the Dark*.

I had been vaguely wishing to write a poem about bogland, chiefly because it is a landscape that has a strange assuaging effect on me, one with associations reaching back into early childhood. We used to hear about bog-butter, butter kept fresh for a great number of years under the peat. Then when I was at school the skeleton of an elk had been taken out of a bog nearby and a few of our neighbours had got their photographs in the paper, peering out across its antlers. So I began to get an idea of bog as the memory of the landscape, or as a landscape that remembered everything that happened in and to it. In fact, if you go round the National Museum in Dublin, you will realize that a great proportion of the most cherished material heritage of Ireland was 'found in a bog'. Moreover, since memory was the faculty that supplied me with the first quickening of my own poetry, I had a tentative unrealized need to make a congruence between memory and bogland and, for the want of a better word, our national consciousness. And it all released itself after 'We have no prairies . . .'—but we have bogs.

At that time I was teaching modern literature in Queen's University, Belfast, and had been reading about the frontier and the West as an important myth in the American consciousness, so I set up—or rather, laid down—the bog as an answering Irish myth. I wrote it quickly the next morning, having slept on my excitement, and revised it on the hoof, from line to line, as it came:

> We have no prairies
> To slice a big sun at evening—
> Everywhere the eye concedes to
> Encroaching horizon,
>
> Is wooed into the cyclops' eye
> Of a tarn. Our unfenced country
> Is bog that keeps crusting
> Between the sights of the sun.
>
> They've taken the skeleton
> Of the great Irish Elk
> Out of the peat, set it up
> An astounding crate full of air.
>
> Butter sunk under
> More than a hundred years
> Was recovered salty and white.
> The ground itself is kind, black butter
>
> Melting and opening underfoot,
> Missing its last definition
> By millions of years.
> They'll never dig coal here,
>
> Only the waterlogged trunks
> Of great firs, soft as pulp.
> Our pioneers keep striking
> Inwards and downwards,

Every layer they strip
Seems camped on before.
The bogholes might be Atlantic seepage.
The wet centre is bottomless.

Again, as in the case of 'Digging', the seminal impulse had been unconscious. What generated the poem about memory was something lying beneath the very floor of memory, something I only connected with the poem months after it was written, namely a warning that older people would give us about going into the bog. They were afraid we might drown in pools in the old workings, so they put it about (and we believed them) that *there was no bottom* in the bog-holes. Little did they—or I—know that I would filch it for the last line of a book.

There was also in that book a poem called 'Requiem for the Croppies', written in 1966, when most poets in Ireland were straining to celebrate the anniversary of the 1916 Rising. That insurrection at Easter was the harvest of seeds sown in 1798, when revolutionary republican ideals and national feeling coalesced in the doctrines of Irish republicanism and in the rebellion of 1798 itself—unsuccessful and savagely put down. The poem was born of and ended with an image of resurrection based on the fact that sometime after the rebels were buried in common graves, the graves began to sprout with young barley, growing up from barley corn which the 'croppies' had carried in their pockets to eat while on the march. The oblique implication was that the seeds of violent resistance sown in the Year of Liberty had flowered in what Yeats called 'the right rose tree' of 1916. I did not realize at the time that the original heraldic murderous encounter between Protestant yeoman and Catholic rebel was to be initiated again in the summer of 1969, in Belfast, two months after the book was published.

From that moment the problems of poetry moved from being simply a matter of achieving the satisfactory verbal icon to being a search for images and symbols adequate to our predicament. I do not mean liberal lamentation that citizens should feel compelled to murder one another or deploy their different military arms over the matter of nomenclatures such as 'British' or 'Irish'. I do not mean public celebrations of resistance or execrations of atrocity—although there is nothing necessarily unpoetic about such celebration, if one thinks of Yeats's 'Easter 1916'. I mean that I felt it imperative to discover a field of force in which, without abandoning fidelity to the processes and experience of poetry as I have outlined them, it would be possible to encompass the perspectives of a humane reason and at the same time to grant the religious intensity of the violence its deplorable authenticity and complexity. And when I say religious, I am not thinking simply of the sectarian division. To some extent, the enmity can be viewed as a struggle between the cults and devotees of a god and a goddess. There is an indigenous territorial numen, a tutelar of the whole island, call her Mother Ireland, Kathleen Ni Houlihan, the poor old woman, the Shan Van Vocht, whatever; and her sovereignty has been temporarily usurped or infringed by a new male cult whose founding fathers were Cromwell, William of Orange and Edward Carson, and whose godhead is incarnate in a rex or caesar resident in a palace in London. What we have is the tail-end of a struggle in a province between territorial piety and imperial power.

Now, I realize that this idiom is remote from the agnostic world of economic interest, whose iron hand operates in the velvet glove of 'talks between elected representatives', and remote from the political manoeuvres of power-sharing; but it is not remote from the psychology of the Irishmen and Ulstermen who do the killing, and not remote from the bankrupt psychology and mythologies implicit in the terms 'Irish Catholic' and 'Ulster Protestant'. The question, as ever, is, 'How with this rage shall beauty hold a plea?' And my answer is, by offering 'befitting emblems of adversity'.

Some of these emblems I found in a book that was published in English translation, appositely, the year the killing started, in 1969. And again appositely, it was entitled *The Bog People*. It was chiefly concerned with preserved bodies of men and women found in the bogs of Jutland, naked, strangled or with their throats cut, disposed under the peat since early Iron Age times. The author, P. V. Glob, argues convincingly that a number of these, and in particular the Tollund Man, whose head is now preserved near Aarhus in the museum at Silkeburg, were ritual sacrifices to the Mother Goddess, the goddess of the ground who needed new bridegrooms each winter to bed with her in her sacred place, in the bog, to ensure the renewal and fertility of the territory in the spring. Taken in relation to the tradition of Irish political martyrdom for that cause whose icon is Kathleen Ni Houlihan, this is more than an archaic barbarous rite: it is an archetypal pattern. And the unforgettable photographs of these victims blended in my mind with photographs of atrocities, past and present, in the long rites of Irish political and religious struggles. When I wrote this poem, I had a completely new sensation, one of fear. It was a vow to go on pilgrimage and I felt as it came to me—and again it came quickly—that unless I was deeply in earnest about what I was saying, I was simply invoking dangers for myself.

Learning from Eliot

The majority of poems one outgrows and outlives, as one outgrows and outlives the majority of human passions: Dante's
is one of those which one can only just hope to grow up to at
the end of life.

—T. S. ELIOT

It was the middle of my own life before I began to grow up to T. S.
Eliot, but the story necessarily starts far earlier. As a schoolboy in
a Catholic boarding-school in Derry, I was daunted by the otherness of Eliot and all that he stood for. Nevertheless, when an aunt
of mine offered to buy a couple of books for me, I requested
his *Collected Poems*. It, and *Tales of Mystery and Imagination*,
were the first 'grown-up' books I owned. Name and date—1955—
were duly inscribed, so I was fifteen or sixteen years of age when
the dark-blue linen-bound volume came into my possession:
the British edition of *Collected Poems 1909–1935*, the one that
ended with 'Burnt Norton' and had by then been reprinted fifteen times. It arrived in a food-parcel from home, and it had an
air of contraband about it, because the only reading matter we
were permitted, I am shocked to recollect, was what the sparsely
stocked college library held, or what our course syllabi required.
So there I was in 1955 with my forbidden book in my hand, with
a literary reach that exceeded my grasp, alone with the words on
the page.

For a long time that book represented to me my distance from
the mystery and my unfittedness—as reader or writer—for the vocation it represented. Over the years I could experience in its presence the onset of a lump in the throat and a tightening of the
diaphragm, symptoms which until then had only affected me in
maths class. Now my neurotic symptoms in relation to advanced
algebra and calculus extended to encompass *Collected Poems*. And,
later, during my first year at Queen's University, when I read in
E. M. Forster's *Howard's End* an account of the character called

Leonard Bast as somebody doomed forever to be familiar with the outsides of books, my identification was not with the privileged narrative voice but with Bast himself, pathetic scrambler on the edge of literacy.

Do I exaggerate? Maybe. Maybe not. The fact that I would not then have been able to put the matter to myself in exactly these terms does not mean that the inarticulate ache towards knowing, towards adequacy, towards fitting oneself out as a reader of modern poetry did not truly exist. It did exist and it ached all the more for being unrequited, because one did not need to know any literary thing in particular in the 1950s in order to know that Eliot was the way, the truth and the light, and that until one had found him one had not entered the kingdom of poetry.

Even his name was a buzz-word for obscurity, and the word 'obscurity' was in turn suggestive of 'modern poetry', a term in those days as compelling as the terms 'simony' and 'paralysis' were for the young boy in Joyce's story 'The Sisters'. For the moment, however, the whole burden of this mystery was confined in four pages of the school poetry anthology, a bilious-green compendium entitled *A Pageant of English Verse*. About one quarter of the poems in this book were set each year as part of the official syllabus for the Northern Ireland Senior Certificate of Education, and in our year the syllabus included 'The Hollow Men' and 'Journey of the Magi'. It was the first of these that made the truly odd impression. It was impossible not to be affected by it, yet it is still impossible to say exactly what the effect was:

> Eyes I dare not meet in dreams
> In death's dream kingdom
> These do not appear:
> There, the eyes are
> Sunlight on a broken column
> There, is a tree swinging
> And voices are
> In the wind's singing
> More distant and more solemn
> Than a fading star.

Whatever happened within my reader's skin was the equivalent of what happens in an otherwise warm and well-wrapped body once a cold wind gets at its ankles. A shiver that fleetingly registered itself as more pertinent and more acutely pleasurable than the prevailing warmth. A cheese-wire exactness that revealed to you the cheesy nature of your own standards and expectations. But, of course, we were not encouraged to talk like that in English class, and anyhow, like the girl in *The Importance of Being Earnest* who was pleased to say she had never seen a spade, I had not then ever seen a cheese-wire.

All this is extremely interesting to remember now, for it persuades me that what is to be learned from Eliot is the double-edged nature of poetic reality: first encountered as a strange fact of culture, poetry is internalized over the years until it becomes, as they say, second nature. Poetry that was originally beyond you, generating the need to understand and overcome its strangeness, becomes in the end a familiar path within you, a grain along which your imagination opens pleasurably backwards towards an origin and a seclusion. Your last state is therefore a thousand times better than your first, for the experience of poetry is one which truly deepens and fortifies itself with reenactment. I now know, for example, that I love the lines quoted above because of the pitch of their music, their nerve-end tremulousness, their treble in the helix of the ear. Even so, I cannot with my voice make the physical sound that would be the equivalent of what I hear on my inner ear; and the ability to acknowledge that very knowledge, the confidence to affirm that there is a reality to poetry which is unspeakable and for that very reason all the more piercing, that ability and that confidence are largely based upon a reading of Eliot.

Of course, the rare music of 'The Hollow Men' was never mentioned in school. Disillusion was what we heard about. Loss of faith. The lukewarm spirit. The modern world. Nor do I remember much attention being given to the cadence, or much attempt being made to encourage us to hear rather than abstract a meaning. What we heard, in fact, was what gave us then a kind of herd laughter: the eccentric, emphatic enunciations of our teacher, who came down heavily on certain syllables and gave an undue weight

to the HOLlow men, the STUFFED men. And needless to say, in a
class of thirty boys, in an atmosphere of socks and sex and snig-
gers, stuffed men and prickly pears and bangs and whimpers did
not elevate the mood or induce the condition of stillness which is
the ideally desirable one if we are to be receptive to this poet's bat-
frequency.

I was never caught up by Eliot, never taken over and shown to
myself by his work, my ear never pulled outside in by what it
heard in him. Numerous readers have testified to this sudden kind
of conversion, when the whole being is flushed by a great stroke of
poetry, and this did indeed happen to me when I read Gerard
Manley Hopkins. From the start something in my make-up was
always ready to follow the antique flute of sensuous writing, yet
when this kind of writing made its appearance in Eliot—in *Ash-
Wednesday*, for instance—its very plenitude was meant to render
its beauty questionable. It signalled a distraction from the way of
purgation:

> At the first turning of the third stair
> Was a slotted window bellied like the fig's fruit
> And beyond the hawthorn blossom and a pasture scene
> The broadbacked figure drest in blue and green
> Enchanted the maytime with an antique flute.
> Blown hair is sweet, brown hair over the mouth blown,
> Lilac and brown hair;
> Distraction, music of the flute, stops and steps of the mind over
>   the third stair,
> Fading, fading; strength beyond hope and despair
> Climbing the third stair.

The fact that within the finer tone and stricter disciplines of
Eliot's poetry, these lines represented what he would later call 'the
deception of the thrush' did not prevent me from being deceived
into relishing them. And in that relish two things were combined.
First of all, a single unbewildering image was presented. To read
the passage was to look across a deep lucidity towards a shaggy
solidity, as if in a Renaissance painting of the Annunciation the

window of the Virgin's chamber opened upon a scene of vegetal
and carnal riot. Second, the language of the lines called in a direct
way, in a way that indeed skirted the parodic, upon the traditional
language of poetry. Antique figure. Maytime. Hawthorn. Flute.
Blue and green. The pleasures of recollection were all there. The
consolations of the familiar. So that combination of composed dramatic scene and consciously deployed poetic diction appealed to
the neophyte reader in me. To express the appeal by its negatives,
the poetry was not obscure, neither in what it was describing nor
in the language that did the describing. It fitted happily my expectations of what poetry might be: what unfitted it was all that other
stuff in *Ash-Wednesday* about leopards and bones and violet and
violet. That scared me off, made me feel small and embarrassed. I
wanted to call on the Mother of Readers to have mercy on me,
to come quick, make sense of it, give me the pacifier of a paraphrasable meaning and a recognizable, firmed-up setting:

> Lady, three white leopards sat under a juniper-tree
> In the cool of the day, having fed to satiety
> On my legs my heart my liver and that which had been
>   contained
> In the hollow round of my skull. And God said
> Shall these bones live? shall these
> Bones live?

My panic in the face of these lovely lines was not just schoolboy
panic. It descended again in my late twenties when I had to lecture on *Ash-Wednesday* as part of a course for undergraduates at
Queen's University, Belfast. I had no access to the only reliable
source for such teaching, namely, the experience of having felt the
poem come home, memorably and irrefutably, so the lecture was
one of the most unnerving forty-five minutes of my life. I scram-
bled around beforehand, snatching at F. O. Matthiessen's *The
Achievement of T. S. Eliot* and George Williamson's *A Reader's
Guide to T. S. Eliot* and D. E. S. Maxwell's *The Poetry of T. S. Eliot*.
But whatever they had to say in their commentaries had nothing
to fall upon, or to combine with, on the ground of my reader's

mind. The poem never quite became a gestalt. Nowadays I talk about it more freely because I am not as shy of the subject as I then was: purgation, conversion, the embrace of an air thoroughly thin and dry, joy in a vision as arbitrary and disjunct from the usual as the vision of the leopards and lady in a white gown—all this offers itself far more comprehensively and persuasively to someone in his late forties than to someone in his late twenties:

> The Lady is withdrawn
> In a white gown, to contemplation, in a white gown.
> Let the whiteness of bones atone to forgetfulness.
> There is no life in them. As I am forgotten
> And would be forgotten, so I would forget
> Thus devoted, concentrated in purpose. And God said
> Prophesy to the wind, to the wind only for only
> The wind will listen. And the bones sang chirping
> With the burden of the grasshopper, saying . . .

Those qualities which created resistance in the first place now seem to me the valuable things about this work. The sense that the poem stood like a geometry in an absence was what caused my original bewilderment. I sensed myself like a gross intrusion, all corporeality and blunder in the realm of grace and translucence, and this unnerved me.

Nowadays, however, what gratifies me most is this very feeling of being privy to an atmosphere so chastely invented, so boldly and unpredictably written. Things like bones and leopards—which pop into the scene without preparation or explanation and which therefore discombobulated me at first—these things I now accept not as the poet's mystifying whim but as his gift and visitation. They are not what I at first mistakenly thought them: constituent parts of some erudite code available to initiates. Nor are they intended to be counters for a cannily secluded meaning. Rather, they arose airily in the poet's composing mind and reproduced themselves deliciously, with a playfulness and self-surprising completedness.

Of course, it is true that a reading of the Earthly Paradise cantos of Dante's *Purgatorio* prepares one for the rarefied air of Eliot's scene, just as some familiarity with Dante will take from the unexpectedness of the leopards that start up in the very first line of Section II of *Ash-Wednesday*. Yet it is wrong to see these things simply as references to Dante. They are not hostages taken from *The Divine Comedy* and held by Eliot's art in the ascetic compound of his poem. They actually sprang up in the pure mind of the twentieth-century poet and their in-placeness does not derive from their having a meaning transplanted from the iconography of the medieval one. It is true, of course, that Eliot's pure mind was greatly formed by the contemplation of Dante, and Eliot's dream processes fed upon the phantasmagoria of *The Divine Comedy* constantly, so the matter of Dante's poem was present to him, and Dante had thereby become *second nature* to him. Dante, in fact, belonged in the rag-and-bone shop of Eliot's middle-ageing heart, and it was from that sad organ, we might say, that all his lyric ladders started.

Given the habitual probity, severity and strenuousness of Eliot's mind, one has therefore no difficulty in crediting him with his right to those moments of release when his nerves threw patterns upon the screen of the language. Yet needless to say, back in that window-rattling classroom in Derry in 1956, with rain gusting up the Foyle Estuary and the sound of the chapel bell marking the beginning and end of each forty-minute period, these kinds of thoughts were far in the future for a candidate in A-Level English. All that fellow wanted was to be able to get a foothold on the slippery slope of the prescribed poems. In the case of 'The Hollow Men', his teacher gave him just such a foothold by driving into the poem a huge extraneous spike labelled 'Loss of Faith in Modern World and Consequences for Modern Man'. There at least was one way of subduing the querulous, outcast melodies of the poem to the familiar tolling of the bell of Faith. The modernist canon was to be co-opted by the ideology that rang the college bell, and indeed it must be said that the rhetoric of the poem's distress connived with the complacencies of the college's orthodoxies. The fraying quotations from the Lord's Prayer and the general tone of litany (which was so much part of our daily round of prayers) all tended to co-opt the imaginative strangeness, formal distinctness and fundamental difference of this poetry into the emulsifying element of our doctrinally sound young heads.

Obviously, the domestication of 'Journey of the Magi' was easier still. The three wise kings had been part of the folk-life of our Catholicism, part of the Christmas crib, the Christmas gospel and the Christmas card itself. Moreover, the idea of conversion was also familiar to us. Losing your life to save it, abandoning self to begin the path of illumination—no problem there. And no problem for me in the reek of actual country when a horse rushes away or a dank green valley moisture generously irrigates the reader's nostrils. High modernism, high Anglicanism and the low-lying farmlands of County Derry came together in a pleasing exhalation or—as Eliot himself might have called it—an 'efflux' of poetry. No problem either when three trees on the skyline were said to prefigure the Crucifixion, or when the hands dicing among the empty wineskins prefigured the hands of the Roman soldier dicing for Christ's robe at the foot of the Cross. This poem required no spike driven into it to give us a grip. On the contrary, it seemed so generously provided with doctrinal spikes of its own that we could not help being pinned down by its images and its orthodoxy:

> Then at dawn we came down to a temperate valley,
> Wet, below the snow line, smelling of vegetation;
> With a running stream and a water-mill beating the darkness,
> And three trees on the low sky,
> And an old white horse galloped away in the meadow.
> Then we came to a tavern with vine-leaves over the lintel,
> Six hands at an open door dicing for pieces of silver,
> And feet kicking the empty wine-skins.
> But there was no information, so we continued
> And arrived at evening, not a moment too soon
> Finding the place; it was (you may say) satisfactory.

The familiarity of the matter of this poem gave us the illusion of 'understanding'; or perhaps the 'understanding' was not an illusion, the illusion being that 'understanding' its content and the cri-

sis it embodied was the equivalent of knowing it as a poem; a formal event in the language; an 'objective correlative'. We knew its
correlation with conversion and with Christmas, but not its artistic
objectivity. Those three trees were never allowed time to manifest
themselves in the mind's eye as three trees before they were
turned into images of Calvary; nor were the hands at the wineskins allowed to be written hands-in-themselves before becoming
inscribed symbols of the division of Christ's garments. It was a
paradoxical destiny for a poet such as Eliot, whose endeavour had
been to insist on the poetriness of poetry being anterior to its status
as philosophy or ideas or any other thing.

At Queen's University I packed myself with commentaries
and in particular advanced upon *The Waste Land* with what help
I could muster in the library. I even read chunks of Jessie L.
Weston's *From Ritual to Romance.* I began to hear the music and
to attune myself, but chiefly I obeyed the directives of the commentaries and got prepared to show myself informed. Yet perhaps
the most lasting influence from this time was Eliot's prose, all as-
sembled and digested by John Hayward in a little purple-coloured
Penguin book, the particular tint of purple being appropriately
reminiscent of a confessor's stole. There I read and re-read 'Tradition and the Individual Talent', essays on the metaphysical poets,
on Milton, on Tennyson's *In Memoriam.* On the music of poetry.
On why *Hamlet* doesn't make it as a play, as an objective correlative. But most important of all, perhaps, was a definition of the
faculty which he called 'the auditory imagination'. This was 'the
feeling for syllable and rhythm, penetrating far below the conscious levels of thought and feeling, invigorating every word; sinking to the most primitive and forgotten, returning to the origin
and bringing something back . . . [fusing] the most ancient and the
most civilized mentality'.

It was not in the context of this definition that Eliot commented upon the dramatic efficacy of the lines from *Macbeth*
spoken just before the murder of Banquo:

> Light thickens,
> And the crow makes wing to the rooky wood,
> Good things of day begin to droop and drowse.

Nor did he invoke it when he discussed the exquisitely direct yet profoundly suggestive line spoken by Othello 'Keep up your bright swords, for the dew will rust them.' Nevertheless, Eliot's revelation of his susceptibility to such lines, the physicality of his ear as well as the fastidiousness of its discriminations, his example of a poet's intelligence exercising itself in the activity of listening, all of this seemed to excuse my own temperamental incapacity for paraphrase and my disinclination to engage a poem's argument and conceptual progress. Instead, it confirmed a natural inclination to make myself an echo chamber for the poem's sounds. I was encouraged to seek for the contour of a meaning within the pattern of a rhythm.

In the 'Death by Water' section of *The Waste Land*, for example, I began to construe from its undulant cadences and dissolvings and reinings-in a mimetic principle which matched or perhaps even overwhelmed any possible meaning that might be derived from the story of Phlebas's fate. In the heft and largesse of the poem's music, I thought I divined an aural equivalent of the larger transcendental reality betrayed by the profit-and-loss people of the City of London, those merchants and clerks who come into the poem as a somnolent rhythmic flow of shades over London Bridge. I began to stop worrying about Phlebas's relation to the Drowned Man and the effigy of Osiris cast into the water; all that was important as a structural principle, but the breath of life was in the body of sound:

Phlebas the Phoenician, a fortnight dead,
Forgot the cry of gulls, and the deep sea swell
And the profit and loss.
         A current under sea
Picked his bones in whispers. As he rose and fell
He passed the stages of his age and youth
Entering the whirlpool.
         Gentile or Jew
O you who turn the wheel and look to windward,
Consider Phlebas, who was once handsome and tall as you.

At this stage of readiness to listen, I was also lucky enough to hear Eliot's poetry read aloud by the actor Robert Speaight. I had

made an introductory foray into *Four Quartets* but was finding it
difficult to retain any impression unified and whole in my mind.
The bigness of the structure, the opacity of the thought, the complexity of the organization of those poems held you at bay; yet
while they daunted you, they promised a kind of wisdom—and it
was at this tentative stage that I heard the whole thing read aloud.
That experience taught me, in the words of the poem, 'to sit still'.
To sit, in fact, all through an afternoon in Belfast, in an upstairs flat,
with a couple of graduate students in biochemistry, people with a
less professional anxiety about understanding the poetry than I had,
since in their unprofessional but rewarding way they still assumed
that mystification was par for the course in modern poetry.

What I *heard* made sense. In the opening lines of 'Burnt Norton', for example, the footfall of the word 'time' echoes and repeats
in a way that is hypnotic when read aloud, yet can be perplexing
when sight-read for its meaning only. Similarly, the interweaving
and repetition of the words 'present', 'past' and 'future' goes round
and round, like a linked dance through the ear. Words going forward meet each other coming back. Even the word 'echo' meets itself on the rebound. The effect is one of a turning and a stillness.
Neither from nor towards. At the still point of the turning world:

> Time present and time past
> Are both perhaps present in time future,
> And time future contained in time past.
> If all time is eternally present
> All time is unredeemable.
> What might have been is an abstraction
> Remaining a perpetual possibility
> Only in a world of speculation.
> What might have been and what has been
> Point to one end, which is always present.
> Footfalls echo in the memory
> Down the passage which we did not take
> Towards the door we never opened
> Into the rose-garden. My words echo
> Thus, in your mind.

But to what purpose
Disturbing the dust on a bowl of rose-leaves
I do not know.
Other echoes
Inhabit the garden. Shall we follow?
Quick, said the bird, find them, find them,
Round the corner. Through the first gate,
Into our first world, shall we follow
The deception of the thrush?

By its orchestration of theme and phrase, paraphrase and reprise, its premonitions of the end recoiling into the beginning, this passage is typical of the procedures of *Four Quartets* as a whole. The poetry comes through in a silent reading, of course, since (to quote again from Eliot's own definition of 'auditory imagination') it operates below the level of sense; but it operates much more potently when the words are spoken aloud. Gradually, therefore, I began in the early 1960s to take pleasure in the basement life of Eliot's ear and to teach myself 'to sit still' and let its underworkings work.

These were also years when I was trying to make a start as a poet, and searching for the charge that sets writing energy flowing in a hitherto unwriting system. Yet much as I was learning from Eliot about the right way to listen, he could not be the stimulator of poetry for me. He was more a kind of literary superego than a generator of the poetic libido, and in order for the libidinous lyric voice to get on with its business, it had to escape from his overseeing presence. So I turned towards more familiar, more engageable writers like Patrick Kavanagh, R. S. Thomas, Ted Hughes, John Montague, Norman MacCaig. All of a sudden I was making up for not having read contemporary British and Irish poetry; and that way, I got excited and got started.

Then I came upon C. K. Stead's book *The New Poetic*, with its revelation of Eliot as a poet who trusted the 'dark embryo' of unconscious energy. Stead revealed Eliot as a much more intuitive kind of writer than the commentaries had allowed one to believe. It is not that this lessened one's awareness of the strictness of his mind or the scrupulousness of his withholdings. Eliot was still a *rara avis*, one whose note was uniquely beyond the common scale, a thin pure signal that might not wash genially across the earthy reaches of one's nature but had the capacity to probe in the universe of spirit as far as Pluto. Yet one could grant this inimitable status to his achievement and still recognize the process that produced it as the usual, uncertain, hopeful, needy, half self-surrendering, half self-priming process which the rest of us also experienced.

What one learns ultimately from Eliot is that the activity of poetry is solitary, and if one is to rejoice in it, one has to construct something upon which to rejoice. One learns that at the desk every poet faces the same kind of task, that there is no secret that can be imparted, only resources of one's own that are to be mustered, or not, as the case may be. Many of the things Eliot says about poetic composition are fortifying because they are so authoritatively unconsoling:

> And what there is to conquer
> By strength and submission, has already been discovered
> Once or twice, or several times, by men whom one cannot hope
> To emulate—but there is no competition—
> There is only the fight to recover what had been lost
> And found and lost again and again: and now, under conditions
> That seem unpropitious. But perhaps neither gain nor loss.
> For us, there is only the trying. The rest is not our business.

So, to conclude. If Eliot did not help me to write, he did help me to learn what it means to read. The experience of his poetry is an unusually pure one. You begin and end with the words alone—which is admittedly always the case, but often in the work of other poets the reader can find respites and alibis. With Frost or Yeats or Hardy, for example, there is a corroborative relation between a landscape and a sensibility. The words on the page can function in a way that is supplementary to their primary artistic function: they can have a window effect and open the blinds of language on to subjects and places before or behind the words. But this kind of mutual help does not exist—and is not intended to exist—between the words of Eliot's poetry and the world that gave rise to them. When I visited Burnt Norton, for example, I did indeed find a rose garden and a dry concrete pool; but I also found this very documentary congruence between poem and place oddly disappointing. I realized that I did not really want a landscape to materialize, since I had long since internalized a soundscape.

Perhaps the final thing to be learned is this: in the realm of poetry, as in the realm of consciousness, there is no end to the possible learnings that can take place. Nothing is final, the most gratifying discovery is fleeting, the path of positive achievement leads to the *via negativa*. Eliot forfeited his expressionist intensity when he renounced the lyric for philosophical song. It may even be truer to say that the lyric renounced Eliot. But in accepting the consequences of renunciation with such self-knowledge and in proceeding with such strictness of intent, he proved a truth that we want to believe not perhaps about all poets but about those who are the necessary ones. He showed how poetic vocation entails the disciplining of a habit of expression until it becomes fundamental to the whole conduct of a life.

Belfast

'If a coathanger knocked in a wardrobe / That was a great event' —Derek Mahon's evocation of the unfulfilled expectancy of an old man living in Belfast could be extended to the young men around Queen's in the late 1950s and early 1960s. A lot of people of a generally literary bent were islanded about the place, but they in no way constituted an archipelago. There was Denis Tuohy, Don Carleton, David Farrell, Stewart Parker, Ian Hill, Seamus Deane, John Hamilton, myself and many another, all dabbling. I don't think many of us had a sense of contemporary poetry—Dylan Thomas's records were as near as we seemed to get to the living thing. Laurence Lerner was in the English Department and produced a collection called *Domestic Interior*, but it was somehow remote, none of our business. And as for Philip Larkin, who had just left, I graduated without hearing his name, from student or lecturer. Michael McLaverty was teaching in town, but we never saw him; Roy McFadden had drawn the blinds on *Rann*, John Hewitt was in Coventry. That older generation were perhaps names to us but not voices. *Gorgon* and *Q*, the university literary magazines, were hand-to-mouth affairs, with no real excitement, audience or clique attaching to them. Mary O'Malley, John Boyd, Sam Hanna Bell, Joseph Tomelty and others were at work, but again, they were beyond us. We stood or hung or sleepwalked between notions of writing that we had gleaned from English courses and the living reality of writers from our own place whom we did not know, in person or in print.

Those of us who stayed around saw that state of affairs changed by the mid-1960s, and one of the strongest agents of change was Philip Hobsbaum. When Hobsbaum arrived in Belfast, he moved disparate elements into a single action. He emanated energy, generosity, belief in the community, trust in the parochial, the inept, the unprinted. He was impatient, dogmatic, relentlessly literary: yet he was patient with those he trusted, unpredictably susceptible to a wide variety of poems and personalities and urgent that the social and political exacerbations of our place should disrupt the decorums of literature. If he drove some people mad with his absolutes and hurt others with his overbearing, he confirmed as many with his enthusiasms. He and his wife, Hannah, kept open house for poetry, and I remember his hospitality and encouragement with the special gratitude we reserve for those who have led us towards confidence in ourselves.

I remember especially the first meeting of the group. Stewart Parker read his poems and was the first—and last—writer to stand up as he did so. That ritual of rising up to enounce, that initial formal ratification of the voice, seems emblematic in retrospect. What happened Monday night after Monday night in the Hobsbaums' flat in Fitzwilliam Street somehow ratified the activity of writing for all of us who shared it. Perhaps not everybody needed it ratified—Michael Longley and James Simmons, for example, had been in the swim before they landed—but all of us were part of it in the end. What Hobsbaum achieved, whether people liked it or not, was to give a generation a sense of themselves, in two ways: it allowed us to get to grips with one another within the group, to move from critical comment to creative friendship at our own pace, and it allowed a small public to think of us as The Group, a single, even singular phenomenon. There was his introduction of a number of us to 'The Arts in Ulster', a BBC programme produced by John Boyd. There was an article in the *Telegraph*. There was Mary Holland scooping it all for *The Observer* when she arrived to cover the Festival in 1965. It's easy to be blasé about all that now, for now, of course, we're genuine parochials. Then we were craven provincials. Hobsbaum contributed much to that crucial transformation.

When the Hobsbaums left, we missed the regular coffee and biscuits, the irregular booze, the boisterous literary legislation. One act of the drama had closed down. When the second act opened in my own house, after interludes in the back room of the English Department and the upper room of a pub, some of the old characters had departed, to London, Portrush, Holywood, wherever, and a crowd of gifted boy actors were in the wings to claim the stage. But by then the curtain was about to rise on the larger drama of our politics, and the writers were to find themselves in a play within the play.

CHRISTMAS, 1971

People keep asking what it's like to be living in Belfast, and I've found myself saying that things aren't too bad in our part of the town: a throw-away consolation meaning that we don't expect to be caught in crossfire if we step into the street. It's a shorthand that evades unravelling the weary twisted emotions that are rolled like a ball of hooks and sinkers in the heart. I am fatigued by a continuous adjudication between agony and injustice, swung at one moment by the long tail of race and resentment, at another by the more acceptable feelings of pity and terror. We live in the sickly light of TV screens, with a pane of selfishness between ourselves and the suffering. We survive explosions and funerals and live on among the families of the victims, those blown apart and those in cells apart.

And we have to live with the Army. This morning I was stopped on the Falls Road and marched to the nearest police barracks, with my three-year-old son, because my car tax was out of date. My protests grew limp when the officer in charge said: 'Look, either you go to the police up the road or we take you now to Holywood'—their own ground. It hasn't been named martial law, but that's what it feels like. Everywhere soldiers with cocked guns are watching you—that's what they're here for—on the streets, at the corners of streets, from doorways, over the puddles on demolished sites. At night, jeeps and armoured cars groan past without lights; or roadblocks are thrown up, and once again it's delays measured in hours, searches and signings among the guns and torches. As you drive away, you bump over ramps that are specially designed to wreck you at speed and maybe get a glimpse of a couple of youths with hands on their heads being frisked on the far side of the road.

Just routine. Meanwhile up in the troubled estates street-lights are gone, accommodating all the better the night-sights of sniper and marksman.

If it is not Army blocks, it is vigilantes. They are very efficiently organized, with barricades of new wood and watchmen's huts and tea rotas, protecting the territories. If I go round the corner at ten o'clock to the cigarette machine or the chip shop, there are gentlemen with flashlights, of mature years and determined mien, who will want to know my business. How far they are in agreement with the sentiments blazoned on the wall at the far end of the street I have not yet enquired. But 'Keep Ulster Protestant' and 'Keep Blacks and Fenians out of Ulster' are there to remind me that there are attitudes around here other than defensive ones. All those sentry-boxes where tea and consultation are taken through the small hours add up to yet another slogan: 'Six into Twenty-Six won't go.' I walk back—'Good night now, sir'—past a bank that was blown up a couple of months ago and a car showroom that went three weeks ago. Nobody was killed. Most of the windows between the sites are boarded up still. Things aren't too bad in our part.

There are few enough people on the roads at night. Fear has begun to tingle through the place. Who's to know the next target on the Provisional list? Who's to know the reprisals won't strike where you are? The bars are quieter. If you're carrying a parcel you make sure it's close to you in case it's suspected of being about to detonate. In the Queen's University staff common-room recently, a bomb-disposal squad had defused a bundle of books before the owner had quite finished his drink in the room next door. Yet when you think of the corpses in the rubble of McGurk's Bar such caution is far from risible.

Then there are the perils of the department stores. Last Saturday a bomb scare just pipped me before I had my socks and pyjamas paid for in Marks and Spencer, although there were four people on the Shankill Road who got no warning. A security man cornered my wife in Robinson and Cleaver—not surprisingly, when she thought of it afterwards. She had a timing device, even though it was just an old clock from an auction, lying in the bottom of her shopping bag. A few days previously someone else's timing device had given her a scare when an office block in University Road exploded just as she got out of range.

There are hardly any fairy lights, or Christmas trees, and in many cases there will be no Christmas cards. This latter is the result of a request by the organizers of the civil disobedience campaign, in order that revenue to the Post Office may be cut as much as possible over the joyous season. If people must send cards, then they are asked to get the anti-internment cards which are being produced by the People's Democracy and the Ardoyne Relief Committee to support, among others, the dependants of the internees in Long Kesh camp. Which must, incidentally, be literally the brightest spot in Ulster. When you pass it on the motorway after dark, it is squared off in neon, bright as an airport. An inflammation on the black countryside. Another of our military decorations.

The seasonal appeals will be made again to all men of goodwill, but goodwill for its proper exercise depends upon an achieved self-respect. For some people in this community, the exercise of goodwill towards the dominant caste has been hampered by the psychological hoops they have been made to jump and by the actual circumstances of their lives within the state, British and all as it may have been. A little goodwill in the Establishment here towards the notion of being Irish would take some of the twists out of the minority. Even at this time it is difficult to extend full sympathy to the predicament of that million among us who would ask the other half-million to exalt themselves by being humbled. You see, I have heard a completely unbigoted and humane friend searching for words to cope with his abhorrence of the Provisionals and hitting on the *mot juste* quite unconsciously: 'These . . . these . . . Irish.'

Instead of the Christmas tree, which will be deliberately absent from many homes, people will put the traditional candle in the window. I am reminded of Louis MacNeice, 'born to the Anglican order, banned for ever from the candles of the Irish poor'; and of W. R. Rodgers, whose *Collected Poems* has appeared in time for Christmas; and of John Hewitt, that Ulsterman of Planter stock whose poetry over the years has been an exploration of the Ulster

Protestant consciousness. All three men were born to a sense of 'two nations', and part of their imaginative effort was a solving of their feelings towards Ireland, a new answer to the question that Macmorris asked Fluellen in the Globe Theatre almost four hundred years ago: 'What is my nation?' As Northern Protestants, they each in different ways explored their relationship to the old sow that eats her farrow. They did not hold apart and claim kin with a different litter. Although, in fact, I have never seen farrow eaten by a sow in my life: what usually happens is that the young pigs eat one another's ears.

Last Sunday, at an interdenominational carol service in the university, I had to read from Martin Luther King's famous 'I Have a Dream' speech. 'I have a dream that one day this nation will rise up and live out the full meaning of its creed'—and on that day all men would be able to realize fully the implications of the old spiritual 'Free at last, free at last, Great God Almighty, we are free at last.' But, as against the natural hopeful rhythms of that vision, I remembered a dream that I'd had last year in California. I was shaving at the mirror of the bathroom when I glimpsed in the mirror a wounded man falling towards me with his bloodied hands lifted to tear at me or to implore.

It used to be that you could predict the aftermath of Christmas: 'How did your Christmas go?' 'Oh quiet, very quiet.' There isn't much predictable now, except that the sirens will blare out the old and blare in nothing very new. In some parts of the country they will have killed the wren on St Stephen's Day. In some houses they will still be hoping for a first-footer to bring a change of luck.

Cessation 1994

The announcement by the Provisional IRA last Wednesday changed everything for the better. I listened to the radio all afternoon, hoping to hear words that would be up to the magnitude of what was happening. But while the political leaders and the commentators were (with predictable exceptions) elated, the sheer volume of the talk began to have an almost claustrophobic effect.

I went outside to try to re-collect myself and suddenly a blind seemed to rise somewhere at the back of my mind and the light came flooding in. I felt twenty-five years younger. I remembered what things had felt like in those early days of political ferment in the late sixties. How we all were brought beyond our highly developed caution to believe that the effort to create new movement and language in the Northern context was a viable project.

But as well as feeling freed up, I felt angry also. The quarter century we have lived through was a terrible black hole, and the inestimable suffering inflicted and endured by every party to the conflict has only brought the situation to a point that is politically less promising than things were in 1968.

At that time, there was energy and confidence on the nationalist side and a developing liberalism—as well as the usual obstinacy and reaction—on the unionist side. There was a general upswing in intellectual and social activity, the border was more pervious than it had been, the sectarian alignments less determining.

I remember in particular feeling empowered (although the word was not in vogue then) by a week on the road with David Hammond and Michael Longley in May 1968 when we brought a programme of songs and poems to schools and hotels and libraries in unionist and nationalist areas all over Northern Ireland.

The programme was called 'Room to Rhyme', and I thought about it again last Wednesday. The title was taken from the opening verse of a mummers' play that went 'Room, room, my gallant boys, and give us room to rhyme', a line that expressed perfectly the eagerness and impatience that was in the air at the time. As a member of the 11-Plus generation of Catholic scholarship boys, just recently appointed to the faculty of Queen's University, I knew myself to be symptomatic of a new confidence in the nationalist minority; and on this particular trip, sponsored by the Northern Ireland Arts Council, with David Hammond singing 'The Boys of Mullaghbawn' and Michael Longley writing about 'Leaving Inishmore' and myself reading 'Requiem for the Croppies', I was conscious that an Irish dimension was at last beginning to figure in the official life of the North.

Which is to say that 'diversity' was beginning to be recognized and to find its expression long before it became a buzz-word. Small changes of attitude, small rapprochements and readjustments were being made. Minimal shifts in different areas—artistic, educational, political—were beginning to effect new contacts and concessions. The fact that I felt free to read a poem about the 1798 rebels to a rather staid audience of middle-class unionists was one such small symptom of a new tolerance.

In a few years' time, of course, to have read 'Requiem for the Croppies' in such a venue would have been taken as a direct expression of support for the IRA's campaign of violence. And this was only one tiny instance of the way in which, during the 1970s, artistic and cultural exercises got peeled away from the action of politics.

I remember, for example, in the early stages of the crisis, being invited to contribute a piece to *Hibernia* on poetry and the Troubles, and writing instead about the contribution of John Hume. I had no qualms whatsoever that this might be a 'dangerous intersection', but as the years proceeded and the situation became more devastating, that kind of living exchange between the professional politicians and the cultural workers quickly became a thing of the past.

What I felt last Wednesday, however, was that there was now an opportunity for everybody to get involved again. The excitement being expressed about the new developments was more than hype. Even people on the unionist side were experiencing a fleeting temptation to credit the turn for the better. The Democratic Unionist Party representatives were understandably downbeat, to say the least, and the citizens on the ground in loyalist areas could hardly be expected to clap their hands. But even so, there was enough positive response to suggest that the complete cessation of military activities by the Provos might result in at least a change of mood on that side also.

Not a great change of mood, of course. The refusal to consider any move that might erode the Britishness of the Ulster Protestant way of life is totally ingrained in the loyalist community, and after the past twenty-five years it would be stupid and insulting to expect them to renege on their sense of separate identity. But it is neither stupid nor insulting to ask them to consider consenting to some political adjustments that would give the nationalist minority equally undisputed rights to the grounds of their Irish identity.

The cessation of violence is an opportunity to open a space—and not just in the political arena but in the first level of each person's consciousness—a space where hope can grow. And I mean hope in the sense that Vaclav Havel has defined it, because it seems to me that his definition has the kind of stoical clarity that should appeal to every realist in the North, Planter or Gael, Protestant or Catholic, optimist or pessimist.

Hope, according to Havel, is different from optimism. It is a state of the soul rather than a response to the evidence. It is not the expectation that things will turn out successfully but the conviction that something is worth working for, however it turns out. Its deepest roots are in the transcendental, beyond the horizon. The self-evident truth of all this is surely something upon which a peace process might reasonably be grounded.

Something to Write Home About

The River Moyola flows southeast from a source in the Sperrin Mountains down through County Derry and enters Lough Neagh just a few miles from where I grew up. Over the years, the river has been deepened and straightened, but in the 1940s there was a ford at Lower Broagh and a trail of big stepping-stones led across from one bank to the other, linking the townland of Broagh to the townland of Bellshill. We used to paddle around the gravel bed on the Broagh side and I always loved venturing out from one stepping-stone to the next, right into the middle of the stream— for even though the river was narrow enough and shallow enough, there was a feeling of daring once you got out into the main flow of the current. Suddenly you were on your own. You were giddy and rooted to the spot at one and the same time. Your body stood stock still, like a milestone or a boundary mark, but your head would be light and swimming from the rush of the river at your feet and the big stately movement of the clouds in the sky above your head.

Nowadays when I think of that child rooted to the spot in midstream, I see a little version of the god the Romans called Terminus, the god of boundaries. The Romans kept an image of Terminus in the Temple of Jupiter on Capitol Hill, and the interesting thing is that the roof above the place where the image sat was open to the sky, as if to say that a god of the boundaries and borders of the earth needed to have access to the boundless, the whole unlimited height and width and depth of the heavens themselves. As if to say that all boundaries are necessary evils and that the truly desirable condition is the feeling of being unbounded, of being king of infinite space. And it is that double capacity that we possess as human beings—the capacity to be attracted at one and the same time to the security of what is intimately known and to the challenges and entrancements of what is beyond us—it is this double capacity that poetry springs from and addresses. A good poem allows you to have your feet on the ground and your head in the air simultaneously.

The word 'terminus' appears as *tearmann* in many Irish place-names, meaning the glebe land belonging to an abbey or a church, land that was specially marked off for ecclesiastical use; and even though there were no places called Termon in the Moyola district, I knew in my bones from very early on that the Moyola itself was a very definite *terminus*, a marker off of one place from another. I knew it when I stood on the stepping-stone but also when I stood on the bridge that spanned the river at Castledawson. I loved to hang over the range wall and look directly down at the flow where the trout were darting about and the riverweed waved like a streamer under the stream. On one side of me was the village of Castledawson, where my mother's people lived in a terrace house, with a trellis of roses over the front pathway and a vegetable garden at the back. My grandparents' house in Castledawson could have been in any spick-and-span English mill village, any working-class terrace where the factory workers came and went to the sound of the factory horn. In this case the factory was Clarke's linen mill and the horn blew morning and evening, at eight and at six, first to call the hands in and then to let them go home. Home to New Row and Boyne Row and Station Road, up past the Orange Hall and the Protestant church, up past the entrance to Moyola Park, where the Castledawson soccer team had its pitch, and Moyola Lodge, where the Chichester Clarkes lived their different life behind the walls of their demesne.

All that was mentally on one side of the river; on the other, there was the parish of Bellaghy, or Ballyscullion, where my father's side of the family, the Heaneys and the Scullions, had lived for generations. Their dwellings were thatched rather than slated, their kitchens had open fires rather than polished stoves, the houses stood in the middle of the fields rather than in a terrace, and the people who lived in them listened to the cattle roaring rather than the horn blowing. Somehow, even at that early age, I

knew the Bellaghy side of my life was not only in a different physical location but in a different cultural location as well. There was
no pitch there for soccer, or English Association Football, as the
game was more officially called. In my mind, Bellaghy belonged
not only to Gaelic football but to the much older Gaelic order of
cattle herding and hill forts; the village, for instance, had a fair day
on the first Monday of every month: the streets would be crammed
with cows and heifers and bullocks, the whole place loud and
stinking with the smells of the beasts and their dung. It was impossible to think of any such unruly activity happening on the
main street of Castledawson. Castledawson was a far more official
place altogether, more modern, more a part of the main drag. The
very name of the place is from the orderly English world of the
eighteenth century, whereas Bellaghy is from an older, more obscure origin in Irish. So, as I once said in a poem—a poem called
'Terminus'—*I grew up in between.*

I grew up between the predominantly Protestant and loyalist village of Castledawson and the generally Catholic and nationalist
district of Bellaghy. In a house situated between a railway and a
road. Between the old sounds of a trotting horse and the newer
sounds of a shunting engine. On a border between townlands and
languages, between accents at one end of the parish that reminded
you of Antrim and Ayrshire and the Scottish speech I used to hear
on the Fair Hill in Ballymena, and accents at the other end of the
parish that reminded you of the different speech of Donegal,
speech with the direct, clear ring of the Northern Irish I studied
when I went to the Gaeltacht in Rannafast.

Naturally enough, some of what Philip Larkin would have
called the 'words of my inner mind' come from that world back
there between times and languages. A word like 'hoke', for example. When I hear somebody say 'hoke', I'm returned to the very
first place in myself. It's not a standard English word and it's not
an Irish-language word either, but it's undislodgeably there, buried
in the very foundations of my own speech. Under me like the floor
of the house where I grew up. Something to write home about, as

it were. The word means to root about and delve into and forage for and dig around, and that is precisely the kind of thing a poem does as well. A poem gets its nose to the ground and follows a trail and hokes its way by instinct towards the real centre of what concerns it. And in fact it was the word 'hoked' itself that got me started on 'Terminus':

> When I hoked there, I would find
> An acorn and a rusted bolt.
>
> If I lifted my eyes, a factory chimney
> And a dormant mountain.
>
> If I listened, an engine shunting
> And a trotting horse.
>
> Is it any wonder when I thought
> I would have second thoughts?

It's hard to grow up in Northern Ireland and not be *forced* into second thoughts, sooner or later. With so much division around, people are forever encountering boundaries that bring them up short. Second thoughts are an acknowledgement that the truth is bounded by different *tearmanns*, that it has to take cognizance of opposing claims. If one person says that too many cooks spoil the broth, another maintains that many hands make light work. If one says a stitch in time saves nine, another says there's many a slip 'twixt the cup and the lip. Ulster is British, says one; Ulster is *Uladh*, an ancient province of Ireland, says the other. On one side of the march drain, you say potato. On the other side, I say potatto. Such contradictions are part of being alive as a member of the human species. But in Northern Ireland they have attained a special local intensity.

> When they spoke of the prudent squirrel's hoard
> It shone like gifts at a nativity.
>
> When they spoke of the mammon of iniquity
> The coins in my pockets reddened like stove-lids.

I was the march drain and the march drain's banks
Suffering the limit of each claim.

The word 'march' was one that I used to hear again and again
when I was a youngster—but not in the usual context of protest
marches and Orange marches and Apprentice Boys marches. In
those days, in that place, the marching season was every season because it was the land itself that did the marching. The verb meant
to meet at the boundary, to be bordered by, to be matched up to
and yet marked off from; one farm marched another farm; one
field marched another field; and what divided them was the march
drain or the march hedge. The word did not mean to walk in a
military manner but to be close, to lie alongside, to border upon
and be bordered upon. It was a word that acknowledged division,
but it contained a definite suggestion of solidarity as well. If my
land marched your land, we were bound by that boundary as well
as separated by it. If the whole of the liberating sky was over the
head of the god Terminus, the whole of the solid earth was under
what he stood for, the march hedge and the march drain.

In the kitchen of the house where I grew up there was a cement
floor, and one of my first memories is the feel of its coldness and
smoothness under my feet. I must have been only two or three at
the time, because I was still in my cot and can remember taking
the boards out of the bottom of it in order to step down to the actual floor. The boards were fitted in like slats but they hadn't been
nailed down, and this meant they could be lifted out one by one—
because, I suppose, they needed to be removable for cleaning every
time a child soiled them. At any rate, I'll never forget that contact
of warm skin and cold floor, the immediate sensation of surprise;
and then something deeper, more gradual, a sensation of consolidation and familiarity, the whole reassuring foundation of the
earth coming up into you through the soles of your feet. It was like
a knowledge coming home to you. I was holding on to the rail of
the cot, but it could have been the deckrail of the world. I was in

two places at once. One was a small square of kitchen floor, and the other was a big knowledgeable space I had stepped into deep inside myself, a space I can still enter through the memory of my warm soles on the cold cement. When my feet touched the floor, I knew I was on my way somewhere, but at the time I could not have said exactly where. Nowadays I would say it was to poetic discovery. And I would quote what the seventeenth-century Japanese poet Bashō had to say about the conduct of the poetic life. 'What is important', Bashō wrote,

> is to keep our mind high in the world of true understanding, and returning to the world of our daily experience to seek therein the truth of beauty. No matter what we may be doing at a given moment, we must not forget that it has a bearing upon our everlasting self which is poetry.

Bashō makes the mind sound a bit like that Roman image of Terminus, earthbound and present in the here and now and yet open also to what Bashō calls the everlasting self, the boundlessness of inner as well as outer space.

The Moyola wasn't the only boundary that entered into me when I was a youngster. I used to carry a can of fresh milk in the evenings from our house to the next house down the road from us. This was—like our own—a thatched house, but unlike our house it was also a pub, and it is there still, more or less the same as it was in the 1940s, thatched and whitewashed, your typical picturesque roadside inn.

My journey from home to the back door of this house was short, no more than a couple of hundred yards, and yet in my child's mind I covered a great distance every time, because between the two doorsteps I crossed the border between the ecclesiastical diocese of Derry and the diocese—or more properly, the archdiocese—of Armagh. The diocese of Derry stretched away to the northwest, into Inishowen and Donegal, and the archdiocese of Armagh stretched for nearly a hundred miles southeast to the

River Boyne and the town of Drogheda on the edge of Meath in the Irish Republic; so while I felt safe and sound on that short stretch of the county road, I still experienced a slightly mysterious sense of distance and division.

Delivering the milk was a genuine expedition into an elsewhere. And the expedition gained in strangeness because the line that marked the division between the here and the there of it was more or less invisible. There was no indication on the road that you were leaving one jurisdiction for the other. But underneath the road, in a culvert that you would hardly notice if you didn't know to look for it, there ran a small trickle of water, and this water was part of a long drain or stream that marked the boundary between the townland of Tamniarn and the townland of Anahorish, as well as the boundary between the parish of Bellaghy and the parish of Newbridge, and then, as I said, the boundary between the diocese of Derry and the archdiocese of Armagh. The name of this march drain or boundary stream was the Sluggan, another Irish word meaning a marsh or a quagmire, and the Sluggan ran on down through a low-lying spread of old wet meadows and plantations to become the border between the townlands of Creagh and Leitrim before it emptied into the waters of Lough Beg, a couple of miles away.

Every day on my road to and from school I crossed and recrossed the Sluggan, and every time my sense of living on two sides of a boundary was emphasized. I never felt the certitude of belonging completely in one place, and, of course, from the historical as well as the topographical point of view, I was right: all those townlands and parishes and dioceses that had once belonged firmly within the old pre-Plantation, ecclesiastical geography of Gaelic Ireland had been subsumed in the meantime and been taken over and taken into another system and another jurisdiction. Many of the place-names I have just mentioned appear in a list of lands confiscated by the English after the Elizabethan conquest of Ulster, lands that were subsequently granted to Sir Thomas Phillips, the governor of what was then the county of Coleraine, in the period between the Flight of the Earls and the beginning of the Plantation of Ulster. The part of the grant which concerns me here is the area known as the 'Lands of Moyola' and which included the names of Tamniaran, Leitrim and Shanmullagh—the old Gaelic name for the place we nowadays call Castledawson:

> Two buckets were easier carried than one.
> I grew up in between.
>
> My left hand placed the standard iron weight.
> My right tilted a last grain in the balance.
>
> Baronies, parishes met where I was born.
> When I stood on the central stepping stone
>
> I was the last earl on horseback in midstream
> Still parleying, in earshot of his peers.

One of the great figures of Irish history in the pre-Plantation period was Hugh O'Neill, Earl of Tyrone, the last native leader to hold out against the Tudor armies of Queen Elizabeth I, the last earl to make a stand and one of the first to suffer within himself the claims of the two different political allegiances that still operate with such deadly force inside Northern Ireland to this day. By English law, O'Neill was the Earl of Tyrone and therefore, in the understanding of Queen Elizabeth, the English Queen's loyal representative in the kingdom of Ireland. But by Irish birth and genealogy, O'Neill was descended from the mythic Irish leader Niall of the Nine Hostages, and to the Irish he therefore appeared as the hereditary leader of the Gaelic O'Neills, with a destined role as the defender of the Gaelic interest against the English. This is not the place to go into a history of the Elizabethan wars in Ireland, which ended with the defeat of the Irish under Hugh O'Neill and Red Hugh O'Donnell at Kinsale in 1601; but there is one incident that happened in the course of those long-drawn-out campaigns that never ceases to fascinate me.

The event occurred one day early in September 1599, after O'Neill's forces had drawn the English Army up into his own territory, in the wooded countryside of Louth and Armagh. The leader

of the English expedition was Queen Elizabeth's favourite courtier,
the Earl of Essex, and the Queen had been ordering him into action for months before he had taken this initiative. But O'Neill was
a master negotiator and a great one for putting off the moment of
confrontation, so he contrived to get Essex to come for a parley
with him, on the banks of the River Glyde in what is now County
Louth. O'Neill was on horseback, out in midstream, with the water
up to his horse's belly and his Irish-speaking soldiers behind him,
speaking English to Essex, who was standing facing him on the
other bank. Essex was under orders to pursue O'Neill as a traitor,
but here he was in conversation, more like the old friend he had
once been than the enemy he was destined to become—for O'Neill
had been at the court of Elizabeth a generation earlier, and his patron in England at that time had been Essex's father, Walter Dev-
ereux, the first Earl. So, for each of them, this meeting by the river
was a mysterious turn, a hiatus, a frozen frame in the violent action, a moment when those on either bank could see what was happening but could not hear what was being said. Both men were
alone and exposed to the consequences of their actions; O'Neill was
already regarded as a traitor, and Essex, by agreeing to a truce with
him at this moment, was going to be seen as a betrayer by the
Queen and in fact before the end of the year would be executed for
treason. O'Neill's ultimate defeat lay ahead also, in a couple of
years' time. But for the moment, the balance trembled and held,
the water ran and the sky moved silently above them:

> Baronies, parishes met where I was born.
> When I stood on the central stepping stone
>
> I was the last earl on horseback in midstream
> Still parleying, in earshot of his peers.

There was no way, given their historical circumstances, that
O'Neill and Essex could cross to each other's side. Their march had
turned into something irrevocably military. They were at the terminus, in an extreme sense of that word. There was no room for

two truths. The brutality of power would have to decide the issue, not the play of mind. And yet as we think about the scene, we want each of them to be released from the entrapment of history. We want the sky to open above them and grant them release from their earthbound fates. And even if we know that such a release is impossible, we still desire conditions where the longed-for and the actual might be allowed to coincide. A condition where borders are there to be crossed rather than to be contested:

> Running water never disappointed.
> Crossing water always furthered something.
> Stepping stones were stations of the soul.

I wrote the 'Terminus' poem in the mid-1980s, when the political situation in Northern Ireland was totally locked and blocked; in the post-hunger-strike world, when the IRA's campaign showed no sign of abating and the Thatcher government was prepared to live with what was termed an acceptable level of violence. Maybe that is one reason why the poem ends in stasis, with the Earl arrested in midstream and his opposite out of reach on the bank beyond him; the poem is saying that the inheritance of a divided world is a disabling one, that it traps its inhabitants and corners them in determined positions, saps their will to act freely and creatively. But before that moment and since that moment, things nevertheless were and have been different.

Nearly thirty years ago, for example, long before I gave any thought to Bashō or Terminus or Hugh O'Neill or the Sluggan drain and all that they might mean, I wrote a poem called 'The Other Side'. It began with a recollection of something a Presbyterian neighbour had said about a field of ours that marched a field of his and was divided from it by a little grassy stream, but then the poem went on to play with the notion of separation, of two sides of the march drain being like the two sides of the divided community in Northern Ireland—two sides divided by the way they pray, for example, and in little subtle but real ways (as I was suggesting earlier on) by the way they speak. The poem, however, ended up suggesting that a crossing could be attempted, that stepping-stones could be placed by individuals who wanted to further things.

> Then sometimes when the rosary was dragging
> mournfully on in the kitchen
> we would hear his step round the gable
>
> though not until after the litany
> would the knock come to the door
> and the casual whistle strike up
>
> on the doorstep, 'A right-looking night',
> he might say, 'I was dandering by
> and says I, I might as well call.'
>
> But now I stand behind him
> in the dark yard, in the moan of prayers.
> He puts a hand in a pocket
>
> or taps a little tune with the blackthorn
> shyly, as if he were party to
> lovemaking or a stranger's weeping.
>
> Should I slip away, I wonder,
> or go up and touch his shoulder
> and talk about the weather
>
> or the price of grass-seed?

There were times during the last thirty years when I thought 'The Other Side' might be too consoling. Given the actual conditions on the roads and the streets, I thought it might be too benign, too tender in the face of assassination and explosion, too hopeful. And yet the subject had called words from my inner mind. They had dandered in and reminded me of the possible boundlessness of our sympathies. In the end they reminded me also of what Bashō called 'the world of true understanding', which is always lying just beneath the surface and just beyond the horizon of the actual words we speak. They reminded me that the marching season need not just be the season of parades and provocation but that in the ground of the language and the ground beneath our feet there is another march which promises far more creative conditions for the mind and soul. For it seems to me that the confrontation between O'Neill and Essex represents where we arrive if we walk in a military manner, a condition of stasis and embittered *rigor vitae* that hampers the emergence of a better future; but the encounter at the march drain represents the possibility of going out on the stepping-stone in order to remove yourself from the hardness and fastness of your home ground. The stepping-stone invites you to change the terms and the *tearmann* of your understanding; it does not ask you to take your feet off the ground, but it refreshes your vision by keeping your head in the air and bringing you alive to the open sky of possibility that is within you. And that still seems something to write home about.

Earning a Rhyme

The translation of a text from the Irish language into English by
an English-speaking Irish writer usually involves considerations
other than the strictly literary. The additional contexts are historical, cultural and political, as when a Native American author turns
to material in one of the original languages of the North American continent. In each case, a canonical literature in English creates the acoustic within which the translation is going to be heard;
an overarching old colonial roof inscribed 'The land was ours before we were the land's' is made to echo with some such retort as
'You don't say!'

The translation of an Anglo-Saxon poem by an English writer
is a less complicated affair: what is missing is the element of answering back. The invasion of England by the Normans did bring
about great changes in the language, but what occurred was a mutation rather than an obliteration. Native translations of the Old
English deposits are acts of retrenchment rather than retaliation.
They reinforce the English myth of continuity. They give new
form to that from which English itself has been formed. The newness may be a disruption or countering of settled conventions, but
it will not be a challenge to the deep structure. Hopkins's innova-
tions, for example, though not strictly translations, did in fact employ an Anglo-Saxon stress in order to produce the double-effect I
have just outlined: they went against the grain of contemporary
English verse-craft in a completely salutary way, and at the same
time they went *with* an older English grain of collective memory
and belonging.

When, however, John Millington Synge created a new man-
darin idiom in his plays and in his prose book *The Aran Islands*,
the purpose of the enterprise was very different. It may have

looked the same: an attempt to refresh the language of English literature, one of those periodic returns to the spoken idiom which
Donne and Dryden and Wordsworth had initiated in their times,
and which T. S. Eliot would set in motion shortly after Synge's own
death. But Synge was more concerned to found a new literary tradition than to renovate the old one. The collective memory and
sense of belonging that Synge aspired to resuscitate were not English; on the contrary, his search for a new style was just one of the
several moves afoot at the time to bring about 'the de-anglicization
of Ireland'. For Synge to base his style upon an otherness of usage
in the absent Irish language was therefore more than a mere ex-
oticism: it constituted solidarity with all those other cultural and
political efforts of a separatist nature that were happening in the
1890s.

The Irish Literary Revival is by now, of course, a historical
phenomenon. As are the Tudor Conquest of Ireland and the English colonization of North America. Yet in Northern Ireland in
the late sixties and early seventies those remote occasions began to
assume a new relevance. Questions about identity and cultural difference, which were being raised by Afro-Americans and Native
Americans in the United States, were coming up again urgently
and violently in Ulster; poets were being pressed, directly and indirectly, to engage in identity politics. The whole unfinished business
of the England/Ireland entanglement presented itself at a local
level as a conflict of loyalties and impulses, and as a result the
search was on for images and analogies that could ease the strain of
the present. The poets were needy for ways in which they could
honestly express the realities of the local quarrel without turning
that expression into yet another repetition of the aggressions and
resentments which had been responsible for the quarrel in the first
place.

It was under these circumstances that I began work in 1972 on
Buile Suibhne, a Middle Irish text already well known because of
Flann O'Brien's hilarious incorporation of its central character into
the apparatus of *At Swim-Two-Birds*. And *Buile Suibhne* is indeed
strange stuff—the tale of a petty king from seventh-century Ulster, cursed by a saint, transformed by the shock of battle into a de-

mented flying creature and doomed to an outcast's life in the trees. But what had all this amalgam in verse and prose to do with me or the moment? How could a text engendered within the Gaelic order of medieval Ireland speak to a modern Ulster audience riven by divisions resulting from the final destruction of that order? The very meaning of the term 'Ulster' had been forced. Originally the name of an ancient Irish province and part of a native Gaelic cosmology, it had become through Plantation by the English in the 1620s and partition by the British Parliament in the 1920s the name of a six-county British enclave that resisted integration with the Republic of Ireland, and indulged in chronic discriminatory practices against its Irish nationalist minority in order to maintain the status quo. What had the translation of the tale of a Celtic wild man to do with the devastations of the new wild men of the Provisional IRA?

My hope was that the book might render a unionist audience more pervious to the notion that Ulster was Irish, without coercing them out of their cherished conviction that it was British. Also, because it reached back into a pre-colonial Ulster of monastic Christianity and Celtic kingship, I hoped the book might complicate that sense of entitlement to the land of Ulster which had developed so overbearingly in the Protestant majority as a result of various victories and acts of settlement over the centuries. By extending the span of their historical memory into pre-British time, one might stimulate some sympathy in the unionists for the nationalist minority who located their lost title to sovereignty in that Gaelic dream-place.

I did not, of course, expect *Sweeney Astray* so to affect things that political conversions would break out all over Northern Ireland. I did not even think of my intention in the deliberate terms which I have just outlined. I simply wanted to offer an indigenous text that would not threaten a unionist (after all, this was just a translation of an old tale, situated for much of the time in what is now County Antrim and County Down), but that would fortify a nationalist (after all, this old tale tells us we belonged here always and that we still remain unextirpated). I wanted to deliver a work that could be read universally as the-thing-in-itself but that would also sustain those extensions of meaning that our disastrously complicated local predicament made both urgent and desirable.

II

First time round I went at the work speedily and a little overbearingly. I was actually taking off from J. G. O'Keefe's parallel translation (published in 1913, volume 12 of the Irish Texts Society's editions) more than I was attending to the Irish itself. I was afraid that I might not finish the whole thing, so in order to forestall as far as possible the let-down of such a failure, I hurled myself at the task. My main pitch, day by day, was to keep up an animated rate of production. I could not afford to dwell upon any single eddy of difficulty or subtlety in case it slowed me down to a discouraging rate. Consequently, the first draft was mostly in free verse, bowling along in the malleable quatrains that had become a habit with me in the course of writing *Wintering Out.*

First time round I was also far more arrogant in my treatment of the sense. That is to say, I arrogated to myself the right to follow suggestions in the original, to develop a line of association out of the given elements of the Irish rather than to set down an obedient equivalent. I allowed myself to import echoes from the English literary tradition, from the Bible, to perform in metaphor what the text delivered in statement. O'Keefe, for example, gave the following direct translation of part of a typical Sweeney lament:

> Though I be as I am to-night,
> there was a time
> when my strength was not feeble
> over a land that was not bad.
>
> On splendid steeds,
> in life without sorrow,
> in my auspicious kingship
> I was a good, great king.

In 1972, however, I was in no mood to follow the drab, old-fashioned lead of this kind of thing. It became a much more jacked-up performance altogether:

> Though I am Lazarus,
> there was a time
> when I dressed in purple
> and they fed from my hand.
>
> I was a good king,
> the tide of my affairs
> was rising, the world
> was the bit in my horse's mouth.

Robert Lowell's example was operative here. His trick of heightening the sense by boosting the diction and planting new metaphors into the circuit was not lost on me. Nor was his unabashed readiness to subdue the otherness of the original to his own autobiographical neediness. I began to inflate myself and my situation into Sweeney's, to make analogies between the early medieval Ulsterman who rocketed out of the North, as a result of vehement squabbles there among the petty dynasties, and this poet from County Derry who had only recently come south to County Wicklow for purposes of retreat and composure. It all contributed to a velocity that was its own reward. I cuffed the original with a brusqueness and familiarity that had not been earned but that gave me immense satisfaction. I was using *Buile Suibhne* as a trampoline. I should have been showing it off, but instead it was being pressed into service to show me off.

Naturally, I did not feel this from day to day as I went baling through the stanzas. But I did have a nagging sense that the freedoms being exercised were not going to yield an integrated work. Riff by riff, it felt good, but there was no sense, as the pages piled up, of 'thoughts long knitted to a single thought'. I had wanted the pressure and accumulating oneness which is the reward—and justification—of a sustained writing; what I was getting was a series of lyric highs, exciting enough in themselves but not gathering force between themselves. Nevertheless, since my primary aim had become the completion of a version of the whole text, I forged ahead until that goal was achieved. Then I simply went flat, fell into a kind of post-composition *tristesse*. I knew that it would all have to be done over again but I had not the stamina or the relish necessary for a fresh start.

I cannot remember when I got the idea that the stanzas should be recast in a more hard-edged, pointed way; that they should have the definition of hedges in a winter sunset; that they should be colder, more articulated; should be tuned to a bleaker note; should be more constricted and ascetic; more obedient to the metrical containments and battened-down verbal procedures of the Irish itself. At any rate, it was while I was spending a month on Long Island in 1979, after my first semester at Harvard, that I suddenly started one morning to reshape stanzas from scratch, rhyming them and keeping my eyes as much to the left, on the Irish, as to the right, on O'Keefe's unnerving trot.

It was this closer inspection of the thickets of the Irish that made the second stint a different kind of engagement. Instead of the energy being generated by hurry and boldness, a certain intensity gathered through the steadier, more lexically concentrated gaze at individual words. Instead of the rhythmic principle being one of lanky, enjambed propulsion, the lines hurdling along for fear they might seize up, the unit of composition now became the quatrain itself and the metrical pattern became more end-stopped and boxed in.

The eight lines I quoted earlier sounded now both more literal and more limited within the stanza-shape:

> Far other than to-night,
> far different my plight
> the times when with firm hand
> I ruled over a good land.
>
> Prospering, smiled upon,
> curbing some great-steed,
> I rode high, on the full tide
> of good luck and kingship.

I still tried to get a self-igniting life between the words but kept them flintier and more niggardly than before. My favourite instance of the new asceticism comes at Section 73, where Sweeney praises the setting of a little monastery at Alternan. O'Keefe gives the place its Irish name and renders the relevant stanza as follows:

> Cliff of Farannan, abode of saints,
> with many fair hazels and nuts,
> swift cold water
> rushing down its side.

In my original handling of this, I took fire at the possibility of making the saintliness of the place more resplendent than either the original poet or the unflashy O'Keefe would have dreamed of:

> O the tabernacle of the hazel wood
> on the cliff of Farannan,
> and the cataract glittering
> like the stem of a chalice!

Seven years later, the gilding came off and the exclamation was at least minus its 'O':

> Sainted cliff at Alternan,
> nut grove, hazel wood!
> Cold quick sweeps of water
> fall down the cliff-side.

III

It is nine years since those lines were written, and sixteen since they were done in the freer register, so what I am doing here is re-creating the feel of the writing experience rather than giving a report on the details of the procedure. Yet that feel is the *sine qua non*: the guarantee of the life of the thing. For in spite of the real enough influence of the cultural and political context I referred to earlier, the true anxiety and the true motivations of writing are much more inward, much more to do with freshets that start unexpectedly in moments of intent concentration and hope. Literary translation—or version-making or imitation or refraction or whatever one should call the linguistic carry-over that is mediated through a crib—is still an aesthetic activity. It has as much to do with form-feeling as with sense-giving, and unless the translator experiences the almost muscular sensation that rewards successful original composition, it is unlikely that the results of the text-labour will have life of their own.

The closer, line by line, stanza by stanza, end-stopped, obedient, literal approach finally yielded more. I had a sense of accumulation rather than of truancy—a different satisfaction, not necessarily superior but more consoling in the execution of a long piece of composition. I had also forgotten about the political extensions that were originally intended. In fact, by the time *Sweeney Astray* appeared, I had got fed up with my own mournful bondings to the 'matter of Ulster' and valued more the otherness of *Buile Suibhne* as a poem from beyond. If, in the beginning, I was somewhat surprised that I had taken on the translation at all, in the end I was grateful to feel still somewhat estranged from what I had made of it. In fact, it was only after the translation had been completed for the second time and I had earned that familiarity which I had originally arrogated—it was only then that the work yielded its full reward. The freedom and peremptoriness which I had exercised prematurely returned in a burst of confidence and I produced the speedy poems included in *Station Island* under the general title 'Sweeney Redivivus'. The identification I had made previously between the green man and the rural child was admitted and even exulted in. Sweeney was unreservedly rhymed with Heaney:

> Give him his due, in the end
> he opened my path to a kingdom
> of such scope and neuter allegiance
> my emptiness reigns at its whim.

('Sweeney and the Cleric')

On Poetry and Professing

I have spent much of my life teaching, at very different levels. I began in the early 1960s in St Thomas's Secondary Intermediate School in the Ballymurphy area of Belfast, in front of a class of deprived and disaffected adolescent boys, many of whom would end up a decade later as active members of the Provisional IRA. I proceeded from there to work in a teacher training college, also in Belfast, and to spend time trying to persuade student teachers of the value of imaginative literature and other kinds of creative play in the educational process; I went on to lecture on poetry in Queen's University and ended up in more recent years as a poet in residence at Harvard. In each of these places, members of the audience differed widely in literary awareness, and in the degree of their assent to the idea that poetry was a subject worth discussing at all. I have known both the heckling of the have-nots in St Thomas's and the nods and gleams of the granny glasses in Harvard Hall; in each case there was a desire, repressed in the Belfast context but altogether ardent in Cambridge, a desire to have the worth and meaning of the art confirmed. What was at stake was the credibility of this honoured but hard to define category of human achievement called poetry. Even in Ballymurphy, those boys excluded by their social and cultural background from any contact with literary verse and disposed to regard it as some kind of fancy affectation, even they were curious despite their resistance. There were plenty of influences at work to make them shy away: peer pressure, the macho conventions of the playground in a boys' school, a working-class shyness in the face of anything that smacked of middle-class pretension. Even so, the mystery of the thing interested them, and every now and again during those English classes something steadied and came into focus: for a concentrated moment the words they were attending to made sense and went home as only poetry can.

Another thing that happened during those English classes is also worth recalling. About once a week, and always unexpectedly, the headmaster of the school would suddenly appear in the classroom door. Mr McLaverty was a short-story writer of real distinction, but he was also compulsively a teacher. He was meant to be in his headmaster's office all day, administering, but instead he prowled the corridors in his tweed suit and polished brogues, seeking whom he might interrupt in order to get in a bit of the actual schoolmastering that he missed so much. 'Right, boys', he would exclaim as he hurried across the floor to claim the boys for his own. And then, 'Right, Mr Heaney!' in order to relieve me of responsibility for them, or rather to appoint me as his straight man in a double act which rarely varied. 'Mr Heaney,' he would continue, 'are they working hard for you?' 'Yes, Mr McLaverty', I would answer. 'And are you doing any poetry with them?' 'Oh yes,' I would reply, 'I am indeed.' 'And are you seeing any improvement in them at all?' To which the correct answer was, 'Of course, I am.' And then, climactically, he would turn his attention very deliberately from the class to me and enquire, 'Mr Heaney, when you look at the photograph of a rugby team in the newspaper, don't you always know immediately from the look of the players' faces which ones of them have studied poetry?' And dutifully, unfailingly I would answer, 'Yes, Mr McLaverty, I do know', and McLaverty would nod triumphantly and turn back towards the desks. 'There you are now, boys', he'd say. 'Work hard and don't end up down there with the rest of them, measuring the length of your spits at some street corner! Right, Mr Heaney!' And away he would go in all his peremptory vigour, as memorable and problematical as poetry itself.

When I say problematical, all I mean is that poetry cannot be proved in the way a theorem can. McLaverty could only manage to get away with his proposition that poetry changed people perceptibly for the better because I was ready to connive with him. And anyhow, the boys in the class knew that the whole thing was a masquerade. But it is precisely this masquerade of fictions and ironies and fantastic scenarios that can draw us out and bring us close to ourselves. The paradox of the arts is that they are all made up and yet they allow us to get at truths about who and what we are or might be. In fact, Mr McLaverty's caricature of the humanizing power of poetry was tempting as well as comic, because it was drawing upon two and a half millennia of Western aesthetic and educational theory. From Plato to the present, from the Athenian academy to the parent-teacher meeting at your local primary school, there has been an ongoing debate about the place and the point and the choice of imaginative writing in the curriculum, and about the relevance of such material to the formation of the good citizen's sensibility and behaviour. In fact, McLaverty's performance was in itself a kind of parody or exaggeration of one of the central ideas of this humanist tradition, the idea that there is an essential connection between the good and the beautiful and that the study of the beautiful is actively conducive to virtue. This particular defence of the value of art was disastrously weakened in the last century, of course, by the historical fact of the Holocaust: what good is a devotion to and an appreciation of the beautiful, the question goes, if some of the most cultivated people in a most cultivated nation could authorize mass killings and attend a Mozart concert on the same evening? Yet if it is a delusion and a danger to expect poetry and music to do too much, it is a diminishment and a derogation of them to ignore what they can do.

What they can do is testified to not only by Mr McLaverty but also by Shakespeare's Caliban. In *The Tempest*, Caliban's description of the effect that Ariel's music produces in him could be read as a kind of paean to the effect of poetry itself. You remember the lines: Caliban is telling Stephano and Trinculo not to be worried about the mysterious tune that is coming out of the sky above them and says:

> Be not afeard; the isle is full of noises,
> Sounds and sweet airs, that give delight, and hurt not.
> Sometimes a thousand twangling instruments
> Will hum about mine ears, and sometimes voices,
> That, if I then had wak'd after long sleep,
> Will make me sleep again.

'Sounds and sweet airs, that give delight, and hurt not': that, as a description of the good of poetry and of literature in general, will do. It is not required that the experience of the sounds change Caliban into another kind of creature, or that it have a carry-over effect upon his behaviour. The good of literature and of music is first and foremost in the thing itself, and their first principle is that which William Wordsworth called in his Preface to *Lyrical Ballads* 'the grand elementary principle of pleasure', the kind of pleasure about which the language itself prompts us to say, 'It did me good.'

So: one function of university chairs such as the one we are here to inaugurate this evening is to promote the experience of that particular good. One function of the holder of such a chair is to enter the university in much the same way as Mr McLaverty entered my classroom and to use the occasion in such a way as to reinforce a belief in the fundamental purpose of the spiritual intellect's great work.

II

The essential professing that poets do usually comes about at moments of crisis in their lives; what they have to say about problems they endure or resolve gets expressed first in terms which are personal and urgent, and then these *ad hoc* formulations about the art or the life become familiar reference points, and may even attain the force of prescriptions.

Take Keats's famous letter to his brother George, the one where he simplifies his vision of the poetic destiny to a parable about the education of an intelligence into a soul: a school is needed and that school is the world of pain. This sacred text arose unpredictably from Keats's own desperate need to square his essentially celebratory temperament with what he perceived to be the awful conditions. Or take Osip Mandelstam's head-lightening faith that the poet is 'a stealer of air', and is therefore never a 'worker' in the sense officially demanded by the state, but works only in the sense that lacemakers work to make a design that is 'air, perforations and truancy', or bakers of doughnuts work to produce the antic hole rather than the worthy dough. Mandelstam's reckless brilliance is a profession of poetry's freedom which outstrips anything that is ever likely to be said on a podium; and, of course, it came at a correspondingly higher cost than the usual orthodoxies of the academy.

Nevertheless, if poetry is to be professed within the educational system, it makes sense that this should be done occasionally by the poets themselves; as long as they recognize the fundamental difference between their function as educators and their function as artists, no harm need be done and a lot of good may even flow from their involvement. And anyhow, like everything else in the area of teaching, success will depend more upon the temperament of the poet/professor and his or her capacity to involve the student than upon any innate genius or acquired wisdom. Teaching is as much a mystery as it is a technique, and the aura of the person, his or her intellectual radiance or general trustworthiness, is going to have as much to do with the poet/professor's impact as the size of the reputation or the intrinsic quality of the poetry itself.

The great advantage a poet has is the fact that he or she is likely to possess a credible personal language—and obviously by this I don't mean colourful 'poetic' speech. I mean, rather, that there will be no gap between the professional idiom and the personal recognitions: the way the poet speaks in the corner of a bar, gossiping about the faults and strengths of a poem that has just appeared in *The Irish Times*, will tend to be the way he speaks to the students in the lecture room. Characteristically, there will be a sensitivity to the technical aspects of the work combined with a more down-to-earth recognition that poetry is part of the usual life and an expectation that a poet or a poem should embody a certain amount of gumption and horse sense. Furthermore, in spite of what might be generally assumed, poets are likely to be hard on fancy stuff, on soft-focus 'feeling' and hyped-up rhetoric; they know the dangers of archness and inflation and self-deception to which their ventures are prone, and they are predisposed to be on the lookout for these flaws in the writing of others if not in their own.

Poets are also more likely to attest without self-consciousness to the living nature of poetic tradition and to the demotic life of 'the canon'. Nowadays, undergraduates are being taught prematurely to regard the poetic heritage as an oppressive imposition and to suspect it for its latent discriminations in the realm of gender, its privilegings and marginalizations in the realms of class and power. All of this suspicion may be salutary enough when it is exercised by a mind informed by that which it is being taught to suspect, but it is a suspicion which is lamentably destructive of cultural memory when it is induced in minds without any cultural possessions whatever. On the other hand, when a poet quotes from memory or from prejudice or in sheer admiration, 'the canon' is manifested in an educationally meaningful way. To put it simply, I believe that the life of society is better served by a quotation-bore who quotes out of a professional love than by an 'unmasking'-bore who subverts out of theory.

Not to confuse the artistic with the educational, however, is the main caveat for the poet as professor. The worst thing that such a confusion leads to is arrogant and ridiculous behaviour by the poet in relation to the student: the poet who thinks that excellence in the art excuses ill-manneredness or ill-preparedness in the classroom is offending the human as well as the professional imperatives. I have seen talented men and women so encased in the shining armour of *moi* that they have utterly failed to connect with the group in front of them. This can be merely a case of idiocy and wasted opportunity, but it becomes grievous when the authority which their position confers is used by the poet/professors to overbear the potential and to destroy the confidence of neophyte readers or writers. Whatever the age of the students and whatever the circumstances—primary-school classroom or graduate poetry workshop—the covenant between the teacher and the taught demands a certain stand-off and protectiveness on the part of the empowered figure of the teacher. We have been rightly alerted to all forms of sexual harassment in these contexts, but there can be such a thing as vocational harassment, where the student's hopes and aspirations are unthinkingly assailed. Of course, a fair and honest estimate of the student's gifts—good or bad—has to be communicated, but the communication must be done with respect and a care for the emotional tissues.

What I tend to say at the beginning of the term to my students in poetry workshops is this: I am going to be involved with your *capacities* as writers, but your *destinies* as writers are your own business—after all, you will be receiving grades at the end of the term, so let that be a reminder of the status of our relationship, which is, strictly speaking, pedagogical. But even as I say this, as much for my own protection as for theirs, I recognize that once a personal connection is established with a student by way of my respect for his or her potential or achievement—or vice versa—then one of us has affected, however fleetingly, the other's sense of a destiny in poetry. And this may turn out to be something very positive indeed.

II

Englands of the Mind

One of the most precise and suggestive of T. S. Eliot's critical formulations was his notion of what he called 'the auditory imagination', 'the feeling for syllable and rhythm, penetrating far below the conscious levels of thought and feeling, invigorating every word; sinking to the most primitive and forgotten, returning to the origin and bringing something back', fusing 'the most ancient and the most civilized mentality'. I presume Eliot was thinking here about the cultural depth-charges latent in certain words and rhythms, that binding secret between words in poetry that delights not just the ear but the whole backward and abysm of mind and body; thinking of the energies beating in and between words that the poet brings into half-deliberate play; thinking of the relationship between the word as pure vocable, as articulate noise, and the word as etymological occurrence, as symptom of human history, memory and attachments.

It is in the context of this auditory imagination that I wish to discuss the language of Ted Hughes, Geoffrey Hill and Philip Larkin. All of them return to an origin and bring something back, all three live off the hump of the English poetic achievement, all three, here and now, in England, imply a continuity with another England, there and then. All three are hoarders and shorers of what they take to be the real England. All three treat England as a region—or rather treat their region as England—in different and complementary ways. I believe they are afflicted with a sense of history that was once the peculiar affliction of the poets of other nations who were not themselves natives of England but who spoke the English language. The poets of the mother culture, I feel, are now possessed of that defensive love of their territory which was once shared only by those poets whom we might call colonial—Yeats, MacDiarmid, Carlos Williams. They are aware of their Englishness as deposits in the descending storeys of the literary and historical past. Their very terrain is becoming consciously precious. A desire to preserve indigenous traditions, to keep open the imagination's supply lines to the past, to receive from the stations of Anglo-Saxon confirmations of ancestry, to perceive in the rituals of show Saturdays and race-meetings and seaside outings, of churchgoing and marriages at Whitsun, and in the necessities that crave expression after the ritual of churchgoing has passed away, to perceive in these a continuity of communal ways and a confirmation of an identity which is threatened—all this is signified by their language.

When we examine that language, we find that their three separate voices are guaranteed by three separate foundations which, when combined, represent almost the total resources of the English language itself. Hughes relies on the northern deposits, the pagan Anglo-Saxon and Norse elements, and he draws energy also from a related constellation of primitive myths and world-views. The life of his language is a persistence of the stark outline and vitality of Anglo-Saxon that paid into the Middle English alliterative tradition and then went underground to sustain the folk poetry, the ballads and the ebullience of Shakespeare and the Elizabethans. Hill is also sustained by the Anglo-Saxon base, but his proper guarantor is that language as modified and amplified by the vocabularies and values of the Mediterranean, by the early-medieval Latin influence; his is to a certain extent a scholastic imagination founded on an England that we might describe as Anglo-Romanesque, touched by the polysyllabic light of Christianity but possessed by darker energies which might be acknowledged as barbaric. Larkin then completes the picture, because his proper hinterland is the English language Frenchified and turned humanist by the Norman Conquest and the Renaissance, made nimble, melodious and plangent by Chaucer and Spenser and besomed clean of its inkhornisms and its irrational magics by the eighteenth century.

And their Englands of the mind might be correspondingly characterized. Hughes's is a primeval landscape where stones cry out and horizons endure, where the elements inhabit the mind with a religious force, where the pebble dreams 'it is the foetus of

God', 'where the staring angels go through', 'where all the stars bow down', where, with appropriately pre-Socratic force, water lies 'at the bottom of all things / utterly worn out utterly clear'. It is England as King Lear's heath, which now becomes a Yorkshire moor where sheep and foxes and hawks persuade 'unaccommo-dated man' that he is a poor bare forked thing, kinned not in a chain but on a plane of being with the animals themselves. There are monoliths and lintels. The air is menaced by God's voice in the wind, by demonic protean crow-shapes; and the poet is a wanderer among the ruins, cut off by catastrophe from consolation and phi-losophy. Hill's England, on the other hand, is more hospitable to the human presence. The monoliths make way for the keeps and chantries, if also for the beheading block. The heath's loneliness is kept at bay by the natural magic of the grove and the intellectual force of the scholar's cell. The poet is not a wanderer but a clerk or perhaps an illuminator or one of a guild of masters: he is in pos-session of a history rather than a mythology; he has a learned rather than an oral tradition. There are wars, but there are also dy-nasties, ideas of inheritance and order, possibilities for the 'true governaunce of England'. His elegies are not laments for the irrev-ocable dispersal of the *comitatus* and the ring-giver in the hall but solemn requiems for Plantagenet kings, whose murderous wars are set in a great pattern, to be understood only when 'the sea / Across daubed rocks evacuates its dead'. And Larkin's England similarly reflects features from the period that his language is hived off. His trees and flowers and grasses are neither animistic nor hallowed by half-remembered druidic lore; they are emblems of mutabilitie. Behind them lies the sensibility of troubadour and courtier. 'Cut grass lies frail; / Brief is the breath / Mown stalks exhale'; his landscape is dominated neither by the untamed heath nor by the totemistic architectures of spire and battlement but by the civic prospects, by roofs and gardens and prospects where urban and pas-toral visions interact as 'postal districts packed like squares of wheat'. The poet is no longer a bardic remnant nor an initiate in curious learning nor a jealous master of the secrets of a craft; he is a humane and civilized member of the customs service or the civil service or, indeed, the library service. The moon is no longer his white goddess but his poetic property, to be image rather than icon: 'high and preposterous and separate', she watches over unfenced existence, over fulfilment's desolate attic, over an England of department stores, canals and floatings of industrial froth, explosions in mines, effigies in churches, secretaries in offices; and she hauls tides of life where only one ship is worth celebration, not a *Golden Hind* or a *Victory*, but a 'black- / Sailed unfamiliar, towing at her back / A huge and birdless silence'.

Hughes's sensibility is pagan in the original sense: he is a haunter of the *pagus*, a heath-dweller, a heathen; he moves by instinct in the thickets beyond the *urbs*; he is neither urban nor urbane. His poetry is as redolent of the lair as it is of the library. The very titles of his books are casts made into the outback of our animal recognitions. *Lupercal*, a word infested with wolfish stinks yet returning to an origin in Shakespeare's *Julius Caesar*: 'You all did see that on the Lupercal / I thrice presented him a kingly crown.' Yet the word passes back through Shakespeare into the Lupercal, a cave below the western corner of the Palatine Hill in Rome; and the Lupercal was also the festival held on 15 February when, after the sacrifice of goats and a dog, youths dressed only in girdles made from the skins of these victims ran about the bounds of the Palatine city, striking those whom they met, especially women, with strips of goatskin. It was a fertility rite, and it was also a ritual beating of the bounds of the city, and in a way Hughes's language is just this also. Its sensuous fetch, its redolence of blood and gland and grass and water, recalled English poetry in the 1950s from a too suburban aversion of attention to the elemental; and the poems beat the bounds of a hidden England in streams and trees, on moors and in byres. Hughes appeared like Poor Tom on the heath, a civilized man tasting and testing the primitive facts; he appeared as 'Wodwo', a nosing wild man of the woods. The volume *Wodwo* appeared in 1967 and carried as its epigraph a quotation from *Sir Gawain and the Green Knight*, and that deliberate affiliation is instructive. Like the art of *Gawain*, Hughes's art is one of clear outline and inner richness. His diction is consonantal, and it snicks through the air like an efficient blade, marking and carving out fast, definite shapes; but within those shapes, mysteries

and rituals are hinted at. They are circles within which he con-
jures up presences.

Hughes's vigour has much to do with this matter of consonants
that take the measure of his vowels like calipers, or stud the line like
rivets. 'Everything is inheriting everything', as he says in one of his
poems, and what he has inherited through Shakespeare and John
Webster and Hopkins and Lawrence is something of that primary
life of stress which is the quick of the English poetic matter. His
consonants are the Norsemen, the Normans, the Roundheads in the
world of his vocables, hacking and hedging and hammering down
the abundance and luxury and possible lasciviousness of the vowels.
'I imagine this midnight moment's forest'—the first line of the
well-known 'The Thought Fox'—is hushed, but it is a hush achieved
by the quelling, battening-down action of the *m*'s and *d*'s and *t*'s: I
iMagine this MiDnighT MoMenT's foresT. Hughes's aspiration in
these early poems is to command all the elements, to bring them
within the jurisdiction of his authoritarian voice. And in 'The
Thought Fox' the thing at the beginning of the poem which lives
beyond his jurisdiction is characteristically fluid and vowelling and
sibilant: 'Something else is alive' whispers of a presence not yet accounted for, a presence that is granted its full vowel music as its
epiphany—'Something more near / Though deeper within dark-
ness / Is entering the loneliness.' It is granted this dilation of its mystery before it is conjured into the possession of the poet-warden, the
vowel-keeper; and its final emergence in the fully sounded *i*'s and *e*'s
of 'an eye, / A widening deepening greenness' is gradually mastered
by the braking action of 'brilliantly, concentratedly' and by the
shooting of the monosyllabic consonantal bolts in the last stanza:

> Till, with a sudden sharp hot stink of fox
> It enters the dark hole of the head.
> The window is starless still; the clock ticks,
> The page is printed.

Next a poem whose subject might be expected to woo the tender
pious vowels from a poet rather than the disciplining consonants.
About a 'Fern':

Here is the fern's frond, unfurling a gesture . . .

The first line is an Anglo-Saxon line, four stresses, three of them picked out by alliteration; and although the frosty grip of those *f*'s thaws out, the fern is still subsumed into images of control and discipline and regal authority:

> And, among them, the fern
> Dances gravely, like the plume
> Of a warrior returning, under the low hills,
>
> Into his own kingdom.

But of course we recognize that Hughes's 'Thistles' are vegetation more kindred to his spirit than the pliant fern. And when he turns his attention to them, they become reincarnations of the Norsemen:

> Bringing their frozen swords, their salt-bleached eyes, their salt-
>   bleached hair,
> The snow's stupefied anvils in rows,
> Bringing their envy,
> The slow ships feelered Southward, snails over the steep sheen of
>   the water-globe.

These are 'The Warriors of the North' as Hughes imagines them, resurrected in all their arctic mail 'into the iron arteries of Calvin', and into 'Thistles'. The thistles are emblems of the Hughes voice as I hear it, born of an original vigour, fighting back over the same ground; and it is not insignificant that in this poem Hughes himself presents the thistles as images of a fundamental speech, uttering itself in gutturals from behind the sloped arms of consonants:

> Every one a revengeful burst
> Of resurrection, a grasped fistful
> Of splintered weapons and Icelandic frost thrust up

From the underground stain of a decayed Viking.
They are like pale hair and the gutturals of dialects.
Every one manages a plume of blood.

Then they grow grey, like men.
Mown down, it is a feud. Their sons appear,
Stiff with weapons, fighting back over the same ground.

The gutturals of dialects, which Hughes here connects with the
Nordic stratum of English speech, he pronounces in another place
to be the germinal secret of his own voice. In an interview published in the *London Magazine* in January 1971 he said:

> I grew up in West Yorkshire. They have a very distinctive dialect
> there. Whatever other speech you grow into, presumably your di-
> alect stays alive in a sort of inner freedom, . . . it's your childhood
> self there inside the dialect and that is possibly your real self or
> the core of it . . . Without it, I doubt if I would ever have written
> verse. And in the case of the West Yorkshire dialect, of course, it
> connects you directly and in your most intimate self to Middle
> English poetry.

In other words, he finds that the original grain of his speech is a
chip off the old block and that his work need not be a new planting but a new bud on an old bough. What other poet would have
the boldness to entitle a collection *Wodwo?* Yet *Sir Gawain and the
Green Knight*, with its beautiful alliterating and illuminated form,
its interlacing and trellising of natural life and mythic life, is probably closer in spirit to Hughes's poetry than Hughes's poetry is
to that of his English contemporaries. Everything inherits everything—and Hughes is the rightful heir to this alliterative tradition, and to the cleaving simplicity of the Border ballad, which he
elevates to the status of touchstone later in that same interview. He
says that he started writing again in 1955:

> The poems that set me off were odd pieces by Shapiro, Lowell,
> Merwin, Wilbur and Crowe Ransom. Crowe Ransom was the one

who gave me a model I felt I could use. He helped me get my words into focus . . . But this whole business of influences is mysterious . . . And after all the campaigns to make it new you're stuck with the fact that some of the Scots Border ballads still cut a deeper groove than anything written in the last forty years. Influences just seem to make it more and more unlikely that a poet will write what he alone could write.

What Hughes alone could write depended for its release on the discovery of a way to undam the energies of the dialect, to get a stomping ground for that inner freedom, to get that childhood self a disguise to roam at large in. Freedom and naturalness and homeliness are positives in Hughes's critical vocabulary, and they are linked with both the authenticity of individual poets and the genius of the language itself. Speaking of Keith Douglas in 1964, Hughes could have been speaking of himself; of the way his language and his imagination alerted themselves when the hunt for the poem in the adult world became synonymous with the hunt for the animal in the world of childhood, the world of dialect:

> The impression is of a sudden mobilizing of the poet's will, a clearing of his vision, as if from sitting considering possibilities and impossibilities he stood up to act. Pictures of things no longer interest him much: he wants their substance, their nature and their consequences in life. At once, and quite suddenly, his mind is whole . . . He is a renovator of language. It is not that he uses words in jolting combinations, or with titanic extravagance, or curious precision. His triumph is in the way he renews the simplicity of ordinary talk . . . The music that goes along with this . . . is the natural path of such confident, candid thinking . . . A utility general purpose style that combines a colloquial prose readiness with poetic breadth, a ritual intensity of music with clear direct feeling, and yet in the end is nothing but casual speech.

This combination of ritual intensity, prose readiness, direct feeling and casual speech can be discovered likewise in the best poems of

Lupercal, because in *The Hawk in the Rain* and indeed in much of *Wodwo* and *Crow*, we are often in the presence of that titanic extravagance Hughes mentions, speech not so much mobilizing and standing up to act as flexing and straining until it verges on the grotesque. But in poems like 'Pike', 'Hawk Roosting', 'The Bull Moses' and 'An Otter' we get this confident, speedy, hammer-and-tongs proficiency. And in this poem from *Wodwo*, called 'Pibroch', a poem uniquely Hughesian in its very title, fetching energy and ancestry from what is beyond the pale and beneath the surface, we have the elements of the Scottish piper's *ceol mor*, the high style, implicit in words like 'dead', 'heaven', 'universe', 'aeon', 'angels' and in phrases like 'the foetus of God', 'the stars bow down'—a phrase which cunningly makes its cast and raises Blake in the pool of the ear. We have elements of this high style, ritual intensity, whatever you want to call it; and we have also the 'prose readiness', the 'casual speech' of 'bored', 'hangs on', 'lets up', 'tryout' and the workaday cadences of 'Over the stone rushes the wind' and 'her mind's gone completely'. The landscape of the poem is one that the Anglo-Saxon wanderer or seafarer would be completely at home in:

> The sea cries with its meaningless voice
> Treating alike its dead and its living,
> Probably bored with the appearance of heaven
> After so many millions of nights without sleep,
> Without purpose, without self-deception.
>
> Stone likewise. A pebble is imprisoned
> Like nothing in the Universe.
> Created for black sleep. Or growing
> Conscious of the sun's red spot occasionally,
> Then dreaming it is the foetus of God.
>
> Over the stone rushes the wind
> Able to mingle with nothing,
> Like the hearing of the blind stone itself.
> Or turns, as if the stone's mind came feeling
> A fantasy of directions.

Drinking the sea and eating the rock
A tree struggles to make leaves—
An old woman fallen from space
Unprepared for these conditions.
She hangs on, because her mind's gone completely.

Minute after minute, aeon after aeon,
Nothing lets up or develops.
And this is neither a bad variant nor a tryout.
This is where the staring angels go through.
This is where all the stars bow down.

Hughes attempts to make vocal the inner life, the simple being-thereness, 'the substance, nature and consequences in life' of sea, stone, wind and tree. Blake's pebble and tiger are shadowy presences in the background, as are the landscapes of Anglo-Saxon poetry. And the whole thing is founded on rock, that rock which Hughes presented in his autobiographical essay as his birthstone, holding his emergence in place just as his headstone will hold his decease:

> This was the *memento mundi* over my birth: my spiritual midwife at the time and my godfather ever since—or one of my godfathers. From my first day it watched. If it couldn't see me direct, a towering gloom over my pram, it watched me through a species of periscope: that is, by infiltrating the very light of my room with its particular shadow. From my home near the bottom of the south-facing slope of the valley, the cliff was both the curtain and backdrop to existence.

I quote this piece because it links the childhood core with the adult opus, because that rock is the equivalent in his poetic landscape of dialect in his poetic speech. The rock persists, survives, sustains, endures and informs his imagination, just as it is the bedrock of the language upon which Hughes founds his version of survival and endurance.

·   ·   ·

Stone and rock figure prominently in the world of Geoffrey Hill's poetry also, but Hill's imagination is not content to grant the mineral world the absolute sway that Hughes allows it. He is not the suppliant chanting to the megalith, but rather the mason dressing it. Hill also beats the bounds of an England, his own native West Midlands, beheld as a medieval England facing into the Celtic mysteries of Wales and out towards the military and ecclesiastical splendours of Europe. His *Mercian Hymns* names his territory Mercia and masks his imagination under the figure of King Offa, builder of Offa's dyke between England and Wales, builder as well as beater of the boundaries. Hill's celebration of Mercia has a double focus: one a child's-eye view, close to the common earth, the hoard of history; and the other the historian's and scholar's eye, inquisitive of meaning, bringing time past to bear on time present and vice versa. But the writing itself is by no means abstract and philosophical. Hill addresses the language, as I say, like a mason addressing a block, not unlike his own mason in Hymn XXIV:

> Itinerant through numerous domains, of his lord's retinue, to Compostela. Then home for a lifetime amid West Mercia this master-mason as I envisage him, intent to pester upon tympanum and chancel-arch his moody testament, confusing warrior with lion, dragon-coils, tendrils of the stony vine.
>
> Where best to stand? Easter sunrays catch the oblique face of Adam scrumping through leaves; pale spree of evangelists and, there, a cross Christ mumming child Adam out of Hell
>
> ('Et exspecto resurrectionem mortuorum' dust in the eyes, on clawing wings, and lips)

Not only must English be kept up here, with its 'spree' and 'scrumping' and 'mumming', but Latin and learning must be kept up too. The mannered rhetoric of these pieces is a kind of verbal architecture, a grave and sturdy English Romanesque. The native undergrowth, both vegetative and verbal, that barbaric scrollwork of fern and ivy, is set against the tympanum and chancel-arch, against the weighty elegance of imperial Latin. The overall pat-

tern of his language is an extension and a deliberate exploitation
of the linguistic effect in Shakespeare's famous 'The multitudinous
seas incarnadine,/Making the green one red,' where the polysyllabic flourish of 'multitudinous' and 'incarnadine' is both set off
and undercut by the monosyllabic plainness of 'making the green
one red', where the Latinate and the local also go hand in glove.
There is in Hill something of Stephen Dedalus's hyperconscious-
ness of words as physical sensations, as sounds to be plumbed, as
weights on the tongue. Words in his poetry fall slowly and singly,
like molten solder, and accumulate to a dull glowing nub. I imagine Hill as indulging in a morose linguistic delectation, dwelling
on the potential of each word with much the same slow relish as
Leopold Bloom dwells on the thought of his kidney. And in *Mercian Hymns*, in fact, Hill's procedure resembles Joyce's not only in
this linguistic deliberation and self-consciousness. For all his references to the 'precedent provided by the Latin prose-hymns or can-
ticles of the early Christian Church', what these hymns celebrate is
the 'ineluctable modality of the audible', as well as the visible, and
the form that celebration takes reminds one of the Joycean
epiphany, which is a prose poem in effect. And it is not only within
the form of the individual pieces that he follows the Joycean example; in the overall organization of the *Hymns*, he does what
Joyce did in *Ulysses*, confounding modern autobiographical material with literary and historical matter drawn from the past. Offa's
story makes contemporary landscape and experience live in the
rich shadows of a tradition.

To go back to Hymn XXIV, the occasion, the engendering moment, seems to involve the contemplation of a carved pediment—
a tympanum is the carved area between the lintel of a door and
the arch above it—which exhibits a set of scenes: one of Eden, one
of some kind of harrowing of hell; and the scenes are supervised
by images of the evangelists. And this cryptic, compressed mode of
presentation in which a few figures on stone can call upon the
whole body of Christian doctrines and mythology resembles
the compression of the piece itself. The carving reminds him of
the carver, a master-mason—and the relevant note reads: 'For the
association of Compostela with West Midlands sculpture of the

twelfth century I am indebted to G. Zarnecki, *Later English Romanesque Sculpture*, London (1953).' This mason is 'itinerant'—a word used in its precise Latin sense, yet when applied to a travelling craftsman, that pristine sense seems to foreshadow its present narrowed meaning of tinker, a travelling tinsmith, a whitesmith. In the first phrases the Latinate predominates, for this is a ritual progress, an itinerary 'through numerous domains, of his lord's retinue', to Compostela. Even the proper name flaps out its music like some banner there. But when he gets home, he is momentarily cut down from his grand tour importance to his homely size, in the simple 'Then home for a lifetime amid West Mercia'; but now the poet/observer of the carving has caught something of the sense of occasion and borrowed something of the mason's excitement. Yet he does not 'see in the mind's eye', like Hamlet, but 'envisages' him, the verb being properly liturgical, 'intent to pester upon tympanum and chancel-arch his moody testament, confusing warrior with lion, dragon-coils . . .' A tympanum, of course, is also a drum, and the verb 'to pester' manages a rich synaesthetic effect; the stone is made to cackle like a kettledrum as the chisel hits it. But 'pester' is more interesting still. Its primary meaning, from the original Latin root, *pastorium*, means to hobble a horse, and it was used in 1685 to mean 'crowding persons in or into'. So the mason hobbles and herds and crowds in warrior and lion, dragon coils, tendrils of the stony vine; and this interlacing and entanglement of motifs is also the method of the poem.

In fact, we can see the method more clearly if we put the poem in its proper context, which is in the middle of a group of three entitled *Opus Anglicanum*. Once again the note is helpful:

> '*Opus Anglicanum*': the term is properly applicable to English embroidery of the period AD 1250–1350, though the craft was already famous some centuries earlier . . . I have, with considerable impropriety, extended the term to apply to English Romanesque sculpture and to utilitarian metal-work of the nineteenth century.

The entanglement, the interlacing, is now that of embroidery, and this first poem, I suggest, brings together womanly figures from

Hill's childhood memory with the ghostly procession of needle-workers from the medieval castles and convents:

XXIII

In tapestries, in dreams, they gathered, as it was enacted, the return, the re-entry of transcendence into this sublunary world. *Opus Anglicanum*, their stringent mystery riddled by needles: the silver veining, the gold leaf, voluted grape-vine, masterworks of treacherous thread.

They trudged out of the dark, scraping their boots free from lime-splodges and phlegm. They munched cold bacon. The lamps grew plump with oily reliable light.

Again, the liturgical and Latinate of the first paragraph are abraded and rebutted by the literal and local weight of 'scraping their boots free from lime-splodges and phlegm'—the boots being, I take it, the boots of labourers involved in this never-ending *Opus Anglicanum*, from agricultural origins to industrial developments. And in order just to clinch the thing, consider the third piece, where the 'utilitarian metal-work' in which his grandmother was involved is contemplated in a perspective that includes medieval embroidress and mason, and a certain 'transcendence' enters the making of wire nails:

XXV

Brooding on the eightieth letter of *Fors Clavigera*, I speak this in memory of my grandmother, whose childhood and prime womanhood were spent in the nailer's darg.

The nailshop stood back of the cottage, by the fold. It reeked stale mineral sweat. Sparks had furred its low roof. In dawn-light the troughed water floated a damson-bloom of dust—

not to be shaken by posthumous clamour. It is one thing to celebrate the 'quick forge', another to cradle a face hare-lipped by the searing wire.

Brooding on the eightieth letter of *Fors Clavigera*, I speak this in
memory of my grandmother, whose childhood and prime
womanhood were spent in the nailer's darg.

Ruskin's eightieth letter reflects eloquently and plangently on the
injustice of the master-and-servant situation, on the exploitation
of labour, on the demeaning work in a nail forge. The Mayor of
Birmingham took him to a house where two women were at work,
labouring, as he says, with ancient Vulcanian skill:

So wrought they,—the English matron and maid;—so it was their
darg to labour from morning to evening—seven to seven—by the
furnace side—the winds of summer fanning the blast of it.

He goes on to compute that the woman and the husband earn altogether £55 a year with which to feed and clothe themselves and
their six children, to reproach the luxury of the mill-owning class
and to compare the wives of industrialists contemplating Burne-
Jones's picture of Venus's mirror 'with these, their sisters, who had
only, for Venus's mirror, a heap of ashes; compassed about with no
forget-me-nots, but with all the forgetfulness in the world'.

It seems to me here that Hill is celebrating his own indomitable
Englishry, casting his mind on other days, singing a clan beaten
into the clay and ashes and linking their patience, their sustaining
energy, with the glory of England. The 'quick forge', after all, may
be what its origin in Shakespeare's *Henry V* declares it to be, 'the
quick forge and working house of thought', but it is surely also the
'random grim forge' of Felix Randal, the farrier. The image shifts
between various points and embroiders a new *opus anglicanum* in
this intended and allusive poem. And the point of the embroider-
ing needle, of course, is *darg*, that chip off the Anglo-Saxon block,
meaning 'a day's work, or the task of a day'.

Mercian Hymns shows Hill in full command of his voice.
Much as the stiff and corbelled rhetoric of earlier work like 'Funeral Music' and 'Requiem for the Plantagenet Kings' stands up
and will stand up, it is only when this rhetoric becomes a press
tightening on and squeezing out of the language the vigour of

common speech, the essential Anglo-Saxon juices, it is only then that the poetry attains this final refreshed and refreshing quality: then he has, in the words of another piece, accrued a 'golden and stinking blaze'.

Finally, to come to Larkin, where what accrues in the language is not a 'golden and stinking blaze', not the rank and fermenting composts of philology and history, but the bright senses of words worn clean in literate conversation. In Larkin's language as in his vision of water, 'any angled light . . . congregate[s] endlessly.' There is a gap in Larkin between the perceiver and the thing perceived, a refusal to melt through long perspectives, an obstinate insistence that the poet is neither a race memory nor a myth-kitty nor a mason but a real man in a real place. The cadences and vocabulary of his poems are tuned to a rational music. It would seem that he has deliberately curtailed his gift for evocation, for resonance, for symbolist *frissons*. He turned from Yeats to Hardy as his master. He never followed the Lawrencian success of his early poem 'Wedding Wind', which ends with a kind of biblical swoon, an image of fulfilled lovers 'kneeling like cattle by all generous waters'. He rebukes romantic aspiration and afflatus with a scrupulous meanness. If he sees the moon, he sees it while groping back to bed after a piss. If he is forced to cry out 'O wolves of memory, immensements', he is also forced to recognize that he is past all that swaddling of sentiment, even if it is 'for others, undiminished, somewhere'. 'Undiminished'—the word, with its hovering balance between attenuated possibilities and the possibility of amplitude, is typical. And Christopher Ricks has pointed out how often negatives operate in Larkin's best lines. Lovers talking in bed, for example, discover it ever more difficult

> to find
> Words at once true and kind,
> Or not untrue and not unkind.

His tongue moves hesitantly, precisely, honestly, among ironies and negatives. He is the poet of rational light, a light that has its own luminous beauty but which has also the effect of exposing clearly the truths which it touches. Larkin speaks neither a dialect nor a pulpit language; there are no 'hectoring large scale verses' in his three books, nor is there the stubbly intimacy of 'oath-edged talk and pipe-smoke' which he nostalgically annotates among the miners. His language would have pleased those Tudor and Augustan guardians who wanted to polish and beautify their speech, to smooth it for art. What we hear is a stripped standard English voice, a voice indeed with a unique break and remorseful tone, but a voice that leads back neither to the thumping beat of Anglo-Saxon nor to the Gregorian chant of the Middle Ages. Its ancestry begins, in fact, when the Middle Ages are turning secular and plays begin to take their place beside the Mass as a form of communal telling and knowing. In the first few lines of Larkin's poem 'Money', for example, I think I hear the cadences of *Everyman*, the querulous tones of Riches reproaching the hero:

> Quarterly, is it, money reproaches me:
>   'Why do you let me lie here wastefully?
> I am all you never had of goods and sex.
>   You could get them still just by writing a few cheques.'

Those end-stopped lines, sliding down to rhymed conclusions, suggest the beginning of that period out of which Larkin's style arises. After *Everyman*, there is Skelton, a commonsensical wobble of rhyme, a humorous wisdom, a practical lyricism:

> Oh, no one can deny
> That Arnold is less selfish than I.
> He married a wife to stop her getting away
> Now she's there all day, . . .

There is as well the Cavalier Larkin, the maker of songs, where the conversational note and the dainty disciplines of a metrical form are in beautiful equilibrium:

> Yet still the unresting castles thresh
> In fullgrown thickness every May.

Last year is dead, they seem to say.
Begin afresh, afresh, afresh.

Even in that short space, by the way, one can see the peculiar Larkin fusion of parsimony and abundance—the gorgeousness of 'unresting castles', the poignant sweetness of 'afresh, afresh' are held in check by the quotidian 'Last year is dead'. Yet it is by refusing to pull out the full stops, or by almost refusing, that Larkin achieves his own brand of negative capability.

As well as the Cavalier Larkin, there is a late Augustan Larkin, the poet of decorous melancholy moods, of twilit propriety and shadowy melody. His poem about superannuated racehorses, for example, entitled 'At Grass', could well be subtitled 'An Elegy in a Country Paddock'. Behind the trees where the horses shelter, there could well rise the spire of Stoke Poges church; and behind the smooth numbers of wind distressing the tails and manes, there is the donnish exactitude of tresses being *dis*tressed:

> The eye can hardly pick them out
> From the cold shade they shelter in
> Till wind distresses tail and mane . . .

And when, at the conclusion of the poem, 'the groom and the groom's boy / With bridles in the evening come', their footsteps surely echo the ploughman homeward plodding his weary way.

There is, moreover, a Tennysonian Larkin and a Hardyesque Larkin. There is even, powerfully, an Imagist Larkin:

> There is an evening coming in
> Across the fields, one never seen before,
> That lights no lamps.
>
> Silken it seems at a distance, yet
> When it is drawn up over the knees and breast
> It brings no comfort.

Where has the tree gone, that locked
Earth to the sky? What is under my hands,
That I cannot feel?

What loads my hands down?

Then there is Larkin the coiner of compounds—which we
may choose to call Hopkinsian or even perhaps, briefly, Shakespearean—who writes of 'some lonely rain-ceased midsummer
evening', of 'light unanswerable and tall and wide', of 'the
million-petalled flower of being here', of 'thin continuous dream-
ing' and 'wasteful, weak, propitiatory flowers'.

And to go from the sublime to the ridiculous, there is the
seaside-postcard Larkin, as true to the streak of vulgarity in the
civilization as he is sensitive to its most delicious refinements: 'Get
stewed: / Books are a load of crap.' Or get this disfigurement of a
poster of a bathing beauty:

Huge tits and a fissured crotch
Were scored well in, and the space
Between her legs held scrawls
That set her fairly astride
A tuberous cock and balls.

And then, elsewhere,

They fuck you up, your mum and dad.
They may not mean to but they do.
They fill you with the faults they had
And add some extra, just for you.

And again, in 'Sad Steps':

Groping back to bed after a piss
I part thick curtains, and am startled by
The rapid clouds, the moon's cleanliness.

But despite the piss, and the snigger of the demotic in all of these places, that title, 'Sad Steps', reminds us that Larkin is solicitous for his Sidney also. He too returns to origins and brings something back, although he does not return to 'roots'. He puts inverted commas round his 'roots', in fact. His childhood, he says, was a forgotten boredom. He sees England from train windows, fleeting past and away. He is urban modern man, the insular Englishman, responding to the tones of his own clan, ill at ease when out of his environment. He is a poet, indeed, of composed and tempered English nationalism, and his voice is the not untrue, not unkind voice of postwar England, where the cloth cap and the royal crown have both lost some of their potent symbolism and the categorical, socially defining functions of the working-class accent and the aristocratic drawl have almost been eroded. Larkin's tones are mannerly but not exquisite, well-bred but not mealy-mouthed. If his England and his English are not as deep as Hughes's or as solemn as Hill's, they are nevertheless dearly beloved, and during his sojourn in Belfast in the late 1950s, he gave thanks, by implication, for the nurture that he receives by living among his own. The speech, the customs, the institutions of England are, in the words of another English poet, domiciled in Ireland, 'wife to his creating thought'. That was Hopkins in Dublin in the 1880s, sensing that his individual talent was being divorced from his tradition. Here is Larkin remembering the domicile in Belfast in the 1950s:

> Lonely in Ireland, since it was not home,
> Strangeness made sense. The salt rebuff of speech,
> Insisting so on difference, made me welcome:
> Once that was recognised, we were in touch.
>
> Their draughty streets, end-on to hills, the faint
> Archaic smell of dockland, like a stable,
> The herring-hawker's cry, dwindling, went
> To prove me separate, not unworkable.
>
> Living in England has no such excuse:
> These are my customs and establishments

It would be much more serious to refuse.
Here no elsewhere underwrites my existence.

Larkin's England of the mind is in many ways continuous with the England of Rupert Brooke's 'Grantchester' and Edward Thomas's 'Adlestrop', an England of customs and institutions, industrial and domestic, but also an England whose pastoral hinterland is threatened by the very success of those institutions. Houses and roads and factories mean that a certain England is 'Going, Going':

> It seems, just now,
> To be happening so very fast;
> Despite all the land left free
> For the first time I feel somehow
> That it isn't going to last,
>
> That before I snuff it, the whole
> Boiling will be bricked in
> Except for the tourist parts—
> First slum of Europe: a role
> It won't be so hard to win,
> With a cast of crooks and tarts.
>
> And that will be England gone,
> The shadows, the meadows, the lanes,
> The guildhalls, the carved choirs.
> There'll be books; it will linger on
> In galleries; but all that remains
> For us will be concrete and tyres.

I think that sense of an ending has driven all three of these writers into a kind of piety towards their local origins, has made them look in, rather than up, to England. The loss of imperial power, the failure of economic nerve, the diminished influence of Britain inside Europe, all this has led to a new sense of the shires, a new valuing of the native English experience. Donald Davie, for example, has published a book of poems with that very title, *The Shires*, which attempts to annex to his imagination by personal memory or historical meditation or literary connections each shire of England. It is a book at once intimate and exclusive, a topography of love and impatience, and it is yet another symptom that English poets are being forced to explore not just the matter of England but what is the matter with England. I have simply presumed to share in that exploration through the medium which England has, for better or worse, impressed upon us all, the English language itself.

Yeats as an Example?

A writer's dedication to his art can often entail some kind of hurt for those who live near and dear to him. Robert Lowell in the final poem of *The Dolphin* used the word 'plotted' to describe something that is questionable in the artistic enterprise:

> I have sat and listened to too many
> words of the collaborating muse,
> and plotted perhaps too freely with my life,
> not avoiding injury to others,
> not avoiding injury to myself—
> to ask compassion . . . this book, half fiction,
> an eelnet made by man for the eel fighting—
>
> my eyes have seen what my hand did.

If there is more than a hint of self-accusation in that last line, there is a strong ring of triumph in it as well, and when Robert Lowell died I remember some of us toyed with it as a possible epitaph for him: it seemed to catch the combination of pride and vulnerability that lay at the roots of his poetic voice.

It would have made a much more rueful tombstone verse than Yeats's:

> Cast a cold eye
> On life, on death.
> Horseman, pass by.

Where Yeats's eye is cold, Lowell's is warm, though by no means wet, sympathetic to the imperfections of living, the eye of a pedestrian rather than the eye of an equestrian. Where Yeats's last poems sang their faith in art and turned in scorn from 'the sort now growing up', Lowell's final work hesitated, and his trust in fictions seemed to waver:

EPILOGUE

Those blessed structures, plot and rhyme—
why are they no help to me now
I want to make
something imagined, not recalled? . . .

Yet why not say what happened?
Pray for the grace of accuracy
Vermeer gave to the sun's illumination
stealing like the tide across a map
to his girl solid with yearning.
We are poor passing facts,
warned by that to give
each figure in the photograph
his living name.

'Accuracy' seems a modest aim, even when it is as richly managed as it is here. Lowell abjures the sublime, that realm where his rhetoric often penetrated, and seeks instead the low-key consolations of the quotidian. He is almost, in Yeats's words, 'content to live'.

Yeats would never have been 'content to live' merely, because that would have meant throwing words away, throwing gesture away, throwing away possibilities for drama and transcendence. From the beginning of his career he emphasized and realized the otherness of art from life, dream from action, and by the end he moved within his mode of vision as within some invisible ring of influence and defence, some bulletproof glass of the spirit, exclusive as Caesar in his tent, absorbed as a long-legged fly on the stream.

Whatever Yeats intends us to understand by 'Long-Legged Fly', we cannot miss the confidence that drives it forward and the energy that underlies it, an energy that exhilarates in the faith that artistic process has some kind of absolute validity. There is a kind of vitreous finish on the work itself that deflects all other truths except its own. Art can outface history; the imagination can disdain happenings once it has incubated and mastered the secret behind happenings. In fact, we can sense a violence, an implacable element in the artistic drive as Yeats envisages and embodies it. The 'yellow eyed hawk of the mind' and the 'ancient, glittering eyes' of the Chinamen in 'Lapis Lazuli' and the 'cold eye' of the tomb-inspecting horseman are all suggestive of sinister appetites. If the act of mind in the artist has all the intentness and amorousness and every bit as much of the submerged aggression of the act of love, then it can be maintained that Yeats's artistic imagination was often in a condition that can only be properly described as priapic.

Is this, then, exemplary? Do we altogether assent to the samurai stare and certainty of 'Cast a cold eye / On life, on death'? Do we say yes to this high-stepping tread? Can we afford to disdain the life that goes on messily and cantankerously? How, in other words, do we regard Yeats's affirmation that the man who sits down to breakfast is a 'bundle of accident and incoherence' and that the man reborn in his poem is 'something intended, complete'?

Personally, I find much to admire in the intransigence of the stance, as I find much to commend and imitate in the two things that Yeats was so often determined to set at loggerheads, his life and his work:

> The intellect of man is forced to choose
> Perfection of the life, or of the work,
> And if it take the second must refuse
> A heavenly mansion, raging in the dark.

What is finally admirable is the way his life and his work are *not* separate but make a continuum, the way the courage of his vision did not confine itself to rhetorics but issued in actions. Unlike Wallace Stevens, for example, that other great apologist of the imagination, Yeats bore the implications of his romanticism into action: he propagandized, speechified, fund-raised, administered and politicked in the world of telegrams and anger, all on behalf of the world of vision. His poetry was not just a matter of printed books making their way in a world of literate readers and critics; it was, rather, the fine flower of his efforts to live as forthrightly as he could in the world of illiterates and politicians. Beside the ringing antithesis of 'The Choice' we must set this other recognition:

> A poet is by the very nature of things a man who lives with entire sincerity, or rather, the better his poetry, the more sincere his life. His life is an experiment in living and those who come after him have a right to know it. Above all, it is necessary that the lyric poet's life be known, that we should understand that his poetry is no rootless flower but the speech of a man; that it is no little thing to achieve anything in any art, to stand alone perhaps for many years, to go a path no other man has gone, to accept one's own thought when the thought of others has the authority of the world behind it . . . to give one's own life as well as one's words (which are so much nearer to one's soul) to the criticism of the world.

I admire the way that Yeats took on the world on his own terms, defined the areas where he would negotiate and where he would not; the way he never accepted the terms of another's argument but propounded his own. I assume that this peremptoriness, this apparent arrogance, is exemplary in an artist, that it is proper and even necessary for him to insist on his own language, his own vision, his own terms of reference. This will often seem like irresponsibility or affectation, sometimes like callousness, but from the artist's point of view it is an act of integrity, or an act of cunning to protect the integrity.

All through his life, of course, and ever since his death, Yeats has been continually rebuked for the waywardness of his beliefs, the remoteness of his behaviour and the eccentricity of his terms of reference. Fairies first of all. Then Renaissance courts in Tuscany and Big Houses in Galway. Then Phases of the Moon and Great Wheels. What, says the reliable citizen, is the sense of all this? Why do we listen to this gullible aesthete rehearsing the delusions of an illiterate peasantry, this snobbish hanger-on in country houses mystifying the feudal facts of the class system, this charlatan patterning history and predicting the future by a mumbo-jumbo of geometry and Ptolemaic astronomy? Our temptation may be to answer on the reliable citizen's terms, let him call the tune and begin to make excuses for Yeats.

'Well,' we might say, 'when he was a youngster in Sligo he heard these stories about fairies from the servants in his grandparents' house; and then when, as a young poet, he sought a badge of identity for his own culture, something that would mark it off from the rest of the English-speaking world, he found this distinctive and sympathetic thing in the magical world-view of the country people. It was a conscious counter-cultural act against the rationalism and materialism of late Victorian England.' To which the citizen replies, 'Anybody who believes in fairies is mad.'

Yeats would not have thanked us for explaining him apologetically. He would want us to affirm him with all the elaborate obstinacy with which he affirmed himself. So for entertainment and instruction, I wish to observe him in action as a young poet, and then as an established poet and public figure; and in each case I hope to make clear what I consider to have been exemplary in his bearing.

The Irish Theosophist, a magazine whose very title is enough to raise the ghosts of the nineties, carried an interview with Mr W. B. Yeats in its issue for 15 October 1893. It had been conducted by the editor, one D. N. Dunlop, who set the scene in his opening paragraphs:

A few evenings ago I called on my friend, Mr W. B. Yeats, and found him alone, seated in his armchair, smoking his cigarette, with a volume of Homer before him. The whole room indicated the style and taste peculiar to its presiding genius. Upon the walls hung various designs by Blake and other less well-known symbolic artists; everywhere books and papers in apparently endless confusion.

In his usual genial way he invited me to have a cup of tea

with him. During this pleasant ceremony little was said, but sufficient to impress me more than ever with the fact that my host
was supremely an artist, much in love with his art.

Yeats was then twenty-eight, and could deploy that elaborate style
he had learned from Pater with as much indolent calculation on a
sofa as in a sentence. If he had not yet formulated his theory of the
mask, he had an instinctive grasp of the potency of his image; and
if he does not altogether ruffle here in a manly pose, there is nevertheless a bit of a peacock display going on. The Homer volume
was a good touch, and so was the cigarette and the 'ceremony' of
the tea.

The young man whose concern for appearances had led him, a
few years earlier, to ink his heels in order to disguise the holes in
his socks had obviously mastered more complex and sure-footed
strategies for holding the line between himself and the world
around him. He had not, to be sure, acquired the peremptory authority which Frank O'Connor was to see in action decades later,
when the poet could silence an argument or buttress a proposition
with a remark such as 'Ah, but that was before the peacock
screamed', but he had about him already a definite atmosphere, a
style that declared allegiance to disciplines and sources of strength
not shared by his contemporaries. He was an artist, devoted to the
beautiful; he was a magician, adept among hidden powers; he was
a Celt, with a lifeline to the mythological depths; he was a propagandist, with a firm line for journalists. He was all these things,
self-consciously and deliberately, yet they did not constitute a dispersal or a confusion of his powers or of his personality; on the
contrary, they concentrated one another, grew from a single root,
and if they were deliberate, the deliberation sprang from an inner
compulsion, an energy discovering itself as vision. Yeats's performances, we might say, then and for the rest of his life, manifested
themselves in the service of creative action. The longer we think
of Yeats, the more he narrows the gap which etymology has forced
between mystery and mastery.

Aspects of the mysterious and the masterful reveal themselves
in one of his coolest strokes during the interview, which was essen-

tially a conversation about Yeats's connection with the Blavatsky Lodge of the Theosophical Society. He had been expelled by Madame Blavatsky, or at least had been asked to resign, about three years earlier. Dunlop asked him:

'Can you remember anything in the nature of a prophecy, Mr Yeats, made by Madame Blavatsky, that might be of interest to record, notwithstanding the fact that you are yet awaiting your prophesied illness?'

'The only thing of that nature', replied Mr Yeats, 'was a reference to England. "The Master told me", said she, "that the power of England would not outlast the century, and the Master never deceived me." '

It seems to me that Yeats cut a sly swath with that answer, enlisting the esoteric fringe to serve the nationalistic heartland, hiding the cultural agitator behind the po-faced dreamer, making a cast across the sleeping pool of historical enmity with a line as neutral as theosophy itself, the calm surface of his speech depth-charged with potential rebellion. The remark leaves a broadening wake in the imagination and operates by the perfect camouflaging of judged intention in an aftermath of overlapping effects; and in this way it rehearses in miniature the more complex orchestration of intention and effect which he was to achieve in *The Wind among the Reeds*, a book whose title was already haunting his mind.

'And what about your present work?' I asked.

'*Celtic Twilight*, a work dealing with ghosts, goblins and fairies, will be out shortly, also a short volume of Blake's poems', he replied. 'Then I am getting ready for publication, next spring, a book of poems, which I intend calling *The Wind Among the Reeds* and, as soon afterwards as possible, a collection of essays and lectures dealing with Irish nationality and literature, which will probably appear under the title of the *Watch Fire*.'

In the event, *Watch Fire* never materialized. His essay on nationality and literature had appeared, however, five months earlier in

The United Irishman and work on similar themes had been published all through the late eighties and continued to be published throughout the nineties. He began with his famous championship of Sir Samuel Ferguson's poetry—'the greatest poet Ireland has produced, because the most central and most Celtic'—and went on to praise James Clarence Mangan, William Allingham and the ballad poets; to sponsor new voices like Katharine Tynan's and AE's; to write for English and Irish magazines bibliographies and reader's guides to the best Irish books; to affirm the validity of that magical world-view implicit in Irish country customs and beliefs; and to rehearse those beliefs and customs in the book he mentions which would give its name to an era, *The Celtic Twilight.*

It was all part of a campaign, and the various suggestions in the word 'campaign' are apposite. It was sustained over a long period and was pursued on a number of fronts: journalistic, political, poetic, dramatic, amatory even, if we think of Maud Gonne as leading lady in *The Countess Cathleen*; it was pursued with the idea of conquest, not of territory perhaps but of imagination—though a successful awakening of the people's imagination would allow them to repossess their territory with a new conviction. As he comes to the end of that part of his autobiography dealing with the years 1887–1891, the note swells as he recollects his purpose:

> I could not endure, however, an international art, picking stories and symbols where it pleased. Might I not, with health and good luck to aid me, create some new *Prometheus Unbound*; Patrick or Colmcille, Oisin or Finn in Prometheus's stead; and, instead of Caucasus, Cro-Patrick or Ben Bulben? Have not all races had their first unity from a mythology that marries them to rock and hill? We had in Ireland imaginative stories, which the uneducated classes knew and even sang, and might we not make those stories current among the educated classes, rediscovering what I have called 'the applied arts of literature', the association of literature, that is, with music, speech and dance; and at last, it might be, so deepen the political passion of the nation that all, artist and poet, craftsman and day-labourer would accept a common design?

If there is something plangent in this proud recollection, there was
nothing of the dying fall in the notes struck by the journalism and
controversy of the eighties and nineties as he pursued that 'common design'. For example, after declaring in his 1886 *Dublin Magazine* article on Sir Samuel Ferguson that of all things the past
bequeaths the future, the greatest are great legends and that it was
therefore the duty of every Irish reader to study those of his own
country, he went on to make clear that this appeal was directed to
the selfless and idealistic young:

> I do not appeal to the professional classes, who, in Ireland, at least,
> appear at no time to have thought of the affairs of their country
> till they first feared for their emoluments—nor do I appeal to the
> shoddy society of 'West Britonism' . . .

That pugnacious thrust never deserted him, although he was to develop a less bare-fisted style, abandoning the short jab in the face
in favour of a long reach for the side of the head.

The point is, however, that no matter how much we have been
led to think of the young Yeats as a dreamer, we must not forget
the practical, driving side of him, driving forward towards
his ideal goal. The founding of libraries, the association with political activists, all this was not undertaken without some reso-
luteness, some ambition, some expense of spirit. And all of this
was by no means the whole story. There were his love affairs, first
with Maud Gonne and then with Olivia Shakespeare, those enhancing and disturbing events in his emotional life that gave him
power in other spheres. There were his more serious literary projects, such as the stories of Red Hanrahan, and those other strange
stories, at once robust and remote, which formed the substance of
The Secret Rose; and there was above all his own secret rose, the
poetry itself.

It is easy to admire this young Yeats: his artistic ambitions, his
national fervour, his great desire to attach himself to a tradition
and a corpus of belief that was communal. For all the activity and
push of the enterprise, the aim of the poet and of the poetry is finally to be of service, to ply the effort of the individual work into

the larger work of the community as a whole, and the spirit of our age is sympathetic to that democratic urge.

It is less than sympathetic, however, to the next stance we find the poet adopting. Twenty years after the *Irish Theosophist* interview in October 1893, in his poem 'September 1913', Yeats's style had evolved a tone for detaching rather than attaching himself, for saying 'I' rather than 'we'. By then, Romantic Ireland's dead and gone. We are in the presence of a poet in his late forties, the Abbey Theatre manager, scorner of middle-class piety and philistinism, mythologizer of aristocratic ceremony and grace. We are in the presence of a man who believes that the redistribution of the Coole Park estate among its tenants would be a step back, not a step forward, in the life of the country. A man stung into superb attitudes by the rude handling meted out to J. M. Synge's *Playboy of the Western World* and by the refusal of Dublin Corporation to provide a gallery for Hugh Lane's collection of Impressionist pictures. All that. An Anglo-Irish Protestant deeply at odds with the mind of Irish Catholic society. A man who is remaking himself, finding a style for resisting his environment rather than a style that would co-opt it, at that thrilling stage of development which he calls, in 'A Dialogue of Self and Soul', 'the finished man among his enemies'. And that poem goes on to ask about this man among his enemies:

> How in the name of Heaven can he escape
> That defiling and disfigured shape
> The mirror of malicious eyes
> Casts upon his eyes until at last
> He thinks that shape must be his shape?

So I want our next image of Yeats to be one that the malicious eyes of George Moore cast into shape when he came to write his classic autobiographical account of the Irish Literary Revival in *Hail and Farewell*. Though 'malicious' is perhaps too severe an adjective. Many of Moore's most quotable jabs at the romantic figure of the poet are more suggestive of affection than of a desire to afflict, as when he describes his laugh as a caw, 'the most melancholy thing in the world', or when he presents a bedraggled Yeats on the margins of Coole Lake looking like an old umbrella left behind after a picnic. Moore's book is finally more of a testimony to Yeats's genius than a worrier of it, sustained and elaborate in its ironies, corrective, accurate in its own way. The following passage occurs after Moore has given his account of the Lane controversy and has reported the text of his own lecture on the Impressionists, a lecture delivered for the edification of the reluctant burghers:

> As soon as the applause died away, Yeats who had lately returned to us from the States with a paunch, a huge stride, and an immense fur overcoat, rose to speak. We were surprised at the change in his appearance, and could hardly believe our ears when, instead of talking to us as he used to do about the old stories come down from generation to generation he began to thunder like Ben Tillett against the middle classes, stamping his feet, working himself into a temper, and all because the middle classes did not dip their hands into their pockets and give Lane the money he wanted for his exhibition. When he spoke the words, the middle classes, one would have thought that he was speaking against a personal foe, and we looked round asking each other with our eyes where on earth our Willie Yeats had picked up the strange belief that none but titled and carriage-folk could appreciate pictures . . .
>
> We have sacrificed our lives for Art; but you, what have you done? What sacrifices have you made? he asked, and everybody began to search his memory for the sacrifices that Yeats had made, asking himself in what prison Yeats had languished, what rags he had worn, what broken victuals he had eaten. As far as anybody could remember, he had always lived very comfortably, sitting down invariably to regular meals, and the old green cloak that was in keeping with his profession of romantic poet he had exchanged for the magnificent fur coat which distracted our attention from what he was saying, so opulently did it cover the back of the chair out of which he had risen . . .

The conscious theatricality of this Yeats, the studied haughtiness, the affectation—this kind of thing has often put people off. This is the Willie Yeats whom his contemporaries could not altogether take seriously because he was getting out of their reach, the Yeats whom Maud Gonne called 'Silly Willie' and whom W. H. Auden also called 'silly', in his 1939 elegy: 'You were silly like us, your gift survived it all.' But in setting the silliness in relation to the gift, Auden went to the heart of the matter—survival. What Moore presents us with is a picture of Yeats exercising that intransigence which I praised earlier, that protectiveness of his imaginative springs, so that the gift would survive. He donned the mantle— or perhaps one should say the fur coat—of the aristocrat so that he might express a vision of a communal and personal life that was ample, generous, harmonious, fulfilled and enhancing. The reactionary politics implied by Yeats's admiration of the Coole Park milieu are innocent in the original sense of that word, not nocent, not hurtful. What is more to the point is the way his experience of that benign, paternalistic regime and of Lady Gregory's personal strengths as conserver of folk culture and choreographer of artistic talent issued in a poetry whose very music is a guarantee of its humane munificence. The silliness of the behaviour is continuous with the sumptuousness of the poetry of the middle period. Yeats's attack upon his own middle class really springs out of disappointment: why aren't they taking the lead culturally now that they are in the lead economically? Of course Moore is right to say he belongs to them, and of course Yeats's pretensions looked ridiculous to his contemporaries. But this was his method of signifying his refusal to 'serve that in which he no longer believed'.

When Joyce rebelled, he left by the Holyhead boat and created his drama by making a fictional character called Stephen Dedalus point up and repeat the terms of his revolt. When Yeats rebelled, he remained—Joyce scorned such 'a treacherous instinct for adaptability'—but he still made a new W. B. Yeats to tread the streets and stage of Dublin, a character who was almost as much a work of imagination as Stephen Dedalus. In order to fly the philistinism of his own class and the pious ignorance of another creed, Yeats remade himself, associated himself with cold, disdainful figures, of whom Charles Stewart Parnell was the archetype and 'The Fisherman' was a pattern. The solitude, the will towards excellence, the courage, the self-conscious turning away from that in which he no longer believes, which is Dublin life, and turning towards that which he trusts, which is an image or dream—all the drama and integrity of his poem 'The Fisherman' depend to a large extent upon that other drama which George Moore so delightedly observed and reported:

> Maybe a twelvemonth since
> Suddenly I began,
> In scorn of this audience,
> Imagining a man,
> And his sun-freckled face,
> And grey Connemara cloth,
> Climbing up to a place
> Where stone is dark under froth,
> And the down-turn of his wrist
> When the flies drop in the stream;
> A man who does not exist,
> A man who is but a dream;
> And cried, 'Before I am old
> I shall have written him one
> Poem maybe as cold
> And passionate as the dawn.'

We are moving from what other people saw to what Yeats himself envisaged. I have said enough, I think, about the outer man and what he intended, so it is time to consider the inwardness of the poems instead of the outwardness of the stance.

Yet the poetry is cast in a form that is as ear-catching as the man was eye-catching, and as a writer, one is awed by the achieved and masterful tones of that deliberately pitched voice, its bare classic shapes, its ability to modulate from emotional climax to wise reflection, its ultimate truth to life. Nevertheless, the finally exemplary moments are those when this powerful artistic control is vulnerable to the pain or pathos of life itself.

But I have to say something about why I put the question mark

after the title of this lecture. 'Yeats as an Example' was the title of
an appreciative but not ecstatic essay that W. H. Auden wrote in
1940, so my new punctuation is partly a way of referring back to
Auden's title. But it is also meant to acknowledge the orthodox
notion that a very great poet can be a very bad influence on other
poets. What Yeats offers the practising writer is an example of
labour, perseverance. He is, indeed, the ideal example for a poet
approaching middle age. He reminds you that revision and slog-
work are what you may have to undergo if you seek the satisfac-
tions of finish; he bothers you with the suggestion that if you have
managed to do one kind of poem in your own way, you should cast
off that way and face into another area of your experience until
you have learned a new voice to say that area properly. He encour-
ages you to experience a transfusion of energies from poetic forms
themselves, reveals how the challenge of a metre can extend the
resources of the voice. He proves that deliberation can be so intensified that it becomes synonymous with inspiration. Above all, he
reminds you that art is intended, that it is part of the creative push
of civilization itself: from 'Adam's Curse' to 'Vacillation' and on until the last poems, his work not only explicitly proclaims the reality
of the poetic vocation but convinces by the deep note of certitude
registered in the proclamation itself.

> No longer in Lethean foliage caught
> Begin the preparation for your death
> And from the fortieth winter by that thought
> Test every work of intellect or faith,
> And everything that your own hands have wrought,
> And call those works extravagance of breath
> That are not suited for such men as come
> Proud, open-eyed and laughing to the tomb.

('Vacillation')

> Malachi Stilt-Jack am I, whatever I learned has run wild,
> From collar to collar, from stilt to stilt, from father to child.
> All metaphor, Malachi, stilts and all. A barnacle goose

Far up in the stretches of night; night splits and the dawn breaks
    loose;
I, through the terrible novelty of light, stalk on, stalk on;
Those great sea-horses bare their teeth and laugh at the dawn.

                                      ('High Talk')

But it is not this vaunting of the special claims of art and the artist
that is finally to be saluted. Rather, it is Yeats's large-minded,
wholehearted assent to the natural cycles of living and dying, his
acknowledgement that the 'masterful images' which compel the
assent of artist and audience alike are dependent upon the 'foul
rag-and-bone shop of the heart', the humility of his artistic mastery before the mystery of life and death. There are several poems
where this tenderness towards life and its uncompletedness is at
odds with and tending to gain sway over the consolations of the artificial work. The tumultuousness and repose of a poem like 'Sailing to Byzantium' come to mind, although there the equilibrium
between the golden bird of art and the tattered scarecrow of life is
just held, as it is held and held in mind, contemplated and celebrated in 'Among School Children'. I am thinking, however, of
quieter poems, more intimate, less gorgeously orchestrated pieces,
such as 'What Then?':

        All his happier dreams came true—
        A small old house, wife, daughter, son,
        Grounds where plum and cabbage grew,
        Poets and Wits about him drew;
        'What then?' sang Plato's ghost. 'What then?'

        'The work is done,' grown old he thought,
        'According to my boyish plan;
        Let the fools rage, I swerved in naught,
        Something to perfection brought';
        But louder sang that ghost, 'What then?'

And the challenge of Plato's ghost is matched and picked up
in that other uncharacteristically introspective poem, 'The Man

and the Echo', where the Echo mocks the Man and where the voice of conscience and remorse opposes itself to the artistic choice that the old man has lived out all his life; this voice of conscience which asks, 'Did that play of mine send out / Certain men the English shot?' is finally symbolized in the anguished cry of a rabbit:

> But hush, for I have lost the theme,
> Its joy or night seem but a dream;
> Up there some hawk or owl has struck,
> Dropping out of sky or rock,
> A stricken rabbit is crying out,
> And its cry distracts my thought.

I want to finish with two poems, one of which sets the dissatisfied poet in the midst of civil war, the other of which sets the violent hero in the middle of the dead. They ask, indirectly, about the purpose of art in the midst of life, and by their movements, their images, their musics they make palpable a truth which Yeats was at first only able to affirm abstractly, in those words which he borrowed from Coventry Patmore: 'The end of art is peace.'

The first is from 'Meditations in Time of Civil War':

> The bees build in the crevices
> Of loosening masonry, and there
> The mother birds bring grubs and flies.
> My wall is loosening; honey-bees,
> Come build in the empty house of the stare.
>
> We are closed in, and the key is turned
> On our uncertainty; somewhere
> A man is killed, or a house burned,
> Yet no clear fact to be discerned:
> Come build in the empty house of the stare.
>
> A barricade of stone or of wood;
> Some fourteen days of civil war;

Last night they trundled down the road
That dead young soldier in his blood:
Come build in the empty house of the stare.

We had fed the heart on fantasies,
The heart's grown brutal from the fare;
More substance in our enmities
Than in our love; O honey-bees,
Come build in the empty house of the stare.

Here the great fur coat of attitude is laid aside, the domineering intellect and the equestrian profile, all of which gain him a power elsewhere, all laid aside. What we have is a deeply instinctive yet intellectually assented-to idea of nature in her benign and nurturant aspect as the proper first principle of life and living. The maternal is apprehended, intimated and warmly cherished and we are reminded, much as Shakespeare might remind us, of the warm eggs in the nest shaking at the impact of an explosion. The stare at Yeats's window and the temple-haunting martlet in Macbeth's castle are messengers of grace.

And if the maternal instincts are the first, perhaps they call us back at the very end also. Yeats lies under Ben Bulben, in Drumcliff Churchyard, under that dominant promontory which I like to think of as the father projected into the landscape, and there is perhaps something too male and assertive about the poem that bears the mountain's name and stands at the end of the *Collected Poems*. If I had my choice I would make the end of that book more exemplary by putting a kinder poem last, one in which the affirmative, wilful, violent man, whether he be artist or hero, the poet Yeats or the headhunter Cuchulain, must merge his domineering voice into the common voice of the living and the dead, mingle his heroism with the cowardice of his kind, lay his grey head upon the ashy breast of death.

I would end with 'Cuchulain Comforted', a poem which Yeats wrote within two weeks of his death, one in which his cunning as a deliberate maker and his wisdom as an intuitive thinker find a rich and strange conclusiveness. It is written in *terza rima*, the metre of Dante's *Commedia*, the only time Yeats used the form, but the proper time, when he was preparing his own death by imagining Cuchulain's descent among the shades. We witness here a strange ritual of surrender, a rite of passage from life into death, but a rite whose meaning is subsumed into song, into the otherness of art. It is a poem deeply at one with the weak and the strong of this earth, full of a motherly kindness towards life, but also unflinching in its belief in the propriety and beauty of life transcended into art, song, words. The language of the poem hallows the things of this world—eyes, branches, linen, shrouds, arms, needles, trees, all are strangely chaste in the context—yet the figure the poem makes is out of this world:

CUCHULAIN COMFORTED

A man that had six mortal wounds, a man
Violent and famous, strode among the dead;
Eyes stared out of the branches and were gone.

Then certain Shrouds that muttered head to head
Came and were gone. He leant upon a tree
As though to meditate on wounds and blood.

A Shroud that seemed to have authority
Among those bird-like things came, and let fall
A bundle of linen. Shrouds by two and three

Came creeping up because the man was still.
And thereupon that linen-carrier said:
'Your life can grow much sweeter if you will

'Obey our ancient rule and make a shroud;
Mainly because of what we only know
The rattle of those arms makes us afraid.

'We thread the needles' eyes, and all we do
All must together do.' That done, the man
Took up the nearest and began to sew.

'Now must we sing and sing the best we can,
But first you must be told our character:
Convicted cowards all, by kindred slain

'Or driven from home and left to die in fear.'
They sang, but had nor human tunes nor words,
Though all was done in common as before;

They had changed their throats and had the throats of birds.

Place and Displacement:
Recent Poetry from Northern Ireland

In his introduction to Jung's psychology, Anthony Storr gives an account of a case that bears closely upon the situation of the poet in Northern Ireland, or anywhere else for that matter:

> Jung describes how some of his patients, faced with what appeared to be an insoluble conflict, solved it by 'outgrowing' it, by developing a 'new level of consciousness'. He writes: 'Some higher or wider interest appeared on the patient's horizon, and through this broadening of his outlook the insoluble problem lost its urgency. It was not solved logically on its own terms but faded out when faced with new and stronger life urge.'
>
> The attainment of this new level of psychological development includes a certain degree of '. . . detachment from one's emotions. One certainly does feel the affect and is shaken and tormented by it, yet at the same time one is aware of a higher consciousness looking on which prevents one from becoming identical with the affect, a consciousness which regards the affect as an object, and can say "I *know* that I suffer." '

All this, Storr is the first to admit, is very general. No example is given by Jung of the 'insoluble problem' which must be outgrown or resolved at a symbolic level but, had he sought one, Jung might have found in Wordsworth's *Prelude* a working model for that evolution of a higher consciousness in response to an apparently intolerable conflict. The last books of the poem worry and circle and ruminate in an effort to discover what had happened in the 1790s when Wordsworth's passion for liberty and human regeneration, awakened by the outbreak of the French Revolution, came into conflict with other elements of his make-up founded upon the land and love of England. When England declared war on Revolutionary France, Wordsworth experienced a crisis of unanticipated intensity which he sought to allay first by addressing himself to the higher reality of Godwin's philosophy and, when that failed, by recourse to a renewed and deepened myth of nature and the human heart. But the crisis itself is described with dramatic and anecdotal power:

> And now the strength of Britain was put forth
> In league with the confederated host;
> Not in my single self alone I found,
> But in the minds of all ingenuous youth,
> Change and subversion from this hour. No shock
> Given to my moral nature had I known
> Down to that very moment—neither lapse
> Nor turn of sentiment—that might be named
> A revolution, save at this one time:
> All else was progress on the self-same path
> On which with a diversity of pace
> I had been travelling; this, a stride at once
> Into another region. True it is,
> 'Twas not concealed with what ungracious eyes
> Our native rulers from the very first
> Had looked upon regenerated France;
> Nor had I doubted that this day would come—
> But in such contemplation I had thought
> Of general interest only, beyond this
> Had never once foretasted the event.
> Now had I other business, for I felt
> The ravage of this most unnatural strife
> In my own heart; there lay it like a weight,
> At enmity with all the tenderest springs
> Of my enjoyments. I, who with the breeze
> Had played, a green leaf on the blessed tree
> Of my beloved country—nor had wished
> For happier fortune than to wither there—
> Now from my pleasant station was cut off,
> And tossed about in whirlwinds. I rejoiced,
> Yes, afterwards, truth painful to record,

Exulted in the triumph of my soul
When Englishmen by thousands were o'erthrown,
Left without glory on the field, or driven,
Brave hearts, to shameful flight. It was a grief—
Grief call it not, 'twas any thing but that—
A conflict of sensations without name,
Of which he only who may love the sight
Of a village steeple as I do can judge,
When in the congregation, bending all
To their great Father, prayers were offered up
Or praises for our country's victories,
And, 'mid the simple worshippers perchance
I only, like an uninvited guest
Whom no one owned, sate silent—shall I add,
Fed on the day of vengeance yet to come!

The Prelude (1805), Book X, 230–74

The good place where Wordsworth had been nurtured and to which his habitual feelings were most naturally attuned has become, for the revolutionary poet, the wrong place. Life, where he is situated, is not as he wants it to be. He is displaced from his own affections by a vision of the good located elsewhere. His political, utopian aspirations displace him from the beloved actuality of his surroundings so that his instinctive being and his appetitive intelligence are knocked out of alignment. He feels like a traitor among those he knows and loves. To be true to one part of himself, he must betray another part. The inner state of man is thus shaken, and the shock waves in the consciousness reflect the upheavals in the surrounding world. Indeed, the whole passage is like a textbook illustration of another of Jung's underlying notions, namely, that the trauma of individual consciousness is likely to be an aspect of forces at work in the collective life, past or present, since, for Jung, Hamlet's exclamation 'O my prophetic soul' has the force of a truism.

It is another truism that the achievement of a work of art is salutary in these circumstances, and we can easily see how the

composition of *The Prelude* was, in itself, part of the symbolic resolution of a lived conflict. Wordsworth admits an inner dialogue
between those inclinations and hopes which landed him in the
impasse he describes. The poem is diagnostic, therapeutic and
didactic all at once. It throws, in a prefiguration of modernist procedures, 'the nerves, as 'twere, in patterns on a screen'. It obeys the
modern demand for psychological realism, and while it often conducts its investigations in a diction that is ornate and elevated,
it does go in fear of abstractions, concentrating instead upon the
story of feelings and aspirations within an individual life, at a
certain place and a certain time. Wordsworth's case is symptomatic of the historical moment, but it is not paraded as being representative: the pressure of the poem's occasion launches it beyond
allegory and exemplum. Its principle of development and its structural and rhetorical life are to be found not in any designs he has
upon a readership, not in self-exculpation or self-dramatization,
but in the autonomous habits of the poet's mind and practice. The
'I' of the poem is at the eye of the storm within the 'I' of the poet.

The extreme of this kind of writing was to come more than a
hundred years later, in *The Waste Land*, another work where the
expression of an acute personal predicament can be read as an expression of the age, and one which enforced a new way of reading
poetry. It taught us to sound the image for its cultural and psychological import, to ponder the allusion for its critical rather than its
decorative weight and to look for the poet's imaginative signature
in the texture of the work, to listen in for the intrinsic poetry
rather than look out for its explicit meaning. *The Waste Land*, we
now know almost too patly, is the resolution at a symbolic level of
conflicts within the consciousness of the poet, but we are free to
read it as a refraction of pressures in the world of postwar Europe,
because we have absorbed Jung's insights quite naturally into our
way of thinking about art.

Like the disaffected Wordsworth, the Northern Irish writers I
wish to discuss take the strain of being in two places at once, of
needing to accommodate two opposing conditions of truthfulness
simultaneously, and at times their procedures are every bit as
cautious and oysterish as those of Eliot. They belong to a place

that is patently riven by notions of belonging to other places. Each person in Ulster lives first in the Ulster of the actual present, and then in one or other Ulster of the mind. The nationalist will wince at the Union Jack and 'God Save the Queen' as tokens of his place in the world; he will withhold assent from the solidarities implicit in those emblems rather as Wordsworth withheld assent from the congregation's prayers for the success of the English armies. Yet, like Wordsworth among his patriotic neighbours, the Northern nationalist conducts his daily social life among unionist neighbours for whom those same emblems have pious and passionate force and to whom his nationalist principles, his hope for a different flag and different anthem, are as traitorous as Wordsworth's revolutionary sympathies. The fountainhead of the unionist's myth springs in the Crown of England, but he must stand his ground on the island of Ireland. The fountainhead of the nationalist's myth lies in the idea of an integral Ireland, but he too lives in an exile from his ideal place. Nevertheless, while he has to concede that he is a citizen of the British state, the nationalist can take comfort in the physical fact of his presence upon the partitioned Irish island, just as the unionist can take comfort in the political reality of the United Kingdom even if he must concede that Ireland is his geographical home.

The condition is chronic and common and not necessarily terminal. It was fully at work in the collective life of Northern Ireland long before the present disruptions occurred. Indeed, it was more radically internalized within the Ulster personality during the years of quiet, and the typically reticent response of many Northern Irish writers to the violent conditions of the last fifteen years has much to do with this very internalization. Like other members of the population, the poets knew the score. Sectarian division, gerrymandering by the majority, discrimination in jobs and housing, all that was recognized as deplorable, and by the mid-1960s I think it would be fair to say that there were nascent attitudes in younger sections of the population, nationalist, republican and unionist, which promised some shift in the shape of things to come. I do not mean that the Unionist Establishment would easily or willingly have changed its ways, but with a more active and

vocal civil rights movement at work and a less blatantly tri-
umphalist generation of Unionist politicians emerging, an evolution towards a better, juster, internal balance might have been
expected to begin.

I think the writers of my generation saw their very emergence
as writers as a part of the leaven. The fact that a literary action
was afoot was in itself a new political condition, and the writers
did not feel the need to address themselves to the specific questions
of politics, because they assumed that the subtleties and tolerances
of their art were precisely what they had to contribute to the
coarseness and intolerances of public life. When Derek Mahon,
Michael Longley, James Simmons and myself were having our
first books published, Paisley was already in full sectarian cry, and,
indeed, Northern Ireland's cabinet ministers regularly massaged
the atavisms and bigotries of Orangemen on the Twelfth of July.
Nothing needed to be exposed: rather, it seemed that conditions
had to be outstripped, and it is probably true to say that the idea of
poetry was itself that higher ideal to which the poets unconsciously had turned in order to survive in the demeaning conditions—demeaned by resentment in the case of the Nationalists, by
embarrassment at least and guilt at best in the case of the Unionists. In fact, that passage from Jung which I quoted earlier does fit
the typical if not fully self-conscious position of the Ulster poet in
the 1960s:

> One certainly does feel the affect and is shaken and tormented by
> it, yet at the same time one is aware of a higher consciousness
> looking on which prevents one from becoming identical with the
> affect . . . which regards the affect as an object.

In our case, we might apply Jung's term 'the affect' to the particular exacerbations attendant on being a native of Northern Ireland,
since this 'affect' means a disturbance, a warp in the emotional
glass which is in danger of narrowing the range of the mind's responses to the terms of the disturbance itself, refracting everything through the warp. Things had advanced when this 'affect'
was observed by a new consciousness that perceived it to be the re-

sult of different history, heritages, cultural identity, traditions, call it what you will. These words provided a perspective on the surge of disruptive feelings which sprang too readily in the collective life, rebellious on the nationalist minority side, overbearing and punitive on the majority side, those unindividuated responses of day-to-day social and political experience.

For a moment, the discovery and deployment of this language allowed us to talk of Planters and Gaels rather than Protestants and Catholics, to speak of different heritages rather than launch accusations and suspicions at one another, to speak of history rather than the skullduggery of the local government. It was a palliative, true in its way, salutary in that it shifted the discourse into a more self-diagnosing frame of reference, but as everyone, including the poets, knew, not true enough. To locate the roots of one's identity in the ethnic and liturgical habits of one's group might be all very well, but for the group to confine the range of one's growth, to have one's sympathies determined and one's responses programmed by it was patently another form of entrapment. The only reliable release for the poet was the appeasement of the achieved poem. In that liberated moment when the lyric discovers its buoyant completion, when the timeless formal pleasure comes to its fullness and exhaustion, in those moments of self-justification and self-obliteration the poet makes contact with the plane of consciousness where he is at once intensified in his being and detached from his predicaments. It is this deeper psychological compulsion which lies behind the typical concern of Northern Irish poets with style, with formal finish, with linguistic relish and play. They knew the truth of Yeats's affirmation that the 'rhetorician would deceive his neighbours,/The sentimentalist himself, while art/Is but a vision of reality'. In other words, politically, topographically and artistically, they knew their place, and it is no accident that Paul Muldoon's first pamphlet, published in Belfast in 1971, was called, in fact, *Knowing My Place*, a punning title which is at once humble and arrogant, slyly allusive to what was expected of the minority to which he belonged and genuinely in sympathy with the idea that everything had its place—art, love, politics, local affections, cultural heritage and, for that matter, the place where a word doubles its meaning or where a line ends on the page.

That is the first point I want to emphasize: the profound relation here between poetic technique and historical situation. It is a superficial response to the work of Northern Irish poets to conceive of their lyric stances as evasions of the actual conditions. Their concern with poetry itself wears well when we place it beside the protest poetry of the 1960s: the density of their verbal worlds has held up, the purely poetic force of the words is the guarantee of a commitment which need not apologize for not taking up the cudgels since it is raising a baton to attune discords which the cudgels are creating. To attune it within the pit of their own consciousness, of course, not in the arena of dustbin lids and shoot-to-kill operations.

The second point to insist on is that the idea of poetry as a symbolic resolution of opposing truths, the idea of the poem as having its existence in a realm separate from the discourse of politics, does not absolve it or the poet from political responsibility. Nobody is going to advocate an ivory tower address for the poet nor a holier-than-thou attitude. Yet 'pure' poetry is perfectly justifiable in earshot of the car bomb, and it can imply a politics, depending on the nature of the poetry. A poetry of hermetic wit, of riddles and slips and self-mocking ironies, may appear culpably miniaturist or fastidious to the activist with his microphone at the street corner, and yet such poetry may be exercising in its inaudible way a fierce disdain of the activist's message or a distressed sympathy with it. But the reading of those political implications is in itself a political activity, separate from the processes that produced the poems, an extension or projection from the artistic endeavour—an endeavour which is not obliged to have any intention beyond its own proper completion.

The poet is stretched between politics and transcendence and is often displaced from a confidence in a single position by his disposition to be affected by all positions, negatively rather than positively capable. This, and the complexity of the present conditions, may go some way towards explaining the large number of poems in which the Northern Irish writer views the world from a great spatial or temporal distance, the number of poems imagined from beyond the grave, from the perspective of mythological or histori-

cally remote characters: Derek Mahon's 'An Image from Beckett' is
an amplification of earlier soliloquies from the other side, by forg-
ers, cowards, tramps, artists, all rehearsing their fates in a note
both wry and plangent. This kind of poem culminates in the beautifully orchestrated 'A Disused Shed in Co. Wexford', where it is
not just a single life that is given voice but a whole Lethe full of
doomed generations and tribes, whispering their unfulfilment and
perplexed hopes in a trickle of masonry, pleading for a hearing in
the great soft gestures of mushroom-growths that strain from the
dark towards a guiding star of light in the keyhole:

> A half century, without visitors, in the dark—
> Poor preparation for the cracking lock
> And creak of hinges, Magi, moonmen,
> Powdery prisoners of the old regime,
> Web-throated, stalked like triffids, racked by drought
> And insomnia, only the ghost of a scream
> At the flash-bulb firing squad we wake them with
> Shows there is life yet in their feverish forms.
> Grown beyond nature now, soft food for worms,
> They lift frail heads in gravity and good faith.
>
> They are begging us, you see, in their wordless way,
> To do something, to speak on their behalf
> Or at least not to close the door again.
> Lost people of Treblinka and Pompeii!
> 'Save us, save us,' they seem to say,
> 'Let the god not abandon us
> Who have come so far in darkness and in pain.
> We too had our lives to live.
> You with your light meter and relaxed itinerary,
> Let not our naive labours have been in vain!'

This is about the need to live and be known, the need for selfhood,
recognition in the eye of God and the eye of the world, and its music is cello and homesick. A great sense of historical cycles, of injustice and catastrophe, looms at the back of the poem's mind. At

its forefront is the pursuit of the logic of its own metaphors growing with the mushrooms in the shed of an old estate that had been
abandoned by an Irish ascendancy family after independence. But
what gives the poem its sorrow and insight is the long perspective,
an intimacy with the clay-floored foetor of the shed kept in mind
and in focus from a point of detached compassion, in another
world of freedom, light and efficiency. To reduce the mushrooms'
lives and appetites to counters for the frustrations and desolations
of lives in Northern Ireland is, of course, one of those political
readings which is perfectly applicable, but we recognize that this
allegorical approach ties the poem too neatly into its place. The
amplitude of its effects, its vault-filling resonance depend upon its
displaced perspective. Those rooted helplessly in place plead with
the capable uprooted visitor, be he poet or photographer. Mahon,
the poet of metropolitan allusion, of ironical and cultivated manners, is being shadowed by his unlived life among the familiar
shades of Belfast. Do not turn your back on us, do not disdain our
graceless stifled destiny, keep faith with your origins, do not desert,
speak for us: the mushrooms are the voices of belonging, but they
could not have been heard so compellingly if Mahon had not created the whispering gallery of absence not just by moving out of
Ireland but by evolving out of solidarity into irony and compassion. And, needless to say, into solitude. These poems of the voice
from beyond are beamed back out of a condition of silence and
Zen-like stillness, an eternity in love with the products of time.
They tenderly evoke the great solace of the natural world and also
the great wounds we make in it and ourselves. 'Ovid in Tomis', for
example, begins with a merry and ecologically indignant identification of the Roman poet with his alienated contemporary:

> What coarse god
> Was the gear-box in the rain
> Beside the road?
>
> What nereid the unsinkable
> Hair conditioner
> Knocking the icy rocks?

They stare me out
With the chaste gravity
And feral pride

Of noble savages
Set down
On an alien shore.

It is so long
Since my own transformation
Into a stone,

I often forget
That there was a time
Before my name

Was mud in the mouths
Of the Danube,
A dirty word in Rome.

Imagine Byron banished
To Botany Bay
Or Wilde to Dawson City

And you have some idea
How it is for me
On the shores of the Black Sea.

Baudelaire's albatross poet, inept upon the deck, mocked by the callous sailors, has nothing on this one, so self-aware and self-mocking, so posthumous to himself, so sceptical of the very effort of poetry that he can say:

I
Have exchanged belief
For documentation.

The Muse is somewhere
Else, not here
By this frozen lake—

Or, if here, then I am
Not poet enough
To make the connection.

Are we truly alone
With our physics and myths,
The stars no more

Than glittering dust,
With no one there
To hear our choral odes?

If so, we can start
To ignore the silence
Of infinite space

And concentrate instead
On the infinity
Under our very noses—

The cry at the heart
Of the artichoke,
The gaiety of atoms.

Better to contemplate
The blank page
And leave it blank

Than modify
Its substance by
So much as a pen-stroke.

Woven of wood-nymphs,
It speaks volumes
No one will ever write.

I incline my head
To its candour
And weep for our exile.

Again, this escapes beyond dramatic monologue and disguised autobiography into contemplation on the nature of artistic satisfac-

tion itself; by the end the poem is abjuring language in a language that offers us that deeply formal sensation of tensions resolved. The speaker laments his exile in such a way that we would not have him rehabilitated. The wound he suffers is to his and our advantage: the local conditions that lie at the roots of the poet's consciousness have been transposed into a symbol.

I don't want to reduce Derek Mahon's poems to this single theme of alienated distance, for his work also abounds in poems where the social voice is up and away on the back of Pegasus, cutting a dash through the usual life of back-kitchens and bar counters, but I would insist that I am not forcing his work to fit a thesis. It is present in all his books, this dominant mood of being on the outside (where one has laboured spiritually to arrive) only to end up looking back nostalgically at what one knows are well nigh intolerable conditions on the inside. It is treated in a number of his best poems, which dwell upon the sufferings of those he called in an early poem 'the unreconciled in their metaphysical pain'. These poems of the displaced consciousness are as rinsed of political and ethnic solidarity as a haiku by Bashō, but their purely poetic achievement is further enriched when we view them against Mahon's own political and ethnic background.

We might say that in order for any place to be credible for Mahon, it has to be re-imagined in the light of other places. In the language of *Star Trek*, it has to be beamed up so that it can be dependably beamed down. Thus, the civil beauty of Penshurst Place, the home of the Sidney family, is evoked by Mahon in terms of the blandishments of Renaissance poetry, music and manners. Nevertheless, while Mahon prizes and yearns for these arcadian harmonies, his mind is haunted by other, more disturbing images. Sir Philip Sidney is one dream, all gilded valour and English patriotic aura, but another dream associated with Penshurst Place is Hugh O'Neill, Earl of Tyrone, leader in the last Irish war against Elizabeth's armies. The line 'The Spanish ships around Kinsale' refers to the Battle of Kinsale, where Hugh O'Neill, arch-traitor in the eyes of the English, the Great O'Neill in the eyes of the Irish, was finally defeated. In other words, the courtliness evoked by the verse and symbolized by Penshurst Place is only one part of the poem's life. Its underlife, its shadow elsewhere, is the Ulster of hill-forts, cattle-raids and rain-sodden gallowglasses where Hugh O'Neill was born and to which, after eight years of being fostered at Penshurst Place in the care of Sir Henry Sidney, he returned. 'Penshurst Place', then, contains Mahon's sense of bilocation, culturally in love with the Surrey countryside, where he was living with his family when this poem was written, but domestically and politically entangled with the country of his first nurture:

> The bright drop quivering on a thorn
> In the rich silence after rain,
> Lute music from the orchard aisles,
> The paths ablaze with daffodils,
> Intrigue and venery in the air
> *A l'ombre des jeunes filles en fleurs*,
> The iron hand and the velvet glove—
> Come live with me and be my love.

> A pearl face, numinously bright,
> Shining in silence of the night,
> A muffled crash of smouldering logs,
> Bad dreams of courtiers and of dogs,
> The Spanish ships around Kinsale,
> The screech owl and the nightingale,
> The falcon and the turtle dove—
> Come live with me and be my love.

Instances of this sort could be multiplied. In a poem about leaving Surrey to return to North Antrim, Mahon imagines himself turning into a tree in an English parkland, 'as if I belonged here too', but he is destined to identify with a very different native bush, a windswept thorn on a high northern clifftop,

> With nothing to recommend it
> But its harsh tenacity
> Between the blinding windows
> And the forests of the sea,

As if its very existence
Were a reason to continue.

Crone, crow, scarecrow,
Its worn fingers scrabbling
At a torn sky, it stands
On the edge of everything
Like a burnt-out angel
Raising petitionary hands.

The petitionary hands of the tree, like the pleading throats of the mushrooms, call upon the poet to identify with 'everything that is the case', in this case his native landscape with all its threshing historical plights. But in a poem called 'Tractatus', which takes off in its first line from a proposition of Wittgenstein's, Mahon insists on the freedom to invent his own case:

'The world is everything that is the case'
From the fly giving up in the coal-shed
To the Winged Victory of Samothrace.
Give blame, praise, to the fumbling God
Who hides, shame-facèdly, His agèd face;
Whose light retires behind its veil of cloud.

The world, though, is also so much more—
Everything that is the case imaginatively.
Tacitus believed mariners could *hear*
The sun sinking into the western sea;
And who would question that titanic roar,
The steam rising wherever the edge may be?

This poem is not in itself as deeply imagined as others I could quote, but it does voice the Mahon approach in quite explicit terms. The imagined hiss and boil of the sun in the sea does not involve a denial of the cosmological facts of the matter; rather, it restores us to a pristine encounter with the cosmos. In a similar way, Mahon's displaced angle of vision is not a Nelson-like ploy to avoid seeing what he prefers not to see but a way of focusing afresh. For all his imaginative ubiquity, his poems enforce the truth he settles upon in the last stanza of a poem called, with stunning plainness, 'A Garage in Co. Cork':

> But we are in one place and one place only,
> One of the milestones of earth-residence
> Unique in each particular, the thinly
> Peopled hinterland serenely tense—
> Not in the hope of a resplendent future
> But with a sure sense of its intrinsic nature.

E. M. Cioran has written: 'Some peoples propose themselves as divine problems: can we believe in ourselves?' 'Certainly not', Paul Muldoon answers, in the Irish context. But it is a negative delivered with a smile which suggests otherwise. In the world of Muldoon's poetry, the reader finds himself in the middle of that old story where the protagonist is faced with two informants, one who always tells the truth and one who always tells lies. The problem, then, is to formulate the question which will elicit an answer from either one that can be reliably decoded. To put it another way, Muldoon's poems do not offer us answers but keep us alive in the middle of the question. And the very question of whether or not this imaginative habit is to be related to his native place and its double-life is posed, obliquely of course, in his short and typically enigmatic poem called 'Blemish':

> Were it indeed an accident of birth
> That she looks on the gentle earth
> And the seemingly gentle sky
> Through one brown, and one blue eye.

The mood of this is neither indicative nor interrogative but conditional. The understood complete sentence goes, 'It would be a blemish, were it indeed . . . etc.', but we cannot be *sure* that it is an accident of birth and hence a hereditary blemish. It might also be a gift of vision, a mark of divine favour, an astonishing boon of being able to see through things as they seem, like the seemingly gentle sky, to things as they are, whatever they are. The poem suggests, indirectly, that the imaginative gifts of Northern Irish writers should not be linked too sociologically to the blemished life of their country. It wanders in and out of the mind like an unremarked soothsayer who drops a remark that flowers with possibility after he has drifted off. And we are still left wondering when we find a character in Márquez's *A Hundred Years of Solitude* with just the blemish that Muldoon describes here: so is this a literary allusion or an archetypal image? All three, Muldoon might well answer from behind the screen of his language.

Language is Muldoon's resolving element, his quick-change gear, his vehicle for getaway. James Joyce, who could invest the very names of punctuation marks with historical riddles when he addressed his people as 'Laities and gentes, full-stoppers and semi-colonials', the Joyce of *Finnegans Wake* who melted time and place into a plasm of rhythms and word-roots, puns and tunes, a slide-show of Freudian slips for the Jungian typesetter, this Joyce would recognize the verbal opportunism of Muldoon as a form of native kenning, a Northern doubling, a kind of daedal fiddling to keep the home fires burning. For example, the protagonist of his long poem 'The More a Man Has the More a Man Wants' is a character called Gallogly. Gallogly's name is related to a previous Muldoon character called Golightly, and also to the Gallowglass warriors of Gaelic Ulster and to the Sioux braves of the Oglala tribe; and he appears in a tale as odd as any one of the Ingoldsby legends. By such verbal means Muldoon makes the stuff of Ulster news headlines—explosions, killings, American aid for the IRA, covert operations of all kinds—the stuff that dreams are made on. All these things which are so much taken for granted that they tend to be thrust to the back of the mind 'in real life' are taken over by Muldoon as the elements of a violent and resourceful fantasy; and by this very relegation to 'fiction' they achieve once again a deadly and unnerving prominence. The old alibis of heritage, tradition, folklore, Planter and Gael, and a whole literature and discourse posited on these distinctions (including poems by his contemporaries), are rifled for tropes and allusions until, within the fiction of the poem, they themselves are imputed with fictional status. By masquerading as a story that is as innocent of high seriousness as an Irish joke, Muldoon's 'The More a Man Has the More a Man Wants' effects what the apostle of high seriousness sought from the serious artist, a criticism of life.

I realize that I am affirming rather than demonstrating all this, but the poem in question is too long to take up in any detail. Indeed, Muldoon's poetry works so much at a symbolic level, by means of parallels, implications, sleights of word, hints and hedgings, that even the shortest lyric may call forth pages of elucidation, or perhaps one should say collusion, 'elucidation' being a word that would imply a meaning too simply and righteously produced from the hat of a poem that might just produce another meaning from up its sleeve.

The poet as conjuror, then, a dab hand at turning tables and spinning yarns, not above innuendo and not without punitive designs upon his audience. Yet the acerbity of Muldoon's intelligence is constantly sweetened by humour and by the natural rhythmic drift of his writing, and nowhere more so than in the self-cancelling narrative of 'Lunch with Pancho Villa', a poem that addresses itself to the relations between 'life' and 'art' as experienced by a poet-protagonist during a certain 'famous revolution' which occurs, to some extent, in 'a back yard'. The poet-narrator is accused by a 'celebrated pamphleteer':

> 'Look, son. Just look around you.
> People are getting themselves killed
> Left, right and centre
> While you do what? Write rondeaux?
> There's more to living in this country
> Than stars, horses, pigs and trees,
> Not that you'd guess it from your poems.
> Do you never listen to the news?'

The poet's response to all this arises from a conviction not unlike Patrick Kavanagh's conviction that for a writer there is nothing as doomed as the important thing, no subject as negligible as the subject with the news-headline status. His narrative is designed to make the words 'famous' and 'celebrated' ring hollow, yet the narrative itself ('All made up as I went along') turns out to be as unreliable as the adjectives:

> My celebrated pamphleteer!
> Of course, I gave it all away
> With those preposterous titles.
> *The Bloody Rose? The Dream and the Drums?*
> The three-day-wonder of the flowering plum!
> Or was I desperately wishing
> To have been their other co-author,
> Or, at least, to own a first edition
> Of *The Boot Boys and Other Battles?*

The flicker of self-doubt in these last four lines gives back to the pamphleteer some of the credence which the whole poem takes away from him, and Muldoon very justly ends with a note of puzzlement, though not without a strong implicit endorsement of the idea that the proper concern of art is with the naming of things rather than with the espousal of causes:

> What should I say to this callow youth
> Who learned to write last winter—
> One of those correspondence courses—
> And who's coming to lunch to-day?
> He'll be rambling on, no doubt,
> About pigs and trees, stars and horses.

If in the Muldoon world we are faced with the liar and the truth teller, searching for the right question, in the poetry of Michael Longley we are with lovers in the dark during a power-failure. It is one of the urban myths that there is a perceptible rise in the birthrate after such a breakdown of services. The couples turn from home life to love life, the delights of touch becoming a natural compensation for the loss of the usual distractions. We recognize the pattern of behaviour as completely credible, the most obvious and delicious in the circumstances.

It is in the light of this parable of the dark that Longley's characteristic erotic music is to be heard. Longley's poetry is often the poetry of direct amorous address, its dramatic voice the voice of indolent and occasionally deliquescent reverie, its subject the whole matter of sexual daydream. But even when the poem is ostensibly about landscape or seascape, about flora and fauna, mythological figures or musical instruments, the intonation of the verse is seductive, its melody allaying and cajoling, its typical mood one of tender insinuation and possibility.

Longley's poems count the phenomena of the natural world with the particular deliberate pleasure of a lover's finger wandering along the bumpy path of the vertebrae. The names for the parts of the body reappear constantly, and even when it is not a body but a flower or a weed that is being touched upon, the contact between the world and the language is lipbrushing or stealthily caressing. As if the back of a hand that has gone to the floor to lift a napkin strayed against the warm limb of a neighbour. Here, almost at random, is a short sequence called 'Botany':

DUCKWEED

Afloat on their own reflection, these leaves,
With roots that reach only part of the way,
Will fall asleep at the end of summer,
Draw in their skirts and sink to the bottom.

FOXGLOVE

Though the corolla dangles upside down,
Nothing ever falls out, neither nectar
Nor loosening pollen grains: a thimble,
Stall for the little finger and the bee.

DOCK

Its green flowers attract only the wind
But a red vein may irrigate the leaf

And blossom into blush or birthmark
Or a remedy for the nettle's sting.

ORCHID

The tuber absorbs summer and winter,
Its own ugly shape, twisted arms and legs,
A recollection of the heart, one artery
Sprouting upwards to support a flower.

These verses are not Longley at his most effulgent, but for that very reason I test my contention against them and find it holds true. The direct sexual analogies are there in drawn skirts, blushes and birthmarks, but the associations in corollas dangling, arteries sprouting upwards to support a flower and little fingers in thimbles and fingerstalls make us feel like lowering our eyes in the presence of these specimens rather than spy upon their little arousals. Yet it is not simply the imagery and the submerged tissue of association that constitute the eroticism of the lines; it is the intent, close-up numbering and savouring of each tiny identifying mark, the cherishing and lingering name laid upon the thing itself.

All this is even more richly evident when we turn to Longley's more fully orchestrated writings; his recent book *The Echo Gate* is full of opulent, classical love poems, one of the best of which is 'The Linen Industry'. By now it is superfluous for me to spell out the connections between the private flax and linen of this poem and the public flax and linen which had been the basis of Belfast's industrial power and its intransigent male-fisted politics, both of which refused the feminine element symbolized by the land of Ireland itself. Again, it is superfluous to insist that Longley has in mind no political allegory of the sort I am sketching, but nevertheless a reading of the poem is possible which sees it as the internalization and affirmation of those feminine powers repressed by man's, and in particular the Ulsterman's, adaptation to conditions in the industrial world:

Pulling up flax after the blue flowers have fallen
And laying our handfuls in the peaty water

To rot those grasses to the bone, or building stooks
That recall the skirts of an invisible dancer,

We become a part of the linen industry
And follow its processes to the grubby town
Where fields are compacted into window-boxes
And there is little room among the big machines.

But even in our attic under the skylight
We make love on a bleach green, the whole meadow
Draped with material turning white in the sun
As though snow reluctant to melt were our attire.

What's passion but a battering of stubborn stalks,
Then a gentle combing out of fibres like hair
And a weaving of these into christening robes,
Into garments for a marriage or funeral?

Since it's like a bereavement once the labour's done
To find ourselves last workers in a dying trade,
Let flax be our matchmaker, our undertaker,
The provider of sheets for whatever the bed—

And be shy of your breasts in the presence of death,
Say that you look more beautiful in linen
Wearing white petticoats, the bow on your bodice
A butterfly attending the embroidered flowers.

That sense of history viewed from a great distance which we found
in Mahon is in this poem too; and that rendering of the world
down to a precipitate of language, typical of Muldoon, is also at
work here, but more candidly, for Longley is more trusting of the
first innocent blush of the word itself, more susceptible to its
purely phonetic body. Here Edward Thomas's English naming
poems rather than Joyce's riddling Irish prose are the sponsoring
presence from the literary tradition, a sponsorship with just as
much political significance as we want to assign it.

To go back to the terms with which I began this lecture and revise them slightly, we might say that Longley's poems are symbolic

dissolutions. Like Faustus in his last hour wishing to be dispersed into the smallest creatures and phenomena in the face of the terror of death, Longley's imagination runs to hide in the multiple details of the natural world. Rapture is imaged by him as the escape of a flock of pigeons from their basket, and the old Elizabethan usage of 'death' as a word for sexual climax comes into play when we find Longley eroticizing even the dissolution of the body after death, in poems like 'Obsequies' and 'Oliver Plunkett'.

I want to end this consideration of the way the energies in Northern Ireland have been transposed or displaced into poetry by looking at Longley's poem 'Self-Heal', from a sequence called 'Mayo Monologues'. Mayo is, of course, in the west, not the north of Ireland, and Longley did not set out to write a poem 'relevant' to the Troubles—which is all to the good. 'Self-Heal' is the name of a flower, and naming it appeases the character in the monologue, a woman who was sexually molested by a mongoloid neighbour, somebody stunted in body and spirit, whose reach out towards beauty and fulfilment brought the full brutal weight of his community's prejudices down upon him; and that violence bred a new violence within himself.

> I wanted to teach him the names of flowers,
> Self-heal and centaury; on the long acre
> Where cattle never graze, bog asphodel.
> Could I love someone so gone in the head
> And, as they say, was I leading him on?
> He'd slept in the cot until he was twelve
> Because of his babyish ways, I suppose,
> Or the lack of a bed: hadn't his father
> Gambled away all but rushy pasture?
> His skull seemed to be hammered like a wedge
> Into his shoulders, and his back was hunched,
> Which gave him an almost scholarly air.
> But he couldn't remember the things I taught:
> Each name would hover above its flower
> Like a butterfly unable to alight.
> That day I pulled a cuckoo-pint apart

To release the giddy insects from their cell.
Gently he slipped his hand between my thighs.
I wasn't frightened; and still I don't know why,
But I ran from him in tears to tell them.
I heard how every day for one whole week
He was flogged with a blackthorn, then tethered
In the hayfield. I might have been the cow
Whose tail he would later dock with shears,
And he the ram tangled in barbed wire
That he stoned to death when they set him free.

As the voice of the woman in this poem recounts her part in the violence for which she is innocently responsible, she begins to gain some detachment from her own suffering and to comprehend the role she played in the larger story. She can see that she was implicated, if unwittingly, in the savage turn of events and does not seek to excuse herself. Her learning process might therefore be analogous to the learning process forced upon poets by events in Northern Ireland. Although in no way personally responsible for the violence that occurred, they comprehend its causes and effects and have been inclined to make their poetry a process of self-healing, neither deliberately provocative nor culpably detached.

The Placeless Heaven:
Another Look at Kavanagh

In 1939, the year that Patrick Kavanagh arrived in Dublin, an aunt of mine planted a chestnut in a jam jar. When it began to sprout she broke the jar, made a hole and transplanted the thing under a hedge in front of the house. Over the years, the seedling shot up into a young tree that rose taller and taller above the boxwood hedge. And over the years I came to identify my own life with the life of the chestnut tree.

This was because everybody remembered and constantly re-peated the fact that it had been planted the year I was born; also because I was something of a favourite with that particular aunt, so her affection came to be symbolized in the tree; and also perhaps because the chestnut was the one significant thing that grew as I grew. The rest of the trees and hedges round the house were all mature and appeared therefore like given features of the world: the chestnut tree, on the other hand, was young and was watched in much the same way as the other children and myself were watched and commented upon—fondly, frankly and unrelentingly.

When I was in my early teens, the family moved away from that house, and the new owners of the place eventually cut down every tree around the yard and the lane and the garden, including the chestnut tree. We deplored all that, of course, but life went on satisfactorily enough where we resettled, and for years I gave no particular thought to the place we had left or to my tree which had been felled. Then, all of a sudden, a couple of years ago, I began to think of the space where the tree had been or would have been. In my mind's eye I saw it as a kind of luminous emptiness, a warp and waver of light, and once again, in a way that I find hard to de-fine, I began to identify with that space just as years before I had identified with the young tree.

Except that this time it was not so much a matter of attaching oneself to a living symbol of being rooted in the native ground; it was more a matter of preparing to be uprooted, to be spirited away into some transparent yet indigenous afterlife. The new place was all idea, if you like; it was generated out of my experience of the old place but it was not a topographical location. It was and remains an imagined realm, even if it can be located at an earthly spot, a placeless heaven rather than a heavenly place.

I am going to suggest here an analogy between the first tree and the last tree as I have just described them and the early and late poetry of Patrick Kavanagh. I also want to talk about that poetry in terms of my earliest and latest responses to it. And I hope that what emerges will be not just a personal record but some kind of generally true account of the nature of Patrick Kavanagh's essential poems.

Briefly, then, I would suggest that the early Kavanagh poem starts up like my childhood tree in its home ground; it is supplied with a strong physical presence and is full of the recognitions which existed between the poet and his place; it is symbolic of affections rooted in a community life and has behind it an imagination which is not yet weaned from its origin, an attached rather than a detached faculty, one which lives, to use Kavanagh's own metaphor, in a fog. Many of those early poems do indeed celebrate the place as heavenly, many more are disappointed that it is not as heavenly as it could or should be, but all of the early Monaghan poetry gives the place credit for existing, assists at its real topographical presence, dwells upon it and accepts it as the definitive locus of the given world.

The horizons of the little fields and hills, whether they are gloomy and constricting or radiant and enhancing, are sensed as the horizons of consciousness. Within those horizons, however, the poet who utters the poems is alive and well as a sharp critical intelligence. He knows that the Monaghan world is not the whole world, yet it is the only one for him, the one which he embosses solidly and intimately into the words of poems. We might say that Kavanagh is pervious to this world's spirit more than it is pervious to his spirit. When the Big Forth of Rocksavage is mentioned, or

Cassidy's Hanging Hill, the reader senses immediately that these are places in the actual countryside which are pressing constantly into memory. In this early period, the experienced physical reality of Monaghan life imposes itself upon the poet's consciousness so that he necessarily composes himself, his poetic identity and his poems in relation to that encircling horizon of given experience.

In the poetry of Kavanagh's later period, embodied first in 'Epic' and then, in the late 1950s, in the Canal Bank Sonnets, a definite change is perceptible. We might say that now the world is more pervious to his vision than he is pervious to the world. When he writes about places now, they are luminous spaces within his mind. They have been evacuated of their status as background, as documentary geography, and exist instead as transfigured images, sites where the mind projects its own force. In this later poetry, place is included within the horizon of Kavanagh's mind rather than the other way around. The country he visits is inside himself:

> I do not know what age I am,
> I am no mortal age;
> I know nothing of women,
> Nothing of cities,
> I cannot die
> Unless I walk outside these whitethorn hedges.

('Innocence')

At the edge of consciousness in a late poem such as this, we encounter the white light of meditation; at the edge of consciousness in the early poems, the familiar world stretches reliably away. At the conclusion of poems like 'Spraying the Potatoes' and 'A Christmas Childhood', self is absorbed by scene:

> And poet lost to potato-fields,
> Remembering the lime and copper smell
> Of the spraying barrels he is not lost
> Or till blossomed stalks cannot weave a spell.

An opposite process, however, is at work at the conclusion of 'Canal Bank Walk'. Here the speaker's presence does not disperse itself in a dying fall, nor does the circumference of circumstances crowd out the perceiving centre. Even though the voice is asking to be 'enraptured', there is no hint of passivity. The rhythm heaves up strongly, bespeaking the mind's adequacy to the task of making this place—or any place—into an 'important place'. Pretending to be the world's servant, Kavanagh is actually engaged in the process of world mastery:

> O unworn world enrapture me, encapture me in a web
> Of fabulous grass and eternal voices by a beech,
> Feed the gaping need to my sense, give me ad lib
> To pray unselfconsciously with overflowing speech
> For this soul needs to be honoured with a new dress woven
> From green and blue things and arguments that cannot be
>   proven.

Similarly, in the pivotal sonnet 'Epic', even though the poem gives the stage over to two Monaghan farmers and successfully sets Ballyrush and Gortin in balance against Munich, it is not saying that the farmers and the Monaghan region are important in them- selves. They are made important only by the light of the mind which is now playing upon them. It is a poem more in praise of Kavanagh's idea of Homer than in praise of Kavanagh's home.

'Epic' appeared in the volume called *Come Dance with Kitty Stobling*, published in 1960 and reprinted three times within the next year. My own copy is one of the fourth impression, and I have dated it 3 July 1963. I did not have many copies of books by living poets at that time, and it is hard now to retrieve the sense of being on the outside of things, far away from 'the City of Kings / Where art music, letters are the real thing'. Belfast at that time had no lit- erary publishers, no poetry readings, no sense of a literary identity. In 1962, while a student at St Joseph's College of Education, I had done an extended essay on the history of literary magazines in Ulster, as though I were already seeking a basis for faith in the pos- sibility of our cultural existence as Northern, Irish and essentially ourselves. It comes as something of a shock nowadays to remember that during four years as an undergraduate in the Queen's University English Department I had not ever been taught by an Irish or an Ulster voice. I had, however, heard Louis MacNeice read his poems there and in 1963 had also listened to Thomas Kinsella read from his second volume, *Downstream*, and from earlier work. Eventually, I got my hands on Robin Skelton's anthology *Six Irish Poets*; on the first edition of John Montague's *Poisoned Lands*, with its irrigating and confirming poem, 'The Water Carrier'; on Alvarez's anthology *The New Poetry*, where I encountered the work of Ted Hughes and R. S. Thomas. All of these things were animating, as were occasional trips to Dublin, where I managed to pick up that emblem of Ireland's quickening poetic life, *The Dolmen Miscellany of Irish Writing*, and to read in it the strong lines of Richard Murphy's 'The Cleggan Disaster'. Meanwhile, my headmaster, Michael McLaverty, himself a Monaghan man by birth but with a far gentler sensibility than Kavanagh's, lent me his copy of *A Soul for Sale* and so introduced me, at the age of twenty-three, to *The Great Hunger*.

Everything, at that time, was needy and hopeful and inchoate. I had had four poems accepted for publication, two by the *Belfast Telegraph*, one by *The Irish Times* and one by *The Kilkenny Magazine*, but still, like Keats in Yeats's image, I was like a child with his nose pressed to a sweetshop window, gazing from behind a barrier at the tempting mysteries beyond. And then came this revelation and confirmation of reading Kavanagh. When I discovered 'Spraying the Potatoes' in the old *Oxford Book of Irish Verse*, I was excited to find details of a life which I knew intimately—but which I had always considered to be below or beyond books—being presented in a book. The barrels of blue potato spray which had stood in my own childhood like holidays of pure colour in an otherwise grey field-life—there they were, standing their ground in print. And there too was the word 'headland', which I guessed was to Kavanagh as local a word as 'headrig' was to me. Here too was the strange stillness and heat and solitude of the sunlit fields, the inexplicable melancholy of distant work-sounds, all caught in a language that was both familiar and odd:

> The axle-roll of a rut-locked cart
> Broke the burnt stick of noon in two.

And it was the same with 'A Christmas Childhood'. Once again, in the other life of print, I came upon the unregarded data of the life I had lived. Potato-pits with rime on them, guttery gaps, iced-over puddles being crunched, cows being milked, a child nicking the doorpost with a penknife and so on. What was being experienced was not some hygienic and self-aware pleasure of the text but a primitive delight in finding world become word.

I had been hungry for this kind of thing without knowing what it was I was hungering after. For example, when I graduated in 1961, I had bought Louis MacNeice's *Collected Poems*. I did take pleasure in that work, especially in the hard-faced tenderness of something like 'Postscript from Iceland'; I recognized his warm and clinkered spirit, yet I still remained at a reader's distance. MacNeice did not throw the switch that sends writing energy sizzling into a hitherto unwriting system. When I opened his book, I still came up against the window-pane of literature. His poems arose from a mind-stuff and existed in a cultural setting which were at one remove from me and what I came from. I envied them, of course, their security in the big world of history and poetry which happened out there, far beyond the world of state scholarships, the Gaelic Athletic Association, October devotions, the Clancy Brothers, buckets and egg-boxes where I had had my being. I envied them, but I was not taken over by them the way I was taken over by Kavanagh.

At this point, it is necessary to make one thing clear. I am not affirming here the superiority of the rural over the urban/ suburban as a subject for poetry, nor am I out to sponsor deprivation at the expense of cultivation. I am not insinuating that one domain of experience is more intrinsically poetical or more ethnically desirable than another. I am trying to record exactly the sensations of one reader, from a comparatively bookless background, who came into contact with some of the established poetic voices in Ireland in the early 1960s. Needless to say, I am aware of a certain partisan strain in the criticism of Irish poetry, deriving from remarks by Samuel Beckett in the 1930s and developed most notably by Anthony Cronin. This criticism regards the vogue for poetry based on images from a country background as a derogation of literary responsibility and some sort of negative Irish feedback. It is also deliberately polemical and might be worth taking up in another context; for the moment, however, I want to keep the focus personal and look at what Kavanagh has meant to one reader, over a period of a couple of decades.

Kavanagh's genius had achieved single-handedly what I and my grammar-schooled, arts-degreed generation were badly in need of—a poetry that linked the small farm life which had produced us to the slim-volume world we were now supposed to be fit for. He brought us back to what we came from. So it was natural that, to begin with, we overvalued the subject-matter of the poetry at the expense of its salutary creative spirit. In the 1960s I was still more susceptible to the pathos and familiarity of the matter of Kavanagh's poetry than I was alert to the liberation and subversiveness of its manner. Instead of divesting me of my first life, it confirmed that life by giving it an image. I do not mean by that that when I read *The Great Hunger* I felt proud to have known people similar to Patrick Maguire or felt that their ethos had been vindicated. It is more that one felt less alone and marginal as a product of that world now that it had found its expression in a work which was regarded not just as part of a national culture but as a contribution to the world's store of true poems.

Kavanagh gave you permission to dwell without cultural anxiety among the usual landmarks of your life. Over the border, into a Northern Ireland dominated by the noticeably English accents of the local BBC, he broadcast a voice that would not be cowed into accents other than its own. Without being in the slightest way political in its intentions, Kavanagh's poetry did have political effect. Whether he wanted it or not, his achievement was inevitably co-opted, north and south, into the general current of feeling which flowed from and sustained ideas of national identity, cultural otherness from Britain and the dream of a literature with a manner and a matter resistant to the central Englishness of the dominant tradition. No admirer of the Irish Literary Revival, Kavanagh was read initially and almost entirely in light of the Revival writers' ambitions for a native literature.

So there I was, in 1963, with my new copy of *Come Dance with Kitty Stobling*, in the grip of those cultural and political pieties which Kavanagh, all unknown to me, had spent the last fifteen years or so repudiating. I could feel completely at home with a poem like 'Shancoduff'—which dated from the 1930s anyhow, as did 'To the Man after the Harrow'—and with 'Kerr's Ass' and 'Ante-Natal Dream'; their imagery, after all, was continuous with the lyric poetry of the 1940s, those Monaghan rhapsodies I had known from the *Oxford Book of Irish Verse*. This was the country poet at home with his country subjects and we were all ready for that. At the time, I responded to the direct force of these later works but did not immediately recognize their visionary intent, their full spiritual daring.

To go back to our original parable, I still assumed Kavanagh to be writing about the tree which was actually in the ground when he had in fact passed on to write about the tree which he held in mind. Even a deceptively direct poem like 'In Memory of My Mother' reveals the change; this does indeed contain a catalogue of actual memories of the woman as she was, and is bound to a true-life Monaghan by its images of cattle and fair days, yet all these solidly based phenomena are transformed by a shimmer of inner reality. The poem says two things at once: mother is historically gone, mother is a visionary presence forever:

> I do not think of you lying in the wet clay
> Of a Monaghan graveyard; I see
> You walking down a lane among the poplars
> On your way to the station, or happily
>
> Going to second Mass on a summer Sunday—
> You meet me and you say:
> 'Don't forget to see about the cattle—'
> Among your earthiest words the angels stray.

Though this is a relatively simple—and sentimentally threatened—manifestation of the change of focus from outer to inner reality, it does have something of that 'weightlessness' which Kavanagh came to seek as an alternative to the weightiness of the poetic substance in, say, *The Great Hunger*. It is silkier and more sinuous than the gravid, powerful roughcast of lines like:

> Clay is the word and clay is the flesh
> Where potato gatherers like mechanized scarecrows move
> Along the sidefall of a hill, Maguire and his men.

And yet, because of its rural content, 'In Memory of My Mother' can almost pass itself off as a poem in the earlier mode. Which could not be said of lines like these, the final stanza of 'Auditors In':

> From the sour soil of a town where all roots canker
> I turn away to where the Self reposes
> The placeless Heaven that's under all our noses
> Where we're shut off from all the barren anger
> No time for self-pitying melodrama
> A million Instincts know no other uses
> Than all day long to feed and charm the Muses
> Till they become pure positive. O hunger
> Where all have mouths of desire and none
> Is willing to be eaten; I am so glad
> To come accidentally upon
> My self at the end of a tortuous road
> And have learned with surprise that God
> Unworshipped withers to the Futile One.

The Self, mentioned twice in those fourteen lines, is being declared the poetic arena and the poetic subject. What is important now is not so much that the world is there to be celebrated, more that the poet is at hand to proceed with the celebration. And this 'celebration' is not just a limp abstraction, a matter of religiose uplift and fine feelings. It is an altogether non-literary act, connected with what the poet began to think of as his 'comic' point of view, an abandonment of a life in order to find more abundant life.

We might say that lyric celebration was to Kavanagh what

witty expression was to Oscar Wilde—in the beginning, a matter
of temperament, a habit of style, a disposition of the artist's fundamental nature, but, in the end, a matter of redemptive force, a
resource that maintained the artist's inner freedom in the face of
worldly disappointments, an infrangible dignity. While both of
them had an admitted appetite for success, neither could bear the
warm breath of success once it offered itself; in order to find their
lives again after what they instinctively sensed as a dangerous
brush with spiritual enslavement to the group, they had to break
with the terms of the group's values; they had to lose themselves.
Wilde joking about wallpaper in his Paris hotel and Kavanagh
walking the fields of Inniskeen, after his lung cancer operation
and his traumatic libel action, are like men in a wise and unassertive afterlife.

There is enormous vigour in the new-found 'comic' conviction
of the poet that he must divest himself of convictions, come to
experience with the pure readiness which an angel brings to the
activity of witnessing reality:

> Away, away away on wings like Joyce's
> Mother Earth is putting my brand new clothes in order
> Praying, she says, that I no more ignore her
> Yellow buttons she found in fields at bargain prices.
> Kelly's Big Bush for a button-hole. Surprises
> In every pocket—the stream at Connolly's corner
> Myself at Annavackey on Armagh border
> Or calm and collected in a calving crisis.
> Not sad at all as I float away away
> With Mother keeping me to the vernacular.
> I have a home to return to now. O blessing
> For the Return in Departure. Somewhere to stay
> Doesn't matter. What is distressing
> Is walking eagerly to go nowhere in particular.

'Walking eagerly' belonged to the old world of ego; now he is in
the new world, where, like the lilies of the field, he considers not
his raiment or what he will put on—Mother Earth, after all, is

putting his brand-new clothes in order. Where Kavanagh had once painted Monaghan like a Millet, with a thick and faithful pigment in which men rose from the puddled ground, all wattled in potato mould, he now paints like a Chagall, afloat above his native domain, airborne in the midst of his own dream place rather than earthbound in a literal field. Or perhaps it would be even truer to say that the later, regenerated poet in Kavanagh does not paint at all, but draws.

Painting, after all, involves one in a more laboured relationship with a subject—or at least in a more conscious and immersed relationship with a medium—than drawing does. Drawing is closer to the pure moment of perception. The blanknesses which the line travels through in a drawing are not evidence of any incapacity on the artist's part to fill them in. They attest rather to an absolute and all-absorbing need within the line itself to keep on the move. And it is exactly that self-propulsion and airy career of drawing, that mood of buoyancy, that sense of sufficiency in the discovery of a direction rather than any sense of anxiety about the need for a destination, it is this kind of certitude and nonchalance which distinguishes the best of Kavanagh's later work also.

This, then, is truly creative writing. It does arise from the spontaneous overflow of powerful feelings, but the overflow is not a reactive response to some stimulus in the world out there. Instead, it is a spurt of abundance from a source within, and it spills over to irrigate the world beyond the self. This is what Kavanagh is talking about in the poem 'Prelude' when he abjures satire, which is a reactive art, an 'unfruitful prayer', and embraces instead the deeper, autonomous and ecstatic art of love itself:

> But satire is unfruitful prayer,
> Only wild shoots of pity there,
> And you must go inland and be
> Lost in compassion's ecstasy,
> Where suffering soars in a summer air—
> The millstone has become a star.

When I read those lines in 1963, I took to their rhythm and was grateful for their skilful way with an octosyllabic metre. But I was too much in love with poetry that painted the world in a thick linguistic pigment to relish fully the line-drawing that was inscribing itself so lightly and freely here. I was still more susceptible to the heavy tarpaulin of the verse of *The Great Hunger* than to the rinsed streamers that fly in the clear subjective breeze of 'Prelude'.

I have learned to value this poetry of inner freedom very highly. It is an example of self-conquest, a style discovered to express this poet's unique response to his universal ordinariness, a way of re-establishing the authenticity of personal experience and surviving as a credible being. So I would now wish to revise a sentence which I wrote ten years ago. I said then that when Kavanagh had consumed the roughage of his Monaghan experience, he ate his heart out. I believe now that it would be truer to say that when he had consumed the roughage of his early Monaghan experience, he had cleared a space where, in Yeats's words, 'The soul recovers radical innocence, / And learns at last that it is self-delighting, / Self-appeasing, self-affrighting, / And that its own sweet will is Heaven's will.' If the price of this learning was too often, in poetic terms, a wilful doggerel, writing which exercised a vindictiveness against the artfulness of art, the rewards of it were a number of poems so full of pure self-possession in the face of death and waste that they prompt that deepest of responses, which the archaic torso of Apollo prompted in Rilke. These poems, with their grievously earned simplicity, make you feel all over again a truth which the mind becomes adept at evading, and which Rilke expressed in a single, simple command: 'You must change your life.'

The Main of Light

E. M. Forster once said that he envisaged *A Passage to India* as a book with a hole in the middle of it. Some poems are like that too. They have openings at their centre which take the reader through and beyond. Shakespeare's Sonnet 60, for example:

> Like as the waves make towards the pebbled shore,
> So do our minutes hasten to their end;
> Each changing place with that which goes before,
> In sequent toil all forwards do contend.
> Nativity, once in the main of light,
> Crawls to maturity, wherewith being crowned,
> Crooked eclipses 'gainst his glory fight,
> And Time that gave doth now his gift confound.

Something visionary happens there in the fifth line. 'Nativity', an abstract noun housed in a wavering body of sound, sets up a warning tremor just before the mind's eye gets dazzled by 'the main of light', and for a split second we are in the world of the *Paradiso*. The rest of the poem lives melodiously in a world of discourse, but it is this unpredictable strike into the realm of sheer being that marks the sonnet with Shakespeare's extravagant genius.

In so far as it is a poem alert to the sadness of life's changes but haunted too by a longing for some adjacent 'pure serene', the sonnet rehearses in miniature the whole poignant score of Philip Larkin's poetry. With Larkin, we respond constantly to the melody of intelligence, to a verse that is as much commentary as it is presentation, and it is this encounter between a compassionate, unfoolable mind and its own predicaments—which we are forced to recognize as our predicaments too—that gives his poetry its first appeal. Yet while Larkin is exemplary in the way he sifts the conditions of contemporary life, refuses alibis and pushes consciousness towards an exposed condition that is neither cynicism nor despair, there survives in him a repining for a more crystalline reality to which he might give allegiance. When that repining finds expression, something opens and moments occur which deserve to be called visionary. Because he is suspicious of any easy consolation, he is sparing of such moments, yet when they come they stream into the discursive and exacting world of his poetry with such trustworthy force that they call for attention.

In his introduction to the reissue of *The North Ship*, Larkin recalls a merry and instructive occasion during the period of his infatuation with Yeats: 'I remember Bruce Montgomery snapping, as I droned for the third or fourth time that evening *When such as I cast out remorse, so great a sweetness flows into the breast . . .* , "It's not his job to cast off remorse, but to earn forgiveness." But then Bruce Montgomery had known Charles Williams.' Larkin tells the anecdote to illustrate his early surrender to Yeats's music and also to commend the anti-Romantic, morally sensitive attitude which Montgomery was advocating and which would eventually issue in his conversion to the poetry of Thomas Hardy. Yet it also illustrates that appetite for sweetness flowing into the breast, for the sensation of revelation, which never deserted him. The exchange between Montgomery and himself prefigures the shape of the unsettled quarrel, which would be conducted all through the mature poetry, between vision and experience. And if it is that anti-heroic, chastening, humanist voice which is allowed most of the good lines throughout the later poetry, the rebukes it delivers cannot altogether banish the Yeatsian need for a flow of sweetness.

That sweetness flows into the poetry most reliably as a stream of light. In fact, there is something Yeatsian in the way that Larkin, in *High Windows*, places his sun poem immediately opposite and in answer to his moon poem: 'Sad Steps' and 'Solar' face each other on the opened page like the two halves of his poetic personality in dialogue. In 'Sad Steps', the wary intelligence is tempted by a moment of lunar glamour. The renaissance moon of Sir Philip Sidney's sonnet sails close, and the invitation to yield to the 'enormous yes' that love should evoke is potent, even for a man who has just taken a piss:

I part thick curtains, and am startled by
The rapid clouds, the moon's cleanliness.

Four o'clock: wedge-shadowed gardens lie
Under a cavernous, a wind-picked sky.

His vulnerability to desire and hope is transmitted in the Tennysonian cadence of that last line and a half, but immediately the delved brow tightens—'There's something laughable about this'—only to be tempted again by a dream of fullness, this time in the symbolist transports of language itself—'O wolves of memory, immensements!' He finally comes out, of course, with a definite, end-stopped 'No'. He refuses to allow the temptations of melody to chloroform the exactions of his common sense. Truth wins over beauty by a few points, and while the appeal of the poem lies in its unconsoled clarity about the seasons of ageing, our nature still tends to run to fill that symbolist hole in the middle.

However, the large yearnings that are kept firmly in their rational place in 'Sad Steps' are given scope to 'climb and return like angels' in 'Solar'. This is frankly a prayer, a hymn to the sun, releasing a generosity that is in no way attenuated when we look twice and find that what is being praised could be as phallic as it is solar. Where the moon is 'preposterous and separate, / Lozenge of love! Medallion of art!', described in the language of the ironical, emotionally defensive man, the sun is a 'lion face', 'an origin', a 'petalled head of flames', 'unclosing like a hand', all of them phrases of the utmost candid feeling. The poem is unexpected and daring, close to the pulse of primitive poetry, unprotected by any sleight of tone or persona. Here Larkin is bold to stand uncovered in the main of light, far from the hatless one who took off his cycle clips in awkward reverence:

Coined there among
Lonely horizontals
You exist openly.
Our needs hourly
Climb and return like angels.

> Unclosing like a hand,
> You give forever.

These are the words of someone surprised by 'a hunger in himself to be more serious', although there is nothing in the poem which the happy atheist could not accept. Yet in the 'angels' simile and in the generally choral tone of the whole thing, Larkin opens stops that he usually keeps muted and it is precisely these stops which prove vital to the power and reach of his work.

'Deceptions', for example, depends upon a bright, still centre for its essential poetic power. The image of a window rises to take in the facts of grief, to hold them at bay and in focus. The violated girl's mind lies open 'like a drawer of knives', and most of the first stanza registers the dead-still sensitivity of the gleaming blades and the changing moods of the afternoon light. What we used to consider in our Christian Doctrine classes under the heading of 'the mystery of suffering' becomes actual in the combined sensations of absolute repose and trauma, made substantial in images which draw us into raw identification with the girl:

> The sun's occasional print, the brisk brief
> Worry of wheels along the street outside
> Where bridal London bows the other way,
> And light, unanswerable and tall and wide,
> Forbids the scar to heal, and drives
> Shame out of hiding. All the unhurried day
> Your mind lay open like a drawer of knives.

It is this light-filled dilation at the heart of the poem which transposes it from lament to comprehension and prepares the way for the sharp irony of the concluding lines. I have no doubt that Larkin would have repudiated any suggestion that the beauty of the lines I have quoted is meant to soften the pain, as I have no doubt he would also have repudiated the Pedlar's advice to Wordsworth in 'The Ruined Cottage' where, having told of the long sufferings of Margaret, he bids the poet 'be wise and cheerful'. And yet the Pedlar's advice arises from his apprehension of 'an

image of tranquillity' which works in much the same way as the
Larkin passage:

> those very plumes,
>> Those weeds, and the high spear grass on the wall,
>> By mist and silent raindrops silvered o'er.

It is the authenticity of this moment of pacification which to some
extent guarantees the Pedlar's optimism; in a similar way the
blank tenderness at the heart of Larkin's poem takes it beyond
irony and bitterness, though all the while keeping it short of facile
consolation: 'I would not dare / Console you if I could'.

Since Larkin is a poet as explicit as he is evocative, it is no surprise to find him coining terms that exactly describe the kind of
effect I am talking about: 'Here', the first poem in *The Whitsun
Weddings*, ends by defining it as a sense of 'unfenced existence'
and by supplying the experience that underwrites that spacious
abstraction:

> Here silence stands
>> Like heat. Here leaves unnoticed thicken,
>> Hidden weeds flower, neglected waters quicken,
>> Luminously-peopled air ascends;
>> And past the poppies bluish neutral distance
>> Ends the land suddenly beyond a beach
>> Of shapes and shingle. Here is unfenced existence:
>> Facing the sun, untalkative, out of reach.

It is a conclusion that recalls the conclusion of Joyce's 'The
Dead'—and indeed *Dubliners* is a book very close to the spirit of
Larkin, whose collected work would fit happily under the title
Englanders. These concluding lines constitute an epiphany, an escape from the 'scrupulous meanness' of the disillusioned intelligence, and we need only compare 'Here' with 'Show Saturday',
another poem that seeks its form by an accumulation of detail, to
see how vital to the success of 'Here' is this gesture towards a
realm beyond the social and historical. 'Show Saturday' remains

encumbered in naturalistic data, and while its conclusion beautifully expresses a nostalgic patriotism which is also an important
part of this poet's make-up, the note achieved is less one of plangent vision, more a matter of liturgical wishfulness: 'Let it always
be so.'

'If I were called in / To construct a religion / I should make use of
water'—but he could make use of 'Here' as well; and 'Solar'; and
'High Windows'; and 'The Explosion'; and 'Water', the poem from
which the lines are taken. It is true that the jaunty tone of these
lines, and the downbeat vocabulary later in the poem involving
'sousing, / A furious devout drench', are indicative of Larkin's un-
ease with the commission he has imagined for himself. But just as
'Solar' and 'Here' yield up occasions where 'unfenced existence'
can, without embarrassment to the sceptical man, find space to reveal its pure invitations, so too 'Water' escapes from its man-of-the-
world nonchalance into a final stanza which is held like a natural
monstrance above the socially defensive idiom of the rest of the
poem:

> And I should raise in the east
> A glass of water
> Where any-angled light
> Would congregate endlessly.

The minute light makes its presence felt in Larkin's poetry, he cannot resist the romantic poet in himself who must respond with
pleasure and alacrity, exclaiming, as it were, 'Already with thee!'
The effects are various but they are all extraordinary, from the
throw-away surprises of 'a street / Of blinding windscreens' or 'the
differently-swung stars' or 'that high-builded cloud / Moving at
summer's pace', to the soprano delights of this stanza from 'An
Arundel Tomb':

> Snow fell, undated. Light
> Each summer thronged the glass. A bright

Litter of birdcalls strewed the same
Bone-riddled ground. And up the paths
The endless altered people came,

—and from that restraint to the manic spasm in this, from
'Livings, II':

Guarded by brilliance
I set plate and spoon,
And after, divining-cards.
Lit shelved liners
Grope like mad worlds westward.

Light, so powerfully associated with joyous affirmation, is even
made to serve a ruthlessly geriatric vision of things in 'The Old
Fools':

Perhaps being old is having lighted rooms
Inside your head, and people in them, acting.

And it is refracted even more unexpectedly at the end of 'High
Windows' when one kind of brightness, the brightness of belief in
liberation and amelioration, falls from the air which immediately
fills with a different, infinitely neutral splendour:

And immediately

Rather than words comes the thought of high windows:
The sun-comprehending glass,
And beyond it, the deep blue air, that shows
Nothing, and is nowhere, and is endless.

All these moments spring from the deepest strata of Larkin's poetic self, and they are connected with another kind of mood that
pervades his work and which could be called Elysian: I am thinking in particular of poems like 'At Grass', 'MCMXIV', 'How Distant' and, most recently, 'The Explosion'. To borrow Geoffrey Hill's

borrowing from Coleridge, these are visions of 'the spiritual, Platonic old England', the light in them honeyed by attachment to a dream world that will not be denied because it is at the foundation of the poet's sensibility. It is the light that was on Langland's Malvern, 'in summer season, when soft was the sun', at once local and timeless. In 'The Explosion' the field full of folk has become a coalfield, and something Larkin shares with his miners 'breaks ancestrally . . . into / Regenerate union':

> *The dead go on before us, they*
> *Are sitting in God's house in comfort,*
> *We shall see them face to face—*
>
> Plain as lettering in the chapels
> It was said, and for a second
> Wives saw men of the explosion
>
> Larger than in life they managed—
> Gold as on a coin, or walking
> Somehow from the sun towards them,
>
> One showing the eggs unbroken.

If Philip Larkin had ever composed his version of *The Divine Comedy*, he would probably have discovered himself not in a dark wood but in a railway tunnel halfway on a journey down England. His inferno proper might have occurred before dawn, as a death-haunted aubade, whence he would have emerged into the lighted room inside the head of an old fool, and then his purgatorial ascent would have been up through the 'lucent comb' of some hospital building where men in hired boxes stared out at a wind-tousled sky. We have no doubt about his ability to recount the troubles of such souls who walk the rising ground of 'extinction's alp'. His disillusioned compassion for them has been celebrated, and his need to keep numbering their griefs has occasionally drawn forth protests that he narrowed the possibilities of life so much that the whole earth became a hospital. I want to suggest that Larkin also had it in him to write his own version of the *Paradiso*. It might well have amounted to no more than an acknowledgement of the need to imagine 'such attics cleared of me, such absences'; nevertheless, in the poems he wrote there was enough reach and longing to show that he did not completely settle for that well-known bargain offer, 'a poetry of lowered sights and patently diminished expectations'.

Atlas of Civilization

At the very end of his life, Socrates' response to his recurring dream, which had instructed him to 'practise the art', was to begin to put the fables of Aesop into verse. It was, of course, entirely in character for the philosopher to be attracted to fictions whose *a priori* function was to expose the shape of things, and it was proper that even this slight brush with the art of poetry should involve an element of didacticism. But imagine what the poems of Socrates would have been like if, instead of doing adaptations, he had composed original work during those hours before he took the poison. It is unlikely that he would have broken up his lines to weep; indeed, it is likely that he would not only have obeyed Yeats's injunction on this score but that he would have produced an *oeuvre* sufficient to confound the master's claim that 'The intellect of man is forced to choose / Perfection of the life or of the work.'

It would be an exaggeration to say that the work of the Polish poet Zbigniew Herbert could pass as a substitute for such an ideal poetry of reality. Yet in the exactions of its logic, the temperance of its tone and the extremity and equanimity of its recognitions, it does resemble what a twentieth-century poetic version of the examined life might be. Admittedly, in all that follows here, it is an English translation rather than the Polish original which is being praised or pondered, but what convinces one of the universal resource of Herbert's writing is just this ability which it possesses to lean, without toppling, well beyond the plumb of its native language.

Herbert himself, however, is deeply attracted to that which does not lean but which 'trusts geometry, simple numerical rule, the wisdom of the square, balance and weight'. He rejoices in the discovery that 'Greek architecture originated in the sun' and that 'Greek architects knew the art of measuring with shadows. The north-south axis was marked by the shortest shadow cast by the sun's zenith. The problem was to trace the perpendicular, the holy east-west direction.' Hence the splendid utility of Pythagoras's theorem, and the justice of Herbert's observation that 'the architects of the Doric temples were less concerned with beauty than with the chiselling of the world's order into stone.'

These quotations come from the second essay in *Barbarian in the Garden*, a collection of ten meditations on art and history which masquerade as 'travel writings' in so far as nine of them are occasioned by visits to specific places, including Lascaux, Sicily, Arles, Orvieto, Siena, Chartres and the various resting places of the paintings of Piero della Francesca. A tenth one also begins and ends at a single pungent site, the scorched earth of an island in the Seine where on 18 March 1314 Jacques de Molay, Grand Master of the Order of the Templars, was burned at the stake along with Geoffroi de Charney and thirty-six brothers of their order. Yet this section of the book also travels to a domain with which Herbert is already too familiar: the domain of tyranny, with its police supervision, mass arrests, tortures, self-inculpations, purges and eradications, all those methods which already in the fourteenth century had begun to 'enrich the repertoire of power'.

Luckily, the poet's capacity for admiration is more than equal to his perception of the atrocious, and *Barbarian in the Garden* is an ironical title. This 'barbarian' who makes his pilgrimage to the sacred places is steeped in the culture and history of classical and medieval Europe. Admittedly, there is situated at the centre of his consciousness a large burnt-out zone inscribed 'what we have learned in modern times and must never forget even though we need hardly dwell upon it', but even so, this very consciousness can still muster a sustaining half-trust in man as a civilizer and keeper of civilizations. The book is full of lines which sing out in the highest registers of intellectual rapture. In Paestum, 'Greek temples live under the golden sun of geometry'. In Orvieto, to enter the cathedral is a surprise, 'so much does the façade differ from the interior—as though the gate of life full of birds and colours led into a cold, austere eternity'. In the presence of a Piero della Francesca: 'He is . . . like a figurative painter who has passed through a cubist phase.' In the presence of Piero's *Death of Adam*

in Arezzo: 'The entire scene appears Hellenic, as though the Old
Testament were composed by Aeschylus.'

But Herbert never gets too carried away. The ground-hugging
sturdiness which he recognizes and cherishes in archaic buildings
has its analogue in his own down-to-earthness. His love of 'the
quiet chanting of the air and the immense planes' does not extend
so far as to constitute a betrayal of the human subject, in thrall to
gravity and history. His imagination is slightly less skyworthy than
that of his great compatriot Czeslaw Milosz, who has nevertheless
recognized in the younger poet a kindred spirit and as long ago as
1968 translated, with Peter Dale Scott, the now reissued *Selected
Poems*. Deliciously susceptible as he is to the *'lucidus ordo*—an
eternal order of light and balance'—in the work of Piero, Herbert
is still greatly pleasured by the density and miscellany of things he
finds in a book by Piero's contemporary, the architect and humanist Leon Battista Alberti:

> Despite its classical structure, technical subjects are mixed with
> anecdotes and trivia. We may read about foundations, building-
> sites, bricklaying, doorknobs, wheels, axes, levers, hacks, and how
> to 'exterminate and destroy snakes, mosquitoes, bed-bugs, fleas,
> mice, moths and other importunate night creatures'.

Clearly, although he quotes Berenson elsewhere, Herbert would be
equally at home with a builder. He is very much the poet of a
workers' republic in so far as he possesses a natural affinity with
those whose eyes narrow in order to effect an operation or a calculation rather than to study a refinement. Discussing the self-
portrait of Luca Signorelli which that painter entered in *The
Coming of the Anti-Christ* (in the duomo at Orvieto) alongside a
portrait of his master, Fra Angelico, Herbert makes a distinction
between the two men. He discerns how Signorelli's eyes 'are fixed
upon reality . . . Beside him, Fra Angelico dressed in a cassock
gazes inwards. Two glances: one visionary, the other observant.' It
is a distinction which suggests an equivalent division within the
poet, deriving from the co-existence within his own deepest self of
two conflicting strains. These were identified by A. Alvarez in his

introduction to the original 1968 volume as the tender-minded and the tough-minded, and it is some such crossing of a natural readiness to consent upon an instinctive suspicion which constitutes the peculiar fibre of Herbert's mind and art.

All through *Barbarian in the Garden*, the tender-minded, desiring side of his nature is limpidly, felicitously engaged. In a church in a Tuscan village where 'there is hardly room enough for a coffin', he encounters a Madonna. 'She wears a simple, high-waisted dress open from breast to knees. Her left hand rests on a hip, a country bridesmaid's gesture; her right hand touches her belly but without a trace of licentiousness.' In a similar fashion, as he reports his ascent of the tower of Senlis Cathedral, the writing unreels like a skein long stored in the cupboard of the senses. 'Patches of lichen, grass between the stones, and bright yellow flowers'; then, high up on a gallery, an 'especially beautiful Eve. Coarse-grained, big-eyed and plump. A heavy plait of hair falls on her wide, warm back.'

Writing of this sort, which ensures, in Neruda's words, that 'the reality of the world should not be underprized', is valuable in itself, but what reinforces Herbert's contribution and takes it far beyond being just another accomplished printout of a cultivated man's impressions is his sceptical historical sense of the world and its unreliability. He is thus as appreciative of the unfinished part of Siena Cathedral and as unastonished by it as he is entranced by what is exquisitely finished: 'The majestic plan remained unfulfilled, interrupted by the Black Death and errors in construction.' The elegance of that particular zeugma should not blind us to its outrage; the point is that Herbert is constantly wincing in the jaws of a pincer created by the mutually indifferent intersection of art and suffering. Long habituation to this crux has bred in him a tone which is neither vindictive against art nor occluded to pain. It predisposes him to quote Cicero on the colonies of Sicily as 'an ornamental band sewn on to the rough cloth of barbarian lands, a golden band that was frequently stained with blood'. And it enables him to strike his own jocund, unnerving sentences, like this one about the Baglioni family of Perugia: 'They were vengeful and cruel, though refined enough to slaughter their enemies on beautiful summer evenings.'

Once more, this comes from his essay on Piero della Francesca, and it is in writing about this beloved painter that Herbert articulates most clearly the things we would want to say about himself as an artist: 'The harmonized background and the principle of tranquillity', 'the rule of the demon of perspective', the viewing of the world as 'through a pane of ice', an 'epic impassiveness', a quality which is 'impersonal, supra-individual'. All these phrases apply, at one time or another, to Herbert's poetry and help to adumbrate the shapes of his 'tough-mindedness'. Yet they should not be taken to suggest any culpable detachment or abstraction. The impassiveness, the perspective, the impersonality, the tranquillity, all derive from his unblindable stare at the facts of pain, the recurrence of injustice and catastrophe; but they derive also from a deep love for the whole Western tradition of religion, literature and art, which have remained open to him as a spiritual resource, helping him to stand his ground. Herbert is as familiar as any twentieth-century writer with the hollow men and has seen more broken columns with his eyes than most literary people have seen in their imaginations, but this does not end up in a collapse of his trust in the humanist endeavour. On the contrary, it summons back to mind the whole dimensions of that endeavour and enforces it once more upon your awareness for the great boon which it is (not *was*), something we may have thought of as vestigial before we began reading these books but which, by the time we have finished, stands before our understanding once again like 'a cathedral in the wilderness'.

Barbarian in the Garden was first published in Polish in 1962 and is consequently the work of a much younger man (Herbert was born in 1924) than the one who wrote the poems of *Report from the Besieged City*. But the grave, laconic, instructive prose, translated with such fine regard for cadence and concision by Michael March and Jaroslaw Anders, is recognizably the work of the same writer. It would be wrong to say that in the meantime Herbert has matured, since from the beginning the look he turned upon experience was penetrating, judicial and absolutely in earnest; but it could be said that he has grown even more secure in his self-possession and now begins to resemble an old judge who has developed the benevolent aspect of a daydreamer while retaining all the readiness and spring of a crouched lion. Where the poems of the reissued *Selected Poems* carry within themselves the battened-down energy and enforced caution of the situation from which they arose in Poland in the 1950s, the poems of *Report from the Besieged City* allow themselves a much greater latitude of voice. They are physically longer, less impacted, more social and genial in tone. They occur within a certain spaciousness, in an atmosphere of winnowed comprehension. One thinks again of the *lucidus ordo*, of that 'golden sun of geometry'; yet because of the body heat of the new poetry, its warm breath which keeps stirring the feather of our instinctive nature, one thinks also of Herbert's eloquent valediction to the prehistoric caves of the Dordogne:

> I returned from Lascaux by the same road I arrived. Though I had stared into the abyss of history, I did not emerge from an alien world. Never before had I felt a stronger or more reassuring conviction: I am a citizen of the earth, an inheritor not only of the Greeks and Romans but of almost the whole of infinity . . .
>
> The road opened to the Greek temples and the Gothic cathedrals. I walked towards them feeling the warm touch of the Lascaux painter on my palm.

It is no wonder, therefore, that Mr Cogito, the poet's alibi/alias/persona/ventriloquist's doll/permissive correlative, should be so stubbornly attached to the senses of sight and touch. In the second section of 'Eschatological Forebodings of Mr Cogito', after Herbert's several musings about his ultimate fate—'probably he will sweep/the great square of Purgatory'—he imagines him taking courses in the eradication of earthly habits. And yet, in spite of these angelic debriefing sessions, Mr Cogito

> continues to see
> a pine on a mountain slope
> dawn's seven candlesticks
> a blue-veined stone

he will yield to all tortures
gentle persuasions
but to the end he will defend
the magnificent sensation of pain

and a few weathered images
on the bottom of the burned-out eye

3

who knows
perhaps he will manage
to convince the angels
he is incapable
of heavenly
service

and they will permit him to return
by an overgrown path
at the shore of a white sea
to the cave of the beginning

The poles of the beginning and the end are crossing, and at the very moment when he strains to imagine himself at the shimmering circumference of the imaginable, Mr Cogito finds himself collapsing back into the palpable centre. Yet all this is lightened of its possible portentousness because it is happening not to 'humanity' or 'mankind' but to Mr Cogito. Mr Cogito operates sometimes like a cartoon character, a cosmic Don Quixote or matchstick Sisyphus; sometimes like a discreet convention whereby the full frontal of the autobiographical 'I' is veiled. It is in this latter role that he is responsible for one of the book's most unforgettable poems, 'Mr Cogito—The Return', which, along with 'The Abandoned', 'Mr Cogito's Soul' and the title poem, strikes an unusually intimate and elegiac note.

Mostly, however, Mr Cogito figures as a stand-in for experimental, undaunted *Homo sapiens*, or, to be more exact, as a representative of the most courageous, well-disposed and unremittingly intelligent members of the species. The poems where he fulfils this function are no less truly pitched and sure of their step than the ones I have just mentioned; in fact, they are more brilliant as intellectual reconnaissance and more deadly as political resistance; they are on the offensive, and to read them is to put oneself through the mill of Herbert's own personal selection process, to be tested for one's comprehension of the necessity of refusal, one's ultimate gumption and awareness. This poetry is far more than 'dissident'; it gives no consolation to papmongers or propagandists of whatever stripe. Its whole intent is to devastate those arrangements which are offered as truth by power's window-dressers everywhere. It can hear the screech of the fighter-bomber behind the righteous huffing of the official spokesman, yet it is not content with just an exposé or an indictment. Herbert always wants to probe past official versions of collective experience into the final ring of the individual's perception and endurance. He does so in order to discover whether that inner citadel of human being is a selfish bolt-hole or an attentive listening-post. To put it another way, he would not be all that interested in discovering the black box after the crash, since he would far prefer to be able to monitor the courage and conscience of each passenger during the minutes before it. Thus, in their introduction, John and Bogdana Carpenter quote him as follows:

> You understand I had words in abundance to express my rebellion and protest. I might have written something of this sort: 'O you cursed, damned people, so and sos, you kill innocent people, wait and a just punishment will fall on you.' I didn't say this because I wanted to bestow a broader dimension on the specific, individual, experienced situation, or rather, to show its deeper, general human perspectives.

This was always his impulse, and it is a pleasure to watch his strategies for showing 'deeper, general human perspectives' develop. In the *Selected Poems*, dramatic monologues and adaptations of Greek myth were among his preferred approaches. There can be no more beautiful expression of necessity simultaneously recognized and lamented than the early 'Elegy of Fortinbras', just as there can be no poem more aghast at those who have power to hurt and who then do hurt than 'Apollo and Marsyas'. Both works deserve to be quoted in full, but here is the latter, in the translation of Czeslaw Milosz:

> The real duel of Apollo
> with Marsyas
> (absolute ear
> versus immense range)
> takes place in the evening
> when as we already know
> the judges
> have awarded victory to the god
>
> bound tight to a tree
> meticulously stripped of his skin
> Marsyas
> howls
> before the howl reaches his tall ears
> he reposes in the shadow of that howl
>
> shaken by a shudder of disgust
> Apollo is cleaning his instrument
>
> only seemingly
> is the voice of Marsyas
> monotonous
> and composed of a single vowel
> Aaa
> in reality
> Marsyas relates
> the inexhaustible wealth
> of his body
>
> bald mountains of liver
> white ravines of aliment
> rustling forests of lung
> sweet hillocks of muscle

joints bile blood and shudders
the wintry wind of bone
over the salt of memory
shaken by a shudder of disgust
Apollo is cleaning his instrument

now to the chorus
is joined the backbone of Marsyas
in principle the same A
only deeper with the addition of rust

this is already beyond the endurance
of the god with nerves of artificial fibre

along a gravel path
hedged with box
the victor departs
wondering
whether out of Marsyas' howling
there will not some day arise
a new kind
of art—let us say—concrete

suddenly
at his feet
falls a petrified nightingale

he looks back
and sees
that the hair of the tree to which Marsyas was fastened

is white
completely

About suffering he was never wrong, this young master. The Polish experience of cruelty lies behind the poem, and when it first appeared it would have had the extra jangle of anti-poetry about it. There is the affront of the subject-matter, the flirtation with horror-movie violence and the conscious avoidance of anything 'tender-minded'. Yet the triumph of the thing is that while it remains set upon an emotional collision course, it still manages to keep faith with 'whatever shares / The eternal reciprocity of tears'. Indeed, this is just the poetry which Yeats would have needed to convince him of the complacency of his objection to Wilfred Owen's work (passive suffering is not a subject for poetry), although, in fact, it is probably only Wilfred Owen (tender-minded) and Yeats (tough-minded) who brought into poetry in English a 'vision of reality' the equal of this one . . . The petrified nightingale, the tree with white hair, the monotonous *Aaa* of the new art, each of these inventions is as terrible as it is artful; each is uttered from the dry well of an objective voice. The demon of perspective rules while the supra-individual principle reads history through a pane of Francescan ice, tranquilly, impassively, as if the story were chiselled into stone.

The most celebrated instance of Herbert's capacity to outface what the stone ordains occurs in his poem 'Pebble'. Once again, this is an *ars poetica*, but the world implied by the poem would exclude any discourse that was so fancied-up as to admit a term like *ars poetica* in the first place. Yet 'Pebble' is several steps ahead of satire and even one or two steps beyond the tragic gesture. It is written by a poet who grew up, as it were, under the white-haired tree but who possessed no sense of either the oddity or the election of his birthright. In so far as it accepts the universe with a sort of disappointed relief—as though at the last minute faith were to renege on its boast that it could move mountains and settle back into stoicism—it demonstrates the truth of Patrick Kavanagh's contention that tragedy is half-born comedy. The poem's force certainly resides in its impersonality, yet its tone is almost ready to play itself on through into the altogether more lenient weather of personality itself.

> The pebble
> is a perfect creature
>
> equal to itself
> mindful of its limits
>
> filled exactly
> with a pebbly meaning

with a scent which does not remind one of anything
does not frighten anything away does not arouse desire

its ardour and coldness
are just and full of dignity

I feel a heavy remorse
when I hold it in my hand
and its noble body
is permeated by false warmth

—Pebbles cannot be tamed
to the end they will look at us
with a calm and very clear eye

This has about it all the triumph and completion of the 'finished man among his enemies'. You wonder where else an art that
is so contained and self-verifying can possibly go—until you open
Report from the Besieged City. There you discover that the perfect
moral health of the earlier poetry was like the hard pure green of
the ripening apple: now the core of the thing is less packed with
tartness, and the whole *oeuvre* seems to mellow and sway on the
bough of some tree of unforbidden knowledge.

There remain, however, traces of the acerbic observer; this, for
example, in the poem where Damastes (also known as Procrustes)
speaks:

I invented a bed with the measurements of a perfect man
I compared the travellers I caught with this bed
it was hard to avoid—I admit—stretching limbs cutting legs
the patients died but the more there were who perished
the more I was certain my research was right
the goal was noble progress demands victims

This voice is stereophonic in that we are listening to it through two
speakers, one from the set-up Damastes, the other from the privileged poet, and we always know whose side we are on. We are
meant to read the thing exactly as it is laid out for us. We stand

with Signorelli at the side of the picture, observantly. We are still, in other words, in the late spring of impersonality. But when we come to the poem on the emperor Claudius, we are in the summer of fullest personality. It is not that Herbert has grown lax or that any phoney tolerance—understanding all and therefore forgiving all—has infected his attitude. It is more that he has eased his own grimness, as if realizing that the stern brows he turns upon the world merely contribute to the weight of the world's anxiety instead of lightening it; therefore, he can afford to become more genial personally without becoming one whit less impersonal in his judgements and perceptions. So, in his treatment of 'The Divine Claudius', the blood and the executions and the infernal whimsicality are not passed over, yet Herbert ends up speaking for his villain with a less than usually forked tongue:

I expanded the frontiers of the empire
by Brittany Mauretania
and if I recall correctly Thrace

my death was caused by my wife Agrippina
and an uncontrollable passion for boletus
mushrooms—the essence of the forest—became the essence of
    death

descendants—remember with proper respect and honour
at least one merit of the divine Claudius
I added new signs and sounds to our alphabet
expanded the limits of speech that is the limits of freedom

the letters I discovered—beloved daughters—Digamma and
    Antisigma
led my shadow
as I pursued the path with tottering steps to the dark land of
    Orkus

There is more of the inward gaze of Fra Angelico here, and indeed, all through *Report from the Besieged City*, Herbert's mind is fixed constantly on last things. Classical and Christian visions of the afterlife are drawn upon time and again, and in 'Mr Cogito—Notes from the House of the Dead', we have an opportunity of hearing how the terrible cry of Marsyas sounds in the new acoustic of the later work. Mr Cogito, who lies with his fellows 'in the depths of the temple of the absurd', hears there, at ten o'clock in the evening, 'a voice // masculine / slow / commanding / the rising / of the dead'. The second section of the poem proceeds:

> we called him Adam
> meaning taken from the earth
>
> at ten in the evening
> when the lights were switched off
> Adam would begin his concert
>
> to the ears of the profane
> it sounded
> like the howl of a person in fetters
>
> for us
> an epiphany
>
> he was
> anointed
> the sacrificial animal
> author of psalms
>
> he sang
> the inconceivable desert
> the call of the abyss
> the noose on the heights
>
> Adam's cry
> was made
> of two or three vowels
> stretched out like ribs on the horizon

This new Adam has brought us as far as the old Marsyas took us, but now the older Herbert takes up the burden and, in a third section, brings the poem further still:

after a few concerts
he fell silent

the illumination of his voice
lasted a brief time

he didn't redeem
his followers

they took Adam away
or he retreated
into eternity

the source
of the rebellion
was extinguished

and perhaps
only I
still hear
the echo
of his voice

more and more slender
quieter
further and further away

like music of the spheres
the harmony of the universe

so perfect
it is inaudible.

Mr Cogito's being depends upon such cogitations (one remembers
his defence of 'the magnificent sensation of pain'), and unlike
Hamlet in Fortinbras's elegy, who 'crunched the air only to vomit',
Mr Cogito's digestion of the empty spaces is curiously salutary.
Reading these poems is a beneficent experience: they amplify im-
mensely Thomas Hardy's assertion that 'If a way to the Better

there be, it exacts a full look at the Worst.' But by the end of the book, after such undaunted poems as 'The Power of Taste'—'Yes taste / in which there are fibres of soul the cartilage of conscience'—and such tender ones as 'Lament', to the memory of his mother—'she sails on the bottom of a boat through foamy nebulas'—after these and the other poems I have mentioned, and many more which I have not, the reader feels the kind of gratitude the gods of Troy must have felt when they saw Aeneas creep from the lurid fires, bearing ancestry on his shoulders and the sacred objects in his hands.

The book's true subject is survival of the valid self, of the city, of the good and the beautiful; or rather, the subject is the responsibility of each person to ensure that survival. So it is possible in the end to think that a poet who writes so ethically about the *res publica* might even be admitted by Plato as first laureate of the ideal republic, though it is also necessary to think that through to the point where this particular poet would be sure to decline the office as a dangerous compromise:

> now as I write these words the advocates of conciliation
> have won the upper hand over the party of inflexibles
> a normal hesitation of moods fate still hangs in the balance
>
> cemeteries grow larger the number of the defenders is smaller
> yet the defence continues it will continue to the end
> and if the City falls but a single man escapes
> he will carry the City within himself on the roads of exile
> he will be the City
>
> we look in the face of hunger the face of fire face of death
> worst of all—the face of betrayal
>
> and only our dreams have not been humiliated

The title poem, to which these lines form the conclusion, is pivoted at the moment of martial law and will always belong in the annals of patriotic Polish verse. It witnesses new developments and makes old connections within the native story and is only one of several poems throughout the volume which sweep the strings of Polish national memory. If I have been less attentive to this domestic witnessing function of the book than I might have been, it is not because I undervalue that function of Herbert's poetry. On the contrary, it is precisely because I am convinced of its obdurate worth on the home front that I feel free to elaborate in the luxurious margin. Anyhow, John and Bogdana Carpenter have annotated the relevant dates and names so that the reader is kept alert to the allusions and connections which provide the book's oblique discharge of political energy. As well as providing this editorial service, they seem to have managed the task of translating well; I had no sense of their coming between me and the poem's first life, no sense of their having interfered.

Zbigniew Herbert is a poet with all the strengths of an Antaeus, yet he finally emerges more like the figure of an Atlas. Refreshed time and again by being thrown back upon his native earth, standing his ground determinedly in the local plight, he nevertheless shoulders the whole sky and scope of human dignity and responsibility. These various translations leave no doubt about the essential function which his work performs, that of keeping a trustworthy poetic canopy, if not a perfect heaven, above our vulnerable heads.

from Envies and Identifications:
Dante and the Modern Poet

T. S. Eliot's work is haunted by the shade of Dante, and nowhere
more tellingly than in the second section of 'Little Gidding'. This
part of *Four Quartets* is set in the dawn, in wartime London, a
modern dream vision, concerned to some extent with strictly literary matters but ultimately involved with the universal sorrows and
penalties of living and ageing. The poet exchanges intense but
oddly formal words with 'a familiar compound ghost' and the section ends like this:

> 'From wrong to wrong the exasperated spirit
>> Proceeds, unless restored by that refining fire
>> Where you must move in measure, like a dancer.'
> The day was breaking. In the disfigured street
>> He left me, with a kind of valediction,
>> And faded on the blowing of the horn.

The phrase 'the blowing of the horn' operates in the same way
that the word 'forlorn' operates in Keats's 'Ode to a Nightingale'. It
tolls us back to our sole selves. It is bleaker than Keats's word because the world outside Eliot's poem is even bleaker than the world
outside Keats's 'Ode'. 'The blowing of the horn' is, in fact, the
sounding of the 'all clear' at the end of an air raid, and it recalls us
to Eliot's historical situation when he was composing the poem and
doing his duty as an air-raid warden during the London Blitz. Indeed, the strange lines at the beginning of the section about 'the
dark dove with the flickering tongue' which passes 'below the horizon of his homing' and the image of 'three districts whence the
smoke arose' are also documentary of the historical moment, in so
far as they suggest the bomber's withdrawal and the burning city
after the raid.

Yet to talk like this about blitz and bombers and air raids and burning cities is out of keeping with the mood and intent of the poetry. That poetry, like the poetry of Keats's 'Ode', is at a third remove from the local, historical moment and is suspended in the ether of a contemplative mind. The language conducts us away from what is contingent; it is mimetic not of the cold morning cityscape but of the calescent imagination. We can say, as a matter of literary fact, that the lines are more haunted by the flocks of Dante's *terza rima* than by the squadrons of Hitler's *Luftwaffe*.

We can also say that the language of the poem is more affected by Eliot's idea of Dante's language than it is by the actual sounds and idioms of those Londoners among whom Eliot lived and over whom he was watching during his 'dead patrol'. The lines have something of the quality which Eliot ascribes to Dante in his 1929 essay on the poet:

> Dante's universality is not solely a personal matter. The Italian language, and especially the Italian language in Dante's age, gains much by being the product of universal Latin. There is something much more *local* about the languages in which Shakespeare and Racine had to express themselves . . . Medieval Latin tended to concentrate on what men of various races and lands could think together. Some of the character of this universal language seems to me to inhere in Dante's Florentine speech; and the localization ('Florentine' speech) seems if anything to emphasize the universality, because it cuts across the modern division of nationality.

In a similar way, the language of the 'Little Gidding' passage seeks for things which 'men of various races and lands could think together'; it tends to eschew the local, the intimate, the word which reeks of particular cultural attachments, and opts instead for words like 'unappeased and peregrine'; 'impelled', 'expiring', 'conscious impotence', 'laceration', 're-enactment', 'exercise of virtue', 'exasperated', 'valediction'. Indeed, at its most primitive and dialect moment, the moment in the animal heat of the byre at milking time, it interposes the smooth and decorous and monosyllabic noun 'pail', as if to distance us from the raucous and parochial energies of the usual 'bucket'.

All this, of course, reinforces one of our perennial expectations from art, that it deliver what Sir Philip Sidney called a 'golden world' to defy the 'brazen world' of nature, that it offer us ideal melodies which transcend and to some extent rebuke the world of sensual music. This hankering for a purely delineated realm of wisdom and beauty sometimes asks literature to climb the stair of transcendence and give us images free from the rag-and-bone-shop reek of time and place. Such an ambition is best served by a language which gives the illusion of an authority and a purity be-yond dialect and tribe, and it is Eliot's achievement in his Dantean stanzas to create just such an illusion of oracular authority by the hypnotic deployment of a vocabulary that is highly Latinate.

The essay on Dante was written six years after the appearance of *The Waste Land*, a poem which arose from personal breakdown and a vision of decline and disintegration in the Europe that was once called Christendom. By the 1940s, however, Eliot was compos-ing his soul rather than rendering images of its decomposition. His critical concerns were less with the strictly verbal and technical as-pects of poetry, more with the philosophical and religious signifi-cances which could be drawn from it and relied upon. The essay on Dante, in fact, ends up as an essay about conversion, and under-standably so, since at the time the intellectual mystery man from Missouri was mutating into the English vestryman. In the essay Eliot is concerned, among other things, with Dante's concentration upon states of purgation and beatitude, his allegorical method, his system of beliefs, even his love of pageantry (corresponding to 'the serious pageants of royalty, of the Church, of military funerals'), and these concerns are symptomatic of his own concerns in 1929. He ends with an evocation of the world of the *Vita Nuova*, of the necessary attempt, 'as difficult and hard as rebirth', to enter it, and bows out with the declaration that 'there is almost a definite mo-ment of acceptance when the New Life begins'.

It is curious that this born-again Anglican and monarchist did not make more of the political Dante, the dreamer of a world obe-dient to the spiritual authority of an uncorrupt Papacy and under the sway of a just emperor, where, without bitterness or compro-mise, Christ and Caesar would be hand in glove. But perhaps we

are meant to deduce this Dante from that praise of 'universal language', the Tuscan speech which transcended its local habitation
because of its roots in classical and ecclesiastical Latin. Eliot's joy
in praising this lucid European instrument springs from his joy in
a writer who speaks not just as himself but as 'the whole mind of
Europe'. By contrast, poets of other European tongues, because
they work further from the pure Latin source, are condemned to a
more opaque idiom and a less than central relevance.

To clinch this argument, Eliot takes those lines of Shakespeare's where Duncan is introduced to Macbeth's castle, lines full
of air and light, and contrasts them with the opening lines of the
Commedia. More is lost, he maintains, in translating Shakespeare
than in translating Dante. 'How can a foreigner find words to convey in his own language just that combination of intelligibility
and remoteness that we get in many phrases of Shakespeare?'

> This guest of summer
> The temple-haunting martlet, does approve
> By his loved masonry that the heaven's breath
> Smells wooingly here: no jutty, frieze,
> Buttress, nor coign of vantage, but this bird
> Hath made his pendant bed and procreant cradle:
> Where they most breed and haunt, I have observed
> The air is delicate.

Agreed. This English is erotic and feels for warmer and quicker
nubs and joints of speech, and as it forages its voice cannot quite
maintain its civil blandishment but lapses into a muttering urgency in 'jutty' and 'buttress', rather like an excited Mellors slip-
ping into dialect. The poetry, in other words, is to a large extent in
the phonetics, in the way the English words waft and disseminate
their associations, the flitting of the swallow being airily present in
phrases like 'they most breed and haunt' and 'The air is delicate',
while the looming stone architecture is conjured by the minatory
solidity of terms like 'masonry' and 'buttress'.

Yet if we look at the opening lines of Dante's poem again, we
might ask ourselves if the Italian is so essentially different in its

operation. Eliot would have us take this as a clean lexical exercise, devoid of any local self-consciousness, and indeed the ghosts of first-declension Latin nouns stand in the open doors of the Italian vowels like sponsors of the much sought universality:

> *Nel mezzo del cammin di nostra vita*
> *mi ritrovai per una selva oscura*
> *che la diritta via era smarrita.*

'*Nostra vita*', '*una selva oscura*', '*la diritta via*': we are in earshot not only of the Vatican but also of the Capitol; and out of that common murmur one voice begins to emerge, the voice of Virgil, a prophetic figure in the medieval mind, the pagan precursor of the Christian dispensation, the poet who had envisaged in an eclogue the world of allegory and encyclical in which Dante had his being. As the great poet of the Latin language, Virgil can walk naturally out of the roots of this Tuscan speech, a figure of completely exemplary force. Virgil comes to Dante, in fact, as Dante comes to Eliot, a master, a guide and authority, offering release from the toils and snares of the self, from the *diserta*, the wasteland. Ladies and leopards begin to appear in Eliot's poems of the late 1920s; the hushed and fragrant possibilities of a heavenly order which we hear in Canto 2 of the *Inferno* are overheard in sections 2 and 4 of *Ash-Wednesday*; the soul's journey as outlined by Marco Lombardo in Canto 16 of the *Purgatorio* is rehearsed in 'Animula'.

It is a moment of crisis, of turning towards and of turning away, when the converting Eliot begins to envy the coherence and certitude, the theological, philosophical and linguistic harmonies available to his great predecessor. Shakespeare he admires, yes, but does not envy. Shakespeare's venturesome, humanist genius, his Elizabethan capacity for provisional and glamorous accommodations between faiths and doubts, his opportunistic dash through the high world of speculation and policy, still fresh from the folk-speech and hedge school of the shires, all this disruptive, unaligned cognition and explorativeness is by now, for Eliot, suspect. It is the symptom of a breakdown which, during his own lifetime, had come out of potential and into the historical convulsion of World War I and its disillusioned aftermath.

But when he makes Dante's confident and classically ratified language bear an almost allegorical force, he does less than justice to the untamed and thoroughly parochial elements which it possesses. To listen to Eliot, one would almost be led to forget that Dante's great literary contribution was to write in the vernacular and thereby to give the usual language its head:

> *Nel mezzo del cammin di nostra vita*
> *mi ritrovai per una selva oscura*
> *che la diritta via era smarrita.*
> *Ahi quanto a dir qual era è cosa dura*
> *esta selva selvaggia e aspra e forte*
> *che nel pensier rinova la paura!*

'*Smarrita.*' *The Concise Cambridge Italian Dictionary* gives 'smarrire, to mislay; to lose; to mislead; to bewilder', yet each of these English equivalents strikes me as less particular, less urgently local than the Italian word, which has all the force of dirt hitting a windscreen. Eliot underplays the swarming, mobbish element in the Italian, which can be just as '*selvaggia e aspra e forte*' as the dark wood itself. Say those first two adjectives aloud and then decide whether they call up the refined *urbs* or the rough-spoken *rus*. '*Selva selvaggia*' is as barbarous as Hopkins, '*aspra e forte*' less suggestive of the composure of the classics than of the struggle with the undergrowth. Dante may be writing about a mid-life crisis within the terms of the allegory, but he is also writing about panic, that terror we experience in the presence of the god Pan, numen of the woods.

Eliot was re-creating Dante in his own image. He had always taken what he needed from the work, and at this stage what he needed was a way of confirming himself as a poet ready to submit his intelligence and sensibility to a framework of beliefs which were inherited and communal. The poet of distress had come to stress the need for acceptance. The poet who earlier in his career could inhabit the phantasmagoria of Canto 3 of the *Inferno*, that

region populated by hollow men, flibbertigibbets blown about after wheeling contradictory standards, whispering together in quiet
and meaningless voices, that poet would now be reborn as the alien
judging figure who walks among them, the thoroughly human
presence who casts a shadow and displaces water when he steps
into Charon's boat.

It is instructive to compare Dante's influence upon *The Waste
Land* and upon the poem published nearly twenty years later. In
the earlier work, the *Commedia* provided Eliot with a theatre
of dreams and gave permission for the symbolist arbitrariness of
oneiric passages such as the famous ending of 'The Burial of the
Dead', a scene which provides a striking contrast with the London
passage in 'Little Gidding'. The influence of the *Inferno* is found
not just in the famous echo of the line from Canto 3 about the
great multitude of the dead, nor in the shocking confrontation
with Stetson, a revenant from the sinister past. It is also to be
found in the sense of bewilderment and somnambulism, of being
caught in a flow of energies that go their predestined and doomed
ways, of losing direction in a foggy populous drift:

> Unreal City,
> Under the brown fog of a winter dawn,
> A crowd flowed over London Bridge, so many,
> I had not thought death had undone so many.
> Sighs, short and infrequent, were exhaled,
> And each man fixed his eyes before his feet.
> Flowed up the hill and down King William Street,
> To where Saint Mary Woolnoth kept the hours
> With a dead sound on the final stroke of nine.
> There I saw one I knew, and stopped him, crying: 'Stetson!
> You who were with me in the ships at Mylae!
> That corpse you planted last year in your garden,
> Has it begun to sprout?'

Here Dante was actually giving Eliot the freedom to surrender to
the promptings of his own unconscious, and the language is more
allied to the Shakespearean-local-associative than to the Latinate-

classical-canonical. For the moment, the imagination is in thrall to romantic expressionism, bewildered on the flood of its own inventiveness.

Twenty years later, things have changed. In the 'Little Gidding' scene, the consecutive thought, the covenant between verse and argument, the tone of gravity and seniority all reflect a rebirth out of the romance of symbolism into the stricter disciplines of *philosophia* and religious orthodoxy. The definitive Dante of the 1929 essay and the definitive Eliot of *Four Quartets* have established a mutually fortifying alliance. The Dante whom Eliot now prefers and expounds walks in the aura of cultural history and representativeness. He is a figure in whom the commentaries on the *Commedia* are implicit; he stands for the thoroughly hierarchical world of scholastic thought, an imagined standard against which the relativity and agnosticism of the present can be judged. For all his talk about Dante's visual imagination—an imagination which sees visions—Eliot's ultimate attraction is to the way Dante could turn values and judgements into poetry, the way the figure of the poet as thinker and teacher merged into the figure of the poet as expresser of a universal myth that could unify the abundance of the inner world and the confusion of the outer. There is a stern and didactic profile to this Dante, and as Eliot embraces a religious faith he turns towards that profile and would re-create it in his own work.

During the 1930s, while Eliot was putting the finishing touches to his classical monument, an image of Dante as seer and repository of tradition, another poet was busy identifying Dante not with the inheritance of culture but with the processes of nature, making him a precursor of the experimental and unnerving poetry of Arthur Rimbaud rather than an heir to the Virgilian *gravitas*. Osip Mandelstam's Dante is the most eager, the most inspiring, the most delightfully approachable re-creation we could hope for, and what I want to do next is to indulge in what Mandelstam says Dante indulges in, 'an orgy of quotations'. These all come from his indispensable essay 'Conversation about Dante', never published in

Russia in his lifetime but available in English translation in *The Complete Prose and Letters of Osip Mandelstam.* The quotations are not in the order in which they appear in the essay, which is a tumultuous affair anyhow, but I have arranged them to give a contrast to Eliot and to suggest the unpredictable intuitive nature of Mandelstam's genius:

> For how many centuries have people been talking and writing about Dante as if he had expressed his thoughts directly on official paper? . . . Dante is discussed as if he had the completed whole before his eyes even before he had begun work and as if he had utilized the technique of moulage, first casting in plaster, then in bronze.

> The process of creating this poem's form transcends our conceptions of literary invention and composition. It would be more correct to recognize instinct as its guiding principle . . . Only through metaphor is it possible to find a concrete sign to represent the instinct for form creation by which Dante accumulated and poured forth his *terza rima.*
>
> We must try to imagine, therefore, how bees might have worked at this thirteen-thousand-faceted form, bees endowed with the brilliant stereometric instinct, who attracted bees in greater and greater numbers as they were required. The work of these bees, constantly keeping their eye on the whole, is of varying difficulty at different stages of the process. Their cooperation expands and grows more complicated as they participate in the process of forming the combs, by means of which space virtually emerges out of itself.

> When I began to study Italian and had barely familiarized myself with its phonetics and prosody, I suddenly understood that the center of gravity of my speech efforts had been moved closer to my lips, to the outer parts of my mouth. The tip of the tongue suddenly turned out to have the seat of honor. The sound rushed toward the locking of the teeth. And something else that struck me was the infantile aspect of Italian phonetics, its beautiful

child-like quality, its closeness to infant babbling, to some kind of eternal dadaism.

It seems to me that Dante made a careful study of all speech defects, listening closely to stutterers and lispers, to nasal twangs and inarticulate pronunciations, and that he learned much from them.

I would very much like to speak about the auditory coloration of canto 32 of the *Inferno*.

A peculiar labial music: 'abbo'—'gabbo'—'babbo'—'Tebe'—'plebe'—'zebba'—'converebbe'. It's as if a nurse had participated in the creation of phonetics. Now the lips protrude in a childish manner, now they extend into a proboscis.

Precisely those who are furthest from Dante's method in European poetry and, bluntly speaking, in polar opposition to him, go by the name Parnassians: Heredia, Leconte de Lisle. Baudelaire is much closer. Verlaine is still closer, but the closest of all the French poets is Arthur Rimbaud. Dante is by his very nature one who shakes up meaning and destroys the integrity of the image. The composition of his cantos resembles an airline schedule or the indefatigable flights of carrier pigeons.

Mandelstam's Dante is more like Eliot's Shakespeare: he is not distinguished by his cultural representativeness, his conservative majesty or his intellectual orthodoxy. Rather, he is fastened upon and shaken into new and disconcerting life as an exemplar of the purely creative, intimate and experimental act of writing itself. This Dante is essentially lyric; he is stripped of the robes of commentary in which he began to vest himself with his epistle to Can Grande, reclaimed from the realm of epic and allegory and made to live as the epitome of a poet's creative excitement. Which is not to say, of course, that Mandelstam is not alive to the historical and literary contexts in which Dante wrote, what he calls the great 'keyboard of references'; but what Mandelstam emphasizes, and what is invaluable in his emphasis, is the thrilling fact that, in the words of W. H. Auden, poetic composition probably feels much the same in the twentieth century A.D. as it did in the twentieth century B.C.

Eliot and Pound envied Dante and to some extent imitated him in the forms and procedures of their poems. Pound's *Cantos* are the great epic homage in English in this century, too large a subject to address here, but they too sway to the authority of Dante the historian, Dante the encyclopaedic mind, the plunderer and harbourer of classical and medieval learning. The *Cantos* are intent upon repeating the *Commedia*'s synoptic feats of inclusion and correspondence; the gigantic is what both attracts and finally daunts Pound—and his reader as well, it could be said. The two Americans at once restored and distanced Dante in the English-speaking literary mind because they both suggested what Mandelstam was at pains to mock, that Dante's poem was written on official paper. They came to Dante early, as students; as young men, they studied him in an academic context; they wore his poem like a magic garment to protect themselves from the contagion of parochial English and American culture; and finally they canonized him as the aquiline patron of international modernism.

What Mandelstam does, on the other hand, is to bring him from the pantheon back to the palate; he makes your mouth water to read him. He possesses the poem as a musician possesses the score, both as a whole structure and as a sequence of delicious sounds. He transmits a fever of excitement in the actual phonetic reality of the work and shares with us the sensation of his poet's delight turning into a sort of giddy critical wisdom. And this personal neediness and rapture which we find in Mandelstam's responses has much to do with the fact that he came to Dante not as an undergraduate but as an exile in his thirties. In her memoir, *Hope against Hope*, Nadezhda Mandelstam tells us that her husband had no copy of Dante until this late stage in his life but that it was one of the few books he took with him when he was banished from his beloved Petersburg to the dark earth of Voronezh. By the time he came to dwell with the *Commedia*, his powers as a lyric poet had been tested and fulfilled, and his destiny as a moral being, in the middle of the journey, was being tragically embraced.

Mandelstam's exile from Petersburg was the result of a poem

he had written against Stalin, an uncharacteristically explicit and publicly directed poem which was reported to the Kremlin by an informer. But this poem had come at the end of four or five years of poetic silence, and the silence was the result of Mandelstam's attempt at connivance, compromise, acceptance—call it what you will; for a number of years he had been trying to make an accommodation with Soviet realities. He had been attempting to quell his essentially subjective, humanist vision of poetry as a kind of free love between the auditory imagination and the unharnessed intelligence, trying to submerge his quarrel with the idea of art as a service, a socialist realist cog in the revolutionary machine. He had worked as a translator; he had attempted to persuade himself that his pre-revolutionary espousal of poetry as an expression of inner freedom, as a self-delighting, self-engendering musical system based upon what he called 'the steadfastness of speech articulation', he had attempted to persuade himself that this vision of art could be maintained and exercised within the Soviet dispensation. For a while he tried to fit in with a system where art had to be, in Joyce's terms, kinetic, directed towards forwarding a cause, ready to forget its covenant with the literary past and the individual's inner sense of the truth. Yet Mandelstam's whole creative being strained against this attempt, and even when he was under the shadow of the death to which Stalin eventually hounded him, he was unable to make the compromise. He tried, a little shamefacedly in his own eyes and, to his credit, entirely unsuccessfully, to write a poem in praise of a hydroelectric dam, but he could manage nothing.

So in order to breathe freely, to allow his lips to move again with poems, which were his breath of life, he had to come clean, spur his Pegasus out of the socialist realist morass and thereby confront the danger of death and the immediate penalty of exile. And his essay on Dante was written in the aftermath of this tragic choice. It is no wonder therefore that Dante is perceived not as the mouthpiece of an orthodoxy but rather as the apotheosis of a free, natural, biological process, as a hive of bees, a process of crystallization, a hurry of pigeon flights, a focus for all the impulsive, instinctive, non-utilitarian elements in the creative life. Mandelstam found a guide and authority for himself also, but a guide who wears no official badge, enforces no party line, does not write paraphrases of Aquinas or commentaries on the classical authors. His Dante is a voluble Shakespearean figure, a woodcutter singing at his work in the dark wood of the larynx.

from The Government of the Tongue

When I thought of 'the government of the tongue' as a general title for these memorial lectures, what I wanted to explore was the idea that poetry vindicates itself through the exercise of its own expressive powers. In this reading, the tongue (representing both a poet's personal gift of utterance and the common resources of language itself) has been granted the right to govern. The poetic art discovers an authority all its own. As readers, we are prepared to be ruled by its rightness, even though that rightness is achieved not by the moral and ethical exercise of mind but by the self-validating operations of what we call inspiration—especially if we think of inspiration in the terms supplied by the Polish poet Anna Swir, who writes of it as a 'psychosomatic phenomenon' and goes on to declare:

> This seems to me the only biologically natural way for a poem to be born and gives the poem something like a biological right to exist. A poet becomes then an antenna capturing the voices of the world, a medium expressing his own subconscious and the collective subconscious. For one moment he possesses wealth usually inaccessible to him, and he loses it when that moment is over.

In this figure of the poem's making, then, we see a paradigm of free action issuing in satisfactorily achieved ends; we see a path projected to the dimension in which, Yeats says, 'Labour is blossoming or dancing where / The body is not bruised to pleasure soul . . .'

But as I warm to this theme, a voice from another part of me speaks in rebuke. 'Govern your tongue', it says, compelling me to remember that my title can also imply a *denial* of the tongue's autonomy and permission. In this reading, 'the government of the tongue' is full of monastic and ascetic strictness. One remembers

Hopkins's 'Habit of Perfection', with its command to the eyes to be 'shelled', the ears to attend to silence and the tongue to know its place:

> Shape nothing, lips; be lovely-dumb:
> It is the shut, the curfew sent
> From there where all surrenders come
> Which only makes you eloquent.

It is even more instructive to remember that Hopkins abandoned poetry when he entered the Jesuits 'as not having to do with my vocation'. This manifests a world where the prevalent values and necessities leave poetry in a relatively underprivileged situation, requiring it to take a position that is secondary to religious truth or state security or public order. It discloses a condition of public and private repressions where the undirected hedonistic play of imagination is regarded at best as luxury or licentiousness, at worst as heresy or treason. In ideal republics, in Soviet republics, in the Vatican and Bible belt, it is a common expectation that the writer will sign over his or her individual, venturesome and potentially disruptive activity into the keeping of an official doctrine, a traditional system, a party line, whatever. In such contexts, no further elaboration or exploration of the language or forms currently in place is permissible. An order has been handed down and the shape of things has been established.

The vitality and insouciance of lyric poetry, its relish of its own inventiveness, its pleasuring strain, always comes under threat when poetry remembers that its self-gratification must be perceived as a kind of affront to a world preoccupied with its own imperfections, pains and catastrophes. What right has poetry to its quarantine? Should it not put the governors on its joy and moralize its song? Should it, as Austin Clarke said in another context, take the clapper from the bell of rhyme? Should it go as far in self-denial as Zbigniew Herbert's poem 'A Knocker' seems to want it to go? This translation, in the Penguin Modern European Poets series, was originally published in 1968:

There are those who grow
gardens in their heads
paths lead from their hair
to sunny and white cities

it's easy for them to write
they close their eyes
immediately schools of images
stream down their foreheads

my imagination
is a piece of board
my sole instrument
is a wooden stick

I strike the board
it answers me
yes—yes
no—no

for others the green bell of a tree
the blue bell of water
I have a knocker
from unprotected gardens

I thump on the board
and it prompts me
with the moralist's dry poem
yes—yes
no—no

Herbert's poem ostensibly demands that poetry abandon its hedonism and fluency, that it become a nun of language and barber
its luxuriant locks down to a stubble of moral and ethical goads.
Ostensibly too, it would depose the tongue because of its cavalier indulgence and send in as governor of the estate of poetry a
Malvolio with a stick. It would castigate the entrancements of poetry, substituting in their stead a Roundhead's plain-spoken counsel. Yet oddly, without the fluent evocation of bells and gardens
and trees and all those things which it explicitly deplores, the

poem could not make the bleak knocker signify as potently as it does. The poem makes us feel that we should prefer moral utterance to palliative imagery, and by making us feel, it carries its truth alive into the heart—exactly as the Romantics said it should. We end up persuaded we are against lyric poetry's culpable absorption in its own process by an entirely successful instance of that very process in action: here is a lyric about a knocker which claims that lyric is inadmissible.

All poets who get beyond the first excitement of being blessed by the achievement of poetic form confront, sooner or later, the question which Herbert confronts in 'A Knocker', and if they are lucky, they end up, like Herbert, outstripping it rather than answering it directly. Some, like Wilfred Owen, outface it by living a life so extremely mortgaged to the suffering of others that the tenancy of the palace of art is paid for a hundredfold. Others, like Yeats, promulgate and practise such faith in art's absolute necessity that they overbear whatever assaults the historical and contingent might mount upon their certitude. Richard Ellmann's statement of the Yeatsian case is finally applicable to every serious poetic life:

> He wishes to show how brute fact may be transmogrified, how we can sacrifice ourselves . . . to our imagined selves which offer far higher standards than anything offered by social convention. If we must suffer, it is better to create the world in which we suffer, and this is what heroes do spontaneously, artists do consciously, and all men do in their degree.

All poets are likely to subscribe to some such conviction, even those who are most scrupulous in their avoidance of the grand manner, who respect the democracy of language and display by the pitch of their voice or the commonness of their subjects a readiness to put themselves on the side of those who are sceptical of poetry's right to any special status. The fact is that poetry is its own reality, and no matter how much a poet may concede to the corrective pressures of social, moral, political and historical reality, the ultimate fidelity must be to the demands and promise of the artistic event.

It is for this reason that I want to discuss 'At the Fishhouses' by Elizabeth Bishop. Here we see this most reticent and mannerly of poets being compelled by the undeniable impetus of her art to break with her usual inclination to conciliate the social audience. This conciliatory impulse was based not on subservience but on a respect for other people's shyness in the face of poetry's presumption: Bishop usually limited herself to a note that would not have disturbed the discreet undersong of conversation between strangers breakfasting at a seaside hotel. Without addressing a question as immense and unavoidable as whether silence rather than poetry is not the proper response in a world after Auschwitz, she implicitly condones the doubts about art's prerogatives which such a question raises.

Elizabeth Bishop, in other words, was temperamentally inclined to believe in the government of the tongue—in the self-denying sense. She was personally reticent, opposed to and incapable of self-aggrandizement, the very embodiment of good manners. Manners, of course, imply obligations to others and obligations on the part of others to ourselves. They insist on propriety, in the good, large original sense of the word, meaning that which is intrinsic and characteristic and belongs naturally to the person or the thing. They also imply a certain strictness and allow the verbs 'ought' and 'should' to come into play. In short, as an attribute of the poetic enterprise, manners place limits on the whole scope and pitch of the enterprise itself. They would govern the tongue.

But Elizabeth Bishop not only practised good manners in her poetry. She also submitted herself to the discipline of observation. Observation was her habit, as much in the monastic, Hopkinsian sense as in its commoner meaning of a customarily repeated action. Indeed, observation is itself a manifestation of obedience, an activity which is averse to overwhelming phenomena by the exercise of subjectivity, content to remain an assisting presence rather than an overbearing pressure. So it is no wonder that the title of Bishop's last collection was that of an old school textbook, *Geography III.* It is as if she were insisting on an affinity between her poetry and textbook prose, which establishes reliable, unassertive relations with the world by steady attention to detail, by equable classification and level-toned enumeration. The epigraph of the book suggests that the poet wishes to identify with these well-tried, primary methods of connecting words and things:

> *What is Geography?*
> A description of the earth's surface.
> *What is the Earth?*
> The planet or body on which we live.
> *What is the shape of the Earth?*
> Round, like a ball.
> *Of what is the Earth's surface composed?*
> Land and water.

A poetry faithful to such catechetical procedures would indeed seem to deny itself access to vision or epiphany; and 'At the Fishhouses' does begin with fastidious notations which log the progress of the physical world, degree by unemphatic degree, into the poet's own lucid awareness:

> Although it is a cold evening,
> down by one of the fishhouses
> an old man sits netting,
> his net, in the gloaming almost invisible,
> a dark purple-brown,
> and his shuttle worn and polished.
> The air smells so strong of codfish
> it makes one's nose run and one's eyes water.
> The five fishhouses have steeply peaked roofs
> and narrow, cleated gangplanks slant up
> to storerooms in the gables
> for the wheelbarrows to be pushed up and down on.
> All is silver: the heavy surface of the sea,
> swelling slowly as if considering spilling over,
> is opaque, but the silver of the benches,
> the lobster pots, and masts, scattered
> among the wild jagged rocks,
> is of an apparent translucence

like the small old buildings with an emerald moss
growing on their shoreward walls.
The big fish tubs are completely lined
with layers of beautiful herring scales
and the wheelbarrows are similarly plastered
with creamy iridescent coats of mail,
with small iridescent flies crawling on them.
Up on the little slope behind the houses,
set in the sparse bright sprinkle of grass,
is an ancient wooden capstan,
cracked, with two long bleached handles
and some melancholy stains, like dried blood,
where the ironwork has rusted.
The old man accepts a Lucky Strike.
He was a friend of my grandfather.
We talk of the decline in the population
and of codfish and herring
while he waits for a herring boat to come in.
There are sequins on his vest and on his thumb.
He has scraped the scales, the principal beauty,
from unnumbered fish with that black old knife,
the blade of which is almost worn away.

Down at the water's edge, at the place
where they haul up the boats, up the long ramp
descending into the water, thin silver
tree trunks are laid horizontally
across the gray stones, down and down
at intervals of four or five feet.

Cold dark deep and absolutely clear,
element bearable to no mortal,
to fish and to seals . . . One seal particularly
I have seen here evening after evening.
He was curious about me. He was interested in music;
like me a believer in total immersion,
so I used to sing him Baptist hymns.
I also sang 'A Mighty Fortress Is Our God'.

He stood up in the water and regarded me
steadily, moving his head a little.
Then he would disappear, then suddenly emerge
almost in the same spot, with a sort of shrug
as if it were against his better judgment.
Cold dark deep and absolutely clear,
the clear gray icy water . . . Back, behind us,
the dignified tall firs begin.
Bluish, associating with their shadows,
a million Christmas trees stand
waiting for Christmas. The water seems suspended
above the rounded gray and blue-gray stones.
I have seen it over and over, the same sea, the same,
slightly, indifferently swinging above the stones,
icily free above the stones,
above the stones and then the world.
If you should dip your hand in,
your wrist would ache immediately,
your bones would begin to ache and your hand would burn
as if the water were a transmutation of fire
that feeds on stones and burns with a dark gray flame.
If you tasted it, it would first taste bitter,
then briny, then surely burn your tongue.
It is like what we imagine knowledge to be:
dark, salt, clear, moving, utterly free,
drawn from the cold hard mouth
of the world, derived from the rocky breasts
forever, flowing and drawn, and since
our knowledge is historical, flowing, and flown.

What we have been offered, among other things, is the slow-motion spectacle of a well-disciplined poetic imagination being tempted to dare a big leap, hesitating and then with powerful sureness actually taking the leap. For about two-thirds of the poem the restraining, self-abnegating, completely attentive manners of the writing keep us alive to the surfaces of a world: the note is colloquial if tending towards the finical, the scenery is chaste, beloved

and ancestral. Grandfather was here. Yet this old world is still being made new again by the sequins of herring scales, the sprinkle
of grass and the small iridescent flies. Typically, detail by detail, by
the layering of one observation upon another, by readings taken at
different levels and from different angles, a world is brought into
being. There is a feeling of ordered scrutiny, of a securely positioned observer turning a gaze now to the sea, now to the fish barrels, now to the old man. And the voice that tells us about it all is
self-possessed but not self-centred, full of discreet and intelligent
instruction, of the desire to witness exactly. The voice is neither
breathless nor detached; it is thoroughly plenished, like the sea
'swelling slowly as if considering spilling over', and then, thrill-
ingly, halfway through, it does spill over:

> Cold dark deep and absolutely clear,
> element bearable to no mortal,
> to fish and to seals . . . One seal particularly . . .

Just a minute ago I said that the habit of observation did not
promise any irruption of the visionary. Yet here it is, a rhythmic
heave which suggests that something other is about to happen—although not immediately. The colloquial note creeps back, and the
temptation to inspired utterance is rebuked by the seal who arrives
partly like a messenger from another world, partly like a deadpan
comedian of water. Even so, he is a sign which initiates a wonder
as he dives back into the deep region where the poem will follow,
wooed with perfect timing into the mysterious. Looking at the
world of the surface, after all, is not only against the better judgement of a seal; it is finally also against the better judgement of the
poet.

It is not that the poet breaks faith with the observed world, the
world of human attachment, grandfathers, Lucky Strikes and
Christmas trees. But it is a different, estranging and fearful element which ultimately fascinates her: the world of meditated
meaning, of a knowledge-need which sets human beings apart
from seals and herrings, and sets the poet in her solitude apart
from her grandfather and the old man, this poet enduring the cold

sea-light of her own *wyrd* and her own mortality. Her scientific impulse is suddenly jumped back to its root in pre-Socratic awe, and water stares her in the face as the original solution:

> If you should dip your hand in,
> your wrist would ache immediately,
> your bones would begin to ache and your hand would burn
> as if the water were a transmutation of fire
> that feeds on stones and burns with a dark gray flame.
> If you tasted it, it would first taste bitter,
> then briny, then surely burn your tongue.
> It is like what we imagine knowledge to be:
> dark, salt, clear, moving, utterly free,
> drawn from the cold hard mouth
> of the world, derived from the rocky breasts
> forever, flowing and drawn, and since
> our knowledge is historical, flowing, and flown.

This writing still bears a recognizable resemblance to the simple propositions of the geography textbook. There is no sentence which does not possess a similar clarity and unchallengeability. Yet since these concluding lines are poetry, not geography, they have a dream truth as well as a daylight truth about them; they are as hallucinatory as they are accurate. They also possess that *sine qua non* of all lyric utterance, a completely persuasive inner cadence which is deeply intimate with the laden water of full tide. The lines are inhabited by certain profoundly true tones, which, as Robert Frost put it, 'were before words were, living in the cave of the mouth', and they do what poetry most essentially does: they fortify our inclination to credit promptings of our intuitive being. They help us to say in the first recesses of ourselves, in the shyest, pre-social part of our nature, 'Yes, I know something like that too. Yes, that's right; thank you for putting words on it and making it more or less official.' And thus the government of the tongue gains our votes, and Anna Swir's proclamation (which at first may have sounded a bit overstated) comes true in the sensation of reading even a poet as shy of bardic presumption as Elizabeth Bishop:

A poet becomes then an antenna capturing the voices of the world, a medium expressing his own subconscious and the collective subconscious.

In conclusion, I want now to offer two further texts for meditation. The first is from T. S. Eliot. Forty-four years ago, in October 1942, in wartime London, when he was at work on 'Little Gidding', Eliot wrote in a letter to E. Martin Browne:

> In the midst of what is going on now, it is hard, when you sit down at a desk, to feel confident that morning after morning spent fiddling with words and rhythms is justified activity—especially as there is never any certainty that the whole thing won't have to be scrapped. And on the other hand, external or public activity is more of a drug than is this solitary toil which often seems so pointless.

Here is the great paradox of poetry and of the imaginative arts in general. Faced with the brutality of the historical onslaught, they are practically useless. Yet they verify our singularity; they strike and stake out the ore of self which lies at the base of every individuated life. In one sense the efficacy of poetry is nil—no lyric has ever stopped a tank. In another sense, it is unlimited. It is like the writing in the sand in the face of which accusers and accused are left speechless and renewed.

I am thinking of Jesus' writing as it is recorded in Chapter Eight of John's Gospel, my second and concluding text:

> And the scribes and Pharisees brought unto him a woman taken in adultery; and when they had set her in the midst,
>
> They say unto him, Master, this woman was taken in adultery, in the very act.
>
> Now Moses in the law commanded us, that such should be stoned: but what sayest thou?
>
> This they said, tempting him, that they might have to accuse him. But Jesus stooped down, and with his finger wrote on the ground, as though he heard them not.

So when they continued asking him, he lifted up himself, and said unto them, He that is without sin among you, let him first cast a stone at her.

And again he stooped down, and wrote on the ground.

And they which heard it, being convicted by their own conscience, went out one by one, beginning at the eldest, even unto the last: and Jesus was left alone, and the woman standing in the midst.

When Jesus had lifted up himself, and saw none but the woman, he said unto her, Woman, where are those thine accusers? hath no man condemned thee?

She said, No man, Lord. And Jesus said unto her, Neither do I condemn thee: go, and sin no more.

The drawing of those characters is like poetry, a break with the usual life but not an absconding from it. Poetry, like the writing, is arbitrary and marks time in every possible sense of that phrase. It does not say to the accusing crowd or to the helpless accused, 'Now a solution will take place'; it does not propose to be instrumental or effective. Instead, in the rift between what is going to happen and whatever we would wish to happen, poetry holds attention for a space, functions not as distraction but as pure concentration, a focus where our power to concentrate is concentrated back on ourselves.

This is what gives poetry its governing power. At its greatest moments it would attempt, in Yeats's phrase, to hold in a single thought reality and justice. Yet even then its function is not essentially supplicatory or transitive. Poetry is more a threshold than a path, one constantly approached and constantly departed from, at which reader and writer undergo in their different ways the experience of being at the same time summoned and released.

from Sounding Auden

Auden was hungering for a form. In his unformed needs and impulses he was rehearsing the scenario which Martin Buber outlines
in *I and Thou*:

> This is the eternal source of art: a man is faced by a form which
> desires to be made through him into a work. This form is no off-
> spring of his soul but is an appearance which steps up to it and
> demands of it the effective power. The man is concerned with an
> act of his being. If he carries it through, if he speaks the primary
> word out of his being to the form which appears, then the effec-
> tive power streams out, and the work arises.

That is actually a firm account of what in experience is elusive
and tenebrous; and in its conception of power streaming out and
the work arising as the primary word is spoken, it represents a
way of acknowledging the kind of governing power to which the
young Auden's tongue gained access when acts of his being issued
in his own words, those entirely compelling, if estranged and estranging words of his famous earliest poems.

This new lyric was dominated by a somewhat impersonal pro-
noun which enclosed much that was fabulous, passional and occasionally obscure. Its manifestations were an 'I' or 'we' or 'you' that
could arrest, confuse and inspect the reader all at once. He or she
seemed to have been set down in the middle of a cold landscape,
blindfolded, turned rapidly around, unblindfolded, ordered to
march and to make sense of every ominous thing encountered
from there on. The new poem turned the reader into an accom-
plice, unaccountably bound to the poem's presiding voice by an insinuation that they shared a knowledge which might be either
shameful or subversive. In Samuel Hynes's terms, it presented an
alternative world. Even Eliot's openings, startling as they were,

could not equal Auden's for defamiliarizing abruptness. Eliot still pushed the poem out with the current of rhythmic expectation, the words sailed off relatively unhampered towards attainable syntactical or scenic or narrative destinations:

> Let us go then, you and I,
> When the evening is spread out against the sky . . .
>
> > *All right, then. Let's go.*
>
> April is the cruellest month, breeding
> Lilacs out of the dead land, mixing
> Memory and desire, stirring . . .
>
> > *OK. Keep talking. What else*
> > *was bothering you?*
>
> Here I am, an old man in a dry month
> Being read to by a boy, waiting for rain.
>
> > *Sure, Granpa! Of course you are.*

Auden's openings, on the other hand, were launched against the flow. The craft itself felt shipshape, but its motion seemed unpredictable, it started in mid-pitch and wobbled:

> Who stands, the crux left of the watershed,
> On the wet road between the chafing grass . . .
>
> > *Between grass? What do you*
> > *mean? Where is this anyway?*
>
> Taller to-day, we remember similar evenings,
> Walking together in the windless orchard . . .
>
> > *Taller what? Whose orchard*
> > *where?*

These famous early poems gave me enormous trouble when I was an undergraduate. Confident teachers spoke of Geoffrey Grigson's advice to Thirties poets to 'Report well. Begin with objects and events.' These poets were socially concerned, we were told; they were tempted by communism, wanted to open some negotiation with popular culture and to include the furniture of the modern technological world in their lyrics. Fine. This was okay for the nude giant girls behind Spender's pylons and the knockabout farce of Louis MacNeice's 'Bagpipe Music'. But Auden was supposed to be the main man, so where did all this lecture-note stuff get you when in the solitude of your room you faced the staccato imperatives of a passage like this:

> Go home, now, stranger, proud of your young stock,
> Stranger, turn back again, frustrate and vexed:
> This land, cut off, will not communicate,
> Be no accessory content to one
> Aimless for faces rather there than here.
> Beams from your car may cross a bedroom wall,
> They wake no sleeper; you may hear the wind
> Arriving driven from the ignorant sea
> To hurt itself on pane, on bark of elm
> Where sap unbaffled rises, being spring;
> But seldom this. Near you, taller than grass,
> Ears poise before decision, scenting danger.

My teachers had used the word 'telegraphese', so I assumed I was in its presence here, the enigma and abruptness of the thing suggesting as much the actual chattering of a machine relaying signals as the condensed idiom of a decoded, printed message. So, all right, telegraphese. Yet to what end? I felt excluded. I had indeed been blindfolded and turned around, only to find myself daunted by a landscape that both convinced me and shrugged me off.

It would have been better had those teachers been in a position to quote what Geoffrey Grigson wrote four decades later, in the volume of memorial tributes edited by Stephen Spender. There, talking about the first poem of Auden's which he had encountered, one never to be republished, Grigson spoke of its having arisen out of an 'Englishness' until then unexpressed or not isolated in a poem:

In the poem, he [Auden] saw the blood trail which had dripped from Grendel after his arm and shoulder had been ripped off by Beowulf. The blood shone, was phosphorescent on the grass . . . It was as if Auden . . . had given imaginative place and 'reality' to something exploited for the Examination Schools, yet rooted in the English origins.

Grigson also spoke of 'assonances and alliterations coming together to make a new verbal actuality as it might be of rock or quartz', which is precisely what this slab of verse felt like to me when I first encountered it, and why I still rejoice in it. It is responses and formulations such as Grigson's, which have little to say about the young poet's shifting allegiances to Marx and Freud, that are the ones which count for most in the long poetic run, because they are the most sensitive to the art of language . . .

A new rhythm, after all, is a new life given to the world, a resuscitation not just of the ear but of the springs of being. The rhythmic disjunctions in Auden's lines, the correspondingly fractured elements of narrative or argument, are wakenings to a new reality, lyric equivalents of the fault he intuited in the life of his times. 'The Watershed' is, according to Edward Mendelson's introduction to *The English Auden*, the earliest of the poems preserved in the standard *Collected Poems*, and reads in places as if a landslide had happened while the lines were being formed or a slippage had occurred between mind and page:

> This land, cut off, will not communicate,
> Be no accessory content to one
> Aimless for faces rather there than here.

What bothered and excluded me when I read this as an undergraduate still excludes me but bothers me no more. The difference is that I am now content that Auden should practise such resistance to the reader's expectations; I take pleasure in its opacity and am ready to accept its obscurity—even if it is wilful—as a symptom of this poet's deliberate insistence upon the distance between art and life. This is not to say that there is no relation between art

and life but to insist, as Lazarus in bliss insisted to Dives in tor-
ment, that a gulf does exist . . .

The usual poem keeps faith with the way we talk at the table,
even more with the way we have heard other poems talk to us before. 'Out on the lawn I lie in bed, / Vega conspicuous overhead / In
the windless nights of June.' Yes, yes, we think; more, more; it's
lovely, keep it coming. The melody allays anxiety, the oceanic feeling of womb-oneness stirs, joy fills the spirit's vault like the after-
echo of a choir in a cathedral:

> That later we, though parted then,
> May still recall these evenings when
> Fear gave his watch no look;
> The lion griefs loped from the shade
> And on our knees their muzzles laid,
> And Death put down his book.

This exemplifies the hymn-singing effect of poetry, its action as a
dissolver of differences, and so long as it operates in this mode, poetry functions to produce a sensation of at-homeness and trust in
the world. The individual poem may address particular occasions
of distress such as a death or a civil war or a recognition of the
sad fact of betrayal between lovers, but as long as its tune plays
into the prepared expectations of our ear and our nature, as long as
desire is not disallowed or allowed only to be disappointed, then
the poem's effect will be to offer a sense of possible consolation. It
is perhaps because of Auden's susceptibility to this tremblingly
delicious power of poetry that he constantly warns against it. 'In
so far as poetry, or any other of the arts, can be said to have an
ulterior purpose, it is, by telling the truth, to disenchant and disin-
toxicate.'

Auden, however, practised more enchantment than this pro-
nouncement would suggest, so it is no wonder that he was impelled to keep the critical heckler alive in himself. After the
mid-1930s, the iambic melodies and traditional formal obedience
of his poems—the skilful rather than sensual deployment of
Anglo-Saxon metre in *The Age of Anxiety*, for example—would

certainly suggest a weakening of his original refusal of the conventional musics, and a consequent weakening of the newness and otherness of his contribution to the resources, if not to the supply, of poetry itself. As he matured, he may have regretted the scampishness with which he played around in his younger days when, as Christopher Isherwood reports,

> He was very lazy. He hated polishing and making corrections. If I didn't like a poem, he threw it away and wrote another. If I liked one line, he would keep it and work it into a new poem. In this way whole poems were constructed which were simply anthologies of my favourite lines, entirely regardless of grammar or sense. This is the simple explanation of much of Auden's celebrated obscurity.

No doubt, this practice (in so far as Isherwood's blithe account is to be credited) betrays an irresponsibility with regard to comprehensibility, but it does represent a strong life-urge in the artist himself. To avoid the consensus and settlement of a meaning which the audience fastens on like a security blanket, to be antic, mettlesome, contrary, to retain the right to impudence, to raise hackles, to harry the audience into wakefulness—to do all this may be not only permissible but necessary if poetry is to keep on coming into a fuller life. Which is why, as I said, I am now ready to attend without anxiety to those oddly unparaphrasable riffs in the very earliest work.

At the beginning of 'The Watershed' the wind is 'chafing', a word which until this occasion had seemed bereft of onomatopoeic life: now it allows us to hear through its lingering vowel and caressing fricative the whisper and friction of wind along a hillside. But this unresisted passage of breath is complicated by the meaning of something rubbing, being fretted and galled and hence inflamed. The word suggests that the topographical crux (of the watershed) which has been left behind is now being experienced as and replaced by a psychological crux, a condition of being subject to two contradictory states, of having to suffer at the same time an utter stillness and a *susurrus* of agitation. Similarly, the

grammatical peace of this present participle is disturbed by a lurk-
ing middle voice: the grass is chafing, active, but in so far as the
only thing being chafed is itself, it is passive. Then, too, the participle occupies a middle state between being transitive and being
intransitive, and altogether functions like a pass made swiftly, a
sleight of semantic hand which unnerves and suspends the reader
above a valley of uncertainty. By the second line the reader is already made into that 'stranger' who will be addressed in line 19. In
fact, the first two words put the reader to the test, for we are not
immediately sure whether 'Who stands' initiates a question or a
noun clause. This deferral of a sense of syntactical direction is a
perfect technical equivalent for that lack of certitude and intuition
of imminent catastrophe which give the poem its soundless climax
and closure.

Yet for all the rightness of 'chafing' there is no sense of its having been chosen; it is completely free of that unspoken 'Here be
sport for diction-spotters' which hangs over the more deliberate,
lexicon-oriented Auden of the last years, when he had begun to resemble in his own person an ample, flopping, ambulatory volume
of the *OED* in carpet slippers. Remember the unravelling wool of
the title poem in *Thank You, Fog*:

> Sworn foe to festination,
> daunter of drivers and planes
> volants, of course, will curse You,
> but how delighted I am
> that You've been lured to visit
> Wiltshire's witching countryside
> for a whole week at Christmas.

That 'witching' is beautiful, permissive, wryly and latecomerly literary, yet its very relish of its own dexterity is tinged with tedium,
even for the poet (and the same holds, only more so, for 'festina-
tion' and 'volants'). Whereas 'chafing' strikes the rock of language
and brings forth sudden life from the rift, these later words are col-
lector's items, lifted in huffing pleasure but without the need and
joy which attended the earlier discovery.

Happily, there is no necessity to go on about this. Later Auden is a different kind of poetry; by then, the line is doctrinaire in its domesticity, wanting to comfort like a thread of wool rather than shock like a bare wire. Attendant upon the whole performance, there is an unselfpitying air of 'Let us grieve not, rather find / Strength in what remains behind', and I quote the fog passage only to remind you again of the extent to which Auden's poetry changed its linguistic posture over four decades. In the very beginning, the stress of Anglo-Saxon metre and the gnomic clunk of Anglo-Saxon phrasing were pulled like a harrow against the natural slope of social speech and iambic lyric. The poem did not sail with the current; it tangled and hassled, chafed, 'hurt itself on pane, on bark of elm'. What was happening in such rare musical eddies was what T. S. Eliot called 'concentration', a term which he employed when addressing the ever-pressing question of the relation between emotions actually experienced by the poet and the emotions which get expressed—or better, get invented—in a poem. 'We must believe that "emotion recollected in tranquillity" is an inexact formula', Eliot wrote in 'Tradition and the Individual Talent', and went on:

> For it is neither emotion, nor recollection, nor, without distortion of meaning, tranquillity. It is a concentration, and a new thing resulting from the concentration, of a very great number of experiences; it is a concentration which does not happen consciously or of deliberation. These experiences are not 'recollected', and they finally unite in an atmosphere which is 'tranquil' only in that it is a passive attending upon the event.

We are in the presence of such concentration when we read a poem like 'Taller To-day'. This lyric is obviously not meant to fall into step with our usual commonsensical speech-gait, nor is it eager to simulate the emotional and linguistic normality of 'a man speaking to men'; rather, it presents us with that 'new thing' which abides, as I suggested, adjacent and parallel to lived experience but which, in spite of perfect sympathy for those living such experience, has no desire to dwell among them:

> Noises at dawn will bring
> Freedom for some, but not this peace
> No bird can contradict: passing, but is sufficient now
> For something fulfilled this hour, loved or endured.

The tranquillity of this has as much to do with what the words achieve as with what they recollect. Not, perhaps, the peace which surpasseth understanding, more that which resisteth paraphrasing; a peace, anyhow, 'No bird can contradict'.

But then, after all, does a bird's motion not equal a disturbance or 'contradiction' even within such deep stillness and fulfilment? Yet somehow the bird in the passage hardly attains enough physical presence to be able to contradict anything. For example, if we put it beside Hardy's dew-fall hawk 'crossing the shades to alight / Upon the wind-warped upland thorn', we know Hardy's to be a dark transience of wing-beat, a palpable, air-lofted glide, a phenomenon *out there*, in the twilight, whereas Auden's bird is an occurrence *in here*, an ignition of energy which happens when certain pert, thin, clicking vowels are combined in a swift reaction: 'but not this peace / No bird can contradict: passing, but is sufficient now / For something fulfilled this hour, loved or endured.' The contrapuntal, lengthened-out, interrupted see-saw movement of those lines is as important as their beautifully elaborated and uncomplicating meaning. The hammer of modern English metre, what Robert Graves called the smith-work of *ti-tum, ti-tum*, is going on during the deeper, longer oar-work of Old English, and the ear, no matter how ignorant it may be of the provenance of what it is hearing, attends to the contest. This contest, perfectly matched, undulant yet balanced, is between the navigating efforts of a singular, directed intelligence and the slug and heave of the element in which it toils, the element of language itself . . .

Those obscure early poems had been unaccommodating and involuntary efforts to speak the primary and utterly persuasive word. They were, in both the literal and slangier senses of the phrase, 'far out'—even at the times when they kept tight in to the metrical rule and spoke the first language of the child's story-book:

Starving through the leafless wood
Trolls run scolding for their food,
Owl and nightingale are dumb,
And the angel will not come.

Cold, impossible, ahead
Lifts the mountain's lovely head
Whose white waterfall could bless
Travellers in their last distress.

Although this does not strike back at a rhythmical angle against the expectation of the well-tuned ear, its metaphysical geography remains very different from the consoling contours of the 'real world' of the familiar. Long before the parable poetry of postwar Europe, Auden arrived at a mode that was stricken with premonitions of an awful thing and was adequate to give expression to those premonitions by strictly poetic means. But this unified sensibility fissured when Auden was inevitably driven to extend himself beyond the transmission of intuited knowledge, beyond poetic indirection and implication, and began spelling out those intuitions in a more explicit, analytic and morally ratified rhetoric. In writing a poem like 'Spain', no matter how breathtaking its condensation of vistas or how decent its purpose, or a poem like 'A Summer Night', no matter how Mozartian its verbal equivalent of *agape*, Auden broke with his solitude and his oddity. His responsibility towards the human family became intensely and commendably strong and the magnificently sane, meditative, judicial poems of the 1940s, 1950s and 1960s were the result. We might say that this bonus, which includes such an early masterpiece as 'Letter to Lord Byron' and such a later one as 'In Praise of Limestone', represents an answer to the question posed in 'Orpheus'. That answer inclines to say that 'song' hopes most of all for 'the knowledge of life' and inclines away from the 'bewildered' quotient in the proffered alternative 'to be bewildered and happy'. To put it another way, Auden finally preferred life to be concentrated into something 'rich' rather than something 'strange', a preference which is understandable if we consider poetry's constant impulse to be all Prospero, harnessed to the rational project of settling mankind into a cosmic security. Yet the doom and omen which characterized the 'strange' poetry of the early 1930s, its bewildered and unsettling visions, brought native English poetry as near as it has ever been to the imaginative verge of the dreadful and offered an example of how insular experience and the universal shock suffered by mankind in the twentieth century could be sounded forth in the English language. In his later poetry, moreover, when a similar note is struck, the poetry inevitably gains in memorability and intensity:

> Unendowed with wealth or pity,
> Little birds with scarlet legs,
> Sitting on their speckled eggs,
> Eye each flu-infected city.
>
> Altogether elsewhere, vast
> Herds of reindeer move across
> Miles and miles of golden moss,
> Silently and very fast.

Lowell's Command

Years ago Michael Longley wrote an essay on poets from Northern Ireland in which he made a distinction between igneous and sedimentary modes of poetic composition. In geology, igneous rocks are derived from magma or lava solidified below the earth's surface, whereas sedimentary ones are formed by the deposit and accumulation of mineral and organic materials, worked on, broken down and reconstituted by the action of water, ice and wind. The very sound of the words is suggestive of what is entailed in each case. Igneous is irruptive, unlooked-for and peremptory; sedimentary is steady-keeled, dwelt-upon, graduated.

If, however, a name exists for the process which begins igneous and ends up sedimentary, it would be the one to apply to the poetry of Robert Lowell. Lowell was a poet who had a powerful instinct for broaching the molten stuff early, but then he would keep coming back to work it over with the hot and cold weathers of his revising intelligence, sometimes even after it had appeared in a book. He was very much alive to the double nature of the act of writing: 'A poem is an event,' he declared to his classes, 'not the record of an event'—equating what I have called 'igneous' with 'event', and 'sedimentary' with 'record'. The distinction comes to light in another form in his *Writers at Work* interview, where he says, 'The revision, the consciousness that tinkers with a poem— that has something to do with teaching and criticism. But the impulse that starts a poem and makes it of any importance is distinct from teaching.' And again, 'I'm sure that writing isn't a craft, that is, something for which you learn the skills and go on turning out. It must come from some deep impulse, deep inspiration.'

Yet his awareness of this distinction between the essential self-engendered impulse and what he would call in the end 'those blessèd structures, plot and rhyme', did not lead Lowell to disdain those structures. His conviction that poetry could not be equated with craft did not diminish his respect for craft. Craft, after all, represents a poet's covenant with the literary tradition of his language, with ancestry and posterity, a covenant based on an understanding that the poetic venture is ultimately serviceable no matter how solipsistic it might at first appear. Lowell was searching for a way of writing that would be an anatomy of his own predicament and of the age. His obsessive subjectivity did not signify an absconding from the usual life with its ethical codes and its various obligations. On the contrary, Lowell deliberately took upon himself—sometimes by public apostrophe and rebuke, sometimes by introspective or confessional example—the role of the poet as conscience of his society. Conscience, if we press upon its etymology, can mean our capacity to know the same thing together, yet such knowledge also makes us vulnerable to poetry as a reminder of what, together, we may have chosen to forget, and this admonitory function is one which Robert Lowell exercised, more or less deliberately, all his life.

When I speak of his 'command', however, I am thinking not just of his arrogation of the right to speak to or for an audience but of the way this arrogation is validated by the note of his writing, its particular 'command' over literary tradition and the illiterate ear. Until full middle age, Lowell achieved this authority by tuning his lines in accordance with traditional practice, bringing them to a pitch of tension and intensity by means of musical climax, dramatic gesture or ironical plotting, constantly recalling himself and his reader to an encounter with a formal shape, a firmly decided outline.

It is true that during this first movement of his career, Lowell abandoned his ambition to write a standoffish, self-sufficient poetry and aimed instead to achieve a more face-to-face contact with his reader and his reader's world. Yet he was always seeking to outfox if not to overwhelm the usual, to sound oracular or at least ungainsayable: 'The Lord survives the rainbow of his will.' 'Your old-fashioned tirade—/Loving, rapid, merciless—/breaks like the Atlantic Ocean on my head.' 'You usually won—/motionless/ as a lizard in the sun.' Closing lines like these would tremble in the ear like an arrow in a target. A sense of something utterly com-

pleted vied with a sense of something startled into scope and freedom. The reader was permitted the sensation of a whole meaning
simultaneously clicking shut and breaking open, a momentary illusion that the fulfilments which were being experienced in the
ear encapsulated meanings and fulfilments available in the world.
So, no matter how much the poem had to do with breakdown or
the evacuation of meaning from experience, its fall towards a val-
ueless limbo was broken by the perfectly stretched net of poetic
form itself.

Life Studies, for example, noted at first for its extreme candour,
for the private, almost taboo nature of its contents, now stands as
unembarrassed and approachable as a public monument. It silhou-
ettes its figures against the life of the times; its hard, intelligent
lines and well-braced speech imply that there is a social dimension
to what it is voicing. It trusts that it has an audience and hence is
able to proceed to the outrageous or unnerving business of autobiography with a certain decorousness. Lowell may write:

> Terrible that old life of decency
> without unseemly intimacy
> or quarrels, when the unemancipated woman
> still had her Freudian papà and maids!

Yet the decorum of *Life Studies* is continuous with that old life
even as it reveals its disintegration, its inadequate hauteur in the
face of locked razors, mad soldiers and electric chairs. This decorum, the book's technical mastery and its drive towards impersonality are as much part of Lowell's birthright as his patronymic. As
an artist, he was the proper Bostonian with his back to a wall of
tradition. His poetic art, however self-willed it might on occasion
be, could never escape from the demand that it be more than self-
indulgence. There had to be something surgical in the incisions
he made, something professional and public-spirited. The whole
thing was a test, of himself and of the resources of poetry, and in
Life Studies those resources proved to be capable of taking new
strains, in both the musical and the stressful sense of that word.

Lowell did not innocently lisp in numbers. Innocence was not something he set much store by, anyhow, either in himself or in others, and his whole *oeuvre* is remarkably free of the sigh for lost Eden. Everything begins outside the garden, in the learning process, in sweat and application. No lisps. The voice has broken by the time it speaks. It has been to school, literally as well as figuratively. Lowell's first style, it should not be forgotten, was formed in the English Departments of Kenyon College, Vanderbilt College and Louisiana State University. His mentors, true enough, were poets and knew poetry inside out, yet they were equally and more famously teachers, New Critics driven by a passion to pluck out the last secret of any poem by unearthing, if necessary, its seventh ambiguity. No wonder, then, that Lowell, in a late poem, wryly and accurately likened his early work to the seven-walled fortress of Troy, where meaning lay immured behind rings of highly wrought art. But at least that meant that he wrote, in the words of F. W. Dupee, 'as if poetry were still a major art and not merely a venerable pastime'. Among a strenuous and brilliant generation of poet-critics, praying to be obsessed by writing and having their prayers answered, Lowell not only strove to hold his own by mastering the classical, English, European and American poetic canons; he also strove to outstrip the level best of his peers by swerves that were all his own: doctrinal, ancestral, political. Doctrinal, when he converted to the Roman Catholic Church and betrayed not just a faith but a civic solidarity. Ancestral, when he invoked his dynastic right derived from the Winslows and the Lowells and presumed to rebuke the President. Political, when he went to gaol as a conscientious objector in 1943, having nevertheless volunteered (without response) for the Navy and the Army in the previous year.

It was in this act of conscientious objection that doctrine, ancestry and politics fused themselves in one commanding stroke and Lowell succeeded in uniting the aesthetic instinct with the obligation to witness morally and significantly in the public realm. Moreover, with what William Meredith once called his 'crooked brilliance', Lowell had combined political dissent with psychic liberation; the refusal of the draft was an affront to his family, another strike in the war of individuation and disengagement which he had so forcefully initiated when he flattened his father with one rebellious blow during his first year at Harvard in the late 1930s. Altogether, the refusal to enlist arose from some deep magma and had an igneous personal scald to it. It may have been the manic statement of a 'fire-breathing CO', but it did burn with a powerful disdainful rhetoric of election and recrimination.

President Roosevelt was first of all morally wrong-footed in Lowell's covering letter—'You will understand how painful such a decision is for an American whose family traditions, like your own, have always found their fulfillment in maintaining . . . our country's freedom and honor.' Then, in the public statement called 'Declaration of Personal Responsibility', the whole of American democracy was arraigned because of its Machiavellian contempt for the laws of justice and charity between nations. In its determination to wage a war 'without quarter or principles, to the permanent destruction of Germany and Japan', the United States was allying itself with 'the demagoguery and herd hypnosis of the totalitarian tyrannies' and had criminalized the good patriotic war begun in response to aggression in 1941. The usual summaries of this document tend to focus on Lowell's outrage at the Allies' immense indifference to the lives of civilians when they bombed Hamburg and the Ruhr; the main drift, as I understand it, is to accuse the United States of becoming like the tyrannies which it set out to oppose. Therefore, the statement concludes:

> after long deliberation on my responsibilities to myself, my country, and my ancestors who played responsible parts in its making, I have come to the conclusion that I cannot honorably participate in a war whose prosecution, as far as I can judge, constitutes a betrayal of my country.

Not unexpectedly, one detects here something of the note of a speech from the dock. Yet even granting that the profile is carefully posed for chivalric effect and that there is a certain strut to the moral carriage of the rhetoric, Lowell does achieve a credible and dignified withdrawal of assent. He is not unlike Yeats, on the first night of Sean O'Casey's *The Plough and the Stars*, rebuking the audience of the Abbey Theatre for disgracing themselves 'again'—which meant, of course, that they had thereby disgraced *him*. In each case, the habit of command was something which issued from the poet's caste. Admittedly, neither Yeats nor Lowell came from a family immediately involved in government or public affairs, but they nevertheless carried with them a sense of responsibility for their country, their culture and the future of both.

It was entirely characteristic of Lowell to have manoeuvred himself into a position where he could speak with superior force. It was rarely with him a case of 'Let this cup pass', but rather a matter of 'How can I get my hands *on* the cup?' Between the stylistic ardour of his early poems and such thoroughly plotted and savoured moments as the draft refusal, there is a discernible connection. It has to do with the determination to force an issue by pressure of will, by the plotting instinct which he would ultimately castigate in himself because it meant he ended up 'not avoiding injury to others' or to himself; it had to do, in other words, with the tactical, critical revising side of his nature. Lowell was always one to call out the opposition, to send the duelling note: there was an imperious strain even in his desire to embrace the role of witness. Yet the desire was authentic, and his conscientious objection can bear comparison with a corresponding instance of collision between individual moral conscience and the demands of the historical moment in the life of Osip Mandelstam.

Mandelstam, of course, lived in a tyranny and Lowell lived in a democracy. That is literally a vital distinction. Nevertheless, I think it is illuminating to set the crisis faced by Lowell in 1943 beside the crisis faced by the Russian poet in the early 1930s. At that time, after five years of poetic silence during which he had tried to make some inner accommodation with the Soviet system, Mandelstam had done something quite uncharacteristic. He had written his one and only poem of direct political comment, a set of couplets contemptuous of Stalin; and he compounded the crime by composing another document of immense rage and therapeutic force called 'Fourth Prose'. Both were self-cleansing acts and tragic preparations. Even though they dared not present themselves as public statements like Lowell's 'Declaration of Personal Responsibility', poem and prose were fatal declarations of that very responsibility and would lead not to prison but to death. It was as if Mandelstam were cutting the hair off his own neck in a gesture that signified his readiness for the guillotine; yet this was the only way in which his true voice and being could utter themselves, the only way in which his self-justification could occur. After this moment, the hedonism and jubilation of purely lyric creation developed an intrinsically moral dimension. The poet's double responsibility to tell a truth as well as to make a thing would henceforth be singly discharged in the formal achievement of the individual poem.

It would be an exaggeration and a presumption to equate Lowell's gesture with Mandelstam's sacrifice; yet I would suggest that Lowell's justification of his specifically poetry-writing self was won by his protest and his experience of gaol—in the same way as Mandelstam's airy liberation was earned at an even more awful price. Gaol set the *maudit* sign upon the brow of the blue-blooded boy. It made him the republic's Villon rather than its Virgil. It permitted him to feel that the discharge of violent energy from the cauldron of his nature had a positive witnessing function, that by forging the right poetic sound he was forging a conscience for the times.

The robust Symbolist opacity of the first books probably derives at least in part from some such personally authenticated conviction about poetry's rights and prerogatives. West Street Jail and the Danbury Correction Center provided the poet with a spiritual licence to withdraw from the language of the compromised tribe. From now on, the poetic task would be a matter of dense engagement with the medium itself. The percussion and brass sections of the language orchestra are driven hard and, in a great set piece like 'The Quaker Graveyard in Nantucket', the string section hardly gets a look-in. Distraught woodwinds surge across the soundscape; untamed and inconsolable discords ride the blast. Hart Crane, Dylan Thomas, Arthur Rimbaud, Lycidas himself—resurrected as a language of turbulent sea-sound—all of them press in at the four corners of the page, taut-cheeked genii of storm, intent on blowing their power into the centre of an Eastern Seaboard chart. The reader is caught in a gale-force of expressionism and

could be forgiven for thinking that Aeolus has it in for him personally. Here is, for example, Section V of the poem:

> When the whale's viscera go and the roll
> Of its corruption overruns this world,
> Beyond tree-swept Nantucket and Woods Hole
> And Martha's Vineyard, Sailor, will your sword
> Whistle and fall and sink into the fat?
> In the great ash-pit of Jehoshaphat
> The bones cry for the blood of the white whale,
> The fat flukes arch and whack about its ears,
> The death-lance churns into the sanctuary, tears
> The gun-blue swingle, heaving like a flail,
> And hacks the coiling life out: it works and drags
> And rips the sperm-whale's midriff into rags,
> Gobbets of blubber spill to wind and weather,
> Sailor, and gulls go round the stoven timbers
> Where the morning stars sing out together
> And thunder shakes the white surf and dismembers
> The red flag hammered in the mast-head. Hide,
> Our steel, Jonas Messias, in Thy side.

It is thrilling to put out in these conditions, to feel what Yeats
called 'the stirring of the beast', to come into the presence of sovereign diction and experience the tread of something metrical,
conscious and implacable. To say that such poetry has designs upon
us is about as understated as to say that Zeus introduced himself to
Leda in fancy dress. 'Take note, Hopkins', it cries. 'Take note,
Melville. And reader, take that!' Yet to enter a poetic career at this
pitch was to emulate Sam Goldwyn's quest for the ultimate in
movie excitement—something beginning with an earthquake and
working up to a climax. It was to create a monotone of majesty
which was bound to drown out the human note of the poet who
had aspired to majesty in the first place. Lawrence had talked
about the young poet putting his hand over his daimon's mouth,
but Lowell actually handed the daimon a megaphone. Somehow
the thing would have to be toned down, or else the command

established would quickly devolve into cacophony, something un-modulated and monomaniacal.

During the next decade, while a new style was readying itself, the shape of Lowell's life was also being established. In spite of the cruel cycles of mania, maybe even because of them, Lowell wrote extraordinarily and achieved eminence. By the time of his marriage to Elizabeth Hardwick and his entry upon the New York scene, he was a consolidated literary phenomenon, with the Pulitzer Prize and the Poetry Consultancy at the Library of Congress already behind him. One cannot ever be sure to what extent the crenellated mass of the early verse was a defence against the illness of his mind, or an emanation of it, but there is no doubting the strength of the work itself. What I want to focus upon now, however, is the not uncommon spectacle of a poet with just such a dear-won individual style facing into his forties and knowing that it will all have to be done again. Words by Anna Swir, whom I quoted in '*from* "The Government of the Tongue" ' (page 197), are again apposite:

> The goal of words in poetry is to grow up to the contents, yet that goal cannot ever be attained, for only a small part of the psychic energy which dwells in a poet incarnates itself in words. In fact, every poem has the right to ask for a new poetics . . . We could say in a paradoxical abbreviation that a writer has two tasks. The first—to create one's own style. The second—to destroy one's own style. The second is more difficult and takes more time.

Lowell did this second thing twice in his poetic life, and on each occasion knew what he was doing—which made it both more purposeful and more painstaking. When I say that he knew what he was doing, I don't mean that he had a prearranged programme of what he wished to achieve, some poetic equivalent of the blueprint in a painting-by-numbers kit. It is, rather, that the critical, teaching side of his mind was so unremittingly active that his command as a poet was never without self-consciousness, without—in the good Elizabethan sense—cunning; yet only a sensibility with a core of volcanic individual genius could have overcome his own artfulness. He could easily have got himself jammed in a Parnassian impasse, but instead the epoch-making *Life Studies* appeared in 1959, when Lowell was forty-two. Anna Swir's law was being proved for the first time in his career. He was later to recollect this period in a well-known account of his experience of reading his symbol-ridden, wilfully difficult early poems in California, to audiences accustomed to the loose-weave writing of the Beats. Already he had sensed 'that most of what [he] knew about writing was a hindrance', that his old work was 'stiff, humorless and encumbered by its ponderous stylistic armor'.

I am not going to rehearse further the attributes of the masterful new poetry which broke from the tegument of his old rhetoric. The main point to insist on is its freedom from the anxiety to sound canonical, the way it no longer stakes its right to be heard on the invocation and assimilation of literary tradition. A phrase of Mandelstam's will once again do critical service here, one taken from his prose work *Journey to Armenia*, where he exclaims: 'If I believe in the shadow of the oak and the steadfastness of speech articulation, how can I appreciate the present age?'

'The steadfastness of speech articulation': it characterizes the dominant music of Lowell's poetic prime, from *Life Studies* through *For the Union Dead* and *Near the Ocean*. But it also directs us to the very source of that music, in his conviction of the tongue's right to speak freely and soundingly, and a further conviction of its capacity, if not to unveil reality, then significantly to enrich it. These books often tangle with a great heavy web of subject-matter, autobiographical, cultural and political, yet they are not primarily interested in commentary or opinion about such subject-matter. Nor are they primarily interested in building stanzas like warehouses to store it. Rather, they are interested in how to make an event of it, how to project forms and energies in terms of it. They are not, of course, successful all the time, but when they do succeed, they rest their claims upon no authority other than the jurisdiction and vigour of their own artistic means.

The patrician repose of 'middle Lowell', the distance travelled from the anxious majesty of the early style, shows up significantly when we compare the protest Lowell made against his society's

waging of war in the 1940s with the one he made against the Vietnam War in the 1960s. On this later occasion, his refusal of an invitation to President Johnson's White House was done without
much clamour or histrionics. It was no longer a case of the writer
putting himself to the test by taking on the role of bard and scape-
goat. It was now rather the President who was to be on the defensive. Poetry, in the figure of this silvered Brahmin from Boston,
was calling upon policy to account for itself. Yet Lowell's authority
now resided in the mystery of his achieved art rather than in his
ancestry or in the justice of any public controversy he might
choose to initiate:

> When I was telephoned last week and asked to read at the White
> House Festival of the Arts on June fourteenth, I am afraid I ac-
> cepted somewhat rapidly and greedily. I thought of such an occa-
> sion as a purely artistic flourish, even though every serious artist
> knows that he cannot enjoy public celebration without making
> subtle public commitments. After a week's wondering, I have
> decided that I am conscience-bound to refuse your courteous in-
> vitation.

The books of Lowell's middle years, like this grave and well-
judged political protest, are wise to the world and wise about it.
'For the Union Dead' and 'Waking Early Sunday Morning' are two
of the finest public poems of our time, but they do not address the
world in order to correct it. They Lowellize it instead, make it ring,
make it a surface against which the poet's voice strikes, is caught
and thereby either amplifies itself or glances off. Here it is, ampli-
fying, at the conclusion of 'Waking Early':

> Pity the planet, all joy gone
> from this sweet volcanic cone;
> peace to our children when they fall
> in small war on the heels of small
> war—until the end of time
> to police the earth, a ghost
> orbiting forever lost
> in our monotonous sublime.

And here it is, in 'Middle Age', glancing off:

> Father, forgive me
> my injuries,
> as I forgive
> those I
> have injured!
>
> You never climbed
> Mount Sion, yet left
> dinosaur
> death-steps on the crust,
> where I must walk.

There will be more to say about this less assertive voice before we finish, but for the moment let us salute it as a good victory by Lowell over his ruling passion for sounding victorious, his temptation to raise the trumpet or let the left hand reinforce the right with a strongly affirmative or discordant bass. As he himself well knew, there was an 'incomparable wandering voice' within him which he often and habitually made the captive of what he also called his 'maze of iron composition'.

Those phrases came from the lovely, limber final sonnet in Lowell's book *The Dolphin* and form the last lines of the massive triptych composed in his fifties, comprising ultimately the three books called *History, For Lizzie and Harriet* and *The Dolphin*. If I here skim over the mighty heave of this work, it is not because I miss Lowell's command in the sound of its lines. On the contrary. These astonishingly, wilfully strong lines are too much under the sway of an imposed power. There is no doubt about the good artistic intentions of what he is doing, and no doubt about the foundry heat in which scores of the standard-mould, fourteen-line, unrhymed poem-ingots are being smelted and cast. To change the metaphor, one admires once again the spectacle of a poet taking the crowbar to a perfected style: these new, unmelodious, dumped-down forms are deliberate rebukes to the classical cadences of the volumes of the 1960s. Line by line, in local manifestations, the genius and sinuousness are still alive and well, but to confront the whole triptych is to confront a phalanx. I feel driven off the field of my reader's freedom by the massive riveted façade, the armoured tread, the unconceding density of it all.

What I wish to dwell upon instead is the gentler, autumnal work in Lowell's last collection, *Day by Day*. The effect of coming to it after the twelve-tone scale of these previous books is of moving from a works-floor ringing with the occasional treble beauty of that busy crowbar to a room full of canvases by, say, Bonnard. A roseate benevolence in the pigment, an unextinguished but ungreedy sensuality in the air, a warm-bloodedness at the centre or in the offing. The voice comes from pillow level rather than from a podium, indulgent but unfooled, schooled by mutuality but not yet schooled into mutuality, more inclined to wryness than pathos. It can cover a great distance in a single shift of tone or image or line. The typical effects are of ruminant talk ('Marriage' and 'Last Walk') or skewed proverbial wisdom ('For Sheridan') or a cross-cutting of these styles into each other ('Ants'). All of this does come, as a character in one of the poems desires it to, 'a little nearer / the language of the tribe', but its primary purpose is neither to curry favour with the reader nor to keep in ideological step with writing in the American grain. The poems proceed by free association, as Helen Vendler has observed; they are as tousled, amiably importunate and comfortably unpredictable as lovers weaving through warm rooms at the end of a slightly erotic, slightly drunken party.

All the same, the tone is not familiar or insinuatingly personal. There is a curious sensation of being kept at a remove while still being close enough to feel the excitement of impulses translating themselves into phrases. The mode pretends to dramatic personal utterance—Lowell talking to his wife, best friends, his son, himself—yet it keeps breaking into a note which is random, impersonal and oracular; 'things thrown in air', as one poem says, 'alive in flight', things resembling the scrapings that fly when 'the immortal is scraped unconsenting from the mortal'.

Lowell always had an inclination to launch such single lines and phrases across the sky of the poem and indeed in the blank sonnets had so tried to make poems blaze line by line that the reader could feel at times he was out bareheaded in a meteor

shower. Those poems were not so much loaded with ore as packed
with gold fillings, grinding in order to gleam. In *Day by Day*,
however, his ferocity has been calmed and replaced by a temperate
waft of either image or generalization. 'The elder flower is cham-
pagne', says one line which sails above the discourse of 'Milgate'.
'A false calm is the best calm', says an orphaned line in 'Suburban
Surf'. And so on: 'If you keep cutting your losses, / you have no loss
to cut' ('In the Ward'). 'If they have you by the neck, a rope will be
found' ('Domesday Book').

We have come far indeed from the kind of command this poet
sought and exercised in the early work, where the work was pile-
driven by metre and condensed allusions. Now the command is
achieved by the oddly tilted wisdom of the propositions, their
oblique clarity and applicability, their wistful strangeness. The
tone is not forced or forcing, the voice of the poem does not come
down upon you but rises towards its own surface. There is an aque-
ous rather than an igneous quality now to the poem's beginnings
and emergence, nowhere more so than in the opening poem of the
volume, called 'Ulysses and Circe', especially in Section V. This is
my favourite moment in the book. In the opening lines, Lowell retains an old bravura and at the end touches a muted Homeric note
of landfall. What happens in between is kaleidoscopic, a progress
of gnomic stanzas, little poem fragments in themselves, held together by the memory and voice of Ulysses.

This Ulysses comes on as a man on the verge of being posthumous to himself, ventriloquizing (through the autobiographical
voice of Robert Lowell) about his interlude with Circe, his sensual
self-knowledge and his appeased curiosities. Ulysses begins the
poem as a drowsy voluptuary and will end it as a killer about to
strike, thus acting as a kind of correlative for the poet caught between his marriages and his manias. The poem is spoken in a middle voice, neither dramatic monologue exactly nor confessional
lyric: enclosed in quotation marks, it rides an eddying course between the near shore of autobiography and the farther shore of
myth:

'Long awash and often touching bottom
by the sea's great green go-light

I found my exhaustion
the light of the world.

Earth isn't earth
if my eyes are on the moon,
her likeness caught
in the split-second of vacancy—

duplicitous,
open to all men, unfaithful.

After so many millennia,
Circe,
are you tired
of turning swine to swine?

How can I please you,
if I am not a man?

I have grown bleak-boned with survival—
I who hoped to leave the earth
younger than I came.

Age is the bilge
we cannot shake from the mop.

Age walks on our faces—
at the tunnel's end,
if faith can be believed,
our flesh will grow lighter.'

This poem does have its openness, yet at its core there is an intransigently charmless streak, and it is the combination of neuter stillness at the centre with something more tolerant and glamorous on the surface which makes it continuous with one of the loveliest and strangest moments in Lowell's early work. I am thinking of the Walsingham section of 'The Quaker Graveyard in Nantucket', where the locus of stillness was in the face of the statue of the Virgin, which, 'expressionless, expresses God'. Around this pivot of the unlovely, the oceanic symphonies swayed and thundered, and

they depended upon the statue's quietude more than upon the
massed instruments of the vocabulary for their ultimate effects of
turbulence and tragedy. The face was like a star whose light was
forever at the moment of arrival, an energy source. Why this figure of the Virgin should enter the poem could be explained
intellectually by contrasting her with the predatory, Calvinist,
blood-spilling whalers; poetically speaking, however, we sense its
rightness as a matter of emotional effect, a result of its timing and
placing. What it supplies is what T. S. Eliot was wanting to supply
in 'Little Gidding' when he wrote to John Hayward: 'The defect of
the whole poem, I feel, is the lack of some acute personal reminiscence (never to be explicated, of course, but to give power from
well below the surface).' It is just this sensation of power coming
from below the surface, without any need for explication, which
the reader finds in the Walsingham section of 'The Quaker Graveyard'.

I have digressed because I want to suggest that the virtue of the
best poems in *Day by Day* derives from their being similarly sustained by the up draught of energy from 'acute personal reminiscence'. Yet the reminiscence is itself unmysterious, coming from a
recent past or a just-sped present: what is uncanny is the feeling of
being at the eye of an agitation, in an emotional calm that is completely impersonal, a condition evenly distanced from the infinite
indifference on the minus side of the graph and the infinite serenity at the other extreme. At his best, Lowell can find the co-
ordinates for this point and beam in on a state that is neither stasis
nor crisis, more dynamic than the former, less precarious than the
latter. At less inspired moments, this genuine impassiveness is sim-
ulated: we encounter in its place an unremitting verbal determination to secure our dazed attention—something which happens
often enough in the books of blank sonnets to make the experience
of reading them disorienting.

Nothing disorienting about the poetry we have just read, however, *qua* poetry, no matter how disconcerting the things it has to
say about ageing and ending: 'Age is the bilge / we cannot shake
from the mop.' Repudiation, ripeness, greyness, aggravation—it's
all there, in the very mouthing of the syllables, from the fruity

corruption of 'age is the bilge', with its custardy vowels and gelati-
nate consonants, to the shudder and ineffectual vigour of 'we cannot shake from the mop'. This is heady and disintoxicating all at
once, exactly the kind of wisdom to vindicate the earlier claim to
preternatural clarity: 'I found my exhaustion/the light of the
world.' This poem manages to begin and carry on from the point
where *Samson Agonistes* ended in 'calm of mind, all passion spent'.
It is the poetic anti-world to the world of Sam Goldwyn's apocalyptic beginnings. Unlike the post-modern voice that speaks in
Derek Mahon's 'Lives' and 'knows too much to know anything any
more', Lowell's Ulysses retains a kind of ultimate heuristic joy.
Even though the single-mindedness of Dante's Ulysses would
seem to him simple-minded, and the rhetoric of Tennyson's in-
credible, the omniscient tone of this veteran sexual campaigner
does not preclude the possibility of further excitements. If the cadences do not move with any great long-swelled promise, neither
have they cancelled all expectation of a renewed shock from
experience.

It all represents the reappearance, fully developed, of a style
that had sweetened sour subjects a decade and a half earlier in *For
the Union Dead.* There, in poems of 'acute personal reminiscence',
such as 'Water' and 'The Old Flame', and in that seemingly casual
gloss called 'Middle Age', Lowell relaxed the method of decisive
confrontation which he had pursued in *Life Studies.* The readiness
for combat which characterized much of the earlier work was replaced by a mood still vigilant and nervy but not as feral or intensely directed.

This 'relaxed' poetry in *For the Union Dead* prefigures the
achievement of the best work in *Day by Day.* It wakens rather
than fixes. A few strokes, a notation, a bestirring and a saluting,
such casual means are typical of writing which is not in itself just
casual notation: little riddling units are lifted up into the condition
of poetry. These poems are pre-eminently events rather than the
record of events—as that wonderfully chaste and bare-handed
poem 'Fall 1961' demonstrates:

> All autumn, the chafe and jar
> of nuclear war;

we have talked our extinction to death.
I swim like a minnow
behind my studio window.

Our end drifts nearer,
the moon lifts,
radiant with terror.
The state
is a diver under a glass bell.

A father's no shield
for his child.
We are like a lot of wild
spiders crying together,
but without tears.

At such a moment, Lowell's poetry is beautifully equal to its occasion. It does not flex its literary muscle. Its tone is unemphatic, yet it derives from a kind of wisdom which knows itself to be indispensable even as it takes itself for granted. I suggest that Lowell's command finally came to reside in this self-denial, this readiness not to commandeer the poetic event but to let his insights speak their own riddling truths:

Past fifty, we learn with surprise and a sense
of suicidal absolution
that what we intended and failed
could never have happened—
and must be done better.

from The Indefatigable Hoof-Taps:
Sylvia Plath

The great appeal of Sylvia Plath's *Ariel* and its constellated lyrics is the feeling of irresistible given-ness. There inheres in this poetry a sense of surprised arrival, of astonished being. The poems were written quickly and they transmit to the reader something of the unexpectedness of their own becoming. There is the pressure of absolute *fiat* behind them; a set of images springs into presence and into motion as at a whimsical but unignorable command. They represent the extreme extension of the imagist mode, which Pound characterized as expressing an emotional and intellectual complex in a moment of time. Their metamorphic speed and metaphoric eagerness are boosted by the logic of their own associative power, and they rush towards whatever conclusions are inherent in their elements. These poems are the vehicles of their own impulses, and it was entirely right that the title which gathered them together should recall not only Shakespeare's pure spirit but also the headlong gallop of a runaway horse. They are full of exhilaration in themselves, the exhilaration of a mind that creates in some sort of mocking spirit, outstripping the person who has suffered. They move without hesitation and assume the right to be heard; they, the poems, are what we attend to, not the poet. They are, in Lowell's words, events rather than the records of events, and as such represent the triumph of Sylvia Plath's romantic ambition to bring expressive power and fully achieved selfhood into congruence. The tongue proceeds headily into its role as governor; it has located the source where the fixed stars are reflected and from which they transmit their spontaneous and weirdly trustworthy signals.

But before all this could occur, Plath's tongue was itself governed by the disciplines of metre, rhyme, etymology, assonance, enjambment. Even if her husband had not given us an image of her as the obedient neophyte, we could have deduced it from the procedures of her early verse. 'She wrote her early poems very slowly,' Ted Hughes tells us, 'thesaurus open on her knee, in her large, strange handwriting, like a mosaic, where every letter stands separate within the work, a hieroglyph to itself . . . Every poem grew complete from its own root, in that laborious inching way, as if she were working out a mathematical problem, chewing her lips, putting a thick dark ring of ink around each word that stirred her on the page of the thesaurus.' That would have been in the late 1950s, when Sylvia Plath was preparing the volume which would be published in 1960 in England as *The Colossus*, in the course of which she gradually focused her poetic attention inward and found a characteristic method of self-exploration.

This was sometimes based on the allegorization of personal experience into an emblem or icon, sometimes on the confounding of the autobiographical and the mythological. 'Full Fathom Five' and 'Lorelei', two poems based on her reading of Jacques Cousteau, are typical examples of this latter procedure. The autobiographical matter they draw upon includes the death of her father when she was a child of eight and the family's subsequent move inland from the sea, after which, as Plath wrote in 'Ocean 1212-W', 'those first nine years of my life sealed themselves off like a ship in a bottle— beautiful, inaccessible, obsolete, a fine, white flying myth.' The autobiographical element also includes a recognition of her suicide attempt in August 1953, and obviously takes some cognizance of the psychiatric treatment which ensued, with its conscious attempts at self-comprehension and self-renewal. But all this is secluded behind the literary and mythological aspects of the poems themselves, which are the products of a ripening skill . . .

I find in her poetic journey three stages which seem to exemplify three degrees of poetic achievement, and since I have always found it instructive to read a famous passage of Wordsworth as a parable of these three stages, I shall do so here in particular relation to Sylvia Plath's career. The passage in question is the one where Wordsworth writes about his young self whistling through his fingers to arouse the owls so that they would then call back to him;

but it especially evokes certain moments when he would be imposed upon by the power of the whole natural universe:

> There was a Boy; ye knew him well, ye cliffs
> And islands of Winander!—many a time,
> At evening, when the earliest stars began
> To move along the edges of the hills,
> Rising or setting, would he stand alone,
> Beneath the trees, or by the glimmering lake;
> And there, with fingers interwoven, both hands
> Pressed closely palm to palm and to his mouth
> Uplifted, he, as through an instrument,
> Blew mimic hootings to the silent owls,
> That they might answer him.—And they would shout
> Across the watery vale, and shout again,
> Responsive to his call,—with quivering peals,
> And long halloos, and screams, and echoes loud
> Redoubled and redoubled; concourse wild
> Of jocund din! And, when there came a pause
> Of silence such as baffled his best skill:
> Then sometimes, in that silence, while he hung
> Listening, a gentle shock of mild surprise
> Has carried far into his heart the voice
> Of mountain-torrents; or the visible scene
> Would enter unawares into his mind
> With all its solemn imagery, its rocks,
> Its woods, and that uncertain heaven received
> Into the bosom of the steady lake.

The first task of the poet—if I may proceed with my allegorization of this memorable passage—is to learn how to entwine his or her hands so that the whistle comes out right. This may seem a minimal achievement, yet those of you who have a memory of attempting to get it right will also remember the satisfaction and justification implicit in that primary act of sounding forth. People who learned to whistle on their thumbs, to trumpet and tu-whit, tu-whoo in the back seats of classrooms and the back seats of buses, would then be happy to perform this feat for its own sake, repeatedly, self-forgetfully and tirelessly. It was an original act of making, the equivalent in the oral/aural sphere of mud pies in the tactile/plastic sphere, and, as has been well observed, one of the chief pleasures of life is when I show you the mud pies I have made and you show me the mud pies you have made. In this trope, the little magazine can be understood as an echo chamber of owl whistles or a gallery of mud-pie life, and many a poetic career begins and ends with poems which do no more than cry out in innocent primary glee, 'Listen, I can do it! Look how well it turned out! And I can do it again! See?'

Sylvia Plath's first book contains several poems of this kind, beautifully tuned, half-rhymed and assonantal. In them, her craft-conscious fingers are twined and lifted at a careful angle, and her poetic breath is evenly, deliberately exhaled. Of course, it is not the only kind of work in *The Colossus*, but it is what is most immediately in evidence; on every page, a poet is serving notice that she has earned her credentials and knows her trade. Relish it along with me, she insinuates; isn't this well done? And it is indeed a pleasure to savour the dull, sea-clap music of a poem like 'Mussel Hunter at Rock Harbour':

> I came before the water-
> Colourists came to get the
> Good of the Cape light that scours
> Sand grit to sided crystal
> And buffs and sleeks the blunt hulls
> Of the three fishing smacks beached
> On the bank of the river's
>
> Backtracking tail. I'd come for
> Free fish-bait: the blue mussels
> Clumped like bulbs at the grass-root
> Margin of the tidal pools.
> Dawn tide stood dead low. I smelt
> Mud stench, shell guts, gull's leavings;
> Heard a queer crusty scrabble

Cease, and I neared the silenced
Edge of a cratered pool-bed.
The mussels hung dull blue and
Conspicuous, yet it seemed
A sly world's hinges had swung
Shut against me. All held still.
Though I counted scant seconds,

Enough ages lapsed to win
Confidence of safe-conduct
In the wavy otherworld
Eyeing me. Grass put forth claws;
Small mud knobs, nudged from under,
Displaced their domes as tiny
Knights might doff their casques . . .

This is a poem in syllabics, seven syllables to the line, seven lines to the stanza; it inches itself forward as the crabs do, as Ted Hughes said her poems did in the beginning, felicity by felicity. The movement is steady, onward, purposeful, yet we are also being encouraged to hesitate in this 'wavy otherworld' and to appreciate the slubbed texture of lines like 'The mussels hung dull blue and / Conspicuous, yet it seemed / A sly world's hinges had swung / Shut against me.' We are invited to indulge the poet ever so slightly, to allow her to raise her eye a fraction from the level of crabs to the level of casques. 'Casque', a word chivalric, plump and metallic, takes our eye off the object for a millimoment. We are, of course, happy to be so richly distracted, and the poem is not so fanatically engaged with its own purposes that it has not the leisure to take us by the elbow and point us towards the riches of its own linguistic estate. Indeed, the reader's pleasure comes from just this sense of being on a linguistic tour where the point of the outing is as much to relish the guide's vocabulary as to see what is being talked about.

So the poem goes about its business, which, like the crab's business, isn't 'fiddling'; but neither is it absolutely engaged until its final stanzas . . .

High on the airy thatching
Of the dense grasses I found
The husk of a fiddler-crab,
Intact, strangely strayed above

His world of mud—green colour
And innards bleached and blown off
Somewhere by much sun and wind;
There was no telling if he'd
Died recluse or suicide
Or headstrong Columbus crab.
The crab-face, etched and set there,

Grimaced as skulls grimace: it
Had an Oriental look,
A samurai death mask done
On a tiger tooth, less for
Art's sake than God's. Far from sea—
Where red-freckled crab-backs, claws
And whole crabs, dead, their soggy

Bellies pallid and upturned,
Perform their shambling waltzes
On the waves' dissolving turn
And return, losing themselves
Bit by bit to their friendly
Element—this relic saved
Face, to face the bald-faced sun.

Something really comes to life when we get to the husk of
that voyager beyond the herd's track, the 'headstrong Columbus
crab' . . . The skull image, the death mask, are here strangely vital.
What is truly malignant is that sea full of 'claws / And whole crabs,
dead, their soggy / Bellies pallid and upturned', performing 'their
shambling waltzes'. It is not necessary to know about Sylvia Plath's
1953 suicide attempt and her intent enterprise of self-renewal to
discover in the conclusion of this poem a drama of survival, the attainment of a dry, hard-won ledge beyond the welter and slippage

of Lethean temptations. And the convincing thing, poetically, is that all this is guaranteed by an energy beyond that mustered by the individual will. It seems managed 'less for/Art's sake than God's'. It is as if in obeying the dictates of her imagination and fastening upon the dead crab, Plath is orienting herself towards the dry hard pitch she will attain in the end, in poems like 'Words'. The crab husk is an art shape and a talisman, something we accept at a level deeper than the beautifully presented 'mussels/Clumped like bulbs'. These latter were literary owl-calls made through the careful fingers, but the crab husk awakens the owl-life in *us*, calls up answering calls in the twilight of our psyche and brings the poem over into the second level of poetic attainment which is implicit in Wordsworth's narrative.

When the vale fills with the actual cries of owls responding to the boy's art, we have an image of the classically empowered poet, the one who has got beyond scale-practising, the one who, as Wordsworth says in his Preface, rejoices in the spirit of life that is in him and is delighted to contemplate similar volitions and passions as manifested in the goings-on of the universe. This represents the poetry of relation, of ripple-and-wave effect upon audience; at this point, the poet's art has found ways by which distinctively personal subjects and emotional necessities can be made a common possession of the reader's. This, at its most prim, is a matter of the old 'what oft was thought but ne'er so well expressed' kind of thing. At its most enriching, it operates by virtue of skeins of language coming together as a dream-web which nets psyche to psyche in order to effect what Frost called 'a clarification', 'a momentary stay against confusion'—precisely the kind of moment which occurs at the end of 'Mussel Hunter at Rock Harbour'.

Ted Hughes has written about Sylvia Plath's breakthrough into her deeper self and her poetic fate: he locates the critical moment in her writing at the composition of the poem called 'Stones' . . . In this middle stretch of her journey, she practises the kind of poem adumbrated by Pound—in Canto I, for example—in which a first voice amplifies the scope of its utterance by invoking classical or legendary parallels. These poems are serenely of their age, in that the conventions of modernism and the insights of psychology are relayed in an idiom intensely personal, yet completely available. When we read, for example, the opening lines of 'Elm', the owls in our own dream branches begin to halloo in recognition:

> I know the bottom, she says. I know it with my great tap root:
> It is what you fear.
> I do not fear it: I have been there.

In his edition of the *Collected Poems*, Ted Hughes provides a note to 'Elm', and an earlier draft from which this deeply swayed final version emerged. There are still twenty-one worksheets to go, so the following represents only what Hughes calls 'a premature crystallization'. (The wych-elm which occasioned the poems grows on the shoulder of a moated prehistoric mound outside the house where Plath and Hughes lived.)

> She is not easy, she is not peaceful;
> She pulses like a heart on my hill.
> The moon snags in her intricate nervous system.
> I am excited seeing it there
> It is like something she has caught for me.
>
> The night is a blue pool; she is very still.
> At the centre she is still, very still with wisdom.
> The moon is let go, like a dead thing.
> Now she herself is darkening
> Into a dark world I cannot see at all.

The contrast between this unkindled, external voice and the final voice of 'I know the bottom, she says' is astonishing. The draft is analytical and unaroused, a case of ego glancing around on the surface of language. In fact, what Plath is doing here is packaging insights she had arrived at in another definitive tree poem called 'The Moon and the Yew Tree', a subject set by Ted Hughes, who writes in his 'Notes on the Chronological Order of Sylvia Plath's Poems':

Early one morning, in the dark, I saw the full moon setting on to a large yew that grows in the churchyard, and I suggested she make a poem of it. By midday, she had written it. It depressed me greatly. It's my suspicion that no poem can be a poem that is not a statement from the powers in control of our life, the ultimate suffering and decision in us.

'Elm' clearly comes from a similar place, from the ultimate suffering and decision in Sylvia Plath, but access to that place could not occur until the right rhythm began to turn under her tongue and the sentence-sounds started to roll like flywheels of the poetic voice. The ineffectual wing-beats of 'The night is a blue pool; she is very still. / At the centre she is still, very still with wisdom' are like the bird of poetry at the glass pane of intelligence, seeing where it needs to go but unable to gain entry. But the window glass is miraculously withdrawn, and deep free swoops into the blue pool and into the centre are effected with effortless penetration once the new lines begin to run:

> Is it the sea you hear in me,
> Its dissatisfactions?
> Or the voice of nothing, that was your madness?
>
> Love is a shadow.
> How you lie and cry after it.
> Listen: these are its hooves: it has gone off, like a horse.

Here too is dramatic evidence of another mark of high achievement, the interweaving of imaginative constants from different parts of the *oeuvre*. These hooves are related to the hooves of the runaway Ariel, just as they are also pre-echoes of the phantom hoof-taps of 'Words'.

The elm utters an elmy consciousness; it communicates in tree-speak: 'This is the rain now, this big hush'. But the elm speaks poet-consciousness also. What is exciting to observe in this poem is the mutation of voice; from being a relatively cool literary performance, aware of its behaviour as a stand-in for a tree, it gradually turns inward and intensifies. Somewhere in the middle, between a stanza like:

> I have suffered the atrocity of sunsets.
> Scorched to the root
> My red filaments burn and stand, a hand of wires

—between this immensely pleasurable mimesis and the far more disturbing expressionism of

> I am terrified by this dark thing
> That sleeps in me;
> All day I feel its soft, feathery turnings, its malignity

—between these two stanzas the poem has carried itself—and the poet, and the reader—from the realm of tactful, estimable writing to the headier, less prescribed realm of the inestimable. It is therefore no surprise to read in Ted Hughes's notes of 1970 that he perceives 'Elm' as the poem which initiates the final phase, that phase whose poems I attempted to characterize earlier as seeming to have sprung into being at the behest of some unforeseen but completely irresistible command.

I wish now to reapproach those last poems in terms of Wordsworth's passage. The third kind of poetry I find suggested there is that in which the poem's absolute business is an unconceding pursuit of poetic insight and poetic knowledge. We have passed the first stage, where poetic making was itself an end and an anxiety; and we have come through the second stage of social relation and emotional persuasion, where the owl-cry of the poems stimulates the answering owl-dream in the audience and 'strikes . . . as a remembrance'. In terms of the Wordsworth story, we have arrived at the point where the boy cannot make any noise with his hands:

> . . . And, when there came a pause
> Of silence such as baffled his best skill:
> Then sometimes, in that silence, while he hung
> Listening, a gentle shock of mild surprise

Has carried far into his heart the voice
Of mountain-torrents; or the visible scene
Would enter unawares into his mind
With all its solemn imagery, its rocks,
Its woods, and that uncertain heaven received
Into the bosom of the steady lake.

Here the boy—call him the poet—has his skill mocked; skill is no use any more; but in the balked silence there occurs something more wonderful than owl-calls. As he stands open like an eye or an ear, he becomes imprinted with all the melodies and hieroglyphs of the world; the workings of the active universe, to use another phrase from *The Prelude*, are echoed far inside him. This part of the story, then, suggests that degree of imaginative access where we feel the poem as a gift arising or descending beyond the poet's control, where direct contact is established with the image-cellar, the dream-bank, the word-hoard, the truth-cave—whatever place a poem like Yeats's 'Long-Legged Fly' emerges from. What Sylvia Plath wrote in those days of somnambulist poetic certitude belongs with that *kind* of poetry. There is an absoluteness about the tone and a sudden in-placeness about the words and all that they stand for, as in the poem 'Edge'. This is perhaps the last she wrote, perhaps the second last, one of two completed on 5 February 1963, six days before her suicide:

> The woman is perfected.
> Her dead
>
> Body wears the smile of accomplishment,
> The illusion of a Greek necessity
>
> Flows in the scrolls of her toga,
> Her bare
>
> Feet seem to be saying:
> We have come so far, it is over.
>
> Each dead child coiled, a white serpent,
> One at each little

Pitcher of milk, now empty.
She has folded

Them back into her body as petals
Of a rose close when the garden

Stiffens and odours bleed
From the sweet, deep throats of the night flower.

The moon has nothing to be sad about,
Staring from her hood of bone.

She is used to this sort of thing.
Her blacks crackle and drag.

Here is an objectivity, a perfected economy of line, a swift, sure-handed marking of the time and space which had been in waiting for this poem. 'Boldness in face of the blank sheet', which Pasternak declared one of the attributes of talent, was never more in evidence. The firmed-up quality of the writing, its implacably indicative mood, mimes the finality of the woman's death. Even though consoling images of grave goods and children enfolded as petals are given due admittance, the overall temperature is that of a morgue. The bone-hooded moon and the bare feet share a chilly sort of dead-weight factuality. Never were the demands of Archibald MacLeish's 'Ars Poetica' so thoroughly fulfilled:

A poem should be palpable and mute
As a globed fruit,

Dumb
As old medallions to the thumb . . .

A poem should be equal to:
Not true . . .

A poem should not mean
But be.

There is a mute, palpable, equal-to 'being' about 'Edge' which insists that we read it as a thing sufficient within itself, which it certainly is. But it is also problematically something else. A suicide note, to put it extremely. An act of catharsis and defence, maybe, or maybe an act of preparation. The 'being' of this poetry, in other words, is constantly being pressed with meanings that sprang upon it the moment Sylvia Plath died by her own hand. Even an image like the dead crab, strayed headstrongly beyond his fellows, is retrospectively canvassed to serve the plot of suicide's progress. I would prefer to read the crab image as I believe the poem wants us to read it: as a relic that saved face, a talisman which helped the protagonist to face the bald-faced sun, an earnest of art's positively salubrious resistance to the shambling pull of the death-wish. I would also want to contend that the most valuable part of the late Plath *oeuvre* is that in which bitterness and the embrace of oblivion have been wrestled into some kind of submission or have been held at least in momentary equilibrium by the essentially gratifying force of the lyric impulse itself. A poem like 'Daddy', however brilliant a *tour de force* it can be acknowledged to be, and however its violence and vindictiveness can be understood or excused in light of the poet's parental and marital relations, remains, nevertheless, so entangled in biographical circumstances and rampages so permissively in the history of other people's sorrows that it simply overdraws its rights to our sympathy . . .

There is nothing *poetically* flawed about Plath's work. What may finally limit it is its dominant theme of self-discovery and self-definition, even though this concern must be understood as a valiantly unremitting campaign against the black hole of depression and suicide. I do not suggest that the self is not the proper arena of poetry. But I believe that the greatest work occurs when a certain self-forgetfulness is attained, or at least a fullness of self-possession denied to Sylvia Plath. Her use of myth, for example, tends to confine the widest suggestions of the original to particular applications within her own life. This is obviously truer at the beginning of her career, and does not apply to such firsthand 'mythic' occasions as 'Elm'. Nevertheless, her clued-in literary intelligence never quite ceased to inspect the given emotional and biographical matter for its translatability into parallel terms of literature or legend. In a poem like 'Ariel', the rewards are patent: the original allusion both swallows and is swallowed by the autobiographical occasion, and there is no sense of one element commandeering the other. In 'Lady Lazarus', however, the cultural resonance of the original story is harnessed to a vehemently self-justifying purpose, so that the supra-personal dimensions of knowledge—to which myth typically gives access—are slighted in favour of the intense personal needs of the poet.

But even as one searches for a way to express what one senses as a limitation, one remembers this poet's youth and remembers also that it was precisely those 'intense personal needs' which gave her work its unprecedented pitch and scald. Her poems already belong to the tradition not just because they fulfil the poetic needs I outlined at the beginning—those considerations of tone, speech and dramatic enactment—but also because they are clearly acts of her being, words from which, in Buber's terms, effective power streams. They demonstrate the truth of Wordsworth's wonderful formulation, in his 1802 Preface to *Lyrical Ballads*, of the way poetic knowledge gets expressed. Wordsworth's account is the finest I know of the problematic relation between artistic excellence and truth, between Ariel and Prospero, between poetry as impulse and poetry as criticism of life. The following quotation includes a perhaps overfamiliar sentence, and may show some syntactical strain, but it covers a lot of the essential ground:

Not that I mean to say, that I always began to write with a distinct purpose formally conceived; but I believe that my habits of meditation have so formed my feelings, as that my description of such objects as strongly excite those feelings, will be found to carry along with them a *purpose*. If in this opinion I am mistaken, I can have little right to the name of a poet. For all good poetry is the spontaneous overflow of powerful feelings: but though this is true, poems to which any value can be attached, were never produced on any variety of subjects but by a man, who being possessed of more than usual organic sensibility, had also thought long and deeply. For our continued influxes of feeling are modified and directed by our thoughts, which are indeed the representatives of all our past feelings; and, as by contemplating the relation of these general representatives to each other we discover what is really important to men, so by the repetition and continuance of this act, our feelings will be connected with important subjects, till at length, if we be originally possessed of much sensibility, such habits of mind will be produced, that, by obeying blindly and mechanically the impulses of those habits, we shall describe objects, and utter sentiments, of such a nature and in such connection with each other, that the understanding of the being to whom we address ourselves, if he be in a healthful state of association, must necessarily be in some degree enlightened, and his affections ameliorated.

Essentially, Wordsworth declares that what counts is the quality, intensity and breadth of the poet's concerns between the moments of writing, the gravity and purity of the mind's appetites and applications between moments of inspiration. This is what determines the ultimate human value of the act of poetry. That act remains free, self-governing, self-seeking, but the worth of the booty it brings back from its raid upon the inarticulate will depend upon the emotional capacity, intellectual resource and general civilization which the articulate poet maintains between the raids.

The Place of Writing

The usual assumption, when we speak of writers and place, is that the writer stands in some directly expressive or interpretative relationship to the milieu. He or she becomes a voice of the spirit of the region. The writing is infused with the atmosphere, physical and emotional, of a certain landscape or seascape, and while the writer's immediate purpose may not have any direct bearing upon the regional or national background, the background is sensed as a distinctive element in the work.

This filial relationship with region did indeed work for the young Yeats, and the Sligo countryside should arguably be called the Young Yeats Country. But in this lecture I am concerned with the poet from the age of fifty onward, establishing an outpost of poetic reality in the shape of a physical landmark, a poet with a domineering rather than a grateful relation to place, one whose poems have created a country of the mind rather than the other way round (and the more usual way), where the country has created the mind which in turn creates the poems.

Consider, for example, Thomas Hardy's home in Dorset, in the hamlet of Upper Bockhampton. Set among the trees, deep at the centre of a web of paths and byroads, in the matured stillness of an old garden, small-windowed, dark-ceilinged, stone-floored, hip-thatched, the Hardy birthplace embodies the feel of a way of life native to the place. It suggests a common heritage, an adherence to the hearth world of Wessex. If it is secret, it is not singular. We recognize a consonance between the inside and outside of that house and the centre and circumference of Hardy's vision. Hardy country, in other words, predated Hardy. It awaited its expression. Its ballad memory, its Romano-Celtic twilights and nineteenth-century dawns, all of which are part of the phantasmagoria of

Hardy's work, were already immanent there and were part of that from which Hardy sprang. He did not impose Hardyness upon his landscape the way Yeats imposed Yeatsness upon his. He was patient rather than peremptory, bearing the given life rather than overbearing it. Hardy's eye was as watchful and withdrawn as the little window at the back of his birthplace through which his mason father doled out wages to the workmen. But it was nevertheless an eye which functioned within its community as unremarkably as the hatch functioned in the wall.

Or take Max Gate, the house Hardy designed and had built for himself on the outskirts of Dorchester, the house that proclaimed him the distinguished writer rather than the son of a Bockhampton builder: here the emblematic meaning is greatly different from the meaning of the tower which Yeats restored for himself and his wife at a corresponding moment of his career. Even if we recognize a significance in its alignment with the birthplace across the fields, Max Gate does not seek the status of monument. It is a red-brick dwelling place which belongs to the fashion of its period and maintains the decorum of its suburb. It both embraces and embodies ordinariness, if only as a camouflage or a retreat; it certainly does not proclaim itself or its inhabitant as an original, a founder, a keeper, a sentry or a besieged one.

Yeats admittedly spent most of his life in houses which were equally machines for living in. The house where he was born on Sandymount Avenue in Dublin remains the usual semi-detached, mid-Victorian, bay-windowed, steps-and-basement type of residence which would be hard to mythologize beyond its solid bourgeois respectability. The same is true of his apartments in Bloomsbury and the town house in Dublin's Merrion Square which was his main base during the very time when the later tower poems were being written. These addresses were not significant and would not be made to signify in terms of Yeats's imagining. They remained structures which would never become symbols. They were places where Yeats would remain his unwritten self.

But a Norman keep in the Barony of Kiltartan, dating from the thirteenth or fourteenth century, descending from the great line of the de Burgos and registered in *The Booke of Connaught* at the end of the sixteenth century, this was a very different matter. Even though Yeats bought it for £35 from a government body called, with an unromantic grimness, the Congested Districts Board, it retained for him the aura of its historically resonant past and became a verifying force within his mind. It sponsored an attitude and a style, attained in his books a fabulous second dimension that would eventually transform its original status as a picturesque antiquity in the fields of Ballylee . . .

Three years had passed between Yeats's purchase of the tower in 1916 and that summer of 1919 when he and his wife, George, moved in; but even then, the residence was never to be permanent. Thoor Ballylee remained a kind of summer home, occupied occasionally by the family between 1919 and 1928, after which date their visits ceased altogether. By then, Yeats's health had begun to fail. Moreover, in 1928 the volume of poems entitled *The Tower* appeared, and its sequel, *The Winding Stair* (1933), had been conceived. The tower had now entered so deeply into the prophetic strains of his voice that it could be invoked without being inhabited. He no longer needed to live in it since he had attained a state in which he lived *by* it.

To call it a summer home, then, is really slightly off the mark, since it is obvious that the tower's first function was not domestic. Here he was in the place of writing. It was one of his singing schools, one of the soul's monuments of its own magnificence. His other addresses were necessary shelters, but Ballylee was a sacramental site, an outward sign of an inner grace. The posture of the building corresponded to the posture he would attain. The stone in all its obstinacy and stillness, the plumb bulk and resistant profile of the keep, the dream form and the brute fact simultaneously impressed on mind and senses, all this transmission of sensation and symbolic aura made the actual building stones into touchstones for the work he would aspire to. And that work would have to be a holding action in the face of old age, death and the disintegrating civilization which he, 'Heart smitten with emotion', perceived in its decline.

One of the first functions of a poem, after all, is to satisfy a

need in the poet. The achievement of a sufficient form and fulfilling music has a justifying effect within his life. And if the horizons
inside which the poet lives are menacing, the need for the steady-
ing gift of finished art becomes all the more urgent. So it is in the
light of just such a constantly flickering horizon of violence and
breakdown that we must read the tower poems and much else of
Yeats's work at this period.

The Easter Rising had occurred in Dublin a few months before
his negotiations with the Congested Districts Board in 1916. The
Battle of the Somme was fought that summer also. The Russian
Revolution broke out in 1917. From 1919 onward, the war of independence was in full swing in Ireland, and between 1922 and 1923
the civil war got close enough to Ballylee for the builder Thomas
Rafferty to get shot, for the bridge outside the tower to get blown
up and for the mind of this most public-spirited of poets to be
darkened by a sense of personal danger and civic collapse.

In the title poem of *The Tower* volume, Thoor Ballylee is a
podium from which the spirit's voice is resolutely projected. In the
third section, the tower's stoniness is repeated in the lean, clean-
chiselled, high-built verse-form; its head-clearing airiness is present in the rise and enjambment of the three-stressed line. Indeed,
the tower is now not just an embodied attitude or symbol of loyalties but also a locus of energy. Inevitably, it continues to affiliate
Yeats with his Anglo-Irish caste and casts him as its self-appointed
panegyrist. But it also marks an original space where utterance and
being are synonymous. This section of 'The Tower' so strives to
transcend its personal and historical occasion that it reminds us of
the exultation and absolutism of another tower-dwelling visionary,
Rainer Maria Rilke. It was Rilke who declared in his third sonnet
to Orpheus, written in 1922, only a few years before Yeats's poem,
that *Gesang ist Dasein*, singing is being, or song is reality, phrases
that could easily stand as epigraph to Yeats's superb peroration:

> Now shall I make my soul,
> Compelling it to study

In a learned school
Till the wreck of body,
Slow decay of blood,
Testy delirium
Or dull decrepitude,
Or what worse evil come—
The death of friends, or death
Of every brilliant eye
That made a catch in the breath—
Seem but the clouds of the sky
When the horizon fades;
Or a bird's sleepy cry
Among the deepening shades.

One brilliant eye which had made a catch in the breath in nineteenth-century Ballylee was the beauty Mary Hynes, celebrated in song by the blind poet Anthony Raftery. Both of them are invoked in an earlier part of 'The Tower', but all through this period of his writing, Yeats was in the situation dramatized by Raftery in the last stanza of his most famous poem:

Féach anois mé,
Mo chúl le balla,
Ag seinm ceoil
Le póchaí folaimh.

Look at me now,
My back to a wall,
Playing the music
To empty pockets.

When he quartered himself and his poetry in Thoor Ballylee, Yeats, too, had been backed into an extreme position. He was being compelled by his years and his times into a new awareness of himself as his own solitary protagonist out on the mortal arena, and then suddenly, in that needy space, a tower ascended. Not a tree, as in Rilke's first sonnet to Orpheus, not a natural given miracle, but a built-up, lived-with, deliberately adhered-to tower. Yet by now that tower is as deep inside our hearing as the temple which Rilke imagines the god Orpheus building inside the consciousness of the listening creatures. Before the visitation of the god's song, their ear was full of humble, unselftrusting creaturely life, shabby huts full of common speech and unpoetic desultoriness. But his song brought about a marvel:

A tree ascended there. Oh pure transcendence!
Oh Orpheus sings! Oh tall tree in the ear!
And all things hushed. Yet even in that silence
a new beginning, beckoning, change appeared.

Creatures of stillness crowded from the bright
unbound forest, out of their lairs and nests:
and it was not from any dullness, not
from fear, that they were so quiet in themselves,

but from simply listening. Bellow, roar, shriek
seemed small inside their hearts. And where there had been
just a makeshift hut to receive the music,

a shelter nailed up out of their darkest longing,
with an entryway that shuddered in the wind—
you built a temple deep inside their hearing.

(Translation by Stephen Mitchell)

That sense of a temple inside the hearing, of an undeniable acoustic architecture, of a written vaulting, of the firmness and in-placeness and undislodgeableness of poetic form, that is one of Yeats's great gifts to our century; and his ability to achieve it was due in no small measure to the 'beckoning', the 'new beginning', the 'pure transcendence' of an old Norman castle in Ballylee, a place that was nowhere until it was a written place.

Yet we must go further, since Yeats himself went further. Another of his gifts was his own boldness to question the final value and trustworthiness of this powerfully composed tower in the ear—for it is a mark of fully achieved poetry that it shirks none of the challenges that the fully awakened intelligence can offer it. The last stanza of 'All Souls' Night', for example, represents all the positive force that Yeats's tower-schooled mind could command: his prayer for concentration is itself focused and shining with an inward, self-illuminating ardour:

> Such thought—such thought have I that hold it tight
> Till meditation master all its parts,
> Nothing can stay my glance
> Until that glance run in the world's despite
> To where the damned have howled away their hearts,
> And where the blessed dance;
> Such thought, that in it bound
> I need no other thing,
> Wound in mind's wandering
> As mummies in the mummy-cloth are wound.

I have talked about this kind of centred, purposeful writing because it is what we rejoice in most immediately in Yeats's poems. Here conviction arises out of the very words in which it is sought, and stamina has been conjured by the strong expression of the poet's need for it. But, as Richard Ellmann has insisted, the credibility of this art is ultimately guaranteed by Yeats's readiness to doubt its efficaciousness. The very power of his desire for foundedness should alert us to the fear of unfoundedness which lurks beneath it. It is Yeats's greatest triumph that he could acknowledge this possibility and yet maintain a resolute faith in the worth of artistic creation. In a late poem like 'The Man and the Echo', the much-vaunted insulation of the tower-dweller is helpless against the unaccommodated cry of suffering nature. The man's composure is certainly assailed by the mocking echo of his own doubting mind, but it is finally most vulnerable to the yelp of pain in a hurt creature:

> But hush, for I have lost the theme,
> Its joy or night seem but a dream;
> Up there some hawk or owl has struck,

> Dropping out of sky or rock,
> A stricken rabbit is crying out,
> And its cry distracts my thought.

It is the triumph of this art to confront a despair at the very notion of art *as* triumph. Yet it also manages to wrest from the confrontation with such despair a margin of trust that makes the renewal of artistic effort contemplatable. Behind the large firm gestures of Yeats's last poems, where the humanist effort is racked upon a wheel that is a paradigm of hollowness, we can already make out the shuffling, unappeasable decrepitude of Beckett's heroes going on refusing to go on . . .

'The Black Tower' is the last poem which Yeats composed. It dramatizes, with deliberate offhandedness, a dialectic between the spirit's affirmative impulses and the mind's capacity to ironize and mock those impulses as self-serving fictions. Indomitable spirit is reflected in an ancient image of warriors buried in a standing position, signifying their eternal vigilance and oath-bound fidelity to the cause that unified them during their lives. The ironist and questioner is their old cook, who represents a kind of unheroic life-force, a scuttling principle of survival and self-preservation. He embodies all that Cuchulain had come to terms with in 'Cuchulain Comforted', the poem where Yeats sends the hero into the underworld and makes him consort with ' "Convicted cowards . . . by kindred slain / Or driven from home and left to die in fear." ' Yet the cook's scepticism is resisted by the *comitatus*; they persist at their post even as they are pestered by his rumours and heckling. They are like T. S. Eliot's magi journeying towards an ambiguous epiphany with voices singing in their ears that this may be all folly:

> Say that the men of the old black tower
> Though they but feed as the goatherd feeds,
> Their money spent, their wine gone sour,
> Lack nothing that a soldier needs,
> That all are oath-bound men:
> Those banners come not in.

There in the tomb stand the dead upright,
But winds come up from the shore:
They shake when the winds roar,
Old bones upon the mountain shake.

In this final appearance of Thoor Ballylee in Yeats's poetry, it stands fast and Yeats stands by it. Both tower and poet stand, as Macbeth and Macbeth's castle once stood, suspended in art time, ratified by prophetic utterance. In Shakespeare's play, Macbeth's sense of inviolable sanctuary was based on oracles delivered to him when the witches prophesied that he would be safe until Birnam Wood should come to Dunsinane. Yeats, on the other hand, had written his own oracles to himself and created a fortified space within the rooms of many powerfully vaulted stanzas. But just as the witches equivocated and the world as a wood of trees moved unthinkably to dislodge Macbeth, so in the end the Yeatsian keep of tragic commitment and loyalty is assailed by mutinous doubts about the ultimate value of what there is to keep. Nevertheless, the Yeatsian drama ends with the poet as Macbeth, still pacing the battlements, just acknowledging the tremor on the fringes of Birnam but refusing to allow his countenance to quail. The tower as emblem of adversity, as the place of writing, has taken on a final aspect as icon of the absurd.

2. ON THOMAS KINSELLA

If Paul Muldoon has rewritten the Yeatsian *immram* and punished the longing and complaint of *The Wanderings of Oisin* with his prodigiously knowledgeable longer poems such as 'Immram' itself and 'The More a Man Has the More a Man Wants', it is Thomas Kinsella, his senior by some twenty-odd years, who has engaged the mature Yeats's compulsion to be in love and to love what vanishes. Since the late 1960s, this deeply responsible poet has been absorbed in a slowly purposeful, heroically undeflected work of personal and national inquisition. From his early, formal and syntactically compact poems of the 1950s, when he defined his purpose as the quest for honesty in love and art, to his more recent open-weave, semi-expressionist explorations of the roots of consciousness, the muscle tone of Kinsella's poetry has always been in perfect order. The subject of much of his work is found in the ever-present wash of acedia and inanition round the edges of a life or a purpose, yet the pitch of the work is antithetically intense and capable.

Two short poems from different periods of his career will be enough to show how Kinsella's technical and imaginative processes have developed. The first is from a sequence of tightly rhymed and strictly argued epigrams entitled *Moralities*, which appeared in 1960. The sequence has four divisions subtitled, with challenging bareness, 'Faith', 'Love', 'Death' and 'Song'. Halfway through, between the emblem poems on love and those on death, comes this quotation, out of series, entitled 'Interlude':

> Love's doubts enrich my words; I stroke them out.
> To each felicity, once. He must progress
> Who fabricates a path, though all about
> Death, Woman, Spring, repeat their first success.

To encounter 'Death, Woman, Spring,' especially in this capitalized state, is to be reminded of Robert Graves's grammar of poetic myth, *The White Goddess*; there Graves elaborates his conviction that there is one theme, one story and one story only, behind true poems, since they all recount some episode in the eternal struggle between the god of the waxing year and the god of the waning year for the hand of the goddess. This is another way of expressing what Yeats was seeking to give shape to in his model of reality as two interpenetrating cones or gyres, the one waning to an apex where the other waxes to a base. It is also another aspect of the cornucopia developing its image out of its negative in the empty shell. Kinsella comes through as a poet helplessly burdened with all the recognitions that these schemes hold up to the mind's eye for contemplation.

The first line of his 'Interlude' keeps the ball of meaning in the air, fleetly bouncing back off the wall of one possibility to the opposite wall, to and fro across a definitely placed caesura: 'Love's doubts enrich my words; I stroke them out.' So does he stroke out the words or does he stroke out the doubts? If he strokes out the doubts and keeps the enriched words, there is no honesty either in the words or in the love. If he strokes out the words, there is no honest acknowledgement that love's doubts are the corollary of love's enrichments. It is a bind from which he would not be released because of an imposed discipline of understanding. The voice of that discipline is the true voice of Kinsella's muse; in the contexts of sexual and domestic love, biological and spiritual survival, physical and psychological exhaustions and renewals—all of which Kinsella takes for granted as what he calls simply 'the ordeal'—this muse speaks the same command over and over again throughout Kinsella's poetry. Deeper, she says. Further. Don't repose in the first resolution of your predicament. That resolution too is a predicament. What more? 'Nothing will come of nothing. Speak again.' Forge on. Fabricate the path.

> Love's doubts enrich my words; I stroke them out.
> To each felicity, once. He must progress
> Who fabricates a path, though all about
> Death, Woman, Spring, repeat their first success.

The formal ancestry of 'Interlude' may include the Auden of 'Death of a Tyrant' and the epigrammatic side of Pope and Donne and Jonson. But the formal ancestry of the later short poem which I will read goes back to early Irish glosses, those brief rhapsodies of the scribe in the margin as he turns from the illumination of the Latin of Holy Writ to make free in the Old Irish vernacular. Often these verses catch a glimpse of a creature—a blackbird or a seal or a cat—or of a joyful moment in the wood. The radiance of a God-filled and divinely ordained nature is implicit in each little pleasure-spurt from the hermit's pen. In Kinsella's gloss, on the other hand, a post-Darwinian nature instructs the self in the necessity of constant self-digestion: this is a necessary condition of self-creation, a law of psychic life that is discernible analogically at the extremes of the biological life. The poem is entitled 'Leaf-Eater':

On a shrub in the heart of the garden,
On an outer leaf, a grub twists
Half its body, a tendril,
This way and that in blind
Space: no leaf or twig
Anywhere in reach; then gropes
Back on itself and begins
To eat its own leaf.

This appeared in Kinsella's volume *Nightwalker and Other Poems* (1968). In that book, he was negotiating his transition from an earlier poetry that had been informed by the regular strains of the English poetic line and operated within an English tradition of meditative or witty poems of definite closure. *Nightwalker* moved towards a different poetry of the open, modernist, Poundian sort, responsive and ongoing, disinclined to the sedateness of traditional stanzaic articulation, content to be fluid and fragmented, yet never mistaking the randomness of this method for permission to slacken the intellectual grip. The more open Kinsella's poetry becomes formally, the more insistent and integrated becomes its obsession with 'the theme'. His recoil from the entropic conditions of the modern Irish scene into the nutrient original deposits of early Irish literary and legendary matter finds its analogue in the leaf-eater's recoil as a solution to its predicament. 'I feed upon it still, as you see', he declares in another context. In yet another, the grub's energies that waved with exploratory zeal on the edge of a leaf are mirrored in an image of a questing, founding consciousness: 'A maggot of the possible / wriggled out of the spine / into the brain.'

These lines are taken from 'Finistère', a poem in Kinsella's strong late manner. In it, Kinsella deliberately embarks upon the mythic method of Pound's early cantos, where psychic and literary faring forth is commingled with the venturings of Homeric and Ovidian heroes. In Kinsella's case, the mythic history of Ireland, as told in the early part of *The Book of Invasions*, provides the wave on which his individual poetic voice can row along. In particular, Kinsella fixes on the arrival in Ireland of the sons of Mil, the sup-planters not only of the Formorian denizens but also of the Tuatha Dé Danaan. Along with Mil and his people there arrives, as the voice of their collective wisdom and purpose, the bard Amergin, ur-poet of the island of Ireland. Through the reappropriation of Amergin's old lines, Kinsella once again rehearses the motif of re-newal at the point of exhaustion; the tremor of development ar-rives involuntarily out of the detritus of a previous life: 'A maggot of the possible / wriggled out of the spine / into the brain.' This is an image of the stirred power experienced by Amergin when he set foot on the land and spoke the prophetic lines which Kinsella appropriates in order to transmit a feeling of his own empower-ment. This new capacity for accommodating (within the ordering principle of the archetype) both the data of the contemporary and the poet's own autobiographical projects has vastly extended Kin-sella's poetic scope and produced a body of work that marks an important stage in the evolution not just of Irish poetry but of modern poetry in English.

The peculiar modernity of it has much to do with the enforce-ment of a recognition which Ellmann pointed to in Yeats—that nothingness could be pregnant as well as empty. This recognition is orchestrated fully in a strange poem called 'Hen Woman', the anecdotal base of which is quickly stated. In a local yard, on a still,

sunlit afternoon, a child watches with eye-popping, almost erotic
fascination as an egg begins to be laid by a hen. The thing is played
in slow motion; the egg appears in the sphincter, the woman of the
house rushes to catch it, misses, the egg falls and breaks on an iron
grating, spills down into the sewage, is wasted, gone, lost, like seed
that falls on barren ground, like spilled potential, obliterated possibility, whatever. Yet just as the fall of a sparrow is to the heavenly
Father a matter of infinite concern, to be cherished throughout all
eternity, so the fall of an egg places absolute demands upon poetic
imagination and tests its ability to plump the shell with its own
ghostly plenitude:

> I feed upon it still, as you see;
> there is no end to that which,
> not understood, may yet be noted
> and hoarded in the imagination,
> in the yolk of one's being, so to speak,
> there to undergo its (quite animal) growth,
> dividing blindly,
> twitching, packed with will,
> searching in its own tissue
> for the structure
> in which it may wake.
> Something that had—clenched
> in its cave—not been
> now was: an egg of being.
> Through what seemed a whole year it fell
> —as it still falls, for me,
> solid and light, the red gold beating
> in its silvery womb,
> alive as the yolk and white
> of my eye; as it will continue
> to fall, probably, until I die,
> through the vast indifferent spaces
> with which I am empty.

'I only know things seem and are not good', says Kinsella, in the
first line of 'Nightwalker'. And in the last, 'I think this is the Sea of

Disappointment.' And he once confessed, in relation to his annual moves between a home in Dublin and a professorship at Temple University in Philadelphia, that while he found it more and more necessary to return to Ireland, he also found it less and less rewarding. All this is of a piece with the extremity and exactions that characterize his poetic achievement. Indeed, when Yeats declared, 'Those men that in their writings are most wise / Own nothing but their blind, stupefied hearts', he was giving us a way of reading Kinsella, a poet who has discovered a completely satisfactory form for his dissatisfactions and sense of incompleteness.

This is not the place to explicate the coherence of Kinsella's *oeuvre*. Suffice it to say that he has ingested loss—of a literature in the Irish language, of a political vision in post-independence Ireland, of all that time robs from the original resources of the individual psyche—and has remembered it in an art that has the effect of restitution. The place of waste, the place of renewal and the place of writing have become coterminous within his poetry— and nowhere more luminously than in the concluding lines of 'His Father's Hands'. This poem recounts, among other things, how the child poet used to hammer into a wooden block little nails which his cobbler grandfather used for shoe repairs; in the end, even these unregarded trivia are made to swarm with larval possibility, retrieved by memory and hatched into a second life by the intent imagination:

> Extraordinary . . . The big block—I found it
> years afterward in a corner of the yard
> in sunlight after rain
> and stood it up, wet and black:
> it turned under my hands, an axis
> of light flashing down its length,
> and the wood's soft flesh broke open,
> countless little nails
> squirming and dropping out of it.

This delicacy and vigor of notation are essential to Kinsella's poetry, as is the amplification of suggestion that occurs when we connect those squirming nails with 'a maggot of the possible' and a grub that twists and gropes back on itself. Each poetic occasion in this *oeuvre* is situated within a deliberated perspective. One is aware of a strong objective intellect and an indignant sensibility cleaving to a purpose that is intensely personal and yet is proffered as a standard and a reminder. Kinsella is, in fact, the representative Irish poet in that his career manifests the oath-bound, unrewarded plight of the *comitatus* in Yeats's black tower. In his work, we can watch the ancient correspondence between the nation's possibilities and the imagination of its poet—represented originally by the Milesian bard Amergin—discover itself again in a modern drama of self-knowledge and self-testing.

Edwin Muir

In Edwin Muir's *An Autobiography* some of the most evocative passages recall moments of great serenity experienced by the poet during his childhood on Orkney. One brief recollection of what it was like in the cradle goes as follows: 'I was lying in some room watching a beam of slanting light in which dusty, bright motes slowly danced and turned, while a low murmuring went on somewhere, possibly the humming of flies.' After childhood, as he confesses a few lines further on, that sense of a slow unending dance, 'the sense of deep and solid peace', came back to him only in dreams. And so, not unexpectedly, it is dream states that underlie and are induced by his most characteristic poems. Muir's level best involves access to a far-off, slightly somnambulist plane of consciousness, in poems where the reader is gratified by the entranced atmosphere but also a little unnerved by the eerie placidity of it all. This kind of effect, which I shall illustrate presently, is what I call his level best; but his very best combines the lucent presentation of such states with a simultaneous apprehension of menace.

Again, an early moment in *An Autobiography* provides a clue to these more complex and commanding achievements. He tells how he felt terror on hearing of the death of a farmer who used to bring him sweets in his snuff-lined pockets, and then goes on:

> In a child's mind there is at moments a divination of a hidden tragedy taking place around him, that tragedy being the life which he will not live for some years still, though it is there, invisible to him, already.

This apprehension of broken harmonies, of the entry of contradiction into life, is what we expect from the highest art, and we expect it precisely as it is manifested here—not as a great accumulation of negative data, not as an assault by the bad evidence, but as an intuited, endangering pressure of reality, a true weighing of things as they are dreaded against things as they are desired. The odd thing about Muir as a twentieth-century poet is that he had more than enough experience of his own to tilt the scales towards a negative reading of the human condition but he nevertheless maintained his innate, positive disposition. His critics have properly resisted him when the thrust of his poetic uplift too easily overwhelmed the actual gravity of the lived conditions; but it must be acknowledged that without his habitual distancing, his way of incorporating abstract joy and pondered sorrows, Muir could never have established the peculiar balance between substance and sonorousness which distinguishes his finest work.

To read a poem like 'Merlin', however, from his 1937 volume, *Journeys and Places*, is to find him working at his level best:

> O Merlin in your crystal cave
> Deep in the diamond of the day,
> Will there ever be a singer
> Whose music will smooth away
> The furrow drawn by Adam's finger
> Across the meadow and the wave?
> Or a runner who'll outrun
> Man's long shadow driving on,
> Break through the gate of memory
> And hang the apple on the tree?
> Will your magic ever show
> The sleeping bride shut in her bower,
> The day wreathed in its mound of snow
> And Time locked in his tower?

The needle on the scale trembles deliciously here. On one side, the balance inclines to whimsicality and wish-fulfilment, the kind of hygienic never-never land that Walt Disney could film without the slightest adaptation and market as something indistinguishable from his own kind of product. All the elements of escapist fantasy are there: magicians, bowers, brides, towers. Yet the usualness of these things is fleetingly renewed by the unusualness of the imagining. 'And hang the apple on the tree', for example, has an unexceptionable allegorical significance, but as a phrase it possesses a simplicity and unexpected clarity that give it the buoyancy and superficies of language-life which distinguish poetry. The same is true of the second line, 'Deep in the diamond of the day,' and also of the penultimate one, 'The day wreathed in its mound of snow'. These incline the balance away from whimsical fantasy towards something more human and poignant; so even if the poem does not expose us to what Robert Frost called the 'desert places between stars', it does at least intimate a receptivity to 'the still, sad music of humanity'. And it does so by the liturgical, unhurriable procession of vowels in a line like 'Deep in the diamond of the day'.

That secure, lucid place evoked in 'Merlin' is surely related to the one where the young Muir knelt at family prayers; just as the note of the poem must surely bear some resemblance to the note which the boy's father struck on these occasions, described in the autobiography as 'a sort of mild chant'. In fact, the overall effect of 'Merlin' on the reader is probably much the same as that experienced by the child-poet when he heard his father enunciate the following words, for which, he claimed, he always waited: 'A house not made with hands, eternal in the heavens'.

Mild chants of houses not made with hands: from beginning to end Muir composed poems that approximated to that kind of thing. Poems with a steady metrical beat, such as 'The Ring', 'The Window', 'The Toy Horse', 'Telemachos Remembers'—the list could be extended. And yet these poems, for all their admissible harmonies and temperate affirmativeness, impose the order of art a little too amiably upon the disorders of experience. A pane of Tennysonian glass, such as intervened between the Lady of Shalott and the traffic on the road, keeps the thick-witted world at a remove. Not unexpectedly, there is even an unashamed echo of Tennyson in 'Telemachos Remembers':

> The weary loom, the weary loom,
> The task grown sick from morn to night,
> From year to year. The treadles' boom
> Made a low thunder in the room.
> The woven phantoms mazed her sight.

This is beguilingly skilful, and nobody is going to suggest that a poem of impeccable verbal order must necessarily misrepresent the complexities of living. A reading of Muir's poem 'The Combat' would be enough to give the lie to such an oversimple equation of verbal melody with spiritual or intellectual gullibility. Nevertheless, Muir's faith in the immortality of the soul and his hard-won if high-toned perspective on personal and historical suffering come through in these poems as a shade too readily available. The poems dwell too calmly in the written place, within the imagined circle. They are of course the bonus of Muir's personal journey, but they are Parnassian, understanding 'Parnassian' according to Hopkins's famous definition in his letter to A. W. M. Baillie. For Hopkins, the term denoted a kind of poetry that was second to the poetry of inspiration:

> It can only be spoken by poets but it is not in the highest sense poetry . . . It is spoken *on and from* the level of the poet's mind, not, as in the other case, when the inspiration . . . raises him above himself.

One thinks here too of Auden's definition of inspiration as that which has occurred when a poet writes better than we could have reasonably expected. The poems by Muir just mentioned are not of this inspired sort. They do not do the whole work of art; they do not move a personal force through an artistic distance. Instead, they tread the force with stationary efficiency and produce a strain in the melodious rather than in the laborious sense of that word. They return us, a little too unscathed, to the mote-lit stillness of the cradle and the chant-filled circle of the prayers.

They return us, in fact, to Eden; and as Peter Butter rightly insists in his study of Muir, Eden as a destination is less poetically rewarding than Eden as a starting-point. From there, the poetic imagination ventures most rewardingly outwards into fallen time; its project is most forceful and its achievements most bracing when it stands with only 'one foot in Eden'. In the poem of that name, appropriately, Muir's music is a combination of primal song chant and the differentiated, alienated precisions of the modern world. There is a haulage job being done by the metre; the rhymes are like a system of pulleys over which the argument drags forward a positive meaning. And allied to this metrical vitality is a brisk diction which keeps the poem from indulging in *longueurs* or relishing its own effects:

> Yet still from Eden springs the root
> As clean as on the starting day.
> Time takes the foliage and the fruit
> And burns the archetypal leaf
> To shapes of terror and of grief
> Scattered along the winter way.
> But famished field and blackened tree
> Bear flowers in Eden never known.
> Blossoms of grief and charity
> Bloom in these darkened fields alone.
> What had Eden ever to say
> Of hope and faith and pity and love
> Until was buried all its day
> And memory found its treasure trove?
> Strange blessings never in Paradise
> Fall from these beclouded skies.

'One Foot in Eden' and other 'chant' poems such as 'The Annunciation'—the one beginning 'The angel and the girl are met'—and 'The Return of the Greeks' and 'The Child Dying' demonstrate the possibility of bringing off that most delicate and difficult of feats: writing a poem in which good wins a points-victory over the opposition, which somehow always starts out the favourite. But then, that feat is only worthwhile when the opposition is fairly admitted—as it is beginning to be in these poems.

In a review of Robert Frost that appeared in *The Listener* in 1943 (reprinted by Peter Butter in *The Truth of Imagination*), what Muir says of the American poet can be said with equal truth of Muir himself:

> [He] is one of those poets who so evidently succeed in doing what they wish to do that they tempt everyone to point out their limitations. The limitation is so clearly there, as it is not in poets who

undertake more than they can manage. But when one examines [his] limitation one finds that it rises from proportion, and that his proportion in turn is rooted in character. If he were to say more than he says, as people sometimes wish he would, it would destroy the balance of his view of life. As for the character itself, it has the soundness and natural distortion of growing things which have already grown sufficiently to possess a distinctive shape.

Muir, by the time he started to write poetry in the 1920s, had also grown sufficiently to produce a distinctive shape. At that moment of beginning he could have declared what he declared in his last unfinished poem:

> I have been taught by dreams and fantasies
> Learned from the friendly and the darker phantoms
> And got great knowledge and courtesy from the dead
> Kinsmen and kinswomen, ancestors and friends.

If there is an echo of Yeats's rhetoric in these lines, there is also a memory of Wordsworth's image of himself as 'an inmate of this active universe'. Indeed, Muir's career as a poet has about it something of Wordsworth's indeflectable purpose. For both of them, poetry was a necessary part of an effort at self-restoration and self-integration, an aspect of the attempt to align powers of the self with powers of the cosmos. Edwin and Willa starting out in Czechoslovakia and Germany in the 1920s remind one of Dorothy and William withdrawn to the south of England in the 1790s; and the simplicity of Wordsworth's ballad poems of that season, in which the greening of vegetation and the startle of birdsong are analogies for the shoots of self-healing he was experiencing—such simplicity is reminiscent of early work by Muir. There is a similar mirroring of outer and inner things in an early Muir poem like 'October at Hellbrunn'. Of this and other poems composed in Salzburg, Willa Muir says, 'they read like notes made by a child-like melancholy observer', and they 'have an overtone of gentle sadness'. This is quite true, but I believe that 'October at

Hellbrunn' is of a higher order than her affectionate references suggest:

> The near-drawn stone-smooth sky, closed in and grey,
> Broods on the garden, and the turf is still.
> The dim lake shines, oppressed the fountains play,
> And shadowless weight lies on the wooded hill.
>
> The patient trees rise separate, as if deep
> They listened dreaming through the hollow ground,
> Each in a single and divided sleep,
> While few sad leaves fall heedless with no sound.
>
> The marble cherubs in the wavering lake
> Stand up more still, as if they kept all there,
> The trees, the plots, in thrall. Their shadows make
> The water clear and hollow as the air.
>
> The silent afternoon draws in, and dark
> The trees rise now, grown heavier is the ground,
> And breaking through the silence of the park
> Farther a hidden fountain flings its sound.

This park scene has become what Wordsworth called 'a prospect of the mind'; the images dwell in two places at one time. The trees, for example, sleep a 'divided sleep' between earth and air, and the cherubs standing in air are reflected in water. Here we are not just dealing with a gentle evocation of literary melancholy; we have entered an element suggestive of that state of consciousness which Muir recollected from childhood, when the child's mind divines 'a hidden tragedy taking place . . . that tragedy being the life he will not live for some years still, though it is there, invisible to him, already'. 'October at Hellbrunn', then, is certainly a poem of tranquil restoration, in that there is fullness and curativeness in the crafting of its stanzas, but I would argue that it is also a poem of the apprehensive and imperilled consciousness.

Obviously, this is not to suggest that Edwin Muir had foreknowledge of what the fate of Europe would be two decades later.

But there was a place in him prepared for what did occur. When catastrophe came out of the borderlands of dread into the actual events of history, Muir's poetic strength revealed itself in being able to co-ordinate the nightmare of history with that place in himself where he had trembled with anticipation. The solitary boy who at the age of five or six on the island of Wyre was filled with fear and wonder at horses and herons was being fostered by this notably Wordsworthian ministry for the vocation of poetry. The heron would come back in a dream, grey and shining, and behind the stiff hedge of its unlikely tail feathers it would transform into a beast on four feet that were padded like a leopard's or a tiger's. The rest of the dream story is given in *An Autobiography*:

> Then, confronting it in the field, there appeared an ancient, dirty, earth-coloured animal with a head like that of an old sheep or a mangy dog. Its eyes were soft and brown; it was alone against the splendid-tailed beast; yet it stood its ground and prepared to fight the danger coming towards it, whether that was death or merely humiliation and pain. From their look I could see that the two animals knew each other, . . . and that the dark, patient animal would always be defeated, and the bright, fierce animal would always win. I did not see the fight, but I knew it would be ruthless and shameful, with a meaning of some kind perhaps, but no comfort.

From that given lump of psychic matter Muir fashioned his poem 'The Combat', a poem with a meaning but no comfort, unless there is comfort to be found in a disconsolate renewal of effort. 'The Combat' can be read politically as a parable about the war against Nazism or, more particularly and far less satisfactorily, about the Battle of Britain. It can be read—also too trimly—within a Christian framework of redemption through suffering. It can, at any rate, be recognized as an entirely satisfactory image of reality.

'The Combat' has something of the quality which Muir attributed to the ballads. It belongs 'on the other side of the great plateau of the eighteenth century, with its humanitarian passion and its great hopes for mankind'. It 'has no sentimental appeal' but

operates 'on the level of tragic acceptance'. Its heraldic apparatus is
animated by a strong rhythmic energy. In it Muir manages to do in
his rather abstract way what Keith Douglas managed to do by
radically different means in a poem like 'Vergissmeinicht'—he
combines the contradictory demands of tough-mindedness and
compassion:

> A while the place lay blank, forlorn,
> Drowsing as in relief from pain.
> The cricket chirped, the grating thorn
> Stirred, and a little sound was born.
> The champions took their posts again.
>
> And all began. The stealthy paw
> Slashed out and in. Could nothing save
> These rags and tatters from the claw?
> Nothing. And yet I never saw
> A beast so helpless and so brave.

This is well beyond Muir's level best. Its applicability as parable is
not gained at the expense of intensity. It almost possesses the 'rich,
dark wintry magic' which the child Muir recognized in a sketch of
Burns.

Wintriness, however, is not the natural weather of Muir's work.
When it is not exercising the singing note, his music is fuller, more
like the half-consoling roll-away of summer thunder, more like
that 'deepening drumming' which hoofbeats make on an evening
road in his poem 'The Horses'. 'The Horses' is another of his indis-
putable achievements and too well known to require any further
comment here. I would just want to observe that it strikes a note
which is Muir's alternative to the metrical chant; this we might
characterize as a rounded eloquence, closer to the pitch of the pulpit than the pub, at its best when it arises from an intent concentration on place or story—as in, say, 'The Return of Odysseus'
or 'The Labyrinth'. The slightly dazed purposefulness of 'The
Labyrinth' is doubly right: the bewilderments of Theseus drama-
tize the predicament both of consciousness seeking a meaning

within its own complexities and of consciousness seeking relation with the cosmos beyond itself. Once again, there is a finely held balance between Muir's temperamental impulse to foreclose with a hopeful QED (drawn from a vision of the gods) and his artistic sense which demands that he follow the less sanguine logic of his own metaphor. We must be grateful that in 'The Labyrinth' this urge to correct Kafka by a dose of Browning is resisted. So, in the last lines, the word 'deceits' is linked with 'the wild-wood waste of falsehoods', but equally it refers back to and qualifies the speaker's conviction that his soul 'has bird wings to fly free'.

> Oh these deceits are strong almost as life.
> Last night I dreamt I was in the labyrinth,
> And woke far on. I did not know the place.

This good surrender to the logic of his fictions doesn't always occur in Muir's mythological and allegorical scenarios. Often his composing head remains at a privileged, plotting distance and cannot resist having designs upon the reader. This tendency can produce lines full of resolute wisdom, but it can also produce a loose-weave, mournful prosiness.

In his 1949 volume, *The Labyrinth*, Muir's unfashionable poetic ways were finally rewarded. His metaphysical habit of mind and mythological disposition had kept him out of the political swim of Thirties English poetry. There seemed to be nothing up-to-date about him. But in the 1940s, and especially in this 1949 volume, we can watch the gratifying spectacle of a solitary poetic endeavour attaining representative status; or to put it another way, by then Muir's subject was everybody's subject. His stand-off with modernity had preceded the general postwar dismay at human destructiveness and a new recognition of human frailty in the atomic age. His experiences in Austria and Czechoslovakia that had kept him at a slight remove from English literary culture in the pre-war years now gave him a unique personal perspective and enabled him to write a poetry recognizably akin to that being written by the tragic ironists and parablists in postwar Eastern Europe.

Still, Muir was not a Middle European. He was Orcadian, then

Scottish, then a creature of the English literary tradition. And within that tradition, I would see him as an heir of the Wilfred Owen who wrote 'Strange Meeting', the Owen who combined a religious temperament with a wounded social conscience, the Owen who was working as a vicar's assistant in Dunsden at about the same time as Muir was going through the scandal of his labours in the bone factory in Greenock. Both men were seared by contact with poverty, and both developed a rhetoric that was somnolent, elegiac and yet politically purposeful. If nothing in Muir's poetry equals the awful documentary content in Owen's, his essential achievement nevertheless corresponds to the kind of thing Owen managed in poems such as 'Miners' and 'Strange Meeting'—poems which display a mixture of visionary breadth and particular social witness.

Both men succeed in giving expression to a sensibility that is deeply affected by Christianity and almost too susceptible to the appeal of passive suffering. It is for this reason that Muir's early period of Nietzschean 'hardness' is so important, and Owen's period of somewhat vindictive outrage and protest. These experiences surely contributed to their fully developed poetic styles, for it is true, as Yeats says, that style is the equivalent of self-conquest in a writer. When, for example, they address the futility and moral beauty of the victim in poems as different as Owen's 'The Send-Off' and Muir's 'The Combat', they both do so with a proper indignation against a world that seems not only to condone but even to ordain such brutality and pain. At these moments, they are both wary of pathos, and their poems represent a victory over common tendencies towards resignation. So, if technically, as a composer of lines, Muir never ceased to belong to the pre-modern world of Rupert Brooke, imaginatively he did cross 'The Bridge of Dread', both inside himself and in the wider field of the times he lived through.

But you may well be wondering, 'Why all this about the English tradition? Is Edwin Muir's place not in Scotland?' And the answer to this latter question, in spite of objections lodged long ago by Hugh MacDiarmid, is yes. Assailable in previous days because it didn't manifest a sufficiently nationalist fervour or sport the correct ethnic regalia, Muir's Scottishness is best appreciated in the light of a much older alliance between Scotland and Europe. More important than the pious local colour of a poem such as 'Scotland's Winter' is the Pictish bareness of 'Prometheus's Grave', more convincing than the pious historical roll-calling of 'Scotland 1941' is Muir's tragic sense (in a poem like 'Troy') of an abandoned culture being frantically and absurdly guarded. And then there are those border ballads of an utterly contemporary sort, frontier poems like 'The Interrogation'. These, and others such as 'The Combat' and 'The Horses', open a path where there is free coming and going between the local conditions and the broader historical realities of the age. In them, Muir addressed the same matters as haunted the Thirties poets but he didn't employ their topical political idiom or rhetoric of concern. By displaying little anxiety about English cultural hegemony, by accepting with equanimity the resources it made available and then walking a little dreamily off to one side and into Europe, Muir oriented himself towards the future and left an example that still awaits full appreciation.

To make this claim is not to suggest that Muir consciously did what I say he did. Nor is it to deny the rightness of MacDiarmid's procedures or the largeness of his achievements. MacDiarmid's was obviously a volcanic genius, more lavish, more impassioned and renegade and far more influential in the literary and political history of Scotland than Muir's. To make the claim is, rather, to state a supplementary truth. I would say that as the old sureties are leached from Europe's vernacular cultures, east and west, as a new permeability and capacity for absorption develop in their hitherto self-absorbed art and politics, Muir's simultaneous at-homeness and abroadness become exemplary, and his work more and more deserves to be re-read and remembered.

from The Redress of Poetry

Professors of poetry, apologists for it, practitioners of it, from Sir Philip Sidney to Wallace Stevens, all sooner or later are tempted to show how poetry's existence as a form of art relates to our existence as citizens of society—how it is 'of present use'. Behind such defences and justifications, at any number of removes, stands Plato, calling into question whatever special prerogatives or useful influences poetry would claim for itself within the *polis*. Yet Plato's world of ideal forms also provides the court of appeal through which poetic imagination seeks to redress whatever is wrong or exacerbating in the prevailing conditions. Moreover, 'useful' or 'practical' responses to those same conditions are derived from imagined standards too: poetic fictions, the dream of alternative worlds, enable governments and revolutionaries as well. It's just that governments and revolutionaries would compel society to take on the shape of their imagining, whereas poets are typically more concerned to conjure with their own and their readers' sense of what is possible or desirable or, indeed, imaginable. The nobility of poetry, says Wallace Stevens, 'is a violence from within that protects us from a violence without'. It is the imagination pressing back against the pressure of reality.

Stevens, as he reaches this conclusion in his essay 'The Noble Rider and the Sound of Words', is anxious to insist that his own words are intended to be more than merely sonorous, and his anxiety is understandable. It is as if he were imagining and responding to the outcry of some disaffected heckler in the crowd of those whom Tony Harrison calls 'the rhubarbarians', one crying out against the mystification of art and its appropriation by the grandees of aesthetics. 'In our time', the heckler protests, echoing something he has read somewhere, 'the destiny of man presents itself in political terms.' And in his understanding, and in the understanding of most people who protest against the ascription to poetry of any metaphysical force, those terms are going to derive from the politics of subversion, of redressal, of affirming that which is denied voice. Our heckler, in other words, will want poetry to be more than an imagined response to conditions in the world; he or she will urgently want to know why it should not be an applied art, harnessed to movements which attempt to alleviate those conditions by direct action.

The heckler, therefore, is going to have little sympathy with Wallace Stevens when he declares the poet to be a potent figure because the poet 'creates the world to which we turn incessantly and without knowing it, and . . . gives life to the supreme fictions without which we are unable to conceive of [that world]'—meaning that if our given experience is a labyrinth, its impassability can still be countered by the poet's imagining some equivalent of the labyrinth and presenting himself and us with a vivid experience of it. Such an operation does not intervene in the actual, but by offering consciousness a chance to recognize its predicaments, foreknow its capacities and rehearse its comebacks in all kinds of venturesome ways, it does constitute a beneficent event, for poet and audience alike. It offers a response to reality which has a liberating and verifying effect upon the individual spirit, and yet I can see how such a function would be deemed insufficient by a political activist. For the activist, there is going to be no point in envisaging an order which is comprehensive of events but not in itself productive of new events. Engaged parties are not going to be grateful for a mere image—no matter how inventive or original—of the field of force of which they are a part. They will always want the redress of poetry to be an exercise of leverage on behalf of *their* point of view; they will require the entire weight of the thing to come down on their side of the scales.

So, if you are an English poet at the front during World War I, the pressure will be on you to contribute to the war effort, preferably by dehumanizing the face of the enemy. If you are an Irish poet in the wake of the 1916 executions, the pressure will be to revile the tyranny of the executing power. If you are an American poet at the height of the Vietnam War, the official expectation will be for you to wave the flag rhetorically. In these cases, to see the German soldier as a friend and secret sharer, to see the British government as a body who might keep faith, to see the South-East Asian expedition as an imperial betrayal, to do any of these things is to add a complication where the general desire is for a simplification.

Such countervailing gestures frustrate the common expectation of solidarity, but they do have political force. Their very power to exacerbate is one guarantee of their effectiveness. They are particular instances of a law which Simone Weil announced with typical extremity and succinctness in her book *Gravity and Grace*. She writes there:

> If we know in what way society is unbalanced, we must do what we can to add weight to the lighter scale . . . we must have formed a conception of equilibrium and be ever ready to change sides like justice, 'that fugitive from the camp of conquerors'.

Clearly, this corresponds to deep structures of thought and feeling derived from centuries of Christian teaching and from Christ's paradoxical identification with the plight of the wretched. And in so far as poetry is an extension and refinement of the mind's extreme recognitions, and of language's most unexpected apprehensions, it too manifests the workings of Weil's law.

'Obedience to the force of gravity. The greatest sin.' So Simone Weil also writes in *Gravity and Grace*. Indeed her whole book is informed by the idea of counterweighting, of balancing out the forces, of redress—tilting the scales of reality towards some transcendent equilibrium. And in the activity of poetry too, there is a tendency to place a counter-reality in the scales—a reality which may be only imagined but which nevertheless has weight because it is imagined within the gravitational pull of the actual and can therefore hold its own and balance out against the historical situation. This redressing effect of poetry comes from its being a glimpsed alternative, a revelation of potential that is denied or constantly threatened by circumstances . . .

Poetry cannot afford to lose its fundamentally self-delighting inventiveness, its joy in being a process of language as well as a representation of things in the world. To put it in W. B. Yeats's terms, the will must not usurp the work of the imagination. And while this may seem something of a truism, it is nevertheless worth repeating in a late-twentieth-century context of politically approved themes, post-colonial backlash and 'silence-breaking' writing of all kinds. In these circumstances, poetry is understandably pressed to give voice to much that has hitherto been denied expression in the ethnic, social, sexual and political life. Which is to say that its power as a mode of redress in the first sense—as agent for proclaiming and correcting injustices—is being appealed to constantly. But in discharging this function, poets are in danger of slighting another imperative, namely, to redress poetry *as* poetry, to set it up as its own category, an eminence established and a pressure exercised by distinctly linguistic means . . .

The *OED* has four entries for 'redress' as a noun, and I began by calling upon the first sense which it provides: 'Reparation of, satisfaction or compensation for, a wrong sustained or the loss resulting from this.' For 'redress' as a verb the dictionary gives fifteen separate entries, all of them subdivided two or three times and almost all of the usages noted as obsolete. I have also taken account of the first of these obsolete meanings, which is given as 'To set (a person or a thing) upright again; to raise again to an erect position. Also *fig.* to set up again, restore, re-establish.'

But in following these rather sober extensions of the word, in considering poetry's possible service to programmers of cultural and political realignment or in reaffirming poetry as an upright, resistant and self-bracing entity within the general flux and flex of language, I don't want to give the impression that its force must always be exercised in earnest, morally premeditated ways. On the contrary, I want to profess the surprise of poetry as well as its reliability; I want to celebrate its given, unforeseeable thereness, the way it enters our field of vision and animates our physical and intelligent being in much the same way as those bird-shapes stencilled on the transparent surfaces of glass walls or windows must suddenly enter the vision and change the direction of the real

birds' flight. In a flash the shapes register and transmit their unmistakable presence, so the birds veer off instinctively. An image
of the living creatures has induced a totally salubrious swerve in
the creatures themselves. And this natural, heady diversion is also
something induced by poetry and reminds me of a further (obsolete) meaning of 'redress', with which I would conclude, a meaning which comes in entry 4 of the verb, subsection (*b*): '*Hunting*.
To bring back (the hounds or deer) to the proper course.' In this
'redress' there is no hint of ethical obligation; it is more a matter of
finding a course for the breakaway of innate capacity, a course
where something unhindered, yet directed, can sweep ahead into
its full potential.

from Extending the Alphabet:
Christopher Marlowe

It will soon be the 400th anniversary of the death by stabbing of Christopher Marlowe at a tavern in Deptford. The minutes of the coroner's inquest tell how he and three other men spent the afternoon of 30 May 1593 'in quiet sort' in a room of the inn, and how after supper a dispute arose about the bill—the famous 'reckoning'. Marlowe is then said to have made a sudden attack on one of his companions, a character called Ingram Friser, who fought back and killed the poet with his knife in self-defence.

The story has always had a slightly sinister feel to it, something to do with the mystery that hangs over those four companions withdrawn quietly out of the early summer day, the stealth of their privacy, the hovering possibility of underhand exchanges or undercover deeds. And, of course, the fascination of the event was every bit as potent for Marlowe's contemporaries, for it did not escape their notice that the whole thing had been vaguely foreshadowed in the dramatist's own writing. At the conclusion of his play *Doctor Faustus*, for example, the Chorus speaks these famous lines which combine the inexorability of high poetry with the melodrama of popular preaching:

> Cut is the branch that might have grown full straight,
> And burnèd is Apollo's laurel-bough,
> That sometime grew within this learned man.
> Faustus is gone: regard his hellish fall,
> Whose fiendful fortune may exhort the wise,
> Only to wonder at unlawful things,
> Whose deepness doth entice such forward wits
> To practise more than heavenly power permits.

Given the disconsolate note of this passage and its significant placing as the curtain line of the play, it is no wonder that it was read as Marlowe's own self-epitaph and was seized upon after his murder in much the same way as the late poems of Sylvia Plath were seized upon after her suicide. Both deaths made sensational news and resulted in the poets becoming legendary figures; their tragic ends were seen to have been implicit in their writings all along. Preachers even rigged the Marlowe knifing so that it presented an instructive symmetry; they gave out that the dagger that killed him had been his own and that the fatal wound had been in his head, the very seat of the talent which had made him one of those damnably 'forward wits'. It was only to be expected, therefore, that the Chorus's lament for an overweening intellectual cut off in his prime should have been understood afterwards as a sort of prediction. To a hot-breathed public, high on murder gossip that carried with it the mingled whiff of religious, sexual and political scandal, the note of doom was not only audible: it was ominous and prophetic of Marlowe's fate.

That fate, moreover, had been predicted by others besides himself. Robert Greene's deathbed pamphlet, *Greene's Groats-worth of Wit, Bought with a Million of Repentance*, had been written nine months before Marlowe was stabbed at Deptford. The pamphlet is most famous for its attack on Shakespeare, but before Greene takes his side-swipe at the 'upstart crow', he has already warned a number of his peers about their own destinies, and although he does not use Marlowe's name, there is no doubt that the 'tragedian' being singled out in his deeply minatory address is indeed the same scandalous, atheistical and morally reprehensible university wit, associate of Sir Walter Raleigh and student of the School of Night. Marlowe's intellectual effrontery, in other words, had been enough to put the wind up a man on his deathbed and take a repentant sinner's mind off his own predicament—which is to say that the figure Marlowe cut in the minds of his contemporaries in the late 1580s and early 1590s was utterly exciting. The carouser who had been gaoled for a couple of weeks after being on the spot at a fatal street-fight, the university student who had tasted the thrills of espionage among the Catholic recusants of Reims, the blasphemer who seemed to be out to break every taboo and to transgress extravagantly in the realms of both religion and sex—this figure, a star in his late twenties, a kind of cross between Oscar Wilde and Jack the Ripper, moved in an aura of glamorous immorality and political danger and was so riveting and marked that the dying Greene felt free to finger him as the next to go.

And, of course, the danger was not just an aura. Atheism and blasphemy could be as fatal in late-sixteenth-century London as anti-revolutionary sympathies were in Moscow in the 1930s. Marlowe was denounced to the Privy Council, and the depositions of the informers have survived. Even if they are perused with the suspicion that such documents always warrant, they still conjure up the image of a man operating at full tilt, both exhilarated and inflammatory. The whole performance was one of great daring, and the reports of it still transmit something of its original subversive headiness, partly exhibitionistic, partly intellectually driven, but altogether inevitable and unstoppable.

In Marlowe's case, therefore, as in Plath's, the daring of the work and the transgressions which it encompassed were the first things to be emphasized in the aftermath of their deaths. Its ironies and complications were relatively neglected; what got highlighted were the points where it conformed to current expectations generated by the extreme behaviour of the writer. In Plath's case, the image of victimized woman was immediately in place as a consequence of her tragic suicide; in Marlowe's, it was the image of the sinner's fall, of divine retribution for blasphemous presumptions. In each instance, the work was read with more regard to what the posthumously created stereotype might have been expected to produce than what the writer actually delivered. *Doctor Faustus*, for example, was regarded for a very long time as a casebook of humanist 'overreaching' before it was reconsidered as an anatomy of Christian despair. And Plath was celebrated as the author of the vindictive 'Daddy' and the morgue-cold 'Edge' while other, more positively inspired works were ignored.

It is hardly news to be reminded of all this. Original poets can obviously sustain a variety of interpretations and answer to very different times and needs. What remains mysterious, however, is the source of that original strength, the very fact of poetic power itself, the way its unpredictability gets converted into inevitability once it has manifested itself, the way a generation recognizes that they are in the presence of one of the great unfettered events which constitute a definite stage in the history of poetry. It is the manifestation of this power in Marlowe's verse, in the first language-life of the poetry itself, that I wish to praise. If I begin by acknowledging that the conditions of a poet's reception and the history of subsequent responses to his or her work do indeed become a part of the work's force and meaning, it is only to indicate that I am as aware as the next person that the import of poetry is affected by several different agencies. But I remain convinced by what my own reading experience tells me; namely, that some works transmit an immediately persuasive signal and retain a unique staying power over a lifetime. Some works continue to combine the sensation of liberation with that of consolidation; having once cleared a new space on the literary and psychic ground, they go on to offer, at each re-reading, the satisfaction of a foundation being touched and the excitement of an energy being released.

I couldn't have put it that way when I first heard Professor Terence Spencer read from Marlowe's *Tamburlaine*. I was then a First Arts student at Queen's University, Belfast, sharing the benches of a lecture hall with others like me, the wary, needy sons and daughters of 1950s Ulster, all of us recent escapees from the sixth-form grind. Rumour had it that the professor had been a Shakespearean actor, which in itself was enough to engender a mood of anticipation. Certainly, when he appeared, he wasn't into playing down the drive and flourish of the big lines. He stalked to the podium, adjusted his gown, profiled himself a little theatrically and pitched into the Prologue to *Tamburlaine* like a long-jumper going for the record:

> From jigging veins of rhyming mother-wits,
> And such conceits as clownage keeps in pay,
> We'll lead you to the stately tent of war,
> Where you shall hear the Scythian Tamburlaine
> Threatening the world with high astounding terms,
> And scourging kingdoms with his conquering sword.

View but his picture in this tragic glass,
And then applaud his fortunes as you please.

And then we were off:

> Then sit thou down, divine Zenocrate;
> And here we crown thee Queen of Persia,
> And all the kingdoms and dominions
> That late the power of Tamburlaine subdu'd.
> As Juno, when the giants were suppress'd,
> That darted mountains at her brother Jove,
> So looks my love, shadowing in her brows
> Triumphs and trophies for my victories;
> Or as Latona's daughter, bent to arms,
> Adding more courage to my conquering mind.
> To gratify the sweet Zenocrate,
> Egyptians, Moors, and men of Asia,
> From Barbary unto the Western India,
> Shall pay a yearly tribute to thy sire;
> And from the bounds of Afric to the banks
> Of Ganges shall his mighty arm extend.

It was impossible not to be carried away by the sheer rhetorical power of this work, and difficult not to share the headiness of the English Renaissance moment as it declared itself in the untrammelled climb of Marlowe's verse. And even though I have learned to place this poetry's expansionist drive in the context of nascent English imperialism, I am still grateful for the enlargements it offered, the soaring orchestration, the roll-call of place-names and of figures from classical mythology. It was a fundamentally pleasurable experience that need not be reneged on for the sake of any subsequent political correctness.

Ought I to have been less ready to be carried away? Maybe I should have been taught to beware of the military push of the thing, and been reminded that this English pentameter marched in step with the invading English armies of the late Tudor period—those who in the 1580s and 1590s were systematically preparing the conquest of Gaelic Ireland and the future Plantation of Ulster in the 1620s. Yet the movement of the lines was so heady and the rhetoric so thrilling that the temptation to go with it proved irresistible. What I want to do here, therefore, is to find a way of reaffirming the value and rights of Marlowe's poetry in our own post-colonial time. When resistance to works from the canonical 'centre' has replaced formal appreciation as the predominant approach to literary study, it is necessary to find a way of treating the marvellously aspiring note of his work as something more than a set of discourses to be unmasked. When the word 'humanist' has become almost a term of abuse, it is necessary to consider whether we would want to have Marlowe's whole keyboard of classical reference demeaned. Surely it is still possible to take cognizance of the unpredictable artistic excellence of Marlowe's plays and poems while acknowledging that they are bound up with a particular moment of English history, and are thereby implicated with the late-Tudor project of national consolidation at home and colonization abroad. There's no doubt, for example, that an up-to-the-minute commentator would be inclined to regard the Virgilian *longueurs* of Marlowe's early play *Dido Queen of Carthage* as a covert endorsement of the expeditionary drives beginning to take shape in late-sixteenth-century England. Aeneas's mission to found a new Troy, from which he is not to be deflected by the power and distraction of love itself, undoubtedly corroborates in imaginative terms the historical effort that would soon go into the founding of a New England and a London Derry.

Obviously, then, when I re-read *Edward II* for this lecture, I was not only aware of the way it could be adapted by the British film-maker Derek Jarman as a liberationist masquerade and turned into a contemporary parable about the suppression of homosexual love. I was also conscious of the banishment to Ireland of Gaveston, the King's favourite, as something more than a shift of plot. Inevitably, in the present intellectual climate, it was hard not to read in Gaveston's relegation to the status of non-person an equal relegation of Ireland to the status of non-place. By its inclusion within the realm of English influence, late-medieval Ireland had become at once an annexe of the civil conquerors and the locus of a barbarism that had to be held at bay. One of the accusations against King Edward, after all, was that

> The wild O'Neill, with swarms of Irish kerns
> Lives uncontrolled within the English pale.

This wild O'Neill was not the one whose rebellious armies would later drive Edmund Spenser off his three-thousand-acre estate in County Cork, an estate which Spenser took over round about the time of the play's production in London and which had been confiscated from the Irish Earl of Desmond in the aftermath of the recent English campaign in Munster. When Spenser settled in Kilcolman, it was in a country almost depopulated by slaughter and famine. Within the previous half-year an estimated thirty thousand men, women and children had perished; Spenser himself, indeed, when acting as secretary to Lord Grey, had witnessed massacre on a large and systematic scale at Smerwick Harbour, where six hundred Spaniards and Irish had been butchered. And, needless to say, it was also at Smerwick that Sir Walter Raleigh had performed as one of Queen Elizabeth's captains was expected to and, in the words of the old *Spenser Handbook*, 'had done rough work for Lord Grey'.

We have been forced to cast a suspicious eye on the pretensions of Renaissance humanism by having its sacred texts placed in the context of their authors' participation in such brutally oppressive escapades; we have been rightly instructed about the ways that native populations and indigenous cultures disappear in the course of these civilizing enterprises; and we have learned how the values and language of the conqueror demolish and marginalize native values and institutions, rendering them barbarous, subhuman and altogether beyond the pale of cultivated sympathy or regard. But even so, it still seems an abdication of literary responsibility to be swayed by these desperately overdue correctives to a point where imaginative literature is read simply and solely as a function of an oppressive discourse, or as a reprehensible masking. When it comes to poetic composition, one has to allow for the presence, even for the pre-eminence, of what Wordsworth called 'the grand elementary principle of pleasure', and that pleasure comes from the doing-in-language of certain things. One has to allow for the fact that, in the words of Ezra Pound,

> the thing that matters in art is a sort of energy, something more or less like electricity or radio activity, a force transfusing, welding and unifying. A force rather like water when it spurts up through very bright sand and sets it in swift motion. You may make what image you like.

Pound's image does not preclude art's implication in the structures and shifts of power at any given moment, but it does suggest a salubrious role for it within the body politic; and another image which the Czech poet Miroslav Holub uses about theatre may also be adduced here. Holub sees the function of drama, and so by extension the function of poetry and of the arts in general, as being analogous to that of the immunity system within the human body. Which is to say that the creative spirit remains positively recalcitrant in face of the negative evidence, reminding the indicative mood of history that it has been written in by force and written in over the good optative mood of human potential.

This reminding, this work of immunity building, is effected by intrinsically artistic means, for it is obvious that poetry's answer to the world is not given only in terms of the content of its statements. It is given perhaps even more emphatically in terms of metre and syntax, of tone and musical trueness; and it is given also by its need to go emotionally and artistically 'above the brim', beyond the established norms. These things are the artistic manifestation of that affirming spiritual flame which W. H. Auden wanted the good person and the good poet to show, a manifestation which has less to do with argument or edification than with the fact and effort of articulation itself. And this is why I want to focus my remarks upon Marlowe with a consideration of his utterly delightful poem 'Hero and Leander', a work happily in love with its own inventions, written at the height of the young master's powers, a work which exercises itself entirely within the playhouse of erotic narrative in the tradition of the Latin poet Ovid but which remains responsive to and transformative of the real pains of love as they are experienced in 'the house in earnest'.

The story of Leander's love for Hero was told by the Greek poet Musaeus, and Marlowe's version takes off from the Greek original, although it famously does not tell the whole story. It was left incomplete at his death, but its incompleteness is not the only reason why Marlowe's poem is generally agreed to be a late work. George Chapman may have rounded out the first eight-hundred-odd lines of the narrative, yet his longer and graver treatment of the second half of the story is really no more mature than Marlowe's treatment of the first half. It's just that Marlowe's lines are without that earnestness which we too automatically associate with the word 'mature'. Everything in the early stages of the romance suited his gifts—Leander's physical beauty and erotic susceptibility, Hero's delicious combination of chastity and sexuality, Leander's swimming to Hero across the Hellespont and their first rapturous lovemaking. Chapman then took up the post-coital consequences of it all: Leander's return to Abydos, where the goddess Ceremony appears to him and constrains him to due marriage with Hero, Hero's turmoil and eventual preparation for their wedding and finally, after several digressions and postponements, the climactic incident of Leander's drowning and Hero's sacrificing of herself for love. In Chapman's words:

> She fell on her love's bosom, hugg'd it fast
> And with Leander's name she breathed her last.
> Neptune for pity in his arms did take them,
> Flung them into the air, and did awake them
> Like two sweet-birds, surnamed th'Acanthides,
> Which we call thistle-warps, that near no seas
> Dare ever come, but still in couples fly
> And feed on thistle-tops, to testify
> The hardness of their first life in their last:
> The first in thorns of love, and sorrows past.

In the poem as we have it, it is Marlowe who presents the account of the couple's first life when Hero appears as 'Venus' nun' and Leander as her infatuated slave, yet it is hard to find any intimation of the thorn and thistle side of things in Marlowe's version of their situation. What we get instead in the first two sestiads is a rapturous, permissive atmosphere, a *tír na n-óg* where the line between playfulness and transgression is at first confused and then suspended until all the inner partitions of the psyche have been opened. Bisexual cajolement, an indulgent recognition of the predatory within the amatory, a gift for transforming the louche and the lax into a nice stylistic decorum—it all goes to prove that Marlowe does indeed deserve the title 'forward wit', though not in the damning sense in which the Chorus applied the term to Doctor Faustus.

Here, for example, is Marlowe's description of the décor in Venus's temple at Sestos:

> Of crystal shining fair the pavement was;
> The town of Sestos called it Venus glass.
> There might you see the gods in sundry shapes
> Committing heady riots, incest, rapes:
> For know that underneath this radiant floor
> Was Danae's statue in a brazen tower,
> Jove slyly stealing from his sister's bed
> To dally with Idalian Ganymede,
> Or for his love Europa bellowing loud
> Or tumbling with the rainbow in a cloud;
> Blood-quaffing Mars, heaving the iron net
> Which limping Vulcan and his cyclops set;
> Love kindling fire, to burn such towns as Troy;
> Sylvanus weeping for the lovely boy
> That now is turned into a cypress tree,
> Under whose shade the wood gods love to be.

It would be hard to remain a nun of any sort, never mind a nun of Venus, in such an environment; and so indeed it proves to be in Hero's case. But this catalogue of amatory exploits only shows Marlowe limbering up. The poem goes on to deal more delicately and deliciously with the whole matter of sexual attraction, and in this regard 'Hero and Leander' is a boldly liberating work; in it the language of desire, the limits of the possible and the inventions of imagination combine to give a supple and mature image of human life. It is comic in tone but not gullible in perception. It abandons the tragic and heroic pitch of the plays but still manages to keep faith with their project of going over the top. The poetry of 'Hero and Leander' is less sonorous than that of *Tamburlaine*, less shot through by dread and lament than that of *Doctor Faustus*. As other commentators have pointed out, it is nearer to the note of Gaveston's infatuated daydreams in *Edward II*, and truer thereby to the hedonistic and homoerotic impulses that seem to have been so powerful an element in Marlowe's own sensibility.

In 'Hero and Leander' all his energy and subversiveness seem to get transformed into relish and artifice . . . He beguiles rather than confronts. Take, for instance, lines from the very start of the poem, which begin by describing the extraordinarily ingenious workmanship that adorned Hero's footwear, and then go on to elaborate their own erotic daydreams. They are typical of a persistent and very attractive note in Marlowe's writing:

> Buskins of shells all silvered used she,
> And branched with blushing coral to the knee,
> Where sparrows perched, of hollow pearl and gold,
> Such as the world would wonder to behold:
> Those with sweet water oft her handmaid fills,
> Which as she went would chirrup through the bills.
> Some say for her the fairest Cupid pined,
> And looking in her face was strooken blind.
> But this is true, so like was one the other,
> As he imagined Hero was his mother;
> And oftentimes into her bosom flew,
> About her naked neck his bare arms threw,
> And laid his childish head upon her breast,
> And with still panting rocked, there took his rest.
> So lovely fair was Hero, Venus' nun.

Admittedly, this 'rhetoric of enticement' is a very fine development of Marlowe's art . . . [His] suppler, almost Chaucerian way with the line is obviously linked to his early translation of Ovid's *Amores*, done while he was a student. These episodes from the imperial Roman *vie de bohème* are virtuoso work, and deserve far more attention than they tend to get. They have wiliness and sexiness and scholastic panache, and would be as much at home among the cleveralities of James Joyce's university wits in *A Portrait of the Artist as a Young Man* as they must have been among the scholars of sixteenth-century Cambridge. But when we come to the art of 'Hero and Leander', we are closer to the world of Anna Livia Plurabelle, to the hithering-thithering whims of a self-possessed mind, a mind that knows both the penalties of life and its invitations, one closer to the spirit of carnival than to the shock tactics of agitprop . . .

Marlowe's Pegasus has bolted free of the five-act harness and sports himself in a manner at once strenuous and unconstrained. The digressions and ornamental effects which the Ovidian genre more or less requires turn out to be ideal romping spaces. This poetry is in great fettle. It is nimble yet it is by no means lightweight: if you break into its path, you'll come up against enough observation and premeditated meaning to knock you sideways. Just consider, for example, how solidly the images of stripped athletes and gold ingots contribute to the crucial momentum of these famous lines, a momentum that gives the final couplet its irresistible proverbial clinch:

> It lies not in our power to love or hate,
> For will in us is overruled by fate.
> When two are stripped, long ere the course begin
> We wish that one should lose, the other win;
> And one especially do we affect
> Of two gold ingots like in each respect.
> The reason no man knows: let it suffice,
> What we behold is censured by our eyes.
> Where both deliberate, the love is slight;
> Who ever loved, that loved not at first sight?

The verse here is like a thick cable being paid out wittily by an intelligence that is nevertheless the very opposite of thick-witted. In fact, I am reminded of Joseph Brodsky's remarks about intonation in poetry, which appear in his introduction to the work of Aleksandr Kushner: 'In a poem,' Brodsky writes, 'the testimony of spiritual tension is intonation; or, more accurately, intonation in a poem—and not in a poem only—stands for the motion of the soul.' The motion of the soul, then, in 'Hero and Leander' is forward towards liberation and beatitude, but it is a motion countered by an implicit acknowledgement of repression and constraint. This dialectic is expressed formally by the co-existence of a supple voice within a strict metrical pattern and tonally by a note that is modulating constantly between the scampish and the plangent . . .

The maturity I commended earlier is present not as moral *gravitas* but as a fully attained artistic mastery, the casual technical virtuosity of the poetry being the equivalent of a happy inner freedom in the poet. Marlowe is involved here in a show-off performance, operating with real spontaneity and affection, in control of a far greater range of expression than he was at the beginning of his stage career. Obviously, as I've remarked already, the intonation of 'Hero and Leander' is not as ominous or stricken as the great scenes of *Doctor Faustus*, yet it does issue from a kind of seasoned knowledge that is almost unshockable, certainly undupable but still not altogether disenchanted. Its psychological realism insists that too much should not be expected from people, or from life in general, while its artistic virtuosity insists that too much is the least we should expect. The poem is at one and the same time a structure of sounds and sweet airs that give delight and hurt not, a tongue-in-cheek love story and an intimation of a far more generous and desirable way of being alive in the world.

In his *Defence of Poesy*, Sir Philip Sidney linked the creative act of the poet with the pursuit of virtue, 'since our erected wit maketh us know what perfection is, and yet our infected will keepeth us from reaching unto it'. There is, of course, something too simple, perhaps even too phallocentric about that account of the matter, and no honest reader of poems, then or now, would see moral improvement or, for that matter, political education as the end and purpose of his or her absorption in a poetic text. There's more phenomenological accuracy in John Keats's notion that poetry surprises by a fine excess, although it's worth remembering that by 'excess' Keats did not mean just a sensuous overabundance of description. What he also had in mind was a general gift for outstripping the reader's expectation, an inventiveness that cannot settle for the conventional notion that enough is enough but always wants to extend the alphabet of emotional and technical expression. Even a poem as tonally sombre as, say, 'Tintern Abbey' is doing something surprising and excessive, getting further back and deeper in than the poet knew it would, the poet being nevertheless still ready to go with it, to rise to the rhythmic and rhetorical occasion.

At these moments there is always a kind of homoeopathic benefit for the reader in experiencing the shifts and extensions which constitute the life of a poem. An exuberant rhythm, a display of metrical virtuosity, some rising intellectual ground successfully surmounted—experiencing things like these gratifies and furthers the range of the mind's and the body's pleasures and helps the reader to obey the old command: *Nosce teipsum*. Know thyself. If I may quote a stanza from an occasional poem of my own:

> This is how poems help us live.
> They match the meshes in the sieve
> Life puts us through; they take and give
> Our proper measure
> And prove themselves most transitive
> When they give pleasure.

Sidney too was concerned with this tonic effect of poetry when he spoke in his *Defence* of 'the . . . forcibleness or *Energia* (as the Greeks call it) of the writer'; and it is this original forcibleness, this sensation of clear water springing through sand, that makes a work like Marlowe's 'Hero and Leander' so valuable and guarantees its safe passage through a world of accusing ideologies and impugned ideals.

John Clare's Prog

Prog: *Gain or profit in a bargain; booty.*

Almost thirty years ago, in a poem called 'Follower', I wrote about myself as a child dragging along behind my father when he was out ploughing. The poem began:

My father worked with a horse-plough,

and unremarkable as this may have been as a line of verse, it was still the result of some revision. In fact, I had deliberately suppressed the one touch of individuality that had appeared in the first version. Originally I had written:

My father *wrought* with a horse-plough,

because until relatively recently that verb was the common one in the speech of mid-Ulster. Country people used the word 'wrought' naturally and almost exclusively when they talked about a person labouring with certain tools or animals, and it always carried a sense of wholehearted commitment to the task. You wrought with horses or with a scythe or with a plough; and you might also have wrought at hay or at flax or at bricklaying. So the word implied solidarity with speakers of the South Derry vernacular and a readiness to stand one's linguistic ground: why, then, did I end up going for the more pallid and expected alternative 'worked'?

The answer is, I suppose, because I thought twice. And once you think twice about a local usage, you have been displaced from it, and your right to it has been contested by the official linguistic censor with whom another part of you is secretly in league. You have been translated from the land of unselfconsciousness to the suburbs of the *mot juste*. This is, of course, a very distinguished neighbourhood and contains important citizens like Mr Joyce, persons who sound equally at home in their hearth speech and their acquired language, persons who seem to have obliterated altogether the line between self-conscious and unselfconscious usage, and to have established uncensored access to every coffer of the word-hoard. But this spontaneous multivocal proficiency is as far beyond most writers as unbroken residence within the first idiom of a hermetically sealed, univocal home place. Our language may indeed be our world, but our writing, unless we happen to belong with the multitudinous geniuses like Joyce or Shakespeare, or with those whom we might call the monoglot geniuses—like John Clare—our writing is unlikely ever to be entirely co-extensive with that world.

Clare, we might say, wrought at language but did not become overwrought about it. Early in his literary career, he had what is called success. His first, 1820 volume, *Poems Descriptive of Rural Life and Scenery*, was reprinted; he went from Helpston to London; he met the well-known writers of the day; he had respect and learned something about the literary milieu. And then, notoriously, the fashion changed, the celebrity dwindled, the publications got spaced out and were less and less noticed until he ended up in Northamptonshire Asylum for the last twenty years of his life, having spent his late thirties and forties in mental confusion, economic distress and poetic neglect. It was only in 1978, for example, that a publisher brought out the extraordinarily copious collection entitled *The Midsummer Cushion* which Clare had ready for printing in the 1830s.

All regrettably true. But for the purposes of re-reading him today, we might express this truth in a different way and say that after an initial brush with the censor, Clare refused to co-operate. The story of his career, in other words, can be told as follows. Once upon a time John Clare was lured to the edge of his word-horizon and his tonal horizon, looked about him eagerly, tried out a few new words and accents and then, wilfully and intelligently, withdrew and dug in his local heels. Henceforth, he declared, I shall not think twice. It is this wilful strength of Clare's that I want to talk about, how it manifests itself and constitutes the distinctive power of his poetry. And I want to say something also about what his example can mean to poets at the present time, on the eve of his bicentenary year, in social and linguistic conditions of a far more volatile and various sort than those that prevailed when he was negotiating the personal, poetic and historical crises of his prime.

Like all readers, I am indebted to John Barrell's diagnosis of Clare's strengths and complications, in so far as it reveals him as a poet who possessed a secure local idiom but operated within the range of an official literary tradition. And previous to Barrell's work, of course, I read Clare in editions by Geoffrey Summerfield and Eric Robinson. In fact, my only regret in talking about Clare here today is that Geoffrey Summerfield is no longer alive to know about it. His sudden death in February 1991 was a great loss, and not only in the field of Clare studies. But it is some compensation to have his recent Penguin *Selected Clare*, which, taken together with other recent editions by R. K. R. Thornton, Eric Robinson and David Powell, has given us Clare's works in all their unpunctuated vigour. This modern editorial effort prepares the way for a wider recognition of the foundedness of Clare's voice and the sureness of his instinct in cleaving to his original 'sound of sense'. His unmistakable signature is written in most distinctively and sounded forth most spontaneously in the scores of fourteen-line poems which Clare wrote about small incidents involving the flora and fauna of rural Northamptonshire. Some of these poems are indeed conventional sonnets, with an octave and a turn and a sestet or with some gesture either to that Petrarchan shape or to the Shakespearean one. But many of them are like the one I'm going to read now, seven couplets wound up like clockwork and then set free to scoot merrily through their foreclosed motions. He seemed to write this kind of poem as naturally as he breathed:

> I found a ball of grass among the hay
> And proged it as I passed and went away
> And when I looked I fancied something stirred
> And turned agen and hoped to catch the bird
> When out an old mouse bolted in the wheat
> With all her young ones hanging at her teats
> She looked so odd and so grotesque to me

> I ran and wondered what the thing could be
> And pushed the knapweed bunches where I stood
> When the mouse hurried from the crawling brood
> The young ones squeaked and when I went away
> She found her nest again among the hay
> The water oer the pebbles scarce could run
> And broad old cesspools glittered in the sun

Clare progged the ball of grass. With equal metrical ease and lexical efficiency, he could have poked it, or with some slight readjustment of the pentameter he could have prodded it. But had he done either of these things, both he and his readers would have been distanced in a minimal yet essential way from the here-and-nowness, or the there-and-thenness, of what happened. I am reminded of a remark made once by an Irish diplomat with regard to the wording of a certain document. 'This', he said, 'is a minor point of major importance.' In a similar way, the successful outcome of any work of art depends upon the seeming effortlessness and sure-fingeredness with which such minor points are both established and despatched. To take another instance, there is in this poem a very instructive use of the preposition 'at' rather than the more expected 'from' or 'on', in the couplet:

> When out an old mouse bolted in the wheat
> With all her young ones hanging at her teats.

'Hanging on' would have had certain pathetic, anthropomorphic associations that would have weakened the objective clarity of the whole presentation; 'hanging from' would have rendered the baby mice far too passive; 'hanging at' suggests 'catching at' and itself catches the sudden desperate tiny tightening of the mouse-jaws, and so conveys a reaction that is both biologically automatic and instinctively affectionate. (There is also an echo, of course, of the phrase 'at the teat'.) But the real strength, once again, is the way the idiom has sprung into its place in the line without any trace of choice or forethought on the poet's part; and in this it partakes of the poem's overall virtue, which is its notational speed. The cou-

plets hurry in upon themselves as fast as pencil-strokes in an excited drawing, and as in the act of drawing, there is no anxiety
about lines repeating and intersecting with the trajectory of other
lines. This is why the 'ands' and 'whens' and self-contained couplets and end-stopped movement of the lines do not irk as they
might. They are clearly a function of the perception rather than a
fault of the execution. They are eager to grab a part of the action.
They are both a prerequisite and a consequence of one kind of accuracy and immediacy, as delightful in their compulsively acceler-
ating way as the beautiful deceleration of the two final lines:

> The water oer the pebbles scarce could run
> And broad old cesspools glittered in the sun.

Once again, what is achieved in this couplet is not a self-conscious
effect but a complete absorption. The eye of the writing is concentrated utterly upon what is before it but also allows what is before
it deep access to what is behind it. The eye, at any rate, does not lift
to see what effect it is having upon the reader; and this typical
combination of deep-dreaming in-placeness and wide-lens atten-
tiveness in the writing is mirrored by the cesspools as they glitter
in the sun. They too combine a deep-lodged, hydraulic locatedness
within the district with a totally receptive adjustment to the light
and heat of solar distances.

And yet, innocent as the poet's eye may seem, it is worth stress-
ing the point that his poem is as surely made of words as any by
Mallarmé. It has a special realism and reliability because it is a
naturalist's observation, but neither the simplicity of its utterance
nor the solidity of its content line by line should prevent its being
regarded as a poetic achievement of rare finesse and integrity. In
fact, in the water that is scarcely fit to run over the pebbles there is
to be found an analogue for the thirst or ache at the core of Clare's
poetry. This ache comes from his standing at the frontier of writing, in a gap between the unmistakably palpable world he inhabits
and another world, reached for and available only to awakened
language.

The kind of excellence I have been praising in 'The Mouse's

Nest' was not quite allowed for by the critical language Clare inherited from the eighteenth century. He wrote more richly and
strangely than he could have told himself. There is an eerie distance between the materiality of what I have just been discussing
and the abstract primness of the following, also by Clare:

> A pleasing image to its page conferred
> In living character and breathing word
> Becomes a landscape heard and felt and seen
> Sunshine and shade one harmonizing green . . .
> Thus truth to nature as the true sublime
> Stands a mount atlas overpeering time

These lines come from a verse-essay called 'Shadows of Taste', and
they reveal Clare outside the borders of his first world, rehearsing
the new language and aligning himself with the new perspectives
of a world beyond. The footwork here is more self-conscious and
the carriage of the verse more urbane than anything in the sonnet
about the mouse's nest, and it would therefore have been more
acceptable to his first reading public. Naturally enough, his 1820
volume, *Poems Descriptive of Rural Life and Scenery*, was influenced by the modes of landscape writing established by Goldsmith
and Thomson and Gray and Collins. In order to cross the line from
his unwriting self to his writing identity, Clare had to proceed
upon the moving stair of those styles which were the current
styles. An early poem to his native village of Helpston, for example, speaks with the unmistakable accents of Goldsmith's *Deserted
Village*:

> Hail humble Helpstone where thy valies spread
> And thy mean village lifts its lowly head
> Unknown to grandeur and unknown to fame
> No minstrel boasting to advance thy name

and so on. And here is another passage, again taken from 'Shadows
of Taste', which reveals him as an equally resourceful mimic when
it comes to projecting the voice of Alexander Pope:

Styles with fashions vary—tawdry chaste
Have had their votaries which each fancied taste
From Donns old homely gold whose broken feet
Jostles the readers patience from its seat
To Popes smooth rhymes that regularly play
In music stated periods all the way
That starts and closes starts again and times
Its tuning gammut true as minster chimes
From those old fashions stranger metres flow
Half prose half verse that stagger as they go
One line starts smooth and then for room perplext
Elbows along and knocks against the next
And half its neighbour where a pause marks time
There the clause ends what follows is for rhyme

This is really laid-back stuff. For all his reputation as a peasant poet, Clare had mastered the repertoire of prescribed styles and skills: nowadays a poet as capable and informed as this would probably be head-hunted to teach a graduate workshop in versification. The point is, however, that Clare's later, less conventionally correct and less (so to speak) tasteful forays into poetic utterance should really be understood as the redress of poetry in the third sense in which I used the term earlier. (See page 285.) This was a sense that came from the chase, where 'to redress' meant to bring the hounds or the deer back to the proper course, and I associated this meaning of the term with the break-out of innate capacity which marks all true lyric activity.

The excitement of finding oneself suddenly at full tilt on the right path, of having picked up a scent and hit the trail, this kind of sprinting, hurdling joy manifests itself in scores of sonnets and short poems of exclamatory observation which Clare wrote all through his life, but especially in the 1820s and 1830s. And this is the part of his work I am singling out for special praise. Which is not to say that I want to decry the full-dress correctness of other writings by him. The combination of realism, moralism and metrical efficiency when he is on his best Augustan behaviour has to be saluted. These more sententious poems show Clare at work under the influence of the poetry-speak current in England in his day; it would have taken a talent as educated and overbearing as Joyce's to have resisted the orthodoxies then governing nature writing. Some of these were famously expressed in a letter to Clare from his publisher, John Taylor. Taylor was being neither exploitative nor insensitive but simply acting as a mouthpiece for received ideas about correct poetic behaviour when he urged Clare to 'raise his view' and 'speak of the Appearances of Nature . . . more philosophically'. But this is not the writing of Clare's which has worn best. Its excellence is, as I say, characteristic of its time; it moves fluently and adequately, but it moves like water that flows over a mill-wheel without turning it.

On the other hand, the poems of Clare's that still make a catch in the breath and establish a positively bodily hold upon the reader are those in which the wheel of total recognition has been turned. At their most effective, Clare's pentameters engage not just the mechanical gears of a metre: at their most effective, they take hold also on the sprockets of our creatureliness. By which I only mean that on occasion a reader simply cannot help responding with immediate recognition to the pell-mell succession of vividly accurate impressions. No one of these is extraordinary in itself, nor is the resulting poem in any way spectacular. What distinguishes it is an unspectacular joy and totally alert love for the one-thing-after-anotherness of the world. Here, by way of illustration, is another one of Clare's sonnets in couplets—perhaps we should call them *supplets*—picked almost at random from the ones Clare wrote at Northborough during his early and middle forties:

> The old pond full of flags and fenced around
> With trees and bushes trailing to the ground
> The water weeds are all around the brink
> And one clear place where cattle go to drink
> From year to year the schoolboy thither steals
> And muddys round the place to catch the eels
> The cowboy often hiding from the flies
> Lies there and plaits the rushcap as he lies
> The hissing owl sits moping all the day

And hears his song and never flies away
The pinks nest hangs upon the branch so thin
The young ones caw and seem as tumbling in
While round them thrums the purple dragon flye
And great white butter flye goes dancing bye

Rarely has the butteriness of a butterfly been so available. The insect has flown into the medium and survives forever there as a pother of lip movement and a set of substituted feet in the scansion of the line. And the old pond here is like the cesspool in 'The Mouse's Nest', in so far as it embodies for Clare not only the reality of all such places *as* places, with distinct characters and histories, but also their value as a set of memories and affections at the back of his mind. There is dreamwork going on here, as well as photography. The casual rightness and potency of the thing come from a level of engagement well below the visual; in fact, the whole poem acts as a reminder of how integrated and concentrated a poetic response can be. What is unstated can still be felt as a potent charge inside or behind an image or a cadence, and what lies behind the self-possession, the sureness of tone and grip on place in such a poem is Clare's great feat of endurance in the face of historical and personal crises.

So far, for example, I have not mentioned Clare's solidarity with the plight of the rural poor, or taken account of the Enclosure Act that affected Helpston in 1809; I have not commented upon the trauma of the poet's move from his native village at the age of thirty-nine to the nearby parish of Northborough; I have not enumerated his gradually more frequent depressions, lapses of memory, hallucinations and collapses into delusion when he imagined himself Lord Byron or the prizefighter Jack Randall; I have not dwelt upon the desperate love he felt for his childhood sweetheart Mary Joyce or his intermittent conviction that he was married to her as well as to his wedded wife, Martha Turner; nor have I alluded to his voluntary entry into Dr Allen's mental hospital in High Beach in Epping Forest in 1837 and his heartbreaking journey of escape out of there four years later in July 1841. But if I have done none of these things, it is not because I believe that

Clare did not suffer fantastically, fiercely and unrelievedly as a result of them, or that they are not fundamental to his sensibility and achievement as a poet.

On the contrary, the vigour of the poetry is linked to the fact that Clare was harrowed and stricken by personal and historical upheavals all the days of his life, until the two final suspended decades he spent in Northampton Asylum. The poems of these years have understandably been called the 'poems of John Clare's madness', and yet *as poems* they seem to me less terribly keyed than much that came before them. The torsions and distortions reached a climax in 1841, just before and after his escape from Epping Forest and during the opening stages of his final commitment on 29 December of that year. These are the months when he wrote his two Byronic pastiches, *Child Harold* and *Don Juan*, the latter of which once more deploys in wonky but madly convincing ways Clare's old gift for mimicry. In this work, he assumes an antic disposition, taunting the reader with a highly aggressive and transgressive intelligence, making sexual and political hay and mayhem. Enigma and affront are precariously balanced, for example, when he turns his attention to his present whereabouts in Essex:

> There's Doctor Bottle, imp who deals in urine,
> A keeper of state-prisons for the queen
> As great a man as is the Doge of Turin
> And save in London is but seldom seen
> Yclep'd old A-ll-n—mad-brained ladies curing
> Some p-x-d like Flora and but seldom clean
> The new road o'er the forest is the right one
> To see red hell and, further on, the white one

This is good stuff but it is not quite Clare in his element. The work which simultaneously displays the greatest pressure, the greatest sureness and the greatest nonchalance comes in the main in poems written before Northampton. Obviously, nobody is going to deny the apocalyptic pathos of his most famous asylum poem, the one beginning 'I am—yet what I am none cares or knows' and including the line about 'the vast shipwreck of my lifes esteems'; nor is anybody going to undervalue the bonus of indispensable songs and sonnets that belong to this period, especially the very late sonnet 'To John Clare' (and not forgetting 'The Round Oak', 'The Yellowhammer', 'The Wood Anemonie', 'The flag top quivers in the breeze', 'The Thunder mutters louder and more loud' and others). But what crowns the lifetime's effort is the great outpouring in his early middle years of short verse about solitary figures in a landscape, or outcast figures, or threatened creatures, or lonely creatures, or birds and birds' nests or dramatic weather changes, all of which manage to convey uncanny intimations of both vulnerability and staying power. By the very fact of having got themselves written, these poems manifest the efficacy of creative spirit in the face of all the adversity I noticed a moment ago; and they prove once again the truth of Keith Douglas's notion that the work of art inheres in 'stating some truth whose eternal quality exacts the same reverence as eternity itself'.

In this work, Clare is led towards the thing behind his voice and ear which Nadezhda Mandelstam called 'the nugget of harmony'. To locate this phonetic jewel, to hit upon and hold one's true note, is a most exacting and intuitive discipline, but it was particularly difficult for a writer like Clare, whose situation in the 1820s was to some extent the same as Christopher Murray Grieve's a hundred years later; which is to say that Clare, like Grieve, was operating within a received idiom that he half-knew was not the right one for him. Grieve dealt with the problem by inventing synthetic Scots and becoming Hugh MacDiarmid. Perhaps if Clare had changed his name to John Fen or Jack Prog, his wilfulness would have been more clarified, and his awareness of what his poetry had to do would have been more pointed. Even so, one might say that MacDiarmid's theoretical passion in the 1920s fulfilled Clare's poetic intuition of the 1820s—although Clare's was always by far the surer voice, artistically speaking. Everything that MacDiarmid wrote about revitalizing the vernacular, all his aspirations to unblock linguistic access to a reservoir of common knowledge and unacknowledged potential, all his angry regret that English literature maintained 'a narrow ascendancy tradition instead of broad-basing itself on all the diverse cultural elements and splendid variety of languages and dialects, in the British Isles'—all this was a making explicit of what was implicit in much of Clare's practice. And I believe that MacDiarmid would also have recognized some affinity between himself and Clare when it came to the use of the ballad measure.

This was the one poetic beat that had sounded in the ears of both poets from the beginning, the measure in which personal and communal experience could enter each other as indissolubly as two streams, and it was the measure in which Clare's moral outrage got expressed most pungently. When, for example, in one of his most powerful poems, the quarry field known as Swordy Well begins to speak, we recognize immediately that Clare's voice is in a deep old groove and that he is hauling into vivid speech an awareness of injustice for which he has paid a personal price; yet it is also an awareness promoted by the bleak folk wisdom of the ballad tradition and by the high tragic understanding of life shared by the authors of *King Lear* and the Book of Job.

The 1809 Act of Parliament for the Enclosure of Helpston had granted Swordy Well to the overseers of the roads in the parish. The field had thereby lost its independence and become like a pauper, dependent upon parish charity. In Clare's poem, what opens the channels of expression so exhilaratingly is the removal of every screen between the identity of the person and the identity of the place. 'The Lament of Swordy Well' is by no means as extraordinary an achievement as MacDiarmid's *A Drunk Man Looks at the Thistle*, but it still represents a thrilling integration of common idiom and visionary anger of the sort that MacDiarmid longed to reintroduce in Scotland. However, the main point I want to make about it is that the ballad stanza does for Clare what it would do for MacDiarmid; it places him at the centre of his world and keeps his voice on course like a plough in a furrow. Here are a few selected stanzas, where the assailed dignity of the pauper and the fate of the requisitioned ground are mutually expressive of each other's plight:

> I hold no hat to beg a mite
> Nor pick it up when thrown
> Nor limping leg I hold in sight

But pray to keep my own
Where profit gets his clutches in
Theres little he will leave
Gain stooping for a single pin
Will stick it on his sleeve . . .

Alas dependance thou'rt a brute
Want only understands
His feelings wither branch and root
That falls in parish hands
The muck that clouts the ploughman's shoe
The moss that hides the stone
Now Im become the parish due
Is more then I can own . . .

The silver springs grown naked dykes
Scarce own a bunch of rushes
When grain got high the tasteless tykes
Grubbed up trees banks, and bushes
And me they turned me inside out
For sand and grit and stones
And turned my old green hills about
And pickt my very bones

These things that claim my own as theirs
Were born but yesterday
But ere I fell to town affairs
I were as proud as they
I kept my horses cows and sheep
And built the town below
Ere they had cat or dog to keep
And then to use me so . . .

The bees flye round in feeble rings
And find no blossom bye
Then thrum their almost weary winds
Upon the moss and die
Rabbits that find my hills turned o'er
Forsake my poor abode

They dread a workhouse like the poor
And nibble on the road . . .

I've scare a nook to call my own
For things that creep or flye
The beetle hiding neath a stone
Does well to hurry bye
Stock eats my struggles every day
As bare as any road
He's sure to be in somethings way
If eer he stirs abroad . . .

The point of this poem, of course, and of another similar if gentler exercise in dramatic monologue called 'The Lamentations of Round Oak Water', is to make a point. Their social protest and their artistic effort are in perfect step. And if there is an emphatic thump to the metre, this is inherent in the convention: the broad effect comes with the genre. What I want to emphasize is that the ballad stanza kept Clare on the right road poetically by giving him a traditional tune to march to, if not total access to his own 'nugget of harmony'.

That nugget is something more elusive and more individual to a poet than anything comprised by a metre. In Clare's case, it is to be found mostly in the poems that we might call his short takes. These are quick little forays of surprising innocence and accuracy, poems where subjects such as the ones I mentioned earlier—creatures, country scenes and so on—pass in and out of language every bit as fluently as moods and impulses pass between the body and the weather itself. In these poems the nugget of harmony is not present as a virtuosity; the trueness of these 'supplets' has less to do with composed sweetness and nice modulation and deliberate technique than with a spontaneous at-homeness in speech itself. In fact, there is not a great deal of variety in the tunes of the poems, just as there never is any great variety of pitch in the cries that people let out at moments of spontaneous excitement—and the work I'm thinking of can be understood to constitute a succession of just such brief, intense, spontaneous outcries.

The poems about birds' nests belong to this category, especially ones like 'The Wryneck's Nest' and 'The Fern Owl's Nest'. Well-known snapshot works such as 'Hares at Play' belong to it also; and little genre paintings like the sonnet 'The Woodman'; and landscape poems such as 'Emmonsdale Heath'; and, in a deeper register, the short sonnet sequence 'The Badger' and the sonnet-diptych 'The Marten-Cat' and 'The Fox'. The desire to quote all of these is strong, but the time is short and the texts are widely available. Here instead is an incidental example of the kind of excellence I have in mind, a fragment of sorts, just a stray stanza really, and yet its random swoop upon the momentary—its casually perfect close-ups on raindrops, for example—illustrates all over again the fact that the truth of art does lie in those minor points of major importance:

> The thunder mutters louder and more loud
> With quicker motion hay folks ply the rake
> Ready to bust slow sails the pitch black cloud
> And all the gang a bigger haycock make
> To sit beneath—the woodland winds awake
> The drops so large wet all thro' in an hour
> A tiney flood runs down the leaning rake
> In the sweet hay yet dry the hay folks cower
> And some beneath the waggon shun the shower

It's populous, it's unpretentious, it seems effortless, yet it is actually a triumph of compression that manages to combine the shapeliness of nine end-stopped, closed-off lines in rhyme with the totally active movements of clouds and haymakers and raindrops and waterlogged wind. In fact, the movements of the world are here an aspect of the movements of Clare's own vivid spirit; and the lines both illustrate and obey the Wordsworthian imperative that poetry should disclose in the workings of the universe analogues for the working of the human mind and soul. Just because Clare's poetry abounds in actualities, just because it is as full of precise delightful detail as a granary is full of grains, does not mean that it is doomed to pile up and sink down in its own materiality. On the contrary, that which is special and unique about it is its lambency, its skim-factor, its bobbing, unencumbered motion. It is what Lawrence calls the poetry of the living present; and its persistent theme, under many guises, in different subjects and scenes and crises, is the awful necessity of the gift for keeping going and the lovely wonder that it can be maintained—a gift which is tutored by the instinctive cheer and courage of living creatures and heartened by every fresh turn and return of things in the natural world. Clare is always cheering for the victim, always ready to pitch in on the side of whatever is tender and well disposed or whatever is courageous and outnumbered—like the badger:

> He turns about to face the loud uproar
> And drives the rebels to their very doors
> The frequent stone is hurled where eer they go
> When badgers fight and every ones a foe
> The dogs are clapt and urged to join the fray
> The badger turns and drives them all away
> Though scarcly half as big dimute and small
> He fights with dogs for hours and beats them all
> The heavy mastiff savage in the fray
> Lies down and licks his feet and turns away
> The bull-dog knows his match and waxes cold
> The badger grins and never leaves his hold
> He drives the crowd and follows at their heels
> And bites them through. The drunkard swears and reels

Needless to say, in spite of my praise for these vivid shorter poems, I do not wish to underrate performances by Clare of greater rhetorical sweep and more sustained intellectual purpose. His ode 'To the Snipe', for instance, is something of a set piece and exhibits the customary fit between word and thing—the quagmire overgrown 'with hassock tufts of sedge', and the moor with its 'spungy lap'—but what makes it a poem of classical force is the perfect posture it maintains as it moves energetically through the demands of a strict and complex stanza. There's something almost Marvellian about its despatch and articulation. Just because I set such store by

Clare the astonished admirer doesn't mean I don't esteem the more deliberately ambitious poet of lines like these:

> Lover of swamps
> The quagmire overgrown
> With hassock tufts of sedge—where fear encamps
> Around thy home alone
>
> The trembling grass
> Quakes from the human foot
> Nor bears the weight of man to let him pass
> Where he alone and mute
>
> Sitteth at rest
> In safety neath the clump
> Of huge flag-forrest that thy haunts invest
> Or some old sallow stump . . .
>
> For here thy bill
> Suited by wisdom good
> Of rude unseemly length doth delve and drill
> The gelid mass for food

'To the Snipe' is one kind of excellence, and there are others. Nobody would want to slight the balmier, plashier riches of a poem like 'The Summer Shower', or the set pieces in *The Shepherd's Calendar* or those other much praised and thematically central poems of the Northborough period like 'The Flitting' and 'Remembrances'. But it's possible to acknowledge the different orders of excellence which these poems represent and still choose to prize most in Clare's *oeuvre* that attribute which Tom Paulin characterized in another context as 'the now of utterance'.

Paulin has written on Clare in an essay of brilliant advocacy in *Minotaur* (1992), his book about poetry and the nation-state. But here I want to draw attention to the very suggestive remarks he made earlier in his introduction to *The Faber Book of Vernacular Verse* (1990), where he had this to say about Clare's texts as we now have them, restored to their original unpunctuated condition:

The restored texts of the poems embody an alternative social idea. With their lack of punctuation, freedom from standard spelling and charged demotic ripples, they become a form of Nation Language that rejects the polished urbanity of Official Standard.

And then, having alluded to the poet's 'ranter's sense of being trapped within an unjust society and an authoritarian language', Paulin concludes that 'Clare dramatizes his experience of the class system and its codified language as exile and imprisonment in Babylon.' By implication, then, Clare is a sponsor and a forerunner of modern poetry in post-colonial nation languages, poetry that springs from the difference and/or disaffection of those whose spoken tongue is an English which sets them at cultural and perhaps political odds with others in possession of that normative 'Official Standard'. Paulin's contention is that wherever the accents of exacerbation and orality enter a text, be it in Belfast or Brooklyn or Brixton, we are within earshot of Clare's influence and example. What was once regarded as Clare's out-of-stepness with the main trends has become his central relevance: as ever, the need for a new kind of poetry in the present has called into being precursors out of the past.

But still, when we look at Paulin's own poetry, and that of Les Murray, Liz Lochhead, Tony Harrison, Derek Walcott, Edward Kamau Brathwaite and many figures in the dub and reggae tradition, it becomes evident that nobody can any longer belong as innocently or entirely within the acoustic of a first local or focal language as Clare could—*focus* being, you remember, the Latin word for hearth. Nowadays every isle—be it Aran or Orkney or Ireland or Trinidad—is full of broadcast noises, every ear full of media accents and expendable idioms. In the few nooks of dialect I have kept in touch with over the years, the first things children speak nowadays are more likely to be in imitation of TV jingles than of the tones of their parents. So what a poet takes from Clare in these conditions is not an antiquarian devotion to dialect or a nostalgia for folkways; rather, the instructive thing about Clare's practice is the way it shows the necessity for being forever at the ready, always in good linguistic shape, limber and fit to go intelligently with the impulse.

In the shorter poems I have been praising, Clare exhibits the same kind of self-galvanizing, gap-jumping life that sends poems by Tom Paulin and Les Murray catapulting and skimming off and over two or three different language levels. The kind of learned and local words that propel their poems and open them inward and forward, the whole unruly combination of phonetic jolts and associated sidewindings, all this obviously issues from a far more eclectic relish of language than Clare ever developed. Nevertheless, he would have been at home with the verve and impatience which the vocabulary of these poets manifests, their need to body-swerve past the censor and shoulder through decorum, to go on a poetic roll that can turn on occasion into a political rough ride.

Clare, in fact, inspires one to trust that poetry can break through the glissando of post-modernism and get stuck in the mud of real imaginative haulage work. He never heard Mandelstam's famous phrase about Acmeism being a 'nostalgia for world culture', but oddly enough, it makes sense to think of Clare in relation to the arrival of poetry in that longed-for place or state—an arrival which John Bayley has observed in the work of many gifted contemporaries. The dream of a world culture, after all, is a dream of a world where no language will be relegated, a world where the ancient rural province of Boeotia (which Les Murray has made an image for all the outback and dialect cultures of history) will be on an equal footing with the city-state of Athens; where not just Homer but Hesiod will have his due honour. Clare's poetry underwrites a vision like this, where one will never have to think twice about the cultural and linguistic expression of one's world on its own terms since nobody else's terms will be imposed as normative and official. To read him for the exotic flavours of an archaic diction and the picturesque vistas of a bucolic past is to miss the trust he instills in the possibility of a self-respecting future for all languages, an immense, creative volubility where human existence comes to life and has life more abundantly because it is now being expressed in its own self-gratifying and unhindered words.

A Torchlight Procession of One:
Hugh MacDiarmid

Christopher Murray Grieve took the pseudonym Hugh MacDiarmid in 1922 and between then and his death in 1978 turned himself into one of the most excessive writers of the twentieth century. His *Complete Poems*, in two volumes, runs to some fifteen hundred pages and represents only a fraction of his total output; the prose is more voluminous still, for MacDiarmid was a journalist and controversialist from his teenage years and made his living by producing copy for newspapers and undertaking commissions for a variety of full-length books. The work as a whole reveals a disconcerting unevenness, but the quality of his best poetry and the historic importance of his whole endeavour mean that MacDiarmid deserves more attention than he has received outside his native Scotland.

MacDiarmid's position in Scottish literature and culture is in many respects analogous to that of Yeats in Ireland, and the liberationist ambitions of Irish writers were always of great importance to him. His linguistic overweening was hugely encouraged by the example of Joyce, while Yeats and other post-Revival writers continued to be highly influential in his programme of cultural nationalism. One could even say that MacDiarmid achieved for Scotland what the combined efforts of the Gaelic League and the Literary Revival achieved for Ireland: first of all, he effected a reorientation of attitudes to the country's two indigenous languages, the Scots Gaelic of the Highlands and Islands and the vernacular Scots of the Borders and Lowlands. And second, MacDiarmid more or less single-handedly created a literature in one of these languages and acted as an inspiration for the poet who was to change the course of poetry in the other.

In the 1920s, MacDiarmid himself emerged fully fledged as a writer of lyric genius in the language he had invented and which he called Synthetic Scots; in the 1930s, his friendship with Sorley

MacLean helped MacLean to fare forward and become the redemptive genius of modern poetry in Gaelic. Within the contemporary conditions, in other words, MacDiarmid demonstrated the artistic possibilities of the indigenous speech and in so doing brought to the fore what he called 'lapsed or unrealized qualities' in the two linguistic heritages which corresponded 'to "unconscious" elements in a distinctive Scottish psychology'. All in all, his practice and example have had an inestimable influence on the history of Scottish writing in particular and on Scottish culture in general over the last fifty years. There is a demonstrable link between MacDiarmid's act of cultural resistance in the Scotland of the 1920s and the literary self-possession of writers such as Alasdair Gray, Tom Leonard, Liz Lochhead and James Kelman in the 1980s and 1990s. He prepared the ground for a Scottish literature that would be self-critical and experimental in relation to its own inherited forms and idioms, but one that would also be stimulated by developments elsewhere in world literature.

MacDiarmid, then, was an inspirational writer whose artistic achievement remains problematic. He was a communist and a nationalist, a propagandist and a plagiarist, a drinker and a messer, and he carried out all these roles with immense panache. He made enemies with as much flair as he made friends. He was a Stalinist and a chauvinist, he was Anglophobic and arrogant, but the very excessiveness which he constantly manifested, the exorbitant quality that marked everything he did, also charged his positive achievements and gave them real staying power. To put it another way, MacDiarmid possessed that 'forcibleness' which Sir Philip Sidney judged to be the ultimately distinguishing mark of poetry itself, although it was a forcibleness which revealed itself as unmistakably in the aggravations and affronts of his work as in its triumphs.

So the negative things that can be said about MacDiarmid's poetry do not invalidate his achievement, nor would they have greatly disturbed the poet himself. He was very clear-headed about his productions and in the 1960s wrote to a BBC producer as follows: 'My job, as I see it, has never been to lay a tit's egg, but to erupt like a volcano, emitting not only flame, but a lot of rubbish.'

From a person of less abundant capacity and with a less compulsive appetite for overdoing things, this could have sounded like an excuse; from MacDiarmid, however, it emerges as a boast. With him, the speech from the dock is sure to be a roar of defiance. No wonder Norman MacCaig suggested that the anniversary of his death should be marked each year by the observance of two minutes of pandemonium. 'He would walk into my mind', MacCaig said at the graveside in Langholm in 1978, 'as if it were a town and he a torchlight procession of one, lighting up the streets . . .'

Still, although his vitality was epoch-making, MacDiarmid has probably written more disconcertingly than any other major twentieth-century poet. Anybody who wishes to praise the work has to admit straight away that there is an un-get-roundable connection between the prodigality of his gifts and the prodigiousness of his blather. The task for everybody confronted with the immense bulk of his collected verse is to make a firm distinction between the true poetry and what we might call the habitual printout. And then there are the questions that arise because of his magpie habits of composition (or is it modernist collage?): the silent incorporation into his own text of the texts of others, sometimes of a technical nature, sometimes discursive, sometimes even literary, the most notorious case here being the eight-line lyric entitled 'Perfect', which—depending upon how much of a critical Malvolio you want to be—can be regarded as either a found poem or a plagiarism from a story by Glyn Thomas. Even if all that mileage of earnest, pedantic and notoriously problematic verse does not disqualify him from the league of the major talents, it does prevent him from being regarded as 'a master'. If we call a writer a master, it suggests an *oeuvre* with a kind of roundedness and finish that MacDiarmid did not even aspire to. He was more devoted to opening salvos than to finishing touches; and even though as a poet he must have approved the idea that every force evolves its form, he was one of those whose faculties rally more naturally to the banner of force.

So the volcanic image he used about himself was entirely appropriate, and, in fact, MacDiarmid the poet was himself the result of an eruption. In 1922 he emerged like a new and fiery form out of the agitated element of Christopher Grieve's imagination; or it could be said with equal justification that he emerged from the awakened energies of the Scots language itself. These had been long dormant as a literary resource until they were stirred into fresh activity when Grieve encountered a learned monograph entitled *Lowland Scotch as Spoken in the Lower Strathearn District of Perthshire* and wrote his first poem in a new version of that old speech. And it was at this moment that he took the pseudonym Hugh MacDiarmid, as if he knew instinctively that he had been born again, as if his boydeeds as a literary figure were now over and he had discovered his heroic name and destiny. MacDiarmid arrived as a fully developed phenomenon, one who both produced and was produced by the language he wrote in, henceforth to be known variously as Synthetic Scots or Vernacular Scots or the Doric. And the first poem of the new language was called 'The Watergaw':

> Ae weet forenicht i' the yow-trummle
> I saw yon antrin thing,
> A watergaw wi' its chitterin' licht
> Ayont the on-ding;
> An' I thocht o' the last wild look ye gied
> Afore ye deed!
>
> There was nae reek i' the laverock's hoose
> That nicht—an' nane i' mine;
> But I hae thocht o' that foolish licht
> Ever sin' syne;
> An' I think that mebbe at last I ken
> What your look meant then.

The poet's biographer, Alan Bold, records how these lines came about, when Grieve focused upon two pages of Sir James Wilson's book on the speech of Lower Strathearn:

> Most of the words in 'The Watergaw' . . . came from two pages of Wilson's work. Yow-trummle ('cold weather in July after shear-

ing'), watergaw ('indistinct rainbow') and on-ding ('beating rain or snow') are all on one page; the first phrase of the second stanza 'There was nae reek i' the laverock's hoose / That nicht' appears in Wilson's list of Proverbs and Sayings . . . where it is glossed as 'There's no smoke in the lark's house to night (said when the night is cold and stormy).'

The use Grieve made of these found elements was a far cry from the kind of busy transcription out of dictionaries and reference books which would disfigure so much of his later work in English. In 1922, however, what the recorded words and expressions did was to stretch a trip-wire in the path of Grieve's auditory imagination so that he was pitched headlong into his linguistic unconscious, into a network of emotional and linguistic systems that had been in place since childhood. The common speech of his subcultural life as a youngster in Dumfriesshire was suddenly ratified by the authority of scholarship. His little self, the dialect creature at the core of his adult speech, began to hear itself amplified within a larger historical acoustic. Grieve turned into MacDiarmid when he realized that his writing identity depended for its empowerment upon his securing an ever deepening access to those primary linguistic strata in his own and his country's memory. And this sense of a nascent truth, of a something not quite clearly apprehended but very definitely experienced, is exactly what is embodied in 'The Watergaw'. Its real subject is the uncanny.

The watergaw, the faint rainbow glimmering in chittering light, provides a sort of epiphany, and MacDiarmid connects the shimmer and weakness and possible revelation in the light behind the drizzle with the indecipherable look he received from his father on his deathbed. But how the poem sounds is probably more important than what it sees. What constitutes the true originality here is the combined sensation of strangeness and at-homeness which the words create. Each expression, each cadence, each rhyme is as surely and reliably in place as a stone on a hillside. The words themselves are uncanny: whether or not their dictionary meaning is understood, it is hard to resist their phonetic allure, their aura of a meaning which has been intuited but not yet quite formulated. Just as the dying father's look transmitted a definite if mysterious promise of revelation, so, on the verge of its disappearance as a living speech, the old language rallies and delivers a new poetry for the future.

What happened in 'The Watergaw', of course, and in other famous lyrics that followed it, such as 'The Eemis Stane' and 'Wheesht, Wheesht' and 'The Bonnie Broukit Bairn', was what typically happens in lyric poetry of the purest sort. Suddenly the thing chanced upon comes forth as the thing predestined: the unforeseen appears as the inevitable. The poem's words seem always to have belonged together and to have enjoyed a distinct existence apart from all other words. Here, for example, is another one of those lyrics upon which MacDiarmid's fame rests, a very short one called 'The Bonnie Broukit Bairn'. The bairn or baby in question is Earth itself, which is distinguished here from other planets by its ability to 'greet', which is to say its ability to weep or cry like an infant. The crimson aura of Mars and the green luminosity of Venus represent one kind of beauty. But Earth's beauty is different, since Earth is the site of human suffering, and this gives it a more grievous and vulnerable presence in the firmament than any of the other planets. 'Crammasy' means crimson, 'gowden' feathers are golden feathers, 'wheen o' blethers' is a pack of nonsense, 'broukit bairn' is a neglected baby, and the 'haill clanjamfrie' is the whole bloody lot of them:

> Mars is braw in crammasy,
> Venus in a green silk goun,
> The auld mune shak's her gowden feathers,
> Their starry talk's a wheen o' blethers,
> Nane for thee a thochtie sparin',
> Earth, thou bonnie broukit bairn!
> —*But greet, an' in your tears ye'll droun*
> *The haill clanjamfrie!*

When he wrote this poem, Grieve was thirty-one years of age, a working journalist with an intense commitment to cultural and political renewal within Scotland, which for him boiled down to resisting and reversing the influence and impositions of English standards and English ways. Born in 1892 in the town of Langholm in Dumfriesshire, he was the first child of a postman father who died young in 1910. His mother came from farming stock and had revealed her own gift for the demotic when she described the newborn poet as 'an eaten and spewed lookin' wee thing wi' een like twa burned holes in a blanket'. After being educated locally and having read, by his own account, everything in the local Carnegie Library, Grieve went at the age of sixteen to a teacher training college in Edinburgh, an institution from which he was forced to withdraw because of an escapade involving the theft of the headmaster's books. From then on, he made his living as a migrant journalist, although it has to be admitted that the migrancy was helped along by Grieve's innate gift for falling out with bosses and his rapidly developing capacity as a whisky drinker. Be that as it may, between January 1911 (when he quit college in Edinburgh) and July 1915 (when he joined the British Army and went off to serve with the Medical Corps in Salonika) Christopher Grieve had worked with the *Edinburgh Evening Dispatch*, the *Monmouthshire Labour News*, the *Clydebank and Renfrew Press*, the *Fife Herald* and the *Fife Coast Chronicle*. He had also read voraciously and had contributed articles to the journal which was to be central to his whole intellectual development, A. R. Orage's *New Age*. Through contact with Orage and his magazine, he was led to read, among others, Nietzsche and Bergson and found himself as deeply susceptible to the Nietzschean injunction 'Become what thou art' as he was to Bergson's claim that it was creative urge rather than natural selection which promoted the evolutionary process. But for Grieve to become what he was would mean becoming MacDiarmid, which in turn would mean achieving a Scottish identity long repressed by Anglocentric attitudes and standard English speech: the evolutionary process would have to be creative not only at a personal level, but at a political level as well.

He returned from the war with a gradually clarifying programme and developed into a propagandist for a new Scottish Idea, something that would take off from and reflect in literary terms Whitman's democratic American idea and Yeats's cultural nationalism, while in the political sphere, the project for a new Scotland would be fired by Lenin's communism and by a vestigial but emotionally decisive predisposition to the Christian way of redemption through self-sacrifice. Grieve, moreover, had been initiated into the rough-and-tumble of politics during a miners' strike in Wales in 1911, and after that through his contacts with socialist activists in Scotland, people like John MacLean and James Maxton; so naturally he was deeply stirred by the Easter Rising in Dublin in 1916 and the Bolshevik Revolution in Russia the following year, two events which had a powerful impact on the way he would henceforth imagine the future, both nationally and internationally.

There was generosity as well as ferocity in MacDiarmid's espousals, and it is well to be reminded that behind his habitual self-promotions there was a constant desire to be of service. As Douglas Sealy observed in a review, he had a calling which he served rather than a career which he worked at. By 1922, at any rate, Christopher Grieve had perfected his idiom as a polemicist and propagandist and was ready for pupation into Hugh MacDiarmid, a creature he would later variously describe as the 'stone among the pigeons' and 'the catfish that vitalizes the other torpid denizens of the aquarium'. Here he is, getting into his stride in an editorial in the first number of the *Scottish Chapbook*, a journal edited by Grieve and devoted to the creation of a new movement in Scottish literature:

> Scottish literature, like all other literatures, has been *written* almost exclusively by blasphemers, immoralists, dipsomaniacs, and madmen, but, unlike most other literatures, has been *written about* almost exclusively by ministers, with, on the whole, an effect similar to that produced by the statement (of the worthy Dr John McIntosh) that 'as a novelist, Robert Louis Stevenson had the art of rendering his writings interesting', and 'his faculty of description was fairly good'.

This prose was fired off in 1922 and represents Grieve in typically provocative form: zesty, head-on, fiercely devoted to eliciting a response. His polemical writings had all the troublemaking tactics of a dangerman in a bar, stripped to his shirtsleeves and squar-

ing up to anyone and everyone. Protest and crusade rather than
nostalgia and pathos were the hallmarks of his new commitment
to the old words. There was nothing backward-looking in the
impulse, for MacDiarmid was very consciously organizing a new
movement in literature and revealing the ambitions of an experi-
menter: he could never have been accused of subscribing to some
form of arrested linguistic development. Synthetic Scots was not
meant to give audiences the simple pleasures of self-recognition,
for that could lead to the sentimentality and self-indulgence which
MacDiarmid wanted to banish from the culture altogether. Nor
was his first purpose to proclaim the superior vitality of the local
language over the compromised and compromising idiom of stan-
dardized modern English. These things might be incidental to his
effort, but central to it was the challenge of jump-starting a language interrupted by history (as Douglas Dunn has called it) and
getting it into modern running order. In fact, MacDiarmid's ways
with the old words were as revolutionary and self-conscious as the
young Ezra Pound's ways with a diction based upon archaism and
a translatorese derived from Anglo-Saxon, Latin and Chinese originals. And there was also something in his practice which corresponded to the poetics of Robert Frost, in so far as the thing that
MacDiarmid was after in the deep Scottish ear resembled what
Frost called 'the sound of sense', a phonetic patterning which preceded speech and authenticated it, a kind of pre-verbal register to
which the poetic voice had to be tuned.

What gave these ideas and hopes credibility was not, however,
MacDiarmid's forcible personality but rather the astonishing
poem which he published in 1926 called *A Drunk Man Looks at
the Thistle*. The title tells all that a reader needs to know before
plunging in: this is an encounter between an intoxicated imagination and everything which that imagination can invent by meditation upon the national symbol of Scotland. At one moment, for
example, the thistle has a mainly domestic and negative meaning,
and is perceived by the drunk man as part and parcel of Scottish
kitsch, of a piece with tartan for tourists, Burns suppers, haggises,
Harry Lauder and every kind of Caledonian corniness. But at another moment it becomes the Yggdrasil, the world-tree, a cosmic

symbol that allows for poetry that is more visionary than satiric, a poetry of great sweep and intellectual resonance which nevertheless still keeps its ear to the native ground. In these lines towards the end of the poem, for example, you can hear the reassuring democratic measure of the ballad stanza; but you can also hear something more stately and deeply orchestrated. There is a stereophonic scope to the music, as if the *gravitas* of the medieval Scots poet William Dunbar were echoing within the stellar reaches of Dante's *Divine Comedy*. (The word 'hain' here, incidentally, means to keep or preserve, and 'toom' to empty out, but what is more important than these details of sense is the sureness of the tone of the whole passage.)

> The stars like thistle's roses floo'er
> The sterile growth o' Space ootour,
> That clad in bitter blasts spreids oot
> Frae me, the sustenance o' its root.
>
> O fain I'd keep my hert entire,
> Fain hain the licht o' my desire,
> But ech, the shinin' streams ascend,
> And leave me empty at the end.
>
> For aince it's toomed my hert and brain
> The thistle needs maun fa' again.
> —But a' its growth'll never fill
> The hole it's turned my life intill! . . .
>
> Yet hae I silence left, the croon o' a'.

Through the deep reach of this poem's music, through its associative range and its inclusion of haunting translations from Russian and French sources, MacDiarmid served notice that his sympathies and concerns were not confined to the local scene and that his outrage at the condition of Scotland was just an aspect of his longing for a totally transformed life for all human beings on the planet. In other words, if MacDiarmid did have a nostalgia, it was the one which Osip Mandelstam embraced, a 'nostalgia for world culture'.

And yet *A Drunk Man* could hardly be described as a solemn bid in the high-cultural stakes. On the contrary, it is distinguished by an inspired down-to-earthness. It has a huge improvisational energy and is driven forward by an impetuous anti-Establishment urge. Even though this impetuousness is an effect of the poem's style, it seems paradoxically to manifest an impatience with the very idea of style *per se*. The overriding impression is that the poem has too much business to get through to be bothered with merely literary considerations. It can be as close to doggerel as to Dante—and get away with it. Here, for instance, are a few lines from a rough-and-tumble section where the drunk man has a vision of the great cosmic wheel, where Scotland and the *dramatis personae* of Scottish history are at once set up and cut down within the perspectives of infinity:

> I felt it turn, and syne I saw
> John Knox and Clavers in my raw,
> And Mary Queen o' Scots ana',
>
> And Robbie Burns and Weelum Wallace
> And Carlyle lookin' unco' gallus,
> And Harry Lauder (to enthrall us).
>
> And as I looked I saw them a',
> A' the Scots baith big and sma',
> That e'er the braith o' life did draw.
>
> 'Mercy o' Gode, I canna thole
> Wi sic an orra mob to roll.'
> —'Wheesht! It's for the guid o' your soul!'
>
> *
>
> 'But in this huge ineducable
> Heterogeneous hotch and rabble
> Why am *I* condemned to squabble?'
>
> '*A Scottish poet maun assume*
> *The burden o' his people's doom,*
> *And dee to brak' their livin' tomb.*

Mony ha'e tried, but a' ha'e failed.
Their sacrifice has nocht availed.
Upon the thistle they're impaled!'

The mixture of passion and irreverence is everywhere in *A Drunk Man* and relates it to Irish masterpieces like Brian Merriman's *The Midnight Court* and Patrick Kavanagh's *The Great Hunger*, poems which similarly combine the expression of poetic high spirits, personal outrage and social protest. Merriman's metrical vitality and insinuating intelligence remind me of parallel qualities in the MacDiarmid poem; and Kavanagh's rawer expression of personal and social trauma is also akin to much that is going on in the Scottish work. Yet perhaps the main point is that none of these poems is directly confessional; all of them are more than simply therapeutic. They do get something aggrieved out of their authors' systems, but their purpose is as public as it is personal. They act like their society's immunity systems, going to attack whatever unhealthy or debilitating forces are at work in the body politic. And in this, they manifest poetry's high potential, its function as an agent of positive transformation.

This poem is MacDiarmid's masterpiece. Even if his political programme failed to materialize, even if the nationalism and socialism which he espoused found themselves unrealized and unpopular, even if his vernacular republic did not attain constitutional status, the fact is that *A Drunk Man Looks at the Thistle* did achieve the redress of poetry. MacDiarmid created a fully realized, imaginatively coherent work, one that contained such life-enhancing satire, such emotional weight and such specific imaginative gravity that it could be placed in the mind's scales as something both equal to and corrective of the prevailing conditions. It was a magnificent intervention by creative power into a historical situation. Its force was the force of the glimpsed alternative, and it still gives credence to MacDiarmid's wonderfully stirring affirmation in another context that poetry is human existence come to life. In the year of its publication, it may have sold only ninety-nine copies, but already it was on its way to that most important audience of all, 'the reader in posterity'. It released in the Scots language what MacDiarmid accurately called a *vis comica*, a capacity for comedy in the widest sense; it was both a deluge and an overflow, so much so that we might say the poem introduced an almost magical element into Scottish life, the kind represented by the crane bag in old Irish mythology.

The crane bag belonged to Manannan, the god of the sea, and contained every precious thing that he possessed. And then 'when the sea was full, all the treasures were visible in it; but when the fierce sea ebbed, the crane bag was empty.' Similarly, *A Drunk Man Looks at the Thistle* contains all the treasures that might or might not become available and life-enhancing within the personal and national life of Scotland. Indeed, there are moments when the drunk man himself seems to have intimations that the poem he is speaking relates to the crane bag myth. In the following stanza, for example, he says that his 'harns', or brains, respond to the ebb and flow of inspiration as seaweed responds to the ebb and flow of tides. And the poem itself will be forever correspondingly susceptible to the changing capacities of its audience. Like Manannan's marvellous sporran, it will reveal or retain its treasures, depending upon the fullness or emptiness of the imaginative world in which it subsists:

> My harns are seaweed—when the tide is in
> They swall like blethers and in comfort float,
> But when the tide is oot they lie like gealed
> And runkled auld bluid-vessels in a knot.

The tidal wave of MacDiarmid's verse in Vernacular Scots was to keep running long after he completed *A Drunk Man Looks at the Thistle*, and it sustained him through many other astonishing performances, such as 'Water Music' and 'Tarras' and the title poem of the volume in which these appeared in 1932, *Scots Unbound*. In that book, the poet is in his element, hitting the note and holding the tune with all his old resource and exhilaration. But at this point I must take my leave of MacDiarmid the Scots 'makar' *redivivus* and turn, too briefly and in conclusion, to the problematic status of MacDiarmid's vast output of verse in English during the remainder of his always amazing writing life.

I was once told about the entry procedures to be followed at a hospital run by a fundamentalist religious group in Tulsa, Oklahoma: incoming patients are asked to fill out a form which requires them to declare, among other things, the date of their birth, and then, the date of their rebirth. For Grieve, there would have been no problem with this: birth, 1892; rebirth, 1922. But the fact of the matter is that MacDiarmid *qua* MacDiarmid could have come up with two sets of dates also, in so far as he was born in Synthetic Scots in 1922 and reborn in English sometime around 1933.

Personally, I find this period the most moving in the whole of MacDiarmid's life. These were the years when he lived with his second wife, Valda Trevlyn, and his newborn son, Michael, on the small island of Whalsay in the Shetlands. In retreat. Over the top and out of sight, so to speak, both physically and psychologically. Drink, the strain of breaking up with his first wife, political hassles, financial troubles, the tension of personal enmities—in the early 1930s, all of these things brought MacDiarmid to the stage of nervous breakdown. But he survived, and his survival had to do with his getting down to the bedrock of his own resources, a bedrock which was reinforced at the time by contact with the stoical fishermen of the Shetland Islands and his at-homeness in the bleakness of the actual geological conditions. Racked by the huge ambitions he had imagined for himself, he now endured the beginnings of an ordeal in his poetic being, one in which the megalomaniac and the marvel-worker vied for the voice of the bard; where the blether of William McGonagall sporadically overwhelmed the strains of Hugh MacDiarmid; where the plagiarist too readily gained an upper hand over the poet; where the sureness of tone and dramatic inevitability which pervade his masterpiece deserted him and a disconcerting unreliability entered his poetic voice.

This is the MacDiarmid who breaks the heart, because he so often and so enragingly fumbles the job, the poet who can at one moment transport a reader's ear and body into a wonderfully sustaining element, a language pure as air or water, a language which carries the reader (as the truest poetry always does) into the sensation of walking on air or swimming free—but then the air fails or the water drains, a disastrous drop occurs in the vocal and metrical pressure; what was fluent becomes flaccid, what was detail becomes data, and what was poetry becomes pedantry and plagiarism. Such let-downs keep happening at crucial turns in poems which are elsewhere full of lovely clarity and temperate, steady wisdom, poems such as 'Island Funeral' or 'Lament for the Great Music' or 'Direadh III'. And the failure derives in the main from three typical aspects of MacDiarmid's later writing: his increasingly propagandist stance, the uncertainty of his ear outside his native Scots and his more and more compulsive habit of transcription (perhaps in the end a better term than plagiarism, since his habits were by then so well known to his readership and regarded with such indulgence).

When he wrote *A Drunk Man Looks at the Thistle*, MacDiarmid was less tied to the Communist Party line than he would be in years ahead, although there was already a strong admixture of Leninism to corroborate his natural sympathy with the underdog. As time went on, however, Lenin's dream of world revolution gradually became associated in MacDiarmid's mind with the boundary-crossing powers of a new world language, one which he took to be foreshadowed in the experimental, meaning-melting ventures of Joyce's *Finnegans Wake*. Joyce's move from the baby-babble of a Dublin infant at the beginning of *A Portrait of the Artist as a Young Man* to the dream-speak of a world-embracing, multilingual consciousness in *Finnegans Wake* was, for MacDiarmid, a pattern of the way local speech could exfoliate into an all-inclusive world idiom, and be fundamental to the evolution of that higher intellectual and imaginative plane which the revolution would promote. In practice, however, these two writers differed greatly in so far as Joyce's linguistic virtuosity was radically pleasure-seeking and absolved of any didactic purpose, whereas MacDiarmid's attempts at philological inclusiveness were doctrinaire and strenuously politically correct. Unfortunately, too, his identification of himself with the great prophets and projects of modernism led to an astounding self-inflation and to a verse that eventually strayed into megalomaniac fantasy. It even attained a certain monstrous dimension in poems like the 'First Hymn to Lenin', where MacDiarmid declares that the murderous activities of the Cheka (the secret police of the USSR) are a fair price to have to pay for the maintenance of that evolutionary momentum which he and his hero prized so much:

> As necessary, and insignificant, as death
> Wi' a' its agonies in the cosmos still
> The Cheka's horrors are in their degree;
> And'll end suner! What maitters 't wha we kill
> To lessen that foulest murder that deprives
>> Maist men o' real lives?

Doctrinal extremism marred both the nationalist and the internationalist strain in MacDiarmid's thinking all through his life. His Anglophobia, for instance, can be both salubrious and strategic, a natural and allowable consequence of opposition to imperialism and another consequence of his ambition to relocate the focus and idiom of Scottish literature. But unless it is exercised in the service of his more broadly transformative vision of world language and communist order, the Anglophobia only massages a kind of vindictive nativism, the very opposite of the liberated consciousness he intended to promote. And it can, of course, pass beyond the stage of mere prejudice to arrive at the lunacy of something like the following, taken from one of the late poems in English:

> So every loveliness that Scotland has ever known
> Or will know, flies into me now,
> Out of the perilous night of English stupidity,
> As I lie brooding on the fact
> That perchance the best chance
> Of reproducing the ancient Greek temperament
> Would be to 'cross' the Scots with the Chinese.

This flawed poetry of the 1930s and 1940s, with all its technical vocabularies, its Joycean revel in the words and ways of other languages, its insistence on the possibility of harnessing a future-oriented dream of Scottish life to the Gaelic and medieval Scots heritages, its ache to produce a seismic poetry that might include every thing and every language and every discipline—this poetry wanted to go so far beyond the proprieties of English literature that it would come right out the other side of orthodox expression. Yet it is only occasionally that the beautiful, deliberately arcane words with which he confronts the reader attain the kind of inevitability which I praised earlier in the Scots lyrics. Poems such as 'On a Raised Beach' and 'In a Cornish Garden' do surprise by a fine excess, and word by word they possess a unique multitudinous accuracy and psychedelic richness. Even they, however, totter close to self-parody and only get by through the huge appetite their author displays for matching the multiplicity of the phenomena with a correspondingly cornucopic vocabulary. More often, alas, neither MacDiarmid's lavishness nor his originality can move the data across the frontier of writing. Skewed rhythms, egregious diction, encyclopaedic quotation, sheer monotony—MacDiarmid certainly gave his detractors plenty to work with.

Before I end, therefore, I want to suggest very briefly a way of both respecting and admitting the failure of MacDiarmid's immense epic effort, in projects such as 'Cornish Heroic Song' and 'In Memoriam James Joyce'. Historically, it's worth thinking of these works as being all of a piece with the awesome and sometimes terrible projects of twentieth-century Soviet communism; they are like those gigantic dams and steelworks and tyrannically organized communal farms, every one of them the result of cruel effort, every one a breathtaking conception surviving in the world as something both spectacular and uncherished, evidence of actions at once heroic and doomed. If I exaggerate, it is partly to emphasize the huge amount of MacDiarmid's poetry that remains unread and unassimilated. The journalist and the activist in him would not be quieted, and when there was no outlet for them in prose, they invaded the verse without compunction. Sooner or later, however, what happened to Wordsworth will happen to Mac-

Diarmid: the second phase of his career will be rendered down to a series of self-contained, self-sustaining passages of genuine poetry, disentangled at last from the editorials and encyclicals he launched so indefatigably for more than forty years upon the unresponsive world.

Still, MacDiarmid was right to make the leap towards the impossible. With the publication of his short lyrics in the collections called *Sangschaw* and *Penny Wheep* (in 1925 and 1926, respectively), then *A Drunk Man* in 1926, not to mention *To Circumjack Cencrastus* and *Scots Unbound* in the early 1930s—with the publication of all this work he not only had created a language but within a decade had endowed it with enough literature to be going on with. But then, in poetry, enough is never enough. To find its true measure, creative talent must exert itself beyond the limit. If MacDiarmid were to continue with the exploration and experiment that had characterized his great decade, he had to get through the barrier of the very excellence he had created. He had to find an idiom that would not make a fetish of the local but would rather transpose the parochial into the planetary. He therefore strove for an all-inclusive mode of utterance and wrote a slackly strung, discursive, digression-filled verse, prone to offloading miscellaneous information and opinions, constantly punctuated by disconcerting and abrupt shifts of tone. Although his reasons for this were outlined with exhilarating force in 'The Kind of Poetry I Want'—'Poetry of such an integration as cannot be effected / Until a new and conscious organization of society / Generates a new view / Of the world as a whole' and so on—it did not work.

These later poems in Synthetic English generally don't have the intensity or oddity or uncanny inevitability of the early work in Scots, even if here and there they do manage to create that double sensation of sure-footed homecoming and light-headed expedition which only the highest poetry achieves. It is surely time, for example, that anthologies of twentieth-century verse—which almost invariably print W. H. Auden's 'In Praise of Limestone'—carry something from the luminous, almost biblical reveries of 'On a Raised Beach'. Philip Larkin's *Oxford Book of Twentieth-Century*

English Verse ignores it, and Larkin's *Selected Letters* gives us his candid assessment of MacDiarmid in one sentence, as follows: 'I am so averse from his work I can hardly bring my eyes to the page.' That comes in a letter to Dan Davin at Oxford University Press, and a couple of weeks later Larkin is asking Anthony Thwaite: 'Is there any bit of MacD that's noticeably less morally repugnant and aesthetically null than the rest?' Thwaite may have given him a few tips, but unfortunately he doesn't seem to have directed his attention to lines like these:

> Nothing has stirred
> Since I lay down this morning an eternity ago
> But one bird. The widest door is the least liable to intrusion,
> Ubiquitous as the sunlight, unfrequented as the sun.
> The inward gates of a bird are always open.
> It does not know how to shut them.
> That is the secret of its song,
> But whether any man's are ajar is doubtful.
> I look at these stones and I know little about them,
> But I know their gates are open too,
> Always open, far longer open, than any bird's can be,
> That every one of them has had its gates wide open far longer
> Than all birds put together, let alone humanity,
> Though through them no man can see,
> No man nor anything more recently born than themselves
> And that is everything else on the Earth.
> I too lying here have dismissed all else.
> Bread from stones is my sole and desperate dearth,
> From stones, which are to the Earth as to the sunlight
> Is the naked sun which is for no man's sight.
> I would scorn to cry to any easier audience
> Or, having cried, lack patience to await the response.

This scorning to cry to an easy audience is, of course, the secret of MacDiarmid's best work. When he was at his artistic best, his appeal was made to an imagined authority, a court of higher spiritual attainment and more illuminated understanding than any he could find around him. And in this, he fulfilled a poetic demand which always precedes and survives the demands of technique and artistic skills. This is the demand that the artist sacrifice himself or herself to an envisaged standard, and what such a demand entails was expressed with great eloquence and persuasiveness by Richard Ellmann when he wrote of the good poetic example of W. B. Yeats: according to Ellmann, in much of his work Yeats 'wishes to show how brute fact may be transmogrified, how we can sacrifice ourselves . . . to our imagined selves which offer far higher standards than anything offered by social convention. If we must suffer, it is better to create the world in which we suffer, and this is what heroes do spontaneously, artists do consciously, and all [others] do in their degree.'

For all his intellectual arrogance and poetic megalomania, MacDiarmid was an approachable and companionable man. The exorbitance and wilfulness of his poetic persona were partly self-inflationary, but they did arise from his conception of the large prophetic role which poetry had to fulfil in Scotland, and in the world of the future. He did not, however, confuse the greatness of the office with the dimensions of his own life as a citizen. When I met him in his later years, he and Valda lived modestly in their cottage in Biggar in Lanarkshire. Their hospitality was very moving, and they had attained a composure which seemed right after the buffeting they had both undergone forty years earlier, when their extreme poverty only intensified what was already an emotional and vocational ordeal. But then and always MacDiarmid was sustained by a faith older and simpler than the one he professed in Marxism. Lenin's utopian vision was undeniably inspirational for him, but deep down in the consciousness of this child of the Bible-reading Scottish Borders, Christ's commandment to people to love one another was surely equally powerful.

from Dylan the Durable? On Dylan Thomas

Dylan Thomas's 'Do Not Go Gentle into That Good Night' fulfils its promise because its craft has not lost touch with a suffered world. The villanelle form, turning upon itself, advancing and re-tiring to and from a resolution, is not just a line-by-line virtuoso performance. Through its repetitions, the father's remoteness—and the remoteness of all fathers—is insistently proclaimed, yet we can also hear, in an almost sobbing counterpoint, the protest of the poet's child-self against the separation:

> Do not go gentle into that good night,
> Old age should burn and rave at close of day;
> Rage, rage against the dying of the light.
>
> Though wise men at their end know dark is right,
> Because their words had forked no lightning they
> Do not go gentle into that good night.
>
> Good men, the last wave by, crying how bright
> Their frail deeds might have danced in a green bay,
> Rage, rage against the dying of the light.
>
> Wild men who caught and sang the sun in flight,
> And learn, too late, they grieved it on its way,
> Do not go gentle into that good night.
>
> Grave men, near death, who see with blinding sight
> Blind eyes could blaze like meteors and be gay,
> Rage, rage against the dying of the light.
>
> And you, my father, there on the sad height,
> Curse, bless, me now with your fierce tears, I pray.
> Do not go gentle into that good night.
> Rage, rage against the dying of the light.

This poem was written at a late moment in Thomas's life, when he was thirty-seven, almost twenty years after 'Before I Knocked'. A year earlier, in 1950, he had worked on the too deliberate raptures of 'In the White Giant's Thigh' and the never-to-be-completed 'In Country Heaven'. And all the while, on and off, he was fiddling with the genial dreamscape of *Under Milk Wood*. But now, in 1951, at a time when his father was dying from cancer and his relationship with his wife, Caitlin, was in a kind of deep-freeze because of his affair with the American woman whom biographers call 'Sarah', Thomas came through with a poem in a single, unfumbled movement, one with all the confidence of a necessary thing, one in which the fantasy and extravagance of imagery and diction did not dissipate themselves or his theme. Words forking 'lightning', frail deeds dancing 'in a green bay', blind eyes blazing 'like meteors'— these defiant and lavishly affirmative images could conceivably have appeared in the windier ambience of a piece like 'Lament', but within the genuinely desperate rhetoric of the villanelle they are informed with an urgency which guarantees their immunity from the virus of rant and posturing.

'Do Not Go Gentle' is obviously a threshold poem about death, concerned with the reverse of the process which occupied Thomas in 'Before I Knocked'. In that earlier poem, the body is about to begin what Thomas calls elsewhere its 'sensual strut'; here the return journey out of mortality into ghosthood is about to be made, so in fact the recurrent rhymes of the villanelle could as well have been 'breath' and 'death' or 'womb' and 'tomb'—but what we have instead are 'night' and 'light'. And the night is a 'good night'. For once, however, a characteristic verbal tic has become an imaginative strength and not just an irritating cleverness. 'Good night' is a pun which risks breaking the decorum of the utterance but which turns out in the end to embody an essential complexity. The mixture of salutation and farewell in the phrase is a perfect equivalent for the balance between natural grief and the recognition of necessity which pervades the poem as a whole.

This is a son comforting a father; yet it is also, conceivably, the child poet in Thomas himself comforting the old ham he had become; the neophyte in him addressing the legend; the green fuse addressing the burnt-out case. The reflexiveness of the form is the right correlative for the reflexiveness of the feeling. As the poem proceeds, exhortation becomes self-lamentation; the son's instruction to the disappointed father to curse and bless him collapses the distance between the sad height of age and physical decay in the parent and the equally sad eminence of poetic reputation and failing powers in the child. 'Do Not Go Gentle' is a lament for the maker in Thomas himself as well as an adieu to his proud and distant schoolteacher father. The shade of the young man who once expressed a fear that he was not a poet, just a freak user of words, pleads for help and reassurance from the older, sadder literary lion he has become, the one who apparently has the world at his feet.

Not that Thomas intended this meaning, of course. One of the poem's strengths is its outwardly directed address, its escape from emotional claustrophobia through an engagement with the specifically technical challenges of the villanelle. Yet that form is so much a matter of crossing and substitutions, of back-tracks and double-takes, turns and returns, that it is a vivid figure for the union of opposites, for the father in the son, the son in the father, for life in death and death in life. The villanelle, in fact, both participates in the flux of natural existence and scans and abstracts existence in order to register its pattern. It is a living cross-section, a simultaneously open and closed form, one in which the cycles of youth and age, of rise and fall, growth and decay find their analogues in the fixed cycle of rhymes and repetitions.

Indeed, there is something Rilkean in the tendency of 'Do Not Go Gentle', for we are here in the presence of knowledge transformed into poetic action, and the extreme claims that Rilke made for poetry are well enough matched by Thomas on this occasion. The following, which comes from a Rilke letter about his *Duino Elegies*, seems relevant and worth quoting:

> Death is a *side of life* that is turned away from us . . . the true figure of life extends through both domains, the blood of the mightiest circulation drives through *both: there is neither a here nor a beyond, but a great unity*, in which those creatures that surpass us, the 'angels', are at home.

In its canvassing of the idea of a great unity and its employment of the bodily image of circulating blood, this statement by Rilke is reminiscent of the murkier, more biological statements of the young Thomas. Yet in 'Do Not Go Gentle', I would suggest that the old murkiness has been worked through . . . I would also suggest that the mighty vaunt of 'A Refusal to Mourn the Death, by Fire, of a Child in London' has now been made good, and its operatic, death-defying strains have modulated into something even more emotionally persuasive.

Joy or Night: Last Things in the Poetry
of W. B. Yeats and Philip Larkin

To begin with, I want to read a poem by the Czech poet Miroslav Holub. This describes two characters who are like allegorical representations of the different poetic postures adopted by W. B. Yeats and Philip Larkin, not only towards last things, but towards nearly everything. It has the clarity of a blackboard diagram and makes an excellent introduction to what I have to say here about the two poets:

THE DEAD

After the third operation, his heart
pierced like an old carnival target,
he woke in his bed and said,
'Now I'll be fine,
like a sunflower, and by the way
have you ever seen horses make love?'

He died that night.

And another one plodded on for eight
milk and water years
like a long-haired waterplant
in a sour creek,
as if he stuck his pale face out
on a skewer from behind the graveyard wall.
Finally his face disappeared.

In both cases the angel of death
stamped his hob-nailed boot
on their *medulla oblongata*.

I know they died the same death
but I don't think they died
in the same way.

As Philip Larkin once said, readability is credibility: because of the truth-to-life in Holub's presentation of the different ways the two men lived, there is great cogency in his claim that there was a difference in the way they died. Indeed, it's because of this thoroughly persuasive quality that I want to set Holub's poem beside one by Larkin which takes an opposing view and contains the line 'Death is *no* different whined at than withstood' (my italics). Larkin's 'Aubade' is the poem where this dark observation appears, and it constitutes a direct contradiction of Holub in that it treats as mystification any imaginative or rhetorical ploy which might mask the facts of the body's dissolution and the mind's disappearance after death. Religion, courage, philosophy, drink, the routines of work and leisure—all these are regarded by Larkin as placebos. As he aged, his vision got arrested into a fixed stare at the inexorability of his own physical extinction. Human wisdom therefore seemed to him a matter of operating within the mortal limits, and of quelling any false hope of transcending or outfacing the inevitable. The poet in Larkin, in other words, was entirely sympathetic to living as a long-haired waterplant in a sour creek, and the persona he created for himself in the last two decades of his life bore a definite resemblance to that pale face on a skewer sticking out from behind the graveyard wall. So what I want to do here is to consider the implications for poetry of Larkin's attitude, and to ask whether his famous rejection of Yeats's more romantic stance has not been too long and too readily approved of.

Consider Yeats's extraordinary visionary exclamation 'The Cold Heaven'. He once described it as a poem about the mood produced in him by looking at the sky in wintertime, but the poem carries things far beyond mood and atmosphere. It is as much about metaphysical need as it is about the meteorological conditions:

> Suddenly I saw the cold and rook-delighting heaven
> That seemed as though ice burned and was but the more ice,
> And thereupon imagination and heart were driven
> So wild that every casual thought of that and this
> Vanished, and left but memories, that should be out of season
> With the hot blood of youth, of love crossed long ago;

And I took all the blame out of all sense and reason,
Until I cried and trembled and rocked to and fro,
Riddled with light. Ah! when the ghost begins to quicken,
Confusion of the death-bed over, is it sent
Out naked on the roads, as the books say, and stricken
By the injustice of the skies for punishment?

This is an extraordinarily vivid rendering of a spasm of consciousness, a moment of exposure to the total dimensions of what Wallace Stevens once called our 'spiritual height and depth'. The
turbulence of the lines dramatizes a sudden apprehension that
there is no hiding place, that the individual human life cannot
be sheltered from the galactic cold. The spirit's vulnerability, the
mind's awe at the infinite spaces and its bewilderment at the implacable inquisition which they represent—all of this is simultaneously present. The poem could be described in Hopkins's phrase
as 'the swoon of a heart . . . trod / Hard down with a horror of
height', for Yeats has clearly received what Hopkins in another
context called a 'heaven-handling'. He too has gone through his
ordeal on the mind's mountains, on those 'cliffs of fall / Frightful,
sheer, no-man-fathomed'. But the difference is that in Hopkins the
terror has its given co-ordinates; the Deity, doubted though He
may be, does provide a certain theological longitude and latitude
for what is unknown and unknowable. In 'The Wreck of the
Deutschland' and 'The Terrible Sonnets', Hopkins's intensity is the
intensity of dialogue, of blame and beseeching: a 'thou' is being
addressed, a comforter is being called upon (or else a false comforter is being rejected, the carrion comfort, Despair). In Yeats, on
the other hand, this personal God has disappeared, and yet Yeats's
poem still conveys a strong impression of direct encounter. The
spirit still suffers from a sense of answerability, of responsibility, to
a something out there, an intuited element that is as credible as
the 'rook-delighting heaven' itself.

There is, for example, this marvellous sense of both physical
visitation and intellectual apprehension in the phrase 'riddled with
light'. Light as strobing rays and light as spiritual illumination are
here indistinguishable. The 'I' of the poet as a first-person singu-

lar, a self-knowing consciousness, is brilliantly and concretely at one with the eye of the poet as a retina overwhelmed by the visual evidence of infinity and solitude. And this is only one of several instances where the poem's stylistic excellence and its spiritual proffer converge. When, in one place, the verb 'to quicken' is rhymed with the participle 'stricken' and still manages to hold its own against it; and when, in another, the rhyme word 'season' sets its chthonic reliability against the potentially debilitating force of 'reason'—when such things occur, the art of the poem is functioning as a corroboration of the positive emotional and intellectual commitments of the poet. To put it in yet another and perhaps provocatively simple way, 'The Cold Heaven' is a poem which suggests that there is an overall purpose to life; and it does so by the intrinsically poetic action of its rhymes, its rhythms and its exultant intonation. These create an energy and an order which promote the idea that there exists a much greater, circumambient energy and order within which we have our being.

The ghost upon the road, the soul's destiny in the afterlife, the consequences in eternity of the individual's actions in time—traditional concerns like these are profoundly relevant to 'The Cold Heaven', and they are also, of course, typical of the things which preoccupied Yeats for the whole of his life. Whether it was fairy lore in Sligo or Buddhism with the Dublin Hermetic Society or spiritualist séances or Noh dramas which imagined the adventures of Cuchulain's shade in the Land of the Dead, Yeats was always passionately beating on the wall of the physical world in order to provoke an answer from the other side. His studies were arcane, his cosmology was fantastic, and yet his intellect remained undeluded. Rational objections were often rationally allowed by him, if only to be imaginatively and rhetorically overwhelmed. Yeats's embrace of the supernatural, in other words, was not at all naïve; he was as alive as Larkin to the demeaning realities of bodily decrepitude and the obliterating force of death, but he deliberately resisted the dominance of the material over the spiritual. He was, moreover, as complicated as the rest of us when it came to the nature of his beliefs in a supernatural machinery, and nowhere more engagingly so than in his introduction to *A Vision*, that thesaurus of arcane

information and speculation which was in part dictated to him by
beings whom he liked to call his 'ghostly instructors'.

> Some will ask whether I believe in the actual existence of my cir-
> cuits of sun and moon . . . To such a question I can but answer
> that if sometimes, overwhelmed by miracle as all men must be
> when in the midst of it, I have taken such periods literally, my
> reason has soon recovered; and now that the system stands
> out clearly in my imagination I regard them as stylistic arrange-
> ments of experience comparable to the cubes in the drawing of
> Wyndham Lewis and to the ovoids in the sculpture of Brancusi.
> They have helped me to hold in a single thought reality and
> justice.

This is both sonorous and moving, but I would like to supple-
ment it with another, very different illustration of the provisional
nature of Yeats's thinking about last things. This comes from
Lady Dorothy Wellesley's recollection of the poet's conversation
in old age and is an almost deadpan account of one of their
sessions:

> I once got Yeats down to bed-rock on these subjects and we talked
> for hours. He had been talking rather wildly about the after life.
> Finally I asked him: 'What do you believe happens to us immedi-
> ately after death?' He replied, 'After a person dies, he does not re-
> alize that he is dead.' I: 'In what state is he?' W. B. Y.: 'In some
> half-conscious state.' I said: 'Like the period between waking and
> sleeping?' W. B. Y.: 'Yes.' I: 'How long does this state last?' W. B. Y.:
> 'Perhaps some twenty years.' 'And after that,' I asked, 'what hap-
> pens next?' He replied, 'Again a period which is Purgatory. The
> length of that period depends upon the sins of the man when he
> was upon this earth.' And then again I asked: 'And after that?' I do
> not remember his actual words, but he spoke of the return of the
> soul to God. I said, 'Well, it seems to me that you are hurrying us
> back into the great arms of the Roman Catholic Church.' He was
> of course an Irish Protestant. I was bold to ask him, but his only
> retort was his splendid laugh.

The laugh was not really evasive. The laugh, in fact, established a conversational space where the question could move again. It was the social expression of that frame of mind which allowed the venturesomeness of a supernatural faith to co-exist with a rigorously sceptical attitude. It was the comic expression of the tragic perception which Richard Ellmann attributed to Yeats in his important essay entitled 'W. B. Yeats's Second Puberty'. Ellmann wrote that the poet, in his old age, 'was obliged by his inner honesty to allow for the possibility that reality was desolation and justice a figment'. 'The image of life as cornucopia', Ellmann continued, 'was relentlessly undermined by the image of life as empty shell.' Yet it is because of Yeats's fidelity to both perceptions and his refusal to foreclose on either that we recognize in him a poet of the highest attainment. Towards the middle of the twentieth century, he continued to hold the tune which 'the darkling thrush' announced to Thomas Hardy at its very beginning. The thrush's song proclaimed that the basis of song itself was irrational, that its prerogative was to indulge impulse in spite of the evidence; and Hardy, in spite of his temperamental inclination to focus his attention upon the dolorous circumstances, for once allowed his heart in hiding to stir for that particular bird:

> So little cause for carolings
>   Of such ecstatic sound
> Was written on terrestrial things
>   Afar or nigh around,
> That I could think there trembled through
>   His happy good-night air
> Some blessed Hope, whereof he knew
>   And I was unaware.

We might say that Hardy, at this moment, experienced what Yeats says he experienced in the writing of *A Vision*: he too was simply overwhelmed by miracle whilst in the midst of it. But this, for sure, is not the Hardy to whom Larkin was converted after the strong enchantments of Yeats had failed for him. At that crucial point in his artistic development, Larkin turned to Hardy the poet of human sadness rather than to Hardy the witness of irrational hope. It was the 'neutral tones' rather than the 'ecstatic carolings' that attracted him; the disenchantment of Hardy's 'God-curst sun, and a tree / And a pond edged with greyish leaves' carried far more weight and cut more emotional ice with Larkin than any illumination that a positively 'rook-delighting heaven' could offer. At any rate, it is surely a God-curst sun that creates the glassy brilliance at the end of his poem 'High Windows'. Certainly it is the opposite of whatever illuminates the scene where Yeats's protagonist 'cried and trembled and rocked to and fro'. Yeats's cold heaven, as I have tried to demonstrate, is neither frigid nor negative. It is, on the contrary, an image of superabundant life, whereas Larkin's sunstruck distances give access to an infinity as void and neuter as those 'blinding windscreens' which flash randomly and pointlessly in 'The Whitsun Weddings'. 'High Windows' concludes:

And immediately

Rather than words comes the thought of high windows:
The sun-comprehending glass,
And beyond it, the deep blue air, that shows
Nothing, and is nowhere, and is endless.

When Larkin lifts his eyes from nature, what appears is a great absence. Neither justice nor injustice is to be sought in the skies; space offers neither illumination nor terminus. Out there, no encounter is possible. Out there is not our business. And all we have to protect us against these metaphysically Arctic conditions is the frail heat-shield generated by human kindness. Larkin is to be taken very seriously when he writes, in his late poem 'The Mower', 'we should be careful / Of each other, we should be kind / While there is still time.' But this minimal shield is insufficient to ward off the enormous *No* which reality pronounces constantly into the face of human life. Naturally, we would like him to answer back with the enormous *Yes* which love and art might generate, but he is unable to do it because he insists on taking full account of the negative evidence and this finally demoralizes the affirmative impulse. The radiance of a poem like 'Solar' is always going to be qualified by the pallor of one like 'Sad Steps'.

And this, of course, is why Larkin's poetry at its best is read with such gratitude. It too is sensitive to the dialectic between the cornucopia and the empty shell, obliged to try to resolve the imagination's stalemate between the death-mask of nihilism and the fixed smile of a pre-booked place in paradise. As Czeslaw Milosz has observed, no intelligent contemporary is spared the pressure exerted in our world by the void, the absurd, the anti-meaning, all of which are part of the intellectual atmosphere we subsist in; and yet Milosz notices this negative pressure only to protest against a whole strain of modern literature which has conceded victory to it. Poetry, Milosz pleads, must not make this concession but maintain instead its centuries-old hostility to reason, science and a science-inspired philosophy. These views were recorded by Milosz in an article published in 1979 in *Poetry Australia*, and they are intrinsically challenging; but the challenge is all the more pointed because they were made in conjunction with remarks about Larkin's 'Aubade', the poem to which I've already alluded and which I would now like to consider in more detail. Milosz praises the poem as 'a high poetic achievement', yet even that approbation may seem mild to those who remember coming upon it in the *TLS*, two days before Christmas, 1977:

> I work all day, and get half-drunk at night.
> Waking at four to soundless dark, I stare.
> In time the curtain-edges will grow light.
> Till then I see what's really always there:
> Unresting death, a whole day nearer now,
> Making all thought impossible but how
> And where and when I shall myself die.
> Arid interrogation: yet the dread
> Of dying, and being dead,
> Flashes afresh to hold and horrify.
>
> The mind blanks at the glare. Not in remorse
> —The good not done, the love not given, time
> Torn off unused—nor wretchedly because
> An only life can take so long to climb

Clear of its wrong beginnings, and may never;
But at the total emptiness for ever,
The sure extinction that we travel to
And shall be lost in always. Not to be here,
Not to be anywhere,
And soon; nothing more terrible, nothing more true.

This is a special way of being afraid
No trick dispels. Religion used to try,
That vast moth-eaten musical brocade
Created to pretend we never die,
And specious stuff that says *No rational being*
Can fear a thing it will not feel, not seeing
That this is what we fear—no sight, no sound,
No touch or taste or smell, nothing to think with,
Nothing to love or link with,
The anaesthetic from which none come round.

And so it stays just on the edge of vision,
A small unfocused blur, a standing chill
That slows each impulse down to indecision.
Most things may never happen: this one will,
And realization of it rages out
In furnace-fear when we are caught without
People or drink. Courage is no good:
It means not scaring others. Being brave
Lets no one off the grave.
Death is no different whined at than withstood.

Slowly light strengthens, and the room takes shape.
It stands plain as a wardrobe, what we know,
Have always known, know that we can't escape,
Yet can't accept. One side will have to go.
Meanwhile telephones crouch, getting ready to ring
In locked-up offices, and all the uncaring
Intricate rented world begins to rouse.
The sky is white as clay, with no sun.

Work has to be done.
Postmen like doctors go from house to house.

It would be hard to think of a poem more opposed than this one to the life-enhancing symbolism of the Christ child in the Christmas crib. It is as if the mid-winter gleam and promise of medieval carols had been obliterated completely by the dread and dolour of a medieval morality play like *Everyman*. In fact, Larkin's terror here is very reminiscent of the terror suffered by the character Everyman; and Everyman's summoner, the presence whom Larkin calls 'unresting death', stalks the poem every bit as menacingly as he stalks the play. There is, furthermore, a specially vindictive force to the figure of death in 'Aubade' because the adjective 'unresting' had been employed most memorably by Larkin in an earlier poem celebrating the opulence and oceanic vitality of leafy trees, their lush power to revivify both themselves and us, year after year. The last stanza of 'The Trees' reads:

> Yet still the unresting castles thresh
> In fullgrown thickness every May.
> Last year is dead, they seem to say,
> Begin afresh, afresh, afresh.

In this stanza, the word 'unresting' embodies an immense luxuriance and deep-rootedness, but in 'Aubade' it has the rangy hungry speed and relentlessness of a death hound: Larkin unleashes it at line 5 and then for the next forty-five lines it beats the bounds of our mortality, forcing its borders to shrink further and further away from any contact with consoling beliefs. Also in 'Aubade', the word 'afresh' (so joyful in 'The Trees') is relocated in a context of horror, the word 'dread' comes to an almost catatonic confrontation with its full meaning as it rhymes with 'dead', and 'die' is forced to live with its own emotional consequences in the verb 'horrify':

> Unresting death, a whole day nearer now,
> Making all thought impossible but how
> And where and when I shall myself die.

Arid interrogation: yet the dread
Of dying, and being dead,
Flashes afresh to hold and horrify.

One could go on praising the technical aspects of this poem, such as the rhyming of 'vision' with 'indecision', a piece of under-cutting that is characteristically Larkinesque in its implicit refusal of the spiritual upbeat of Yeats's rhymes. Instead of any further detailed commentary, however, I shall confine myself to the obser-vation that this, for me, is the definitive post-Christian English poem, one that abolishes the soul's traditional pretension to im-mortality and denies the Deity's immemorial attribute of infinite personal concern. Moreover, no matter how much or how little readers may at the outset be in sympathy with these views, they still arrive at the poem's conclusion a little surprised at how far it has carried them on the lip of its rhetorical wave. It leaves them like unwary surfers hung over a great emptiness, transported fur-ther into the void than they might have expected to go. It arrives at a place where, in Yeats's words, 'cold winds blow across our hands, upon our faces, the thermometer falls'.

Yeats, however, considered these things to be symptoms not of absence but of the ecstatic presence of the supernatural. Writing near the end of his life, in 'A General Introduction for My Work', Yeats told of his aspiration to a form of utterance in which imagi-nation would be 'carried beyond feeling into the aboriginal ice'. Which ice, needless to say, was the antithesis of the stuff to be found under the mortuary slabs. It represented not so much a frigid exhaustion as an ultimate attainment. It was an analogue of that cold heaven where it 'seemed as though ice burned and was but the more ice'; an analogue also of Yeats's rejection of the body heat of the pathetic and the subjective in art, for his embrace of the dramatic and the heroic, his determination to establish the crystalline standards of poetic imagination as normative for the level at which people should live. For Yeats, there was something both enviable and exemplary about the enlargement of vision and the consequent histrionic equanimity which Shakespeare's heroes and heroines attain at the moment of their death, 'carried beyond feeling into the aboriginal ice'. He wanted people in real life to emulate or at least to internalize the fortitude and defiance thus manifested in tragic art. Where Larkin was all for human beings huddling together in kindness, like refugees from the injustice of the skies, Yeats was all for flourish and theatrical challenge. Larkin might declare:

> Courage is no good:
> It means not scaring others. Being brave
> Lets no one off the grave.
> Death is no different whined at than withstood.

Yeats absolutely disagreed. 'No actress', he maintained, 'has ever sobbed when she played Cleopatra, even the shallow brain of a producer has never thought of such a thing.' Which amounts to saying that death withstood is indeed very different from death whined at and that it is up to poets and actresses to continue to withstand.

So we must imagine Yeats as the reader in eternity who resists Philip Larkin's 'Aubade', high poetic achievement though it may be; and resists it for the same reason as Czeslaw Milosz, who, having conceded the integrity of 'Aubade' as a work that copes with the eternal subject of death 'in a manner corresponding to the sensibility of the second half of the twentieth century', goes on to protest:

> And yet the poem leaves me not only dissatisfied but indignant, and I wonder why myself. Perhaps we forget too easily the centuries-old mutual hostility between reason, science and science-inspired philosophy on the one hand and poetry on the other? Perhaps the author of the poem went over to the side of the adversary and his ratiocination strikes me as a betrayal? For, after all, death in the poem is endowed with the supreme authority of Law and universal necessity, while man is reduced to nothing, to a bundle of perceptions, or even less, to an interchangeable statistical unit. But poetry by its very essence has always been on the side of life. Faith in life everlasting has accompanied man in

his wanderings through time, and it has always been larger and deeper than religious or philosophical creeds which expressed only one of its forms.

Still, when a poem rhymes, when a form generates itself, when a metre provokes consciousness into new postures, it is already on the side of life. When a rhyme surprises and extends the fixed relations between words, that in itself protests against necessity. When language does more than enough, as it does in all achieved poetry, it opts for the condition of overlife and rebels at limit. In this fundamentally artistic way, then, Larkin's 'Aubade' does not go over to the side of the adversary. But its argument does add weight to the negative side of the scale and tips the balance definitely in favour of chemical law and mortal decline. The poem does not hold the lyre up in the face of the gods of the underworld; it does not make the Orphic effort to haul life back up the slope against all the odds. For all its heartbreaking truths and beauties, 'Aubade' reneges on what Yeats called the 'spiritual intellect's great work'.

This phrase comes from Yeats's poem 'The Man and the Echo', with which I am going to conclude. In it, the theme so playfully treated by Holub in the lines I read at the beginning is orchestrated into something far more sombre and vigorous. Both poets present their characters at death's door, but whereas Holub's spunky surrealist affirms his faith in life with a whimsical vision of horses making love, Yeats's seer endures a more strenuous ordeal and is rewarded with a vision of reality that is at once more demanding and more fulfilling. Indeed, what 'The Man and the Echo' implies is something that I have repeatedly tried to establish through several different readings and remarks in the course of these lectures: namely, that the goal of life on earth, and of poetry as a vital factor in the achievement of that goal, is what Yeats called in 'Under Ben Bulben' the 'profane perfection of mankind'.

In order to achieve that goal, therefore, and in order that human beings bring about the most radiant conditions for themselves to inhabit, it is essential that the vision of reality which poetry offers be transformative, more than just a printout of the given circumstances of its time and place. The poet who would be most the poet has to attempt an act of writing that outstrips the conditions even as it observes them. The truly creative writer, by interposing his or her perception and expression, will transfigure the conditions and effect thereby what I have been calling 'the redress of poetry'. The world is different after it has been read by a Shakespeare or an Emily Dickinson or a Samuel Beckett because it has been augmented by their reading of it. Indeed, Beckett is a very clear example of a writer who is Larkin's equal in not flinching from the ultimate bleakness of things, but who then goes on to do something positive with the bleakness. For it is not the apparent pessimism of Beckett's world-view that constitutes his poetic genius: his excellence resides in his working out a routine in the playhouse of his art which is both true to the depressing goings-on in the house of actuality and—more important—a transformation of them. It is because of his transformative way with language, his mixture of wordplay and merciless humour, that Beckett the writer has life and has it more abundantly than the conditions endured by Beckett the citizen might seem to warrant.

We go to poetry, we go to literature in general, to be forwarded within ourselves. The best it can do is to give us an experience that is like foreknowledge of certain things which we already seem to be remembering. What is at work in this most original and illuminating poetry is the mind's capacity to conceive a new plane of regard for itself, a new scope for its own activity. Which is why I turn in conclusion to 'The Man and the Echo', a poem where human consciousness is up against the cliff-face of mystery, confronted with the limitations of human existence itself. Here the consciousness of the poet is in full possession of both its creative impulse and its limiting knowledge. The knowledge is limiting because it concedes that pain necessarily accompanies the cycles of life and that failure and hurt—hurt to oneself and to others—persist disablingly behind even the most successful career. Yet in the poem the spirit's impulse still remains creative and obeys the human compulsion to do that 'great work' of spiritual intellect.

The situation of the man in 'The Man and the Echo' is that of somebody *in extremis*, somebody who wants to make his soul, to bring himself to wholeness, to bring his mind and being into congruence with the divine mind and being. He therefore goes to consult the oracle, not at Delphi, but in a glen on the side of Knocknarea in County Sligo, at a place called Alt; but this rock-face does not issue any message from the gods—all it does is give back an echo. And what the echo communicates, of course, is the man's own most extreme and exhausted recognitions. The echo marks the limits of the mind's operations even as it calls the mind forth to its utmost exertions, and the strenuousness of this dialectic issues in a poem that is as shadowed by death as Larkin's 'Aubade' but is far more vital and undaunted. 'The Man and the Echo' tries to make sense of historical existence within a bloodstained natural world and an indifferent universe. It was written near the end of Yeats's life, when he was reviewing his involvement with the historical events in Ireland over a previous half-century: events such as the founding of the Abbey Theatre and its political impact in the lead-up to the 1916 Rising; the Irish war of independence and the destruction of many of the big houses belonging to the Anglo-Irish gentry; and other, more private, guilt-inducing events, such as the nervous breakdown of a young poet and dancer, Margot Collis, with whom Yeats felt himself half-culpably implicated:

THE MAN AND THE ECHO

Man

In a cleft that's christened Alt
Under broken stone I halt
At the bottom of a pit
That broad noon has never lit,
And shout a secret to the stone.
All that I have said and done,
Now that I am old and ill,
Turns into a question till
I lie awake night after night
And never get the answers right.
Did that play of mine send out
Certain men the English shot?

Did words of mine put too great strain
On that woman's reeling brain?
Could my spoken words have checked
That whereby a house lay wrecked?
And all seems evil until I
Sleepless would lie down and die.

Echo

Lie down and die.

Man

That were to shirk
The spiritual intellect's great work,
And shirk it in vain. There is no release
In a bodkin or disease,
Nor can there be work so great
As that which cleans man's dirty slate.
While man can still his body keep
Wine or love drug him to sleep,
Waking he thanks the Lord that he
Has body and its stupidity,
But body gone he sleeps no more,
And till his intellect grows sure
That all's arranged in one clear view,
Pursues the thoughts that I pursue,
Then stands in judgement on his soul,
And, all work done, dismisses all
Out of intellect and sight
And sinks at last into the night.

Echo

Into the night.

Man

O Rocky Voice,
Shall we in that great night rejoice?
What do we know but that we face
One another in this place?
But hush, for I have lost the theme,

> Its joy or night seem but a dream;
> Up there some hawk or owl has struck,
> Dropping out of sky or rock,
> A stricken rabbit is crying out,
> And its cry distracts my thought.

What we have here is the obverse of the experience of illumination and visitation that Yeats wrote about in 'The Cold Heaven': here he is riddled not so much with light as with dark. And much, much more could be said about the poem—about, for example, the resilience of the man and the vigour of the metre in face of the echo's intransigence. I shall confine myself, however, to one detailed comment and one brief concluding reflection. The detail is the final rhyme, which yokes together the words 'crying out' and 'thought'. It is not a perfect rhyme, nor should it be, for there is no perfect fit between the project of civilization represented by thought and the facts of pain and death represented by the rabbit's 'crying out'. What holds the crying out and the thought together is a consciousness which persists in trying to make sense of a world where suffering and violence are more evidently set to prevail than the virtue of being 'kind'. The rhyme, and the poem in general, not only tell of that which the spirit must endure; they also show *how* it must endure, by pitting human resource against the recalcitrant and the inhuman, by pitting the positive effort of mind against the desolations of natural and historical violence, by making 'rejoice' answer back to the voice from the rock, whatever it says:

> O Rocky Voice,
> Shall we in that great night rejoice?
> What do we know but that we face
> One another in this place?
> But hush, for I have lost the theme,
> Its joy or night seem but a dream;
> Up there some hawk or owl has struck,
> Dropping out of sky or rock,
> A stricken rabbit is crying out,
> And its cry distracts my thought.

There is a strong sense, at the conclusion of this poem, that the mind's options are still open, that the mind's constructs are still vital and reliable, even though its functions may for the moment be suspended. Where Larkin's 'Aubade' ended in entrapment, 'The Man and the Echo' has preserved a freedom and manages to pronounce a final *Yes*. And the *Yes* is valuable because we can say of it what Karl Barth said of the enormous *Yes* at the centre of Mozart's music, that it has weight and significance because it overpowers and contains a *No*. Yeats's poetry, in other words, gives credence to the idea that courage is *some* good; it shows how the wilful and unabashed activity of poetry itself is a manifestation of 'joy' and a redressal, in so far as it fortifies the spirit against assaults from outside and temptations from within—temptations such as the one contained in Larkin's attractively defeatist proposition that 'Death is no different whined at than withstood'.

from Counting to a Hundred:

Elizabeth Bishop

There is nothing spectacular about Elizabeth Bishop's writing, even though there is always something transformative about it. One has a sense of justice being done to the facts of a situation even as the situation is being re-imagined into poetry. She never allows the formal delights of her art to mollify the hard realities of her subjects. For example, in one of her two sestinas—the one she calls, with typical plain-spokenness, 'Sestina'—the six end-words have a thoroughly domestic provenance, and in the first instance they seem all set to keep the poem within comforting emotional bounds. 'House', 'grandmother', 'child', 'stove', 'almanac', 'tears'. They imply a little drama of youth and age, even perhaps of instruction and correction. A Victorian genre piece, almost. A decorous domestic interior, at any rate, in terms both of the setting and of the emotions. The end-words, at one level, do keep bringing to mind a conventional home situation where we would naturally expect to find a father and a mother as well as a child and a grandparent. But gradually and insistently a second realization is forced into consciousness by the inexorable formal recurrences within the poem itself. Gradually, the repetition of 'grandmother' and 'child' and 'house' alerts us to the significant absence from this house of a father and a mother:

> September rain falls on the house.
> In the failing light, the old grandmother
> sits in the kitchen with the child
> beside the Little Marvel Stove,
> reading the jokes from the almanac,
> laughing and talking to hide her tears.
>
> She thinks that her equinoctial tears
> and the rain that beats on the roof of the house

were both foretold by the almanac,
but only known to a grandmother.
The iron kettle sings on the stove.
She cuts some bread and says to the child,

It's time for tea now; but the child
is watching the teakettle's small hard tears
dance like mad on the hot black stove,
the way the rain must dance on the house.
Tidying up, the old grandmother
hangs up the clever almanac

on its string. Birdlike, the almanac
hovers half open above the child,
hovers above the old grandmother
and her teacup full of dark brown tears.
She shivers and says she thinks the house
feels chilly, and puts more wood in the stove.

It was to be, says the Marvel Stove.
I know what I know, says the almanac.
With crayons the child draws a rigid house
and a winding pathway. Then the child
puts in a man with buttons like tears
and shows it proudly to the grandmother.

But secretly, while the grandmother
busies herself about the stove,
the little moons fall down like tears
from between the pages of the almanac
into the flower bed the child
has carefully placed in the front of the house.

Time to plant tears, says the almanac.
The grandmother sings to the marvellous stove
and the child draws another inscrutable house.

Like any successful sestina, this has a touch of virtuosity about it, but its virtuosity is not what engages one's attention. Its immediate effect is as emotionally direct as a fairy tale. Just as Dylan Thomas's villanelle 'Do Not Go Gentle into That Good Night' comes across as a dramatic cry rather than a formal set piece, so the narrative and dramatic interest of Bishop's sestina very quickly deflects attention from its master-class excellence as a technical performance. The poem circles unspoken sorrows, and as it circles them, it manages to mesmerize them and make them obedient to creative will. The short-circuited pain within the grandmother's house, a pain to which the almanac imparts a fatal inevitability, is shut up for the time being inside the inscrutable house which the child draws. In so far as it echoes old tales where the wicked spirit is imprisoned in some box or tree or rock, this conclusion represents a victory over the negative conditions. But viewed from another perspective, it simply returns the situation to its original configuration, where the entrapment is ongoing and resolution is something attainable only in imagination.

In fact, 'Sestina', with its inscrutable house, performs the same reflexive but ultimately salubrious function as the monument performs in an early Bishop poem called (with equal plainness) 'The Monument'. This monument is made of wood, of boxes placed upon boxes; like the sestina it is both enigmatic and entirely satisfactory. It promises nothing beyond what it exhibits, and yet it seems to be standing over something which it also stands *for*. Once again, a withdrawn presence, an inscrutable purpose or missing element is what the resulting structure exists to express or shelter. In fact, the final lines of the poem declare that the monument commemorates something undeclared, something embodying and maintaining a meaning it feels no need to proclaim:

> It is an artifact
> of wood. Wood holds together better
> than sea or cloud or sand could by itself,
> much better than real sea or sand or cloud.
> It chose that way to grow and not to move.
> The monument's an object, yet those decorations,
> carelessly nailed, looking like nothing at all,
> give it away as having life, and wishing;

wanting to be a monument, to cherish something.
The crudest scroll-work says 'commemorate',
while once each day the light goes around it
like a prowling animal,
or the rain falls on it, or the wind blows into it.
It may be solid, may be hollow.
The bones of the artist-prince may be inside
or far away on even drier soil.
But roughly but adequately it can shelter
what is within (which after all
cannot have been intended to be seen).
It is the beginning of a painting,
a piece of sculpture, or poem, or monument,
and all of wood. Watch it closely.

This monument to something which 'cannot have been intended to be seen' finds itself menaced by the very light which goes around it 'like a prowling animal'. Yet in spite of the guardedness which these conditions induce, it still does want 'to cherish something'. And if we watch it closely, as we are counselled to, we shall find that in being an object which has life and 'can shelter/what is within', it resembles the work of the poet who imagined it into being in the first place. For the gratifying thing about Elizabeth Bishop's poetry is that in the end it too overcomes the guardedness of its approach. It may be an observant poetry, but it does not finally, in the colloquial sense of the term, 'watch it', even though the inclination to caution is persistently felt as a condition of the poet's style. Qualification is her natural habit of mind, but even so, the poetry continually manages to go out to greet what is there, to salute what Louis MacNeice called 'the drunkenness of things being various'. And it justifies itself *as* poetry by the thoroughness of its assistance. At its most ardent, it wants to give itself entirely to what it discovers, as when her poem 'Over 2,000 Illustrations and a Complete Concordance' concludes by asking, 'Why couldn't we have . . . looked and looked our infant sight away?'

This is to say that Bishop's famous gift for observation is more than a habit of simply watching; it represents, rather, a certain

self-conquest, the surmounting of a definite temperamental wari-
ness. She is more naturally fastidious than rhapsodic. If she is well
enough disposed towards the phenomena, she is still not exultant.
Her detachment is chronic, and yet the combination of attentive-
ness and precision which she brings to bear upon things is so intense that the detachment almost evaporates. What Bishop does is
to scrutinize and interrogate things as they are before giving her
assent to them. She does not immediately or necessarily glorify
them, being more of a sympathetic adjudicator than a born cheer-
leader, but neither does she refuse them their just measure of
praise. Her sense of reality, to put it another way, is more earthbound than angelic. Her early poem 'Anaphora', for example, is a
morning song in which Bishop does indeed conceive of an angelic
creature, one who represents a part of us that is potentially equal
to the brilliant promises of the morning and the day; yet she is
constrained to acknowledge that this creature is also the one whose
possibilities we nevertheless actually and repeatedly fail to realize.
And so he

> suffers our uses and abuses,
> sinks through the drift of bodies,
> sinks through the drift of classes
> to evening to the beggar in the park
> who, weary, without lamp or book
>   prepares stupendous studies:
>   the fiery event
>   of every day in endless
>   endless assent.

But there is, after all, something marvellous about a beggar assent-
ing to things as they are. For him, the fiery event of every day, be
it the dawn or the sunset, has to be its own reward, since there is
nothing else in it for him. And it is in similar acts of outstripping
one's own deprivation, in not doting upon it, so to speak, but proceeding instead into freely offered celebration—it is in such acts
and attainments of the spirit that Bishop's poetry redresses the
scales that were loaded against her from the start.

The move is not so much from delight to wisdom, although both
of these things figure importantly in the poems; in her case, the
characteristic shift might be more precisely described as being from
self-containment to an acknowledgement of the mystery of the
other, with the writing functioning as an enactment of all the bit-
tersweet deferrals in between. 'The Fish' is an obvious instance of
this, the whole poem hypnotically suspended between the two definite actions reported in the first and last lines: 'I caught a tremen-
dous fish', 'And I let the fish go'. In between, what the poem offers
is a slow-motion replay, sensation by sensation, of the process by
which the fish is recognized as a harbinger of what Hopkins calls
'the glory of God', of that dearest freshness that lives deep down in
things, all that which the poem itself finally calls 'rainbow, rainbow, rainbow'. For once, Bishop seems to go beyond assent, yet in
fact the action of releasing the fish is simply the deepest form
which assent can take, and, in a Cordelia-like way, it speaks more
loudly than the superlative words. The fish is recognized as a kindred spirit, one of the swimming as opposed to the walking
wounded, one who takes things in but prefers to keep his counsel:

> I looked into his eyes
> which were far larger than mine
> but shallower, and yellowed,
> the irises backed and packed
> with tarnished tinfoil
> seen through the lenses
> of old scratched isinglass.
> They shifted a little, but not
> to return my stare.
> —It was more like the tipping
> of an object toward the light.
> I admired his sullen face,
> the mechanism of his jaw,
> and then I saw
> that from his lower lip
> —if you could call it a lip—
> grim, wet, and weaponlike,
> hung five old pieces of fish-line,

or four and a wire leader
with the swivel still attached,
with all their five big hooks
grown firmly in his mouth.

One can imagine this fish and the poet who writes about him recognizing the truth in the reply of the old Eskimo woman who,
when asked why all the songs sung by her tribe were so short,
answered simply: 'Because we know so much.'

Similarly, the cost of Bishop's composure in her poems should
not be underestimated. The rainbow effect is not attained without
some expense of spirit. No writer is more positive in registering
the detailed marvels of the world, yet no writer is more scrupulous
in conceding that there are endangering negative conditions which
must equally and simultaneously be accounted facts of life. I would
like, therefore, to concentrate for a few minutes on a poem which
reveals these characteristic motions of Bishop's mind, both in art
and in life, one which also has about it a touch of comedy and a
hint of self-portraiture. This is her poem about the sandpiper:

The roaring alongside he takes for granted,
and that every so often the world is bound to shake.
He runs, he runs to the south, finical, awkward,
in a state of controlled panic, a student of Blake.

The beach hisses like fat. On his left, a sheet
of interrupting water comes and goes
and glazes over his dark and brittle feet.
He runs, he runs straight through it, watching his toes.

—Watching, rather, the spaces of sand between them,
where (no detail too small) the Atlantic drains
rapidly backwards and downwards. As he runs,
he stares at the dragging grains.

The world is a mist. And then the world is
minute and vast and clear. The tide
is higher or lower. He couldn't tell you which.
His beak is focussed; he is preoccupied,

looking for something, something, something.
Poor bird, he is obsessed!
The millions of grains are black, white, tan, and gray,
mixed with quartz grains, rose and amethyst.

'The roaring alongside he takes for granted', we are told right away; and if we think of that roaring as the noise of the public world as well as the noise of the sea, we can say much the same thing about Elizabeth Bishop. She does not go in for the epic panorama, for large historical treatments, for the synoptic view of cultures and crises so typical of other major twentieth-century poets. She is, of course, deeply aware that every so often the world is bound to shake, and not only with the thunder of waves but also with the thunder of war or of earthquake or the merciless death of a parent or the untimely and guilt-inducing suicide of a beloved friend. In such circumstances, panic is a natural enough reaction, a reflex impulse to escape from the scene altogether. And yet since one cannot escape one's times or one's destiny, such panic has to be controlled, and to control is to set limits, to map a defined space within which one will operate. In the case of the sandpiper, this space is a shifting space of sand, between the tide and the land: it is here that the sandpiper naturally becomes a student of Blake, since William Blake is the poet who urged in 'Auguries of Innocence':

> To see a World in a Grain of Sand,
> And a Heaven in a Wild Flower,
> Hold Infinity in the palm of your hand,
> And Eternity in an hour.

Blake's poem is visionary and prophetic, but even as zealous a student as the sandpiper can never possess its immense bardic confidence. The poor bird is 'finical', a word whose very sound and texture suggest nervousness, primness, petulance; a finical creature will never be in command of the situation, and so, instead of standing his ground, the sandpiper runs:

> He runs, he runs to the south, finical, awkward.

Nevertheless, the poet is instinctively drawn to the bird, and cannot blame him for his twitchiness. There is something detached and concerned in her attitude to his fretful busy scurrying which is not unlike her own attitude to herself as she expressed it in a speech in 1976. 'Yes,' she said then, 'all my life I have lived and behaved very much like that sandpiper—just running along the edges of different countries, "looking for something".' But it's not just Bishop's migrant impulse that links her to the sandpiper. There is also her vigilant, hesitant, yet completely fascinated attention to detail, and her habitual caution in the face of the world. The phrase 'watching his toes', for example, applies in an exact and jokey way to both the bird and the poet. It echoes, obviously, the phrase 'watch your step' while putting a spin on the phrase 'keep on your toes', and in its double encompassing of alertness and caution, of being menaced and being ready, it is consonant both with Elizabeth Bishop's habitual attitudes and with the tiny plight of the sandpiper.

I say 'tiny' plight. But part of the purpose of this writing is to blur the distinction between what is vast and what is tiny. The student of Blake, after all, will see a world in a grain of sand. So this poem will see to it that vast words like 'Atlantic' and 'world' and indeed the word 'vast' itself are matched and balanced and equalled by small words like 'toes' and 'beak' and 'grains'. No detail is too small, as the parenthesis in line 10 insists. 'The world is a mist. And then the world is / minute and vast and clear.' We might in fact go so far as to say that the poem is about the way in which obsessive attention to detail can come through into visionary understanding; the way in which an intense focus can amplify rather than narrow our sense of scope. The last two lines of the poem do transform what is tiny and singular and project it on a cosmic screen. They make radiant and marvellous that which is in danger of being overlooked and disregarded. Again, the small and the great are brought into contact, and the small brings the great into question:

> looking for something, something, something.
> Poor bird, he is obsessed!

> The millions of grains are black, white, tan, and gray,
> mixed with quartz grains, rose and amethyst.

'The millions of grains': we see a pepper-and-salt of grains. A yard of sand is first a gritty texture and then a glittering marvel. And all this is effected without any straining of linguistic muscle. The poem does not raise its voice or overstretch its vocabulary. The words are usual and plain and available to everybody. Yet the poet does to words what she does to details: she makes them beckon us into hitherto unsuspected spaces. Quartz, rose, amethyst: all three of them are now ashimmer, 'minute and vast and clear', as if they had escaped from the light-drenched empyrean of Dante's *Paradiso*. The student of Blake has found not only a world but a whole system of heavens in the grains of sand.

'Sandpiper' is a poem of immense discretion and discreet immensity, and if I appear to be talking it up in excess of its merits, then all I can say is that appearances are deceptive. It is a perfect achievement, one that brings itself and its reader into a renewed awareness of the mysterious otherness of the world. And it brings us to that threshold by following its nose—or its beak—through the old crazy-paving and matter-of-fact of detail. And the same is true of many of Bishop's acknowledged triumphs, especially her great meditative *excursus*, 'At the Fishhouses'. But since I have written at length about that poem in the title essay of *The Government of the Tongue*, I want to draw attention here briefly instead to those two longish late poems, 'The Moose' and 'Crusoe in England'. Each of them is a memory poem, each gives access to a marvellous thing, but neither of them treats the marvellous as other than an achievement of the imagination. When the moose comes out of the woods, when Crusoe remembers the aura which his jackknife once possessed for him, the world does shimmer in a transformed light; and yet both of these poems, in Auden's words, find the mortal world enough. Their characteristic strength comes from Bishop's old gift for raising the actual to a new linguistic power. Their triumph is the redundancy of that power, its capacity to be more than enough. Here is Crusoe, remembering waterspouts:

And I had waterspouts. Oh,
half a dozen at a time, far out,
they'd come and go, advancing and retreating,
their heads in cloud, their feet in moving patches
of scuffed-up white.
Glass chimneys, flexible, attenuated,
sacerdotal beings of glass . . . I watched
the water spiral up in them like smoke.
Beautiful, yes, but not much company.

And here is the almost beautiful moose appearing out of the night as the passengers on a bus talk and talk intimately among themselves on the long journey south out of Nova Scotia, a journey which follows a scheduled bus-route and at the same time retraces in memory the path the poet once took from the pre-reflective world of her childhood:

Talking the way they talked
in the old featherbed,
peacefully, on and on,
dim lamplight in the hall,
down in the kitchen, the dog
tucked in her shawl.

Now, it's all right now
even to fall asleep
just as on all those nights.
—Suddenly the bus driver
stops with a jolt,
turns off his lights.

A moose has come out of
the impenetrable wood
and stands there, looms, rather,
in the middle of the road.
It approaches; it sniffs at
the bus's hot hood.

Towering, antlerless,
high as a church,
homely as a house
(or, safe as houses).
A man's voice assures us
'Perfectly harmless . . .'

Some of the passengers
exclaim in whispers,
childishly, softly,
'Sure are big creatures.'
'It's awful plain.'
'Look! It's a she!'

Taking her time,
she looks the bus over,
grand, otherworldly.
Why, why do we feel
(we all feel) this sweet
sensation of joy?

'Curious creatures,'
says our quiet driver,
rolling his *r*'s.
'Look at that, would you.'
Then he shifts gears.
For a moment longer,

by craning backward,
the moose can be seen
on the moonlit macadam;
then there's a dim
smell of moose, an acrid
smell of gasoline.

Something that the American poet Charles Simic has written in
relation to the work of the artist Joseph Cornell—an artist, incidentally, to whom Elizabeth Bishop was also devoted—seems
worth quoting at this juncture. 'There are really three kinds of
images', Simic writes:

First, there are those seen with eyes open in the manner of real-
ists in both art and literature. Then there are images we see with
eyes closed. Romantic poets, surrealists, expressionists and everyday dreamers know them. The images Cornell has in his boxes
are, however, of the third kind. They partake of both dream and
reality, and of something else that doesn't have a name. They
tempt the viewer in two opposite directions. One is to look and
admire . . . and the other is to make up stories about what one sees
. . . Neither [way] by itself is sufficient. It's the mingling of the
two that makes up the third image.

Simic entitles his short meditation 'The Gaze We Knew as a
Child', which again seems apposite to Bishop's images, for they too
strike us as being both preternaturally immediate and remotely familiar. Their attraction partakes of 'something that doesn't have
a name', as if things known once upon a time in a pre-literate
security were reappearing among the destabilizations of the post-
modern. Her images call consciousness towards recollection. And it
is surely Bishop's successful effort to become utterly receptive in
face of the phenomena and to give a just account of the reactions,
both positive and negative, which they induce—it is surely this peculiar honest gaze, both level and brimming, which has drawn so
many readers to her work over the last couple of decades. Naturally, as a woman poet whose laconic sense of her relegation
through gender was matched only by her sense of entitlement
through achievement, Bishop has rightly gained the advocacy of
feminist critics. Her quietude was a far cry from quietism, and poems like 'Roosters', dating from the early 1940s, were a clear-eyed
and deeply creative response to the impositions of a militaristic,
patriarchal world. Yet she always resisted the pressures to connect
herself politically with activist feminist politics. She was by temperament and choice too much of a loner to subscribe even to the
most urgent of solidarities.

Within recent American poetry, Bishop occupies a position
analogous to that long occupied on the other side of the ocean by
Philip Larkin. In an era of volubility, she seems to demonstrate
that less is more. By her sense of proportion and awareness of tradition, she makes what is an entirely personal and contemporary

style seem continuous with the canonical poetry of the past. She writes the kind of poem that makes us want to exclaim with admiration at its professional thoroughness, its technical and formal perfections, and yet at the same time she tempts us to regard technical and formal matters as something of a distraction, since the poem is so candidly *about* something, engaged with its own business of observing the world and discovering meaning.

All of which is immediately manifest in the poem I want to read and comment upon by way of conclusion. This is a villanelle entitled 'One Art', and since its publication sixteen years ago in Bishop's last volume, it has become one of the most admired examples of her work. This last volume, *Geography III*, was published in 1976 and contains a number of extraordinary poems of summation and benediction—including 'The Moose' and that other hide-and-seek, count-to-a-hundred dramatic monologue, 'Crusoe in England'. These poems arise from a mind that is unembittered but still unappeased, like the sandpiper still 'looking for something, something, something'. They come near the end of a life which Bishop had long contemplated with regard to both its penalties and its blessings. They represent the effort of a memory observing its own contents, a consciousness squaring up to itself and taking the measure of its own strengths and weaknesses. And this reflexive strain, this compulsion of her intelligence to keep standing at an angle to her predicament, finds its natural form in the villanelle. With its repetitions and revisions and nuancings, its shifts and refinements and siftings of what has already been finely sifted, the villanelle is the perfect mould for Bishop's habitual method of coming at a subject in little renewed attempts and sorties. But each little attempt falls short of stating the big sorrow or sorrows which occasioned the poem. Anybody familiar with the outlines of the poet's biography will know that there are plenty of specific occasions from which the poem's general preoccupation with loss could have arisen, but the lines can be read without any special knowledge of the facts of Bishop's life:

> The art of losing isn't hard to master;
> so many things seem filled with the intent
> to be lost that their loss is no disaster.

Lose something every day. Accept the fluster
of lost door keys, the hour badly spent.
The art of losing isn't hard to master.

Then practice losing farther, losing faster:
places, and names, and where it was you meant
to travel. None of these will bring disaster.

I lost my mother's watch. And look! my last, or
next-to-last, of three loved houses went.
The art of losing isn't hard to master.

I lost two cities, lovely ones. And, vaster,
some realms I owned, two rivers, a continent.
I miss them, but it wasn't a disaster.

—Even losing you (the joking voice, a gesture
I love) I shan't have lied. It's evident
the art of losing's not too hard to master
though it may look like (*Write* it!) like disaster.

In this poem, Bishop's ability to write plainly and at the same time
reticently manifests itself *in extremis*. This is wonderful lyric writing; it is impossible to separate the poem's reality as a made thing
from its effect as a personal cry. It is in one way, of course, entirely
formal, preoccupied with its technical procedures, taking delight
in solving the challenges of rhyme, in obeying (and disobeying)
the rules of the highly constraining villanelle form. At the same
time, it is obviously the whimper of a creature who has been hard
done by; or, to be more exact, it is a choked-off whimper, the
learned behaviour of somebody who, without the impersonal demands of an art and an ethic of doughty conduct, might have submitted to self-pity. In fact, the conquest of a temptation to self-pity
is what the poem manages to effect: wit confronts hurt and holds a
balance that deserves to be called wisdom. The writing itself could
be called deadpan-ironical or whimsical-stoical, but it is not exactly either. It is, to quote another famous line of Bishop's, 'like
what we imagine knowledge to be'. By its trust in poetic form and
its abnegation of self, it bears a recognizable relationship to the
work of that seventeenth-century English poet-priest whom Eliza-

beth Bishop so admired, George Herbert. Like Herbert, Bishop
finds and enforces a correspondence between the procedures of
verse and the predicaments of the spirit. She makes rhyme an
analogy for self-control. The first time 'master' and 'disaster' occur,
in stanza one, they are tactfully, elegantly, deprecatingly paired off.
It wasn't a disaster. The speaker is being decorous, good-mannered,
relieving you of the burden of having to sympathize, easing you
out of any embarrassed need to find things to say. The last time
the rhyme occurs, however, the shocking traumatic reality of what
happened almost overbrims the containing form. It *was* a disaster.
It was devastatingly and indescribably so. And yet what the poem
has just managed to do, in the nick of time, is to survive the devas-
tation. The verb 'master' places itself in the scales opposite its twin
noun, 'disaster', and holds the balance. And the secret of the held
balance is given in the parenthesis '(*Write* it!)'. As so often in
Bishop's work, the parenthesis (if you have ears to hear) is the
place to hear the real truth. And what the parenthesis in 'One Art'
tells us is what we always knew in some general way but now
know with an acute pang of intimacy, that the act of writing is an
act of survival:

> I lost two cities, lovely ones. And, vaster,
> some realms I owned, two rivers, a continent.
> I miss them, but it wasn't a disaster.
>
> —Even losing you (the joking voice, a gesture
> I love) I shan't have lied. It's evident
> the art of losing's not too hard to master
> though it may look like (*Write* it!) like disaster.

The pun in that nick-of-time imperative—'*Write* it!'—is in deadly
earnest. The redress of poetry is called upon by one of poetry's
constant votaries; the poem is asked to set the balance *right*. Losses
of all sorts have caused the mind's scales to tilt drastically, and so
they desperately need to be evened out by a redistribution of the
mind's burdens—and the act of writing is depended upon to bring
that redistribution about. The throwaway tone of the thing is rec-

ognizably the tone that accompanies a throw that risks all. In the pun on the word 'write', therefore, and in the harmony which prevails momentarily in the concluding rhyme, we experience the resolving power of deliberately articulated sound in much the same way as it is experienced by the child narrator of Bishop's early story 'In the Village'. There the scream was subsumed in the anvil note; here the 'disaster' is absorbed when it meets its emotional and phonetic match in the word 'master'. Bishop's 'one art' does not after all fail her. For all her caution about overstating its prerogatives and possibilities, she does continually manage to advance poetry beyond the point where it has been helping us to enjoy life to that even more profoundly verifying point where it helps us also to endure it.

Burns's Art Speech

> Poets' real biographies are like those of birds . . . their real
> data are in the way they sound. A poet's biography is in his
> vowels and sibilants, in his meters, rhymes and meta-
> phors . . . With poets, the choice of words is invariably more
> telling than the story they tell . . .
>
> —JOSEPH BRODSKY, *Less Than One*

From the start, the way Robert Burns sounded made me feel close
to him. His choice of words, his rhymes and metaphors, all that
collapsed the distance I expected to feel between myself and the
school-book poetry I encountered first at Anahorish Elementary
School and subsequently at St Columb's College, Derry. I'm almost
certain that I knew his lines 'To a Mouse, On Turning Her Up in
Her Nest, with the Plough, November, 1785' before I went to secondary school, but it wasn't any previous acquaintance with the
poem that gave me a special relationship to it when I met it again
in *The Ambleside Book of Verse*. In those days, when it came to poetry, we all braced ourselves linguistically. And rightly so: everybody should be in good verbal shape when faced with a page of
verse. In our case, however, we expected that the language on the
written page would take us out of our unofficial speaking selves
and transport us to a land of formal words where we would have to
be constantly on our best verbal behaviour. 'Hail to thee, blithe
spirit' fulfilled these expectations perfectly, as did the elevation of
'Tyger, tyger, burning bright'. But next comes this:

> Wee, sleeket, cowran, tim'rous *beastie*,

and this was different. Even before a metre or a melody could be
established, the word 'wee' put its stressed foot down and in one
pre-emptive vocative strike took over the emotional and cultural
ground, dispossessing the rights of written standard English and
offering asylum to all vernacular comers. To all, at least, who

hailed from north of a line drawn between Berwick and Bundoran. 'Wee' came on strong. It was entirely un-twee. It neither beckoned nor beguiled. It was just suddenly and solidly there, and there it remains to this day, like a pebble of the pre-literary and the preliterate stuff, irreducible, undislodgeable and undeniably true. A bit like what Burns himself was like at his best, the Burns whom Walter Scott remembered, for example, as a person 'strong and robust' with 'a sort of dignified plainness and simplicity', expressive of 'perfect self-confidence, without the slightest presumption', and exhibiting thereby a 'perfect firmness, but without the least intrusive forwardness'.

Big claims, you may feel, for a wee word; but not, I would argue, exaggerated claims. Both as a matter of poetic fact and as a matter of personal reminiscence, the opening of Burns's poem to the mouse is a decisive occurrence. It gets into the boundless language of poetry by reason of its unchallengeable rightness as utterance, its simultaneous at-oneness with the genius of English and Scottish speech; and it got under my official classroom guard and into the kitchen life, as it were, of my affections by reason of its truth to the life of the language I spoke while growing up in mid-Ulster, a language where trace elements of Elizabethan English and Lowland Scots are still to be heard and to be reckoned with as a matter of pronunciation and even, indeed, of politics.

'Wee, sleeket, cowran, tim'rous *beastie*'—'sleeket' was something else that slipped under the guard, as a sleeket thing might be expected to, since the word has connotations of plausibility as well as silkiness and slinkiness. And the line built quickly and securely on that 'wee' foundation. The mouse, for example, was not cowering but 'cowran', a participle as careless about its final *g* as we ourselves were in our schoolyard speech. It was a beastie, not a beast, the way a John among us became a Johnnie or a Hugh a Hughie or, indeed, a Robert a Rabbie. And the whole thing, I knew, had to be spoken in a more or less County Antrim accent, an accent I happened to be familiar with from my trips to the fair hill in Ballymena where the farmers said 'yin' and 'twa' for 'one' and 'two' and in general spoke a tongue that was as close to Ayrshire as to County Derry.

There is no need, I suppose, to keep going on in this fashion, because what I am describing is a common enough phenomenon. It is always a pleasure to find your subcultural life being represented with accuracy and without condescension in a high cultural context—and in its own way, in its own time, *The Ambleside Book of Verse* did provide just such a context. Nowadays, however, as well as recognizing the documentary accuracy of the language, I can also rejoice in what we might call its poetic verity. By which I mean its earworthiness, the way it is as firm and as buoyant as a boat beneath an oarsman. 'Wee, sleeket, cowran, tim'rous *beastie*': the line comes on like a reassuring 'There, there, there, there'; the four stresses of the four adjectives establish the largeness and largesse of the human agent on the scene. The poetic feet have a benevolent tread and step into the poem as surely and unthreateningly as the ploughman coming to inspect the ruined nest. Indeed, what is being sounded forth beat by metrical beat is that independence which was so often remarked upon as an attractive and indispensable part of the poet's own make-up—what Scott called his 'perfect firmness'.

Moreover, it is because of the aural trustworthiness of the first line that the rhetorical exclamation of the second one—'O, what a panic's in thy breastie!'—carries real emotional weight. I can, of course, imagine Spike Milligan using a burlesque Scoto-Goonish accent and putting these words through it as through a synthesizer in order to send them up; but the point is that it would indeed require such genuinely comic gifts as Spike's to rock the line on its emotional keel. 'O, what a panic's in thy breastie!' has a scramblier movement than the first line, but it is a movement which springs from sympathy rather than mimicry. There is nothing remotely Disney-like going on here: this is not mere skilful verbal simulation of the behaviour of a frightened mouse but an involuntary outrush of fellow feeling. And as the address to the unhoused mouse continues, the identification becomes more intense, the plough of the living voice gets set deeper and deeper in the psychic ground, dives more and more purposefully into the subsoil of the intuitions until finally it breaks open a nest inside the poet's own head and leaves him exposed to his own profoundest forebodings

about his fate. The last stanza feels weird, in the strictly Anglo-
Saxon sense:

> Still thou art blest compar'd wi' me!
> The present only toucheth thee:
> But, Och! I backward cast my e'e
> On prospects drear!
> An' forward tho' I canna see,
> I guess an' fear.

What has happened here is truly, almost literally, a discovery. From
a hiding place in the foggage of the poet's own consciousness, his
wee, cowran, tim'rous soul has been panicked into a sudden recognition of its destiny. The sturdy, caring figure who overshadowed
and oversaw the panic of the mouse at the beginning has been revealed to himself as someone less perfectly firm, less strong and
robust than he or the reader would have ever suspected. In other
words, Burns's mouse gradually becomes a sibylline rather than a
sentimental element in the poem—so much so that by the end the
reader feels that the bleakness of Lear's heath must have overtaken
the field at Mossgiel on that wintry November day in 1785 when
'crash! the cruel coulter passed / Out thro' thy cell'.

And it is a matter of the profoundest phonetic satisfaction that
the exclamation 'Och' should be at the centre of this semi-
visionary final stanza. For if 'wee' is the monosyllable that takes
possession of the cultural and linguistic ground at the start, 'och' is
a kind of *Nunc Dimittis* positioned near the end. 'Och' springs us
from the domestic into the disconsolate. It is a common, almost
pre-linguistic particle, one of those sounds that 'haven't been
brought to book . . . living in the cave of the mouth'; and while it is
certainly a cry of distress, it is by no means a venting of self-pity. If
'ouch' is the complaint of the ego, 'och' is the sigh of ultimate resignation and illumination. Here, and on the countless occasions
when it has been uttered by men and women *in extremis* since
time immemorial, it functions as a kind of self-relinquishment, a
casting of the spirit upon the mercy of fate, at once a protest and a
cry for help.

Of course, I am aware that I am overdoing it a bit here, but I believe that I am still not misrepresenting the poetic truth of the matter, which has precisely to do with the raising of common speech to the power of art. 'Och' strikes a note of grief and wisdom which the poem as a whole elaborates and orchestrates. It is what Nadezhda Mandelstam called 'the nugget of harmony' and the guarantee of Burns's genius as a poet of the Scots and English tongues, for 'och', like 'wee', also belongs north of that Berwick/Bundoran line, where the language of Shakespeare and the Bible meets the language of Dunbar and the ballads and where new poetic combinations and new departures are still going on.

The language missing in those places is, of course, Gaelic, whether of the Scots or Irish variety, although it is a promising fact that the expression 'och' lies every bit as deep in the Irish larynx as in the Ulster Scots. Twenty-five years ago, for example, when I was trying to coax a few lyric shoots out of the political compost heap of Northern Ireland, I wrote a poem called 'Broagh' which could just as well have been entitled 'Och'. Its immediate subject was my recollection of an outlying part of our farm in the townland of Broagh on the banks of the River Moyola in County Derry, but its purpose was to bring the three languages I've just mentioned—Irish, Elizabethan English and Ulster Scots—into some kind of creative intercourse and alignment and thereby to intimate the possibility of some new intercourse and alignment among the cultural and political heritages which these three languages represent in Northern Ireland.

I very much wanted to affirm the rights of the Irish language to be recognized as part of that Ulster mix, to correct the official, east-of-Bann emphasis on the province's ur-languages as Ulster Scots and Elizabethan English. None of this appeared, however, in the story the poem told: instead, it was all meant to be implicit in the way it sounded, in the vocabulary and voicing of the lines, in the way the poem tapped into the shorthand and coding that are constantly operating beneath the first level of Ulster speech. Ultimately, it all came down to the ability to say 'Broagh', to pronounce that last *gh* as it is pronounced in the place itself; the poem, in other words, was just one tiny move in that big campaign of our times which aims to take cultural authority back to the local ground, to reverse the colonizing process by making the underprivileged speech the normative standard. Whitehall ministers would have called the place *Broa*, but they would have been wrong. Their pronunciation, for once, would have been no sign of entitlement; on the contrary, it would have revealed a certain incapacity. But everyone native to Northern Ireland, Protestant or Catholic, Planter or Gael, whatever their separate myths of linguistic exile from Irish or Ulster Scots—every one of them could say 'Broagh', every one of them was fitted to dwell in at least phonetic amity with the other. I wanted to suggest, therefore, that it was at this first level of utterance that the foundations of a common language were to be sought.

I think, in other words, that we can prefigure a future by re-imagining our pasts. In poetry, however, this prefiguring is venturesome and suggestive, more like a melodic promise than a social programme. It is not like the blueprint for a better world which might spring from the mind of a social engineer. Rather, it arises from the cravings of the spirit as expressed in language, in all of those patiences and impatiences which language embodies. I wish, therefore, that in those days when I was studying *The Ambleside Book of Verse* in my English class, somebody had told me to look at another poem which we would eventually meet in our Irish class and to compare it with Burns's poem to the evicted mouse. This other poem was 'An Bunnán Buí' by the Irish-language poet Cathal Buí Mac Giolla Ghunna, a native of Ulster who followed, according to his most recent editors, 'the career of rake poet', who died three years before Burns was born and whose work is 'marked by a rare humanity' and a 'finely-judged blend of pathos and humour'.

Mac Giolla Ghunna was a significant presence to me in my mid-teens, when I was beginning to be able to read and feel my way into poetry in the Irish language. Significant because he was a Northern voice and part of a group of Ulster poets whose work, like Burns's, was sustained out of the past by a long and learned literary tradition; but this once privileged tradition subsisted in the poets' time as part of a culture that was oral, rural and more and more dislodged from its previous high cultural authority. Mac Giolla Ghunna and his older brothers in the art—Seamus Dall Mac Cuarta and Art Mac Cumhaigh, for example—still retained something of the *techne* and the status of bardic poets, but the Gaelic order which once supported the bardic schools had been shattered in the course of the seventeenth century, beginning with Elizabeth's decisive campaign against Hugh O'Neill, continuing with the Cromwellian depredations and culminating in the Williamite defeat of the Stuart cause at Derry, Aughrim and the Boyne. Loss of patronage by the poets was one consequence of these defeats, but Joseph Brodsky's law applied to them as well, in that their biographies were also present in the way they sounded. Their words and intonations belonged to an Ulster Irish in which I felt completely at home, since it was the Ulster version of the language that had been taught in Derry. Consequently, when I read Mac Cuarta's 'Fáilte do'n Éan' or Mac Cumhaigh's 'Úr Chill Ui Chreagain' or Mac Giolla Ghunna's 'An Bunnán Buí', I experienced something of that domestic familiarity I had known when I first read 'To a Mouse'. What I experienced, in fact, in the work of these Ulster Gaels was what John Hewitt experienced when he read 'The Rhyming Weavers', those local bards of the late eighteenth and early nineteenth centuries who wrote in the Ulster Scots vernacular and who produced in Hewitt 'some feeling that, for better or worse, they were my own people . . .', a feeling issuing from a susceptibility 'in stanza, couplet or turn of phrase, [to] some sense of the humanity that was in them'.

Like everything else in Ulster, the reading of poetry can quickly devolve into an aspect of identity politics, but it would be more rewarding to read 'An Bunnán Buí' alongside 'To a Mouse' as a purely literary exercise. In the Irish poem, the rake poet is in mourning because he has just discovered the carcass of a bird frozen into the ice of a winter lake and this awakens a mood of foreboding, a fear that his addiction to drink will be the end of him. The bird is a mighty one, a yellow bittern, and the tragedy and omen of its death come home to the poet all the more force-fully because its very name—bunnán buí, yellow bittern—echoes his own name, Cathal Buí—Yellow or Fair-haired Cathal or Charles. As in the Burns poem, there is an increasing convergence, as the stanzas proceed, between the tender and the tragic aspects of the situation, a sense of fatal link between the poet exposed to poverty and danger and the creature foraging for dear life until the day of its death; just as there is also the same huge sense of pro-portion, a cosmic perspective within which the man and the mouse or the man and the bird end up as big or as small as each other by the conclusion of the poem. The third and fourth stanzas go like this:

> I am saddened, bittern, and broken-hearted
>   To find you in scrags in the rushy tufts
> And the big rats scampering down the ratpaths
>   To wake your carcass and have their fun.
> If you had got word to me in time, bird,
>   That you were in trouble and craved a sup,
> I'd have struck the fetters off those loch waters
>   And have wet your thrapple with the blow I struck.
>
> Your common birds do not concern me,
>   The blackbird, say, or the thrush or crane,
> But the yellow bittern, my heartsome namesake
>   With my looks and locks, he's the one I mourn.
> Constantly he was drinking, drinking,
>   And by all accounts I am just the same,
> But every drop I get I'll down it
>   For fear I might get my death from drouth.

> (Translation by Seamus Heaney)

And here are those stanzas in the original:

> A bhonnáin óig, is é mo mhíle brón
>   thú bheith romham i measc na dtom,

is na lucha móra ag triall chun do thorraimh
    ag déanamh spóirt is pléisiúr ann;
dá gcuirfeá scéala in am fá mo déinse
    go raibh tú i ngheibheann nó i mbroid fá dheoch,
do bhrisfinn béim ar an loch sin Vesey
    a fhliuchfadh do bhéal is do chorp isteach.

Ni hé bhur n-éanlaith atá mise ag éagnach,
    an lon, an smaolach, ná an chorr ghlas—
ach mo bhonnán buí lán den chroí,
    is gur cosúil liom féin é ina ghné is a dhath;
bhíodh sé choíche ag síoról na dí,
    agus deir na daoine go mbím mar sin seal,
is níl deor dá bhfaighead nach ligfead síos
    ar eagla go bhfaighinnse bás den tart.

Needless to say, it's another source of satisfaction to me that *och* reappears at the phonetic centre of this poem in the word *loch* and the word *deoch*—which happens to mean 'drink' in Irish. It functions like a signal broadcast forward into Broaghville and points towards a future that is implicit in the mutually pronounceable elements of the speech of Planter and Gael. Even if we grant the deeply binary nature of Ulster thinking about language and culture, we can still try to establish a plane of regard from which to inspect the recalcitrant elements of the situation and reposition ourselves in relation to them. And that plane, I believe, can be reliably projected from poems and poetry. I wish, as I said earlier, that somebody had asked me years ago, 'Have you ever noticed how the note deepens in those two poems by Burns and Mac Giolla Ghunna? How poems that might have been merely affecting get closer to something tragic? How their given note arrives out of the literary tradition but ends up in the place that Ted Hughes calls the place of "ultimate suffering and decision in us"?' Moreover, I wish all this not because I believe the reading of the two poems would have helped me into some better civic posture, some higher commitment to the notion of diversity, for example; instead, I wish it because, to quote Joseph Brodsky once more, good poetry is a tonic and defence against that which is the final enemy, namely, 'the vulgarity of the human heart'.

None of us wants fake consolation in the face of real problems. None of us wants Disney when what we need is Dante. But in discovering a similar sense of vulnerability and sympathy in Burns and Mac Giolla Ghunna, and in recognizing that their art speech not only inhabits a similar literary and linguistic middle state but also is capable of prospecting the deeper levels of their poetic being, I believe one is doing more than merely introducing a feel-good factor, some corollary of the old Ulster saw that there are faults on both sides. Poetry operates more opulently than that. The terms of its understanding are not dictated by the circumstances that pertain but are commensurate with the poet's intellectual and imaginative wavelength. Those rats in the Irish poem, for example, for all their anthropomorphic jollity, are every bit as far from Disneyland as Burns's mouse. I feel, indeed, that they could have escaped from Villon or that they might return from the bittern's wake to join up with the rattons Burns hears squeaking under the rigging of the thatch in his poem 'The Vision'. They're a bit macabre and a bit macaronic, archetypal and vernacular all at once, and as such they (and the poem which they inhabit) belong equally to the parish and the universe.

This phrase, 'the parish and the universe', is the title of an essay by Patrick Kavanagh. In it, Kavanagh is concerned with the way in which the local can be winnowed by the boundless and set free within it, the way in which poetry can create conditions where 'the word for family / is also the word for departure'. And it is this very transformation which has concerned me in this essay. I want to do more than state the obvious truth that Burns's poetry is particularly congenial to natives of Ulster, whatever their allegiance, not only because of a common language but also because of a shared feeling of embattledness. Obviously, poetry is a domestic art and finds its most telling reach within the acoustic of its first language and language-group. But I wanted to affirm a supplementary truth, namely, that poems and poets do not become available to their audience on the simple basis of ethnic or linguistic kinship. Burns is a world poet because of his genius, not because of his Scottishness. There is nothing determined about the reach of poetry, either for the writer or for the reader of it: it is, as Keats said, a matter of surprise by fine excess, what Robert Frost calls in 'Birches' a going above the brim, a getting away from earth awhile in order to come back and begin over . . .

What produces the art is not the medium, but what is made of it. For example, I am predisposed to like Burns's 'The Twa Dogs' because of its unfoolable, realistic sense of the world, its uncorny, wily humour and its unmitigated sense of justice, but I could say that about Burns's letters as well; what distinguishes it as a poem is the way it combines reliable tone and technical virtuosity—the pitch of the voice and the musical trueness of it. It is because of a special mixture of intimacy and documentary accuracy in the art speech of the poem that none of the humour is at the expense of the dogs and none of the virtuosity is knowing. And the same is true of the two poems about Poor Mailie, the author's 'pet yowe' that strangled herself at the end of a rope. There is a beautifully limpid quality about the dying words which she wishes to be carried to her master and relayed by him to her family, a quality hard to name, less dewy-eyed than pathos, more sympathetic than irony:

> My poor *toop-lamb*, my son an' heir,
> O, bid him breed him up wi' care!
> An' if he live to be a beast,
> To pit some havins in his breast!
> An' warn him, what I winna name,
> To stay content wi' *yowes* at hame;
> An' no to rin an' wear his cloots,
> Like ither menseless, graceless brutes.
>
> An' niest my *yowie*, silly thing,
> Gude keep thee frae a *tether string*!
> O, may thou ne'er forgather up,
> Wi' onie blastet, moorlan *toop*;
> But ay keep mind to moop an' mell,
> Wi sheep o' credit like thysel!

Even Burns's humorous rhyming is distinguished by a compensatory emotional fidelity to the subjects which are being made fun of. If you compare what he does with what Byron or Auden do in a similar vein, you find that the pair of them tend to be show-offs, and the more deadpan and one-up their performance is, the better. Burns, on the other hand, retains a certain protectiveness towards those very things which bring out the verbal scamp in him. In 'Tam o' Shanter', for example, the poise of the rhymes in the following famous lines is altogether characteristic:

> Nae man can tether time or tide;
> The hour approaches Tam maun ride;
> That hour, o' night's black arch the key-stane,
> That dreary hour he mounts his beast in;
> And sic a night he takes the road in,
> As ne'er poor sinner was abroad in.

There is something as bountiful about the feeling here as there is about the sense of supply. The words are as kind to Tam as they are kinned to one another. That run of feminine rhymes is carried away with itself, as they would say in Ulster, and cannot quite suppress its relish of its own sportiveness; but neither can it forget the suppressed panic in Tam o' Shanter's breast, and it is this double susceptibility in the writing that makes it so beguiling.

Being able to get carried away is, of course, a crucial gift when it comes to poetry. 'What reasonable man', Czeslaw Milosz asks in his poem 'Ars Poetica?', 'would like to be a city of demons, / who behave as if they were at home, speak in many tongues, / and who, not satisfied with stealing his lips or hand, / work at changing his destiny for their convenience?' And the answer expected here, but not necessarily desired, is Plato's answer: no reasonable man or woman would want to be susceptible to that kind of visitation. Control freak a poet cannot afford to be, but must, on the contrary, be prepared to go with the flow. And it is out of the submerged quarrel between the reasonable man in Burns and the city of demons which he contained that his best poems arrive. A great number of Burns's contemporaries thought of those demons as sexual, emissaries from caverns 'grim an' sootie', sent by 'Auld

Hornie . . . Nick, or Clootie', but nowadays we have added to their
horde the geniuses of the different languages that were available
to him. Burns, we gratefully realize, opened his door to a great variety of linguistic callers. He gladly let his lips and hands be stolen
at one moment by the language of Beattie and Thomson and at
the next by the voices of his neighbours. In fact, his subjectivity
only became totally available in situations which were performa-
tive or, if you prefer Milosz's way of thinking, when he was possessed by a spirit. 'Holy Willie's Prayer' is the masterpiece of such
possession and performance, but his gift for it is everywhere. The
first line or two of each epistle, for example, opens the door to different visitors, each one corresponding under the name of Burns
but each displaying different potentialities in the pitch and
rhythm of his utterance. Who, after all, could shut the door on the
agility and genuine accommodation in the voice that addresses
Dr Blacklock?

> Wow, but your letter made me vauntie!
> And are ye hale, and weel, and cantie?
> I kend it still your wee bit jauntie
>   Wad bring ye to:
> Lord send you ay as weel's I want ye,
>   And then ye'll do—

And who could have guessed that such a *jongleur* of the vernacular
could reappear and be equally convincing in the role of minstrel
boy addressing the master minstrel James Lapraik?

> While briers an' woodbines budding green,
> An' Patricks scraichan loud at e'en,
> An' morning Poosie whiddan seen,
>   Inspire my Muse,
> This freedom, in an *unknown* frien',
>   I pray excuse.

Even the songs, perhaps most of all the songs, required a surrender of the Burns who sat down to breakfast (as Yeats would have

called him) to the Burns who had been reborn as the melody of inwardness:

> Had we never lov'd sae kindly,
> Had we never lov'd sae blindly!
> Never met—or never parted,
> We had ne'er been broken hearted.—
>
> Fare-thee-weel, thou first and fairest!
> Fare-thee-weel, thou best and dearest!
> Thine be ilka joy and treasure,
> Peace, Enjoyment, Love and Pleasure!—
>
> Ae fond kiss, and then we sever!
> Ae fareweel, Alas, for ever:
> Deep in heart-wrung tears I'll pledge thee,
> Warring sighs and groans I'll wage thee.—

The drama is one that is played out in every poet between the social self and a deeper self which is the locus of 'the ultimate suffering and decision in us', and I have to confess that when I began re-reading Burns for this essay, I did so with a prejudice . . . From my memories of the poems that I knew, and particularly those in the Standard Habbie metre, I had got it into my head that the social self had been given too much of an upper hand. I remembered the Burns stanza as one which set its cap rather too winsomely at the reader; but in fact Burns's deep poetic self inheres in something much bigger and older and more ballad-fastened, so to speak, something as intimately laid down in him as the insinuation and stealth of both his humour and his sexuality. The potency of his songs is in itself enough to prove how surely he could find his way into a sort of original knowledge, but that feeling of broaching the race's oldest survival-truths is present everywhere. One of my own favourite instances comes in the meeting of the poet with Death in 'Death and Doctor Hornbook', in particular the recognition that Death too has to survive by the sweat of his brow, that he's one of the toilers, that it is an achievement for him too simply to keep going:

'Weel, weel!' says I, 'a bargain be't;
'Come, gies your hand, an' sae we're gree't;
'We'll ease our shanks an' tak a seat,
    'Come, gies your news!
'This while ye hae been mony a gate,
    'At mony a house.'

'Ay, ay!' quo' he, an' shook his head,
'It's e'en a lang, lang time indeed
'Sin' I began to nick the thread,
    'An' choke the breath:
'Folk maun do something for their bread,
    'An' sae maun *Death*.'

The access to world-sorrow comes in the intonation, the sound of sense in that concluding cadence. The utterance matches the contours of immemorial utterances made to the same effect. To call it folk wisdom or proverbial truth is to rob it of its specific emotional gravity within the dramatized setting. Death is a neighbour recognized on the road. He doesn't, for example, cut the thread of life but nicks it, and in that acutely refreshing and totally unshowy vernacular touch, Burns gives a glimpse of the other, more intimate power that he so often broaches. So I want to end by quoting and commenting briefly upon a poem whose subject is, in fact, the poet's middle state not just between Belles Lettres and Braid Scots, or between Ayr and Edinburgh or between 'Ça ira' and 'God Save the King', but between the vocation of poet and the behaviour of a reasonable man, between the call to open the doors of one's life to the demonic and prophetic soul and have one's destiny changed by it, between that choice and the temptation to keep the doors closed and the self securely under social and domestic lock and key. Whether to be the cotter or Saint Paul, as it were. Here, therefore, beginning with the second stanza, is the opening of 'The Vision':

The Thresher's weary *flingin tree*
The lee-lang day had tir'd me;
And when the Day had clos'd his e'e,

Far i' the West,
Ben i' the *Spence*, right pensivelie,
    I gaed to rest.

There, lanely, by the ingle-cheek,
I sat and ey'd the spewing reek,
That fill'd, wi' hoast-provoking smeek,
        The auld, clay biggin;
And heard the restless rattons squeak
        About the riggin.

All in this mottie, misty clime,
I backward mus'd on wasted time,
How I had spent my *youthfu' prime*,
        An' done nae-thing,
But stringing blethers up in rhyme
        For fools to sing.

Had I to guid advice but harket,
I might, by this, hae led a market,
Or strutted in a Bank and clarket
        My *Cash-Account*;
While here, half-mad, half-fed, half-sarket,
        Is a' th' amount.

I started, mutt'ring blockhead! coof!
And heav'd on high my wauket loof,
To swear by a' yon starry roof,
        Or some rash aith,
That I, henceforth, would be *rhyme-proof*
        Till my last breath—

When click! the *string* the *snick* did draw;
And jee! the door gaed to the wa';
And by my ingle-lowe I saw,
        Now bleezan bright,
A tight, outlandish *Hizzie*, braw,
        Come full in sight.

Ye need na doubt, I held my whisht;
The infant aith, half-form'd, was crusht;
I glower'd as eerie 's I'd been dusht,
        In some wild glen;
When sweet, like *modest Worth*, she blusht,
        And stepped ben.

Green, slender, leaf-clad *Holly-boughs*
Were twisted, gracefu', round her brows,
I took her for some SCOTTISH MUSE
        By that same token;
And come to stop those restless vows,
        Would soon been broken.

This is Burns's *aisling*, and its transcultural allegiance to the
Gaelic heritage in Scotland is made clear by his calling each section of it a *duan*, a term he found in Macpherson and which is
simply the word for a poem in Irish and Scots Gaelic. The *aisling*
genre had immense popularity in Ireland during the late seventeenth and eighteenth centuries, although in her Irish setting the
Muse was politicized into an image of the maiden Hibernia, a
Hibernia Tacta, as it were, violated by and in thrall to the heretic
English invader. So the genre's primal function as a vehicle for the
myth of access to poetic power got submerged as it became more
and more a manifestation of the Jacobite strain in Irish politics
during those decades when the Irish Gaels were left without lead-
ership or a plan for resurgence. But the Art Mac Cumhaigh who
wrote an *aisling* about a maiden coming to kiss him awake at dawn
in the churchyard at Killycreggan would surely have recognized
the commingling of the erotic with the local and the national in
Burns's lines. And the sexually entranced Sir Thomas Wyatt,
whose dawn visitor once took him 'in her armes long and smale'
and 'Therewithal sweteley did [him] kiss / And softely said, *dere
hert, howe like you this?*'—Wyatt too would have smiled with a
delicious remembrance 'When click! the *string* the *snick* did
draw; / And jee! the door gaed to the wa'' ...
    And yet it is not the ancient thematic respectability of the 'The

Vision' which makes it such a credible poetic event. There are, of course, echoes of the Muses singing to the farmer Hesiod, of Dante about to give up in the middle of his journey and being saved by Beatrice and of the White Goddess whose presence Robert Graves would have recognized immediately in the lines that I've just quoted. But this poem is not simply a case of an archetype being selected from the myth kitty: the personal expense of Burns's poetic vocation is embodied deeply in its speech and drama. The initiate's fear of the divine call, the poet's temptation to go easy on himself: these are indeed part of the story the poem tells, but they are also present in the way it sounds. The reluctance (call it the rel*och*tance) to face the next move, the desire to let the harp pass, to do a Caedmon and substitute the business of the day-time self for the dreamwork—all this comes through and comes true in the words themselves. And so too does the miraculous light-ening and alleviation of that mood as a brightness comes from the air and everything that is viscous and sluggish yields miraculously to something far more lightsome and visionary. When I read 'The Thresher's weary *flingin tree* / The lee-lang day had tir'd me', the limberness of the flail travels fleetly up my arm only to meet the actual drudgery of farmwork coming leadenly down; but when 'click! the *string* the *snick* did draw', I know that 'the next bright bolt' has fallen and I come through the reasonable man's demur-rals every time. So even though a part of me will always agree with Milosz's admonition at the end of his 'Ars Poetica?' that 'po-ems should be written rarely and reluctantly, / under unbearable duress and only with the hope / that good spirits, not evil ones, choose us for their instrument', I am still nevertheless persuaded that Burns did right to let his door go to the wall and that he did not fail the Muse or us or himself as one of poetry's chosen instruments.

Through-Other Places, Through-Other Times:
The Irish Poet and Britain

Fifty years ago the Northern Irish poet W. R. Rodgers published a poem called 'Armagh' that begins:

> There is a through-otherness about Armagh
> Of tower and steeple,
> Up on the hill are the arguing graves of the kings
> And below are the people.

Rodgers was then working as a BBC producer in London, but until a few years before he had served as the Presbyterian minister in the rural parish of Loughgall. There were several reasons why he moved from being in charge of a meeting-house in County Armagh to being in charge of a microphone in a studio in Broadcasting House, but a central factor was his discovery of himself as a poet. In 1938 his friend John Hewitt, who had been writing verse since he was a teenager, lent Rodgers some books by contemporary poets and the results were seismic. The explanation of what happened was given by Rodgers in his own inimitable way years afterwards, when he was revisiting the Loughgall manse and meeting-house. On that occasion, the story goes, a former parishioner asked him why somebody so naturally gifted as a pastor and a preacher, so much at home in the pulpit and with the people, had abandoned the ministry. 'Ah well, you know,' Rodgers is supposed to have replied, 'too many books spoil the cloth.'

Finding the right expression by wrong-footing the language like that is one way of escaping the bind of the usual; indeed, it is the principal path into poetry, and it became a recognizable feature of Rodgers's style. 'I had a tongue in both my parents' cheeks,' he would write later,

> Could take the word out of two different mouths.

His father he associated with the indigenous Irish stock and his mother with his Scottish Planter ancestry, but he chose, he says,

> my father's slower way of talk
> That had the native tint of wonder in it
> To soften it; though my mother tongue,
> Scots, raucous, quick, followed it hard
> With hints of glottal stops.
> I am Ulster, my people an abrupt people
> Who like the spiky consonants in speech
> And think the soft ones cissy . . .
> And I, born to the purple passage,
> Was heir to all that Adamnation
> And hand-me-down of doom.

I begin with Rodgers and his situation because the way he presents himself is emblematic of a condition I want to explore. One very capable part of Rodgers, the day-job part of him let's call it, the part that was professional and career-making, that part was connected up with the world of official culture and books in London and the BBC; but as well as the day-job part of him there was what we might call the 'return room' part, the return room being not only the room farthest away from the front door in those terrace houses that Rodgers knew in his childhood in Belfast but also the name of a radio programme where he evoked that childhood with typical brio. 'There was a halo of hills round me from the start', the narrator of the broadcast declares, and when he and his family went out in the countryside, 'the duck twirled like a stick on the stream, each gay cloud was off on its own, the very clod sang.' So Rodgers in this self-placing passage again associates something original in himself with the lyrical element in the Irish countryside that had, like his father's speech, the native tint of wonder in it. And if you add the halo of hills to that native tint, you have something vestigially Catholic also. But equally present in the return room at the back of his head was the Scottish inheritance, everything from the Adamnation of the Lowland Covenanters to the Unionist determination that marked the solemn leaguing and covenanting of the Ulster Volunteers in 1912 against Home Rule and Rome Rule. Even as the narrator celebrates the pristine scenery of the countryside, he is longing to be back in the city for the Twelfth of July:

> There would be a bonfire in our back street that night. It would light up the roses of the wallpaper of the return room. It would flicker on the picture of Robbie Burns. It would glimmer on the tallboy with its deep drawers full of treasures—a black silk topper . . . a copy of the Solemn League and Covenant, a Volunteer hat that looked like a cowboy's.

So: where I am heading with all this should be clear enough by now. I am trying to suggest that in the triangulation of Rodgers's understanding of himself between London, Loughgall and the Lowlands, in that three-sided map of his inner being that he provided with its three cardinal points, in all of that there is something analogous to the triple heritage of Irish, Scottish and English traditions that compound and complicate the cultural and political life of contemporary Ulster. For Rodgers, it wasn't a question of the otherness of any one part of his inheritance, more a recognition of the through-otherness of all of them. 'Through-other' is a compound in common use in Ulster, meaning physically untidy or mentally confused, and, appropriately enough, it echoes the Irish-language expression *tré na céile*, meaning things mixed up among themselves, like the cultural and historical mix-up that the poet acknowledges, a bit too winsomely perhaps, in the last two stanzas of 'Armagh':

> Through-other is its history, of Celt and Dane,
> Norman and Saxon,
> Who ruled the place and sounded the gamut of fame
> From cow-horn to klaxon.

> There is through-otherness about Armagh
> Delightful to me,
> Up on the hill are the graves of the garrulous kings
> Who at last can agree.

The Irish for 'Armagh' is 'Ard Mhacha', meaning the heights of Macha, and the garrulous kings are presumably those who once upon a time occupied the legendary royal seat of Emain Macha, home of King Conor and the Red Branch Knights, although they must include as well all those warring lords of the great Gaelic families of Ulster, those O'Neills and O'Donnells and Maguires whose descendants continued to hold sway until the Flight of the Earls in 1607. But obviously, more recent and more rancorous battles between the house of Orange and the house of Stuart are being alluded to in that concluding cadence: 'Up on the hill are the graves of the garrulous kings / Who at last can agree.' The problem is that the dying fall has the effect of settling the argument a bit too quickly and too amicably; it dodges very nimbly past the dangers, so I don't find that it provides the momentary stay against confusion which Robert Frost said a poem should provide and be; the conclusion is more like an evasion, more like saying 'There are faults on both sides'—the old palliative catch-phrase that has got Northern Ireland people through embarrassing situations for years and at the same time got them nowhere.

All the same, a certain amount of evasion is understandable in such a through-other situation. I remember, for example, a moment in Belfast early on in the Troubles, sometime in 1970, when I myself hesitated to face the full force of the sectarian circumstances. I was living then on the wrong side of Lisburn Road, socially speaking, since Lisburn Road was a thoroughfare that divided a wedge of middle-class and university-related housing from a largely working-class barrio that grew more and more boisterous as it ran down, in more senses than one, to its loyalist limit, a district known locally as The Village. The Village in those days was no place for somebody called Seamus, and I wasn't often to be seen there, but I did frequent a lock-up fish-and-chip shop just round the corner from us, on the outer edge of what was still strongly loyalist territory. Anyhow, one night there was a new assistant behind the counter, a young English girl who happened to recognize my face because she'd seen me the night before on some television arts show. 'Oh,' she cried as she lashed on the salt and vinegar, 'I saw you on the box last night, didn't I? Aren't you the Irish poet?' And before I could answer, the owner of the shop turned from her tasks at the boiling oil and corrected her, 'Not at all, dear. He's like the rest of us, a British subject living in Ulster! God,' she went on, addressing me and rolling an eye behind the innocent mainlander's back, 'wouldn't it sicken you! Having to listen to that. Irish poet!' And Irish and all as I was, I'm afraid I hesitated to contradict her.

'What is the source of our first suffering?' the French writer Gaston Bachelard asks, and then answers, 'It lies in the fact that we hesitated to speak. It began in the moment when we accumulated silent things within us.' This quotation I used almost twenty years ago as the epigraph for a pamphlet published in Ireland by Field Day Theatre Company. The title of the pamphlet was *An Open Letter*, and it was one of an initial group of three that dealt with the Britification of 'The Isles', as Norman Davies calls them. We were looking at the intermingled Irish, English and Scottish inheritances of Ulster, in particular the linguistic inheritances, the other two pamphlets being Seamus Deane's *Civilians and Barbarians* and Tom Paulin's *A New Look at the Language Question*. Mine was less furious about British impositions than Deane's but more disaffected than Paulin's. It was a verse epistle addressed to Andrew Motion and Blake Morrison in their capacity as editors of the recently published *Penguin Book of Contemporary British Poetry*, and what I was out to do was to dispute use of the word 'British' as a description of my nationality.

My sense of being Irish was simply a given of my life, something that was with me from the start, something reinforced rather than eroded by the experience of living in a Northern Ireland that insisted that it—and I—was British. Like the rest of the minority, I felt coerced in this regard. Having to take my Jacobite way under the Williamite arches every July was a constant reminder that a settlement had been made, a settlement that was not at all in my favour, and for a long time this definitely had the effect of sharpening a sense of otherness rather than encouraging any notions of through-otherness. Some orientation towards a more tolerant future did occur in the 1960s, but all that was long gone. We had escaped from Lord Brookeborough's sectarian Ulster only to be landed in Margaret Thatcher's. In the early 1980s, we were in the bitter aftermath of dirty protests and hunger strikes, in the middle of the IRA's campaign, and at that polarized moment the Morrison and Motion book was published. I had the feeling that if my British audience were not kept apprised of my stand-off with the 'British' nomenclature, and indeed if my unionist readers were not kept reminded of it, I would be guilty of more than evasiveness.

Like all Northern nationalists of my generation, I accumulated silent things within me whenever incidents like the one in the chip shop occurred. And those things accumulated even more problematically in the mid-1960s, when I started to publish poems and began to be included in anthologies with titles like *Young Commonwealth Poets* and *Young British Poets*. Probably I could have gone on living and hesitating to speak had I gone on living in Northern Ireland and had the question of British versus Irish loyalties not mutated into the deadly complications of our more or less civil war. There were precedents enough and reasons enough to hold one's tongue, to shift through the identity gears and be carried along on the conveyor belt of the times and the customary language. And there was still the possibility, even after the violence broke out in 1968, that a more salubrious political climate would evolve in Northern Ireland, a climate which would be helped by compromise and give and take and irony about ethnicity and origins and identity and all that.

Instead, however, things polarized and the sense of possibility atrophied. And in my own life, things changed also. By 1983, my family and I had been resident for eleven years in the Irish Republic, although I should emphasize that when we moved, it was not in order to flee the violence but in order that I might take advantage of an offer of a house in Wicklow that was a kind of writer's retreat; anyhow, there we were, and in order to make a new coherence between where we were living and who and what I was, I had taken out an Irish passport. In fact, when *The Penguin Book of Contemporary British Poetry* appeared in 1982, I could have said what Hopkins said during his time in Dublin a hundred years earlier, when he described himself as being at 'a third remove'; I was neither in London nor in Belfast and spent much of the time in Cambridge, Massachusetts, where I actually composed *An Open Letter* in the spring of 1983. I remember it as a moment more of solitude than of solidarity. Here, at any rate, are a couple of the stanzas that get to the crux of the naming business:

'Under a common flag', said Larkin.
'Different history', said Haughton.
Our own fastidious John Jordan
    Raised an eyebrow:
How British were the Ulstermen?
    He'd like to know.

Answer: as far as we are part
Of a new commonwealth of art,
Salute with independent heart
    And equally
Doff and flourish in your court
    Of poesie.

(I'll stick to I. Forget the we.
As Livy said, it's *pro se quisque*,
And Horace was exemplary
    At Philippi:
He threw away his shield to be
    A naked I.)

Still, doubts, you'd think, should not arise
When somebody who publishes
In *LRB* and *TLS*,
    The Listener—
In other words, whose audience is,
    Via Faber,

A British one—is characterized
As British. But don't be surprised
If I demur, for, be advised,
    My passport's green.
No glass of ours was ever raised
    To toast *The Queen*.

Custom, Ben Jonson said, is a most sovereign mistress of language, meaning that common usage is what decides the norms and patterns of our ways of speaking. But whatever it is that decides, it is certainly not open letters. If, in the years since the Motion and Morrison anthology appeared, others covering the same ground have included the term 'Irish' or 'Ireland' as well as 'Britain' or 'British' in their titles, that is just another indication that things are moving on. The Anglo-Irish Agreement of the late 1980s which opened up the possibility of new relations between the administrations in London, Dublin and Belfast, the declaration of a cessation of violence by the IRA in 1994, the establishment of a new assembly and the promise of an all-Ireland dimension in the governance of Northern Ireland, the beginnings of devolution in Britain itself—all these circumstances mean that the coercive element in the British nomenclature has been recognized and that the 'equally' adverb in those lines about doffing and flourishing in the court of poetry has begun to apply in other places as well. Custom, in other words, even in Britain, is bound to acknowledge henceforth an Irish as well as a British dimension of Northern Irish reality—and that is now enough said about that. What I have been describing, after all, is just one further instance of the inherited through-otherness that history is to blame for.

We could say, revising Stephen Dedalus, that hegemony was a nightmare from which I was trying to awake, but it would be nearer the mark to say that I was suffering from what might be called the Ledwidge syndrome. It's one thing to find yourself in a British anthology at the time of an Ulster crisis, but it is something else to find yourself in the British Army at the time of an Irish rebellion. Francis Ledwidge's at-homeness in the English lyric could not prevent his feeling of out-of-placeness in a British uniform after soldiers wearing that same uniform executed his friend the poet and 1916 leader Thomas MacDonagh. Like thousands of other Irish nationalists, Ledwidge had joined up in 1914, at a moment when the Home Rule Bill was on the Statute Book and the British Army, in Ledwidge's own words, 'stood between Ireland and an enemy common to our civilization and I would not have her say that she [Britain] defended us while we did nothing at home but pass resolutions'. At the moment of the Rising, however, it must have seemed to Ledwidge that his courage and his honour had been most cruelly mocked. The Rising began on Easter Monday, 24 April, and the previous Thursday, Ledwidge, who was at home on sick-leave after a devastating retreat march to Salonika, had written to Lord Dunsany: 'Coming from Southampton on the train, looking on England's beautiful valleys all white with spring, I thought indeed its freedom was worth all the blood I've seen flow. No wonder England has so many ardent patriots. I would be one of them myself did I not presume to be an Irish patriot.' A couple of weeks later, while he was still convalescing at Slane, that patriotism was put into great distress and confusion when he heard the news of MacDonagh and Joseph Mary Plunkett being sentenced to death in Richmond Barracks, where he had enlisted, and being executed at Arbour Hill. So it is not surprising to find him being court-martialled during this same leave for offensive remarks to a superior officer, drinking more than usual, reporting late for duty and generally displaying the symptoms of a man under great stress. And another of those symptoms of stress, of course, was the composition of the poem for which he is best remembered, called simply 'Thomas MacDonagh':

> He shall not hear the bittern cry
> In the wild sky where he is lain,
> Nor voices of the sweeter birds
> Above the wailing of the rain.
>
> Nor shall he know when loud March blows
> Thro' slanting snows her fanfare shrill,
> Blowing to flame the golden cup
> Of many an upset daffodil.
>
> But when the Dark Cow leaves the moor
> And pastures poor with greedy weeds,
> Perhaps he'll hear her low at morn
> Lifting her horn in pleasant meads.

This poem may at first appear to have little to do with the subject of this lecture: Britain doesn't seem to be anywhere in sight here, but that is only because she, as Ledwidge would have called her, is being repressed. Her idiom, or rather the idiom of English poetry, is being revised in favour of an idiom recommended by the man being elegized. In fact, the poem could equally well have been entitled 'The Upset Daffodil' in so far as it shows Ledwidge's Irish patriotism beginning to reveal itself at a poetic and phonetic level. Given the powerful presence of Wordsworth's daffodils poem within English literary culture, the daffodil in this context could be taken as a kind of synecdoche, and the upset within the poet— his disturbed equanimity as an Irishman—is reflected by the subversion of the flower and a reversion to what MacDonagh had called the Irish mode. Thomas MacDonagh's translation of Cathal Buí Mac Giolla Ghunna's poem 'An Bunnán Buí' imitated the assonance and internal rhyme of the original Irish, and Ledwidge is here following MacDonagh's practice. Take the recurrence of the *o* sounds and the *uh* sounds in his second stanza, for example—'Nor shall he knOW when loud March blOWs/Thro' slanting snOWs her fanfare shrill,/BlOWing to flame the gOlden cUP/Of many an UPset daffOdil'—the melody and method of this are clearly under the sway of MacDonagh's 'The yellow bittern that never broke OUt/In a drinking bOUt might as well have drUNk./His bones are lAIn on the nAked stOne/Where he lived alOne like a hermit mONk.'

What I am getting round to saying is that any account of the Irish poet and Britain must get past politics and into poetry itself, and that will involve poetry not only in English but in Irish, Welsh, Scots and Scots Gaelic, not to mention the work done in what Edward Kamau Brathwaite calls 'Nation Language'. It is not only a poem's explicit political concerns and paraphrasable content that need attending to. A précis of the content, for example, takes no account of literary echoes and allusions which can be fundamental to its poetic energy. In a poem, words, phrases, cadences and images are linked into systems of affect and signification which elude the précis maker. These under-ear activities, as they might be termed, may well constitute the most important business

which the poem is up to and are a matter more of the erotics of
language than of the politics and polemics of the moment. Which
is to say that poetry moves things forward once the poet and the
poem get ahead of themselves and find themselves out on their
own.

So I want to go on now to a poem by someone who has often
been treated more as a cultural witness or as some form of ethnic
or anthropological symptom than as a poet *per se*. The poet is John
Hewitt and the poem where he gets out on his own is one he wrote
early in the 1970s entitled 'The King's Horses'.

> After fifty years, nearly, I remember,
> living then in a quiet leafy suburb,
> waking in the darkness, made aware
> of a continuous irregular noise,
> and groping to the side window to discover
> the shadow-shapes which made that muffled patter
> passing across the end of our avenue,
> the black trees and streetlights shuttering
> a straggle of flowing shadows, endless, of horses.
>
> Gypsies they could have been, or tinkers maybe,
> mustering to some hosting of their clans,
> or horse-dealers heading their charges to the docks,
> timed to miss the day's traffic and alarms;
> a migration the newspapers had not foretold;
> some battle's ragged finish, dream repeated;
> the last of an age retreating, withdrawing,
> leaving us beggared, bereft
> of the proud nodding muzzles, the nervous bodies:
> gone from us the dark men with their ancient skills
> of saddle and stirrup, or bridle and breeding.
>
> It was an end, I was sure, but an end of what
> I never could tell. It was never reported;
> but their echoing hooves persisted. Years after,
> in a London hotel in the grey dawn,
> a serious man concerned with certain duties,

I heard again the metal clatter of hooves staccato
and hurriedly rose to catch a glimpse of my horses,
but the pace and beat were utterly different:
I saw by the men astride these were the King's horses
going about the King's business, never mine.

As a title, 'The King's Horses' is already full of echo. On the one hand, it connects up with the pageantry and military display of royal parades, of 'Rule, Britannia' and Horse Guards' Parade. But somewhere in the background there is also the rollick and frolic of 'Humpty-Dumpty'. Hewitt may not have been wanting to call up that particular association, but it is there 'in the language': 'All the king's horses and all the king's men / Couldn't put Humpty together again.' So it might be possible to construct a tendentious argument claiming that Hewitt perceives himself as a shattered Humpty-Dumpty in that he is a man divided against himself, somebody with deep affiliations to British traditions that come with his Ulster Planter background, and yet equally somebody with a deep desire for regional separateness; one whose sense of social justice wants the minority to receive a better deal but whose philosophical and political disposition puts him out of sympathy with their Catholic faith and long-term nationalist aspirations. And yet to read all that into the title would be to attribute to Hewitt a kind of literary and ideological deliberateness which is absent from this poem. In fact, one reason I chose this particular poem of Hewitt's for discussion is that for once Hewitt does not seem to know from the start where exactly he is going. The lines are distinguished by a drowsy sleepwalking movement, and it is this not-quite-defined, slightly apparitional quality that makes the whole thing so persuasive and attractive. 'The King's Horses' gives credence to the poet's claim, made in an autobiographical essay in 1972: 'My cast of mind is such that I am moved by intuitions, intimations, imaginative realizations, epiphanies . . .'

'The King's Horses' is basically an epiphany, and an epiphany might be defined as a showing forth in an uncanny light of some reality or truth hitherto insufficiently perceived. In Hewitt's poem, a memory transports the figure at the window into a state of unusual awareness during which the last-ditch nature of his solitude and individuality as a human being becomes fleetingly present to him. So, although the poem certainly arises out of Hewitt's complicated feelings as a left-wing Irishman of Planter stock, living in a place that was once a colony and is now a region of Britain, I believe it would be crude to interpret it in a restricted political way, seeing the speaker's repudiation of the King's horses as an expression of anti-monarchical feeling but of nothing much else:

> I saw by the men astride these were the King's horses
> going about the King's business, never mine.

There is, admittedly, something of Hewitt's egalitarianism and Presbyterianism present there, but to my ear what is even more strongly audible is a sense of his calling as a poet.

Even so, 'The King's Horses' is about something more than the poet's recognition of his solitude and individuality: it surely relates to a crisis in the outside world which in turn promoted this crisis within the self. A specific political reading is possible even if it is not the whole story. We know, for example, from the notes in Frank Ormsby's edition of *The Collected Poems of John Hewitt* (Blackstaff Press, 1991, p. 604) that the poem was written in April 1973, which was a time of constitutional crisis in Northern Ireland. Because of the political upheavals caused first by non-violent protest and then by a campaign of bombing and shooting, the old order had come to an end. The British government had stepped in to suspend the operations of the parliament at Stormont; the B-Special Constabulary, an arm of the security forces deeply resented by the nationalist minority, had also been suspended; and a new power-sharing assembly was being envisaged. Hewitt did not need to be a believer in Unionist supremacy to be deeply affected by all this. If the nationalist minority had a sense of an ending as well as a new sense of opportunity, it was inevitable that an Irishman of Planter stock, however left-wing his sympathies, would be affected at the deepest level by cracks in the institutional and constitutional integrity of his region. So, as I say, there is a sound basis for a specific historical and political interpretation of lines like 'It was an end, I was sure, but an end of what / I never could tell', and (perhaps even more so) of the lines about 'some battle's ragged finish, dream repeated; / the last of an age retreating, withdrawing, / leaving us beggared, bereft'.

But there is more to it than 'the breakup of Britain'. Take, for example, the way Hewitt employs the word 'my' in relation to the remembered horses, in a usage that is as tender as it is possessive. There's a sense that something intimate and precious is at stake: some illumination has been received, the animals walk in an otherworldly aura, so there is definite disappointment at the end when the poem moves from the psychic to the physical plane of reality:

> Years after,
> in a London hotel in the grey dawn
> a serious man concerned with certain duties,
> I heard again the metal clatter of hooves staccato
> and hurriedly rose to catch a glimpse of my horses,
> but the pace and beat were utterly different:
> I saw by the men astride these were the King's horses
> going about the King's business, never mine.

That 'my', in fact, connects the poem to another linguistic terminal in D. H. Lawrence's poem 'Snake', where Lawrence recognizes that when he turns on a snake—'my snake'—and drives it violently away from his water-trough in the heat of the Sicilian afternoon, he is also turning on some deep instinctive part of himself and driving *it* underground. In a way similar to Lawrence, Hewitt concedes that the civic part of him, the socially formed 'serious man concerned with certain duties', is a disguise, a kind of false self, and that his real allegiance is to a 'pace and beat' that are 'utterly different', namely, the pace and beat he knows and obeys as a poet. And this is why Hewitt is right to make a strong claim for the importance of 'intimations, imaginative realizations, epiphanies' as not the worst things to rely upon when facing life and the future in what he called 'our bitter hate-riven island'. What a poet can establish in the act of writing a poem is something a reader can get from the completed work, namely, a realization that as persons and as peoples we can get further into ourselves and further out of ourselves than we might have expected; and this is one of the ways that poetry helps things forward.

A poem that comes out ahead will often have crept up from behind. This is certainly what happens in 'Symposium', a recent sonnet by Paul Muldoon, whose title probably mocks the earnest business of seminars on the past, present and future of Northern Ireland's Troubles. At the same time, the title is remembering that the original Greek *symposium* was a gathering where men met in order to drink and talk and where in all likelihood they then proceeded to get well and truly drunk and to talk nonsense. The poem, at any rate, creeps up from behind and comes out ahead. You can read it as a one-off joke, but there's more to it than that. Its verbal fooling, its wrong-footing and double-taking remind us how fed up we have all become listening to the same old stories and the same old arguments repeated and repeated. It tells us that not only do we want more truth than we usually get but we deserve more and should be capable of getting through to it. It is fed up with all the typical contrarinesses and absurdities that sectarian and ideological intransigence can induce. Come to think of it, it might just as easily have been called 'The Stormont Assembly':

> You can lead a horse to water but you can't make it hold
> its nose to the grindstone and hunt with the hounds.
> Every dog has a stitch in time. Two heads? You've been sold
> one good turn. One good turn deserves a bird in the hand.
>
> A bird in the hand is better than no bread.
> To have your cake is to pay Paul.
> Make hay while you can still hit the nail on the head.
> For want of a nail the sky might fall.
>
> People in glass houses can't see the wood
> for the new broom. Rome wasn't built between two stools.
> Empty vessels wait for no man.

A hair of the dog is a friend indeed.
There's no fool like the fool
who's shot his bolt. There's no smoke after the horse is gone.

Here for certain is another poet who can take the word out of two different mouths. This poem would roll its eyes and kick its heels at too earnest a discussion of British and Irish, Scots and Gaelic, Highland and Lowland; but it is nevertheless clued into the realities and deadly consequences of all that and angrily aware that the music of what happens in the usual life will always have to be faced. But, says the poem, maybe it's better to outface it, to think again, to miss a beat and skip a step, to get into a new stride and call a new tune.

I have a dread of pious words like 'diversity', but I believe in what they stand for, so I might note here that when Ted Hughes and I came to edit an anthology called *The School Bag*, a title that meant to mean what it said, one of the things we had in mind was to insist on the diverse and deep traditions that operate through and sustain for good the poetry written in Ireland, England, Scotland and Wales. At the time I had not read Professor Hugh Kearney's study entitled *The British Isles: A History of Four Nations*, but our editorial principles were consonant with Kearney's approach. His book is an attempt to examine 'the interaction of the various major cultures of the British Isles from the Roman period onwards', and it was written 'in the belief that it is only by adopting a Britannic approach that historians can make sense of the particular segment in which they may be primarily interested, whether it be "England", "Ireland", "Scotland", "Wales", Cornwall or the Isle of Man'. This is simple, sensible and relevant. In a context where the word 'British' might function like a political reminder, a mnemonic for past invasions and coercions, there is a wonderful originality, in all senses, about employing instead the word 'Britannic'. 'Britannic' works like a cultural wake-up call and gestures not only towards the past but also towards an imaginable future. Without insistence or contention, 'Britannic' is a reminder of much that the term 'British' managed to occlude. 'Britannic' allows equal status on the island of Britain to Celt and Saxon, to

Scoti and Cymri, to Maldon and Tintagel, to *Beowulf* and the *Gododdin*, and so it begins to repair some of the damage done by the imperial, othering power of 'British'. In fact, one way of describing the era of devolution is to think of it as the moment when Britain went Britannic, a phenomenon which tends, incidentally, to hiberniorize Hibernia.

To go back, however, to *The School Bag*. It is not arranged on chronological or national or thematic lines but sets out to instruct by juxtaposition. So, for example, translated extracts from Brian Merriman's comic masterpiece 'The Midnight Court' (which was written in Irish in 1780) follow Robert Burns's 'Tam o' Shanter', published ten years later in 1790. Lady Gregory's translation of the traditional song 'Donal Oge' precedes the Border ballad 'The Demon Lover' and follows one of the great set pieces of early literature in Scots, Cresseid's lament from Robert Henryson's fifteenth-century *Testament of Cresseid*.

I could go on about these contents, and will, for just a little longer. Kuno Meyer's translation of a quatrain about a wild night on the Irish Sea that will keep the Vikings away from the coast is set between an imaginative account of one such Viking raid by the twentieth-century Orkney poet George Mackay Brown and a translation of the eighteenth-century Alasdair MacMaighstir Alasdair's extraordinary poem in Scots Gaelic called 'MacRanald's Galley', about an epic sea-crossing from the Western Isles to Carrickfergus. 'Dover Beach' with its expression of disappointment at the decline of Christian belief follows James Kearney's translation of the early Irish poem called 'Adze Head', which is essentially an expression of disappointment at the arrival of Christianity. And the anthology begins with Yeats's 'Long-Legged Fly', so that its first line is 'That civilization may not sink', and it ends with a song from a masque by John Dryden, so that the last two lines go, ' 'Tis well an old age is out / And time to begin a new.'

In the post-colonial phase of our criticism and cultural studies, we have heard much about 'the other', but perhaps the moment of the through-other should now be proclaimed, if only because it seems to have arrived. Translation, among other things, has seen to that.

Irish-language poets were probably aware for the past half-century of the achievement of Sorley MacLean in Scots Gaelic, but the publication of Canongate's dual-language edition, which includes the poet's own English versions, has helped to canonize MacLean in the new through-otherness of English and other nation languages. It disturbed a number of tidy Irish assumptions, north and south, to discover that this Gaelic-speaking Free Presbyterian from Raasay and Skye, a passionate socialist whose heroes included James Connolly, had fought with equally passionate conviction as a British soldier in the Western Desert and had written about the heroism of the common Tommy. I think it is only fair to say that in Ireland the native speaker would be presumed to be Catholic and would certainly not be expected to enlist, never mind eulogize the British soldier. Nor is the stereotype of the Irish poet from the Gaeltacht very likely to be confirmed by the life and work of Cathal O'Searcaigh, whose exploration of his homosexuality in 'the first official language' wrong-foots many of the old expectations.

A similar wrong-footing, or perhaps I should say rightifying, of expectations has happened in the case of translations by Paul Muldoon of the poems of Nuala Ní Dhomhnaill. In Ireland for decades we were exercised by a problematic *'ceist na teangan'*, or 'language question', that concerned itself with the contesting claims of Irish and English to be the right language of the country. Now, through the collaboration of these two poets, what was problematic has become productive, even arguably reproductive: when Muldoon translated 'Ceist na Teangan' as 'The Language Issue'—issue having associations not only of new life springing from an old source but of a hand-out of provisions or equipment that you have to make the best of—when he translated the title in this way, new thinking was bred out of the original words, and it seemed as if the two languages were wanting to indulge in the old clandestine pleasures of 'touching tongues'. And Muldoon has further compounded the through-otherness by giving the 1998 Clarendon Lectures on English Literature under the title *To Ireland, I* and then taking his Oxford audience through an A to Z of *Irish* literature from Amergin to Zozimus.

It would be coy of me, I suppose, not to take some account here

of my own bit of translation from the Anglo-Saxon and the desire
I had to complicate things by doing it. Working on *Buile Suibhne*
was one thing, and an expected thing from somebody with my
background, but taking on *Beowulf* was a move away from translation as an expected manifestation of Ulster identity politics. I take
Beowulf to be a poem which is also about facing up to silent things
accumulated within a consciousness. What gives it imaginative
potency and makes it so much more than a digest of the lore and
practices of Scandinavian warrior culture in the late Iron Age is a
brooding sense of what the Anglo-Saxon language calls *wyrd*. This
wyrd, or fate, is a silent thing that is ominously present, lying in
wait in every life, a challenge that should be faced and that probably can't be shirked. People know it as a sense of destiny, and its
presence at the climax of *Beowulf* is recognized once the dragon
has been disturbed in his underground vault and becomes the
deadly threat that the old King must face.

I first encountered *Beowulf* over forty years ago when I was
studying for a degree in English Language and Literature at
Queen's University, and there are those who would argue that this
was in fact a degree of separation from my proper cultural inheritance and that in translating the poem I had studied I was exhibiting all the symptoms of the colonial subject. I can understand
what such commentators are saying, but I could also see what I
myself was doing. I knew what a through-other venture the whole
thing would have to be, but was happy enough to say, So, so be it.
Let *Beowulf* now be a book from Ireland. Let it function in the
world in the same way as the Venerable Bede tells us that books
from Ireland functioned within the Britannic and Hibernian context of his times in the eighth century. Ireland, he tells us in his
Ecclesiastical History of the English People, is far more favoured
than Britain by its mild and healthy climate, and goes on:

> There are no reptiles, and no snake can exist there; for although
> often brought over from Britain, as soon as the ship nears land,
> they breathe the scent of its air, and die. In fact, almost every-
> thing on this isle confers immunity to poison and I have often
> seen that folk suffering from snake-bite have drunk water in

which scrapings of the leaves off books from Ireland have been steeped, and that this remedy checked the spreading poison and reduced the swelling.

One of Bede's editors suggests that this may be an example of the author's po-faced humour and that Bede is here giving a merely ironical credence to a tall tale that must have been in common circulation among the monks and scribes of Northumbria. Either way, it is an example of a writer calling upon a fiction in order to cope with differences between two islands linked and separated in various degrees by history and geography, language and culture. As such, it prefigures much of the work that would be done by Irish poets in the coming times and much that will continue to be done.

III

Stevie Smith's *Collected Poems*

Always inclined to the brisk definition, W. H. Auden once declared that poetry was memorable speech. *The Collected Poems* of the late Stevie Smith prompts one to revise that: poetry is memorable voice. The unknown quantity in my response to the book was the memory of the poet's own performance of her verse, her voice pitching between querulousness and keening, her quizzical presence at once inviting the audience to yield her their affection and keeping them at bay with a quick irony. She seemed to combine elements of Gretel and of the witch, to be vulnerable and capable, a kind of Home Counties *sean bhean bhocht*, with a hag's wisdom and a girl's wide-eyed curiosity. She chanted her poems artfully off-key, in a beautifully flawed plainsong that suggested two kinds of auditory experience: an embarrassed party-piece by a child halfway between tears and giggles, and a deliberate *faux-naif* rendition by a virtuoso.

This raises the whole question of poetry for the eye versus poetry for the ear. Perhaps the 'versus' is an overstatement, yet there are poets whose work is enhanced and amplified in its power to move once we know the characteristic tone and rhythm and texture of the poet's physical voice. The grave inward melodies of Wallace Stevens become more available if we happen to have heard that Caedmon recording of him reading 'The Idea of Order at Key West'. Similarly, Robert Frost's words are enlivened by any memory of his switchback pacing, the hard and fluent contours of his accent. And I am sure that Coleridge's excitement on first hearing Wordsworth read was as much a matter of how the poem sounded as of what it intended.

But in the case of Stevie Smith, it is not simply a matter of extra gratification from the poems on the page if we happen to have heard her. It is the whole question of the relationship between a speaking voice, a literary voice (or style) and a style of speech shared by and typical of a certain social and cultural grouping. In other words, it is essential to bring to the appreciation of these poems an ear aware of the *longueurs* and acerbities, the nuanced understatements and tactical intonations of educated middle-class English speech. The element this work survives in is a disenchanted gentility, and while I can imagine, for example, the Reverend Ian Paisley making a fine job of Yeats's 'Under Ben Bulben', I cannot imagine Stevie Smith's idiosyncratic rhythms and metres surviving the hammer-and-tongue of that vigorous North Antrim emphasis.

One is tempted to use words like 'fey', 'arch' and 'dotty' when faced with these five hundred and seventy pages, and yet such adjectives sell Stevie Smith's work short. These odd, syncopated melancholy poems are haunted by the primitive and compelling music of ballad and nursery rhyme, but it has been transposed by a sophisticated and slightly cosseted poetic ear into a still, sad drawing-room music of humanity:

> He said no word of her to us
> Nor we of her to him,
> But oh it saddened us to see
> How wan he grew and thin.
> We said: She eats him day and night
> And draws the blood from him,
> We did not know but said we thought
> This was why he grew thin.

There is variety and inventiveness, much humour and understanding and a constant poignancy. Her gift was to create a peculiar emotional weather between the words, a sense of pity for what is infringed and unfulfilled, as in the much-anthologized 'Not Waving but Drowning', or in this one, taken almost at random:

> I always remember your beautiful flowers
> And the beautiful kimono you wore
> When you sat on the couch
> With that tigerish crouch
> And told me you loved me no more.

What I cannot remember is how I felt when you were unkind.
All I know is, if you were unkind now I should not mind.
Ah me, the power to feel exaggerated, angry and sad
The years have taken from me. Softly I go now, pad pad.

Stevie Smith reminds you of two Lears: the old King come to
knowledge and gentleness through suffering, and the old comic
poet Edward veering off into nonsense. I suppose in the end the
adjective has to be 'eccentric'. She looks at the world with a mental
squint; there is a disconcerting wobble in the mirror she holds up
to nature.

Death, waste, loneliness, cruelty, the maimed, the stupid, the
innocent, the trusting—her concerns were central ones, her compassion genuine and her vision almost tragic. Yet finally the voice,
the style, the literary resources are not adequate to the sombre
recognitions, the wounded *joie de vivre*, the marooned spirit we
sense they were destined to express. There is a retreat from resonance, as if the spirit of A. A. Milne successfully vied with the
spirit of Emily Dickinson.

The genetic relations which the forms of these poems often
bear to the clerihew and the caricature prevent them from attaining the kind of large orchestration that they are always tempting
us to listen for. And if they are the real thing when measured by
Auden's definition, they miss the absolute intensity required by
Emily Dickinson's definition: when you read them, you don't feel
that the top of your head has been taken off. Rather, you have been
persuaded to keep your head at all costs.

Joyce's Poetry

He wrote to Ibsen and identified with him, he was championed by Pound, he fostered Beckett, he was an outsider from the start—all true. Yet at the very start his dealings were with Yeats and AE and that 'old hake Gregory' because, at the very start, verse was his medium.

The poems were entered in longhand on folio sheets. They were shown to friends, to his brother Stanislaus, to W. B. Yeats, and through Yeats's assistance they made their way to magazines and publishers.

Joyce's first book was a sequence of thirty-six poems published in 1907 as *Chamber Music*. Twenty years later, twelve more poems and a 'Tilly' thrown in appeared for a shilling as *Pomes Penyeach*. And when the *Collected Poems* came out in 1936 there was only one new poem added, the well-known 'Ecce Puer', written on the occasion of his father's death and the birth of his own grandson. This is the canon of his 'official' verse. Unofficially, he released two broadsides, 'The Holy Office' (1904) and 'Gas from a Burner' (1912).

For some novelists—Hardy and Lawrence, for example—verse offers itself as a medium for extending and refining apprehensions that their prose fiction has failed to render altogether satisfactorily. There are poems by Hardy and Lawrence which we would be inclined to keep in preference to certain parts of their novels. The same, however, cannot be said of Joyce. Sure, the poems are well tuned and well turned; there is a technical fastidiousness about them, a touch of elegy and pathos. But their chief interest is that they were written by Joyce, their chief surprise the surprise of contrast with other parts of the *oeuvre*. This stanza from 'Ecce Puer' could be by Francis Ledwidge:

> Of the dark past
> A child is born,

With joy and grief
My heart is torn.

There is a conventional touch to this, a kind of rehearsed tenderness that recalls a Celtic Twilight poem like Padraic Colum's 'O
men from the fields'. The heavy end-stopping of the lines, the regular metre, the candid rhymes—it is an unexpectedly unsophis-
ticated performance from an artist who at the same time was
splitting the linguistic atom in *Finnegans Wake.*

If I seem to be doing Joyce down, he can stand it, because he
himself set the standard by which he must be judged. The great
poetry of the opening chapter of *Ulysses,* for example, amplifies
and rhapsodizes the world with an unlooked-for accuracy and
transport. It gives the spirit freedom to range in an element that is
as linguistic as it is airy and watery, and when the poems are compared with writing that feels so natural, spacious and unstoppably
alive, they are seen to be what Yeats said the earliest of them
were—the work of a man 'who is practising his instrument, taking
pleasure in the mere handling of the stops'.

Perhaps that is the way for us to take pleasure in them—at a
slight aesthetic distance, with a connoisseur's awareness. And that,
in fact, seems to be the way Joyce himself appreciated poetry.
Stephen in *A Portrait of the Artist as a Young Man,* like Joyce in
real life, loves the songs of the Elizabethans, the mournful and
melodious rhythms of Nashe and Dowland and Shakespeare's
songs. It is poetry as the handmaiden of music, as evocation, invitation to dream.

Stephen is not worked upon by the poetry he remembers;
rather, he works upon it, savouring it and transposing it to the keyboard of his own mind and senses. In *Portrait* the shock of recognition for Stephen comes in his encounter with a word like 'suck'
or 'tundish'. Poetry *per se* evokes a less directly sensuous response,
something more cultivated and delicate, and it would seem that
Joyce aimed for just such a response when he wrote his own verse.

What I am saying applies only to the 'official' lyrics. The unofficial satires—those couplets that cut the air sometimes with
the exact deadliness of Toledo steel, sometimes with the thick-
witted ferocity of a faction-fighter's stick—those are a different

case and remind me of one of the many triumphant and possessive insights in Stanislaus Joyce's *My Brother's Keeper*.

Stanislaus there credits Yeats with divining that prose, not verse, would be his brother's medium, and then goes on, 'but I take personal satisfaction in recording that I was the first and perhaps the only one to understand that ruthlessness, not delicacy, would be the keynote of my brother's work.' Right on, as they used to say in the Bay Area.

'Gas from a Burner' and 'The Holy Office' may not be as self-consciously beautiful or as well finished as the lyrics but they are in earnest. The language has all the roused expectation of a loosed ferret. The thing may be hurried, but it has angry momentum. And it is a performance. The connoisseur of styles is showing off, but at the same time the hurt human being is giving vent to his rage. Significantly, this is the stuff that people tend to know by heart:

> 'Twas Irish humour, wet and dry,
> Flung quicklime into Parnell's eye;
> 'Tis Irish brains that save from doom
> The leaky barge of the Bishop of Rome
> For everyone knows the Pope can't belch
> Without the consent of Billy Walsh.
> O Ireland my first and only love
> Where Christ and Caesar are hand and glove!

The instrument is being put to work at last. Stand back there!

Italo Calvino's *Mr Palomar*

Symmetries and arithmetics have always tempted Italo Calvino's imagination to grow flirtatious and to begin its fantastic displays. His new book has three main sections entitled 'Mr Palomar's Vacation', 'Mr Palomar in the City' and 'The Silences of Mr Palomar'. Each main section has three subsections and each subsection three parts, and Mr Calvino has created a numbering system for them. 'The numbers 1, 2, 3 that mark the titles of the index,' he writes,

> whether they are in the first, second, or third position, besides having a purely ordinal value, correspond also to three thematic areas, three kinds of experience and inquiry that, in varying proportions, are present in every part of the book.
>
> Those marked '1' generally correspond to a visual experience . . .
>
> Those marked '2' contain elements that are anthropological, or cultural in the broad sense . . .
>
> Those marked '3' involve more speculative experience, concerning the cosmos, time, infinity, the relationship between the self and the world.
>
> (Translation by William Weaver)

But can this tongue that stays so neutrally in its cheek as it explains the book's structural principles woo us into pleasure and assent all over again in the actual text? Happily, the schema turns out to be not just a prescription; what might have been a grid acts in this case like a springboard. Each of the pieces has the feel of a single inspiration being caught as it rises and then being played for all its life is worth—though not for an instant longer than it takes to exhaust its first energy.

Mr Palomar is a lens employed by his author in order to inspect the phenomena of the world, but the lens is apt to turn into a mirror which reflects the hesitations and self-corrections of Mr Palomar's own reflecting mind. The book consists of a graduated sequence of descriptions and speculations in which the protagonist confronts the problem of discovering his place in the world and of watching those discoveries dissolve under his habitual intellectual scrutiny.

So the very first movement is entitled 'Reading a Wave' and here Mr Palomar attempts to see and describe and kidnap into language the exact nature of a single wave. His precisions, which he must keep revising, are constantly accurate and constantly inadequate; yet it is these very frustrations which constitute the reader's pleasure. By the last movement, however, Mr Palomar has turned his gaze inward and is now, as the title of the piece puts it, 'Learning to Be Dead'. But his appetite for certain knowledge remains equally tantalized and unsatisfied: 'You must not confuse being dead with not being.' In between there are twenty-five other texts, which one hesitates to call prose poems, since it makes them sound much too affected and humourless, or meditations, since that undersells their lovely metaphorical ease and rapture.

Calvino's line whispers and lazes and tautens and sports itself very cajolingly. His gaze, like Mr Palomar's as he contemplates the stars, 'remains alert, available, released from all certitude'. 'In August,' he tells us, 'the Milky Way assumes a dense consistency, and you might say it is overflowing its bed.' The lavish simplicity of that, its double gratitude for the world and for words adequate to the world, its mingled sense of something sweetly and personally discovered yet also something of almost racial memory, this atmosphere of spacious and buoyant reverie is typical of the whole work.

Here is a large unhampered talent sailing a middle course between the sophistication of the avant-garde and the innocence of the primitive poetic imagination, between the kind of intelligence that constructed the medieval bestiaries and the pre-literate intuitiveness that once chanted hunters' prayers. If the persona of Mr Palomar is haunted at times by the petulant shade of Beckett's

Molloy, trying to devise an infallible method by which to rotate his sucking stones from pocket to mouth to pocket, and at other times by the urbane Jorge Luis Borges, softly expatiating upon the question of whether writing gets done by 'Borges' or 'I', the reader is not worried. Nor is Mr Calvino. He knows that everybody ends up worrying about the same things anyhow.

Mr Palomar worries and watches incessantly and in Italian; but William Weaver has me persuaded that I now know his fastidious, easily beguiled and graciously implacable mind in English. The rhythms and savours of Mr Weaver's language can render equally well the punctilio of Mr Palomar's intellectual searches and the civility and eroticism of his daydreams. It is a language that brings us nearer that destination which Mr Palomar constantly aspires to—'a step closer to true knowledge, which lies in the experience of the flavors, composed of memory and imagination at once'.

> Behind every cheese, [he muses,] there is a pasture of a different green under a different sky: meadows caked with salt that the tides of Normandy deposit every evening; meadows scented with aromas in the windy sunlight of Provence; there are different flocks, with their stablings and their transhumances; there are secret processes handed down over the centuries. This shop is a museum: Mr Palomar, visiting it, feels as he does in the Louvre, behind every displayed object the presence of the civilization that has given it form and takes form from it.

Nevertheless, for all its sensual felicity, the writing is philosophically impelled. Mr Palomar, who takes his name from the famous telescope and observatory, is both an 'I' and an 'eye', 'A world looking at the world', as the title of one of Mr Palomar's meditations suggests, a question mark retroactively affecting his own credibility: 'Is he not a piece of the world that is looking at another piece of the world? Or else, given that there is world that side of the window and world this side, perhaps the "I", the ego, is simply the window through which the world looks at the world. To look at itself, the world needs the eyes (and the eyeglasses) of Mr Palomar.'

Which mercifully takes us, Mr Palomar and Italo Calvino

beyond the impasse of solipsism, the distrust of language and the frigid fires of 'experiment'. There may be a problem of knowledge, but the consciousness only comes alive to this problem by suffering those constant irrepressible appetites for experience which want to rampage beyond the prison of the self. Mr Calvino may divide and categorize in triplicate the visual, the cultural and the speculative aspects of Mr Palomar's world, he may prompt and tag and analyse and juxtapose to his (and our) heart's content, but Mr Palomar himself remains wonderfully spontaneous and receptive to the pell-mell of the senses. Lawns, breasts, starlings, planets, lizards, the moon in the afternoon, the blackbird's whistle, the clack of mating tortoises, the fog of memories in 'Two Pounds of Goose Fat', where, 'in the thick, soft whiteness that fills the jars, the clangor of the world is muffled'—all these things and a thousand others keep the mind from its ultimate shadow feast. Mr Palomar may collapse at the end, like the book named for him, in a syllogism, but not before he has outstripped his conclusion in one incandescent apotheosis after another.

If it often seems in the course of this book that Italo Calvino cannot put a foot wrong, this is because he is not a pedestrian writer. Like Robert Frost's, his whole concern is for himself as a performer, but whereas Frost performed at eye-level, as it were, on vocal cords and heartstrings, Calvino is on the high wires, on lines of thought strung out above the big international circus. Yet such high-wire displays engage us only if the performer is in fact subject to gravity and genuinely at risk. A lightweight can throw the same shapes but cannot evince that old, single, open-mouthed stare of hope and wonder which we all still want to be a part of. What is most impressive about *Mr Palomar* is a sense of the safety net being withdrawn at the end, of beautiful, nimble, solitary feats of imagination being carried off not so much to dazzle an audience as to outface what the poet Philip Larkin calls 'the solving emptiness / That lies just under all we do'.

Paul Muldoon's *The Annals of Chile*

Robert Frost, a poet whose roguery and tough-mindedness are admired by Paul Muldoon, once wrote about the art of filling a cup up to the brim 'or even above the brim'. This impulse to go further than is strictly necessary is presented by Frost as the most natural thing in the world. It's why young boys want to climb to the tops of birch trees and why grown-up poets write poems.

John Keats expressed the same thought in another way when he said that poetry should surprise by a fine excess. In poetry, Keats implied, enough is never enough. What's called for is an extra dimension, a way of saying that transports reader and writer (and the subject, too, of course) to a new plane.

Poetry is language in orbit. It may start with recollected emotion or immediate anger or rapture, but once that personal boost has helped a poem to lift off, it runs on its own energy circuit. And the energy coursing in the circuit is generated and flows between the words themselves, between the words and the metre, the metre and the line, the line and the stanza and so on.

Formal and technical excellence in the best poetry is therefore not just a matter of surface finish or verbal ingenuity. It always embodies a transformation of the writer's excitement and is a guarantee of his or her engagement with the subject. Something has been made of something else—that's what artwork entails, after all—and the more that's made of it, the better. Above the brim, in this context, does not mean over the top.

In Paul Muldoon's new book, for example, personal grief and creative glee keep playing into each other's hands. One of several extraordinary poems here is called 'Incantata', a lamentation for the premature death by cancer of a young and gifted artist. This is both a cry of heartbreak and a virtuoso performance. The higher the lift-off that the poem achieves, the deeper the registers it engages. In this, it is a work that resembles Eibhlin Dubh Ní

Chonaill's great 'Caoineadh Airt Uí Laoghaire' and will survive comparison with it. Both poems have an immense rhythmical surge and an overload of immediate grief, the same wild frankness, the same anger at the loss of a loved one and the same ecstatic sense of the dead person's enduring worth.

'Incantata' commemorates the life and work of Mary Farl Powers, an artist who was much cherished because of the intensity of her striving for spiritual and technical perfection. It is an example of what we might call 'the Lycidas syndrome', whereby one artist's sense of vocation and purpose is sent into crisis by the untimely death of another. Here Paul Muldoon is possessed by a subject that puts all his brilliance to the test, with the result that he blossoms into truth and humanizes his song to an extraordinary degree.

But grief is not the only humanizer. Some of the most delightful poems in the book were written to celebrate the birth of the poet's daughter, and once again the metaphorical speed of the invention is a match for the fleetness and sweetness of the emotion. 'The Sonogram', for example, is a meltdown of ancient history, satellite technology and parental joy, and its ease in yoking together these heterogeneous elements is altogether typical of this poet:

> Only a few weeks ago, the sonogram of Jean's womb
> resembled nothing so much
> as a satellite-map of Ireland:
>
> now the image
> is so well-defined we can make out not only a hand
> but a thumb;
>
> on the road to Spiddal, a woman hitching a ride;
> a gladiator in his net, passing judgement on the crowd.

It looks and sounds casual until you look again and find that the shape and the sound that beguiled you are not as casual as they were pretending to be. There are, for example, those nicely placed half-rhymes of 'womb' and 'thumb', 'hand' and 'Ireland', 'ride' and 'crowd'; and there is a whole bitter vision of history in the unex-

pected moment of inversion at the end. In the Roman amphithe-
atre, after all, it was the crowd who gave the thumbs up or the
thumbs down to the gladiator, but here it is the unborn child who
is considering the verdict and seems ready to consign us, the readers, to the ranks of the condemned.

In Muldoon's previous book of poems, *Madoc, A Mystery*, this
fantastic genius was equally in evidence, but it seemed intent upon
short-circuiting itself, producing a chain reaction of blinding daz-
zles, a semaphore of flashes that not only put readers on their met-
tle but put the wind up them as well. Here, however, his gift shines
out in a richer, steadier light. *The Annals of Chile* is by no means a
simple read, but it is his best book so far. There is emotional and
musical fullness, an opulence and maturity which still leave room
for a huge playfulness.

'Yarrow', the very long sequence of linked verses which makes
up most of the book's 180 pages, is one big echoing playroom of allusion, a fantasia in which the death of the poet's mother and the
growth of the poet's mind are superbly orchestrated and richly celebrated. Post-modern in its speed and structure (it channel-surfs,
as it were, upon personal memory and childhood reading and cultural history) but old-fashioned in its obsessive focus upon a beloved home ground ('The bridge. The barn. Again and again . . .'),
'Yarrow' works so beautifully because it is fed by deep personal experiences; and it is no real problem if these are rendered by hints
and glimpses and intimate touches because their function is to give
power, as T. S. Eliot said such experiences should, 'from well below
the surface'.

This work gives the impression of coming clean and being
clandestine at one and the same time. It is Joycean in its combination of the everyday and the erudite, but it is also entirely *sui
generis*, a late-twentieth-century work that vindicates Muldoon's
reputation as one of the era's true originals.

And it does more. *The Annals of Chile* shows that when it
comes to the workings of poetry, Muldoon's virtuosity represents
more than the 'articulation of sweet sounds together', because by
now it also expresses the workings of an ever-maturing and increasingly rhapsodic spirit. The largesse of the writing here justi-

fies the blurb on another recent book of his, *The Prince of the Quo-tidian*, an occasional poem-diary published by Gallery Press. If several of the poems in it can be thought of as muldoodles, others could be ranked as mulboons ('The Sonogram', for example, is in-cluded). There's a lot of the old cleverality and some very cocky snook-cocking in this volume, but the blurb is still right when it speaks of the author as a major poet.

Norman MacCaig, 1910–1996

My first encounter with Norman MacCaig's poetry converted me
to it. In a BBC pamphlet that accompanied *Listening and Writing*,
a Schools Radio series produced in the early 1960s, I came across
'Summer Farm'. 'Straws like tame lightnings lie about the
grass/And hang zigzag on hedges.' Brilliant. A unique continuum
of wiliness and sensuousness. The minimal and the dotty ('A
hen stares at nothing with one eye,/Then picks it up') transposed into a metaphysical key. This was the world of the fairy
tale, the farmyard as it was known in the children's story about
Henny Penny: if an acorn had dropped from an oak tree here-
abouts, it could have meant that the whole sky was about to fall.
In fact, everything that Gaston Bachelard says about childhood
images in his book *The Poetics of Reverie* is deeply germane to
the lyric power of 'Summer Farm' and scores of other MacCaig
poems: 'They are associated with the universe of a season, a season
which does not deceive and which can well be called the *total
season* . . . They are not only spectacles through sight, they are
soul values . . . lasting benefits.'

He was a great fisherman, a master of the cast, of the line that is a
lure. And the angler's art—the art of coming in at an angle—is
there in his poetry too. He could always get a rise out of the
subject. He made it jump beyond itself. There is a metaphorical
gleefulness in his work, yet in the end what this volatile gift
celebrates is the world's stability. The MacCaig creativity is
Pasternakian, the Pasternak of *My Sister Life*, very different
from the tragic elegiac strain that distinguishes the work of his
friend Sorley MacLean or that of their grave contemporary the
poet Czeslaw Milosz; and yet the following lines by Milosz could
stand as an apt commentary upon the MacCaig project: 'I stare

and stare. It seems I was called for this: / To glorify things just
because they are.'

One night in Garech de Brún's house in County Wicklow, after an
evening at the Abbey Theatre to launch *The Way I Say It*, a record
of Norman reading his poems, he was working the table as gleefully
and deliberately as he would have worked a salmon pool. And next
thing, he landed a perfectly baited line in front of me, like a little
test, just to see how I'd jump. 'I can't stand,' he said—the first flex of
the rod—'I can't stand gloomy, ambitious poetry.' Meaning, from another angle, 'This is just a wee jag because of the dark and earnest
moods of your bog poems.' (These were being published here and
there at the time.) Meaning, from yet another angle, 'Robert Lowell's poetry is overrated and you should beware of being influenced
by him.' (Not that I was then.) I don't know what imp inspired me,
but I remember that I managed to leap free and flick back with, 'So
I suppose Robert Herrick is the one for you, Norman.' Cheeky, but
called for. I date our real friendship from that moment.

Norman had the poet's gift for 'flying crooked' down the paths
of irony and surprise. His intelligence was both strict and play-
ful, his whole character equally averse to self-pity and to self-
aggrandizement. Anything too solemn or too obvious (especially
concerning himself) discomfited him, so even praise could be risky.
I knew, for example, that I was testing his patience when he rolled
a big eye in my direction as I introduced him at an arts festival in
Kilkenny in 1975. To give the audience some notion of the quality
of his sensibility, I was talking about early Irish nature poetry. This
was justified partly by the fact that Norman's mother spoke Scottish Gaelic as her native language, partly by certain attributes inherent in his own writing. The clarity of image, the sensation of
blinking awake in a pristine world, the unpathetic nature of nature in his work, all these things are also to be found in the earliest
Irish poetry. The weather in it, as in MacCaig's, is never clammy:
the fish jumps, the bird calls, the berry brightens. And yet there is
(of course) a difference, and Norman wanted the audience to be

aware of that difference as well; he did not want to be presented as some kind of Celto-Caledonian nostalgia kit. For while it is true that many of his ancestors were Gaels, it is also true that his imagination had been sprung into modernity. His poems are discovered in flight, migratory, wheeling and calling. Everything is in a state of restless becoming: once his attention lights on a subject, it immediately grows lambent. As Dr Johnson said of Goldsmith, 'He put a shine on everything he touched.'

One day at a party in Edinburgh, in a room full of smoke and music and flirtation, Norman took me into a corner and began to whistle a totally bewitching air. It was a fragment of *pibroch*, a few orphaned phrases as piercing as a curlew call, but it was also a melody of the soul's loneliness, a tune that was like a piece of secret knowledge. It has grown stronger and clearer in my memory, and nowadays I link it with the clarity of conscience and the moral strength that impelled and sustained MacCaig in the course of his protest as a conscientious objector during World War II. I link it also with his labyrinthine ironies and courtesies, the way in which he maintained a debonair style and yet kept faith with a history of loss. The filament of sound that unspooled from his lips that day was an Ariadne's thread leading into the heart of the Scottish Gaelic maze: in there, at the outback of modernity and English, dwells the foetal shape of defeat and dispersal, language loss and trauma. One side of this is 'Aunt Julia', 'silenced in the absolute black/of a sandy grave/in Luskentyre'. The other is a matter of tone, that habit of joking and jagging which protects the survivor's silence. As in his poem 'Go Away, Ariel', where he says, 'I'd rather be visited by Caliban . . . I'm teaching him to smoke. It soothes him/when he blubbers about Miranda and/goes on about his mother.' But now I can just hear Norman rebuking me for all this, telling me to tone it down. 'Post-colonial cant! Blarney! Blather! Come off it!' And yet, and yet . . .

I first met Norman in February 1973, when my wife and I were travelling to a poetry festival in St Andrew's. On our way through

Edinburgh we had arranged to have coffee with him in a hotel—
The North British, I think—and he then took us round for a dram
and a bite of lunch at The Abbotsford, one of the great literary
pubs of the age. There we had our grilled haddock and were introduced to Gavin Muir, son of the poet Edwin Muir. I could hardly
believe it was all happening. I also remember being instructed that
the Glenmorangie whisky we were drinking was pronounced to
rhyme not with the Italian *piange* (as I had long assumed) but
with the English word—if it exists—'orangey'. Being in his company was always a bracing experience: no false note was permitted,
and 'Boo', mitigated by a giggle, was a term of praise.

Integritas. Consonantia. Claritas. As a master of the light touch,
Norman might feel uneasy about having these heavyweight terms
applied to himself and his work, but as a classicist, he might just
allow them. One of his self-portraits, after all, presents him as an
'Equilibrist', with a burden of joy in his right hand and a burden
of sorrow in his left; which is another way of saying that his poetry
is an element where what Shelley called the 'weight of hours' becomes momentarily buoyant and 'something / tosses the world in
its hand, / judging its weight, / wondering if it's worth keeping' ('A
Matter of Scale').

Joseph Brodsky, 1940–1996

Those who knew Joseph Brodsky were well aware that his heart disease was serious and that it would probably be the death of him, but because he always existed in his friends' minds not just as a person but as some kind of principle of indestructibility, it was difficult for them to admit that he was in danger. The intensity and boldness of his genius plus the sheer exhilaration of being in his company kept you from thinking about the threat to his health; he had such valour and style, and lived at such a deliberate distance from self-pity and personal complaint, you inclined to forget that he was as mortal as the next one. So his death is all the more shocking and distressing. Having to speak of him in the past tense feels like an affront to grammar itself.

There was a wonderfully undoubting quality about Joseph, an intellectual readiness that was almost feral. Conversation attained immediate vertical take-off and no deceleration was possible. Which is to say that he exemplified in life the very thing that he most cherished in poetry—the capacity of language to go farther and faster than expected and thereby provide an escape from the limitations and the preoccupations of the self. Verbally, he had a lower boredom threshold than anyone I have ever known, forever punning, rhyming, veering off and honing in, unexpectedly raising the stakes or switching the tracks. Words were a kind of high-octane for him, and he loved to be propelled by them wherever they took him. He also loved to put a spin on the words of others, whether by inspired misquotation or extravagant retort. Once, for example, when he was in Dublin and complaining about one of our rare heatwaves, I suggested jokingly that he should take off for Iceland, and he replied in a flash, with typical elevation and roguery, 'But I could not tolerate the absence of meaning.'

His own absence will be harder to tolerate. From the moment I met him in 1972, when he was passing through London on the second leg of his journey from dissidence in Russia to exile in the United States, he was a verifying presence. His mixture of brilliance and sweetness, of the highest standards and the most refreshing common sense, never failed to be both fortifying and endearing. Every encounter with him constituted a renewal of belief in the possibilities of poetry. There was something magnificent in his bewilderment at the self-delusion of second-raters and his anger at the sheer ignorance of the technical demands evident in the work of many poets with big reputations; and there was something bracing about what he called 'doing the laundry list' with him, which meant going over the names of contemporaries, young and old, each sticking up for the ones he regarded most. It was like meeting a secret sharer.

But this was a personal bonus, and in the end it is less important than what might be called his impersonal importance. This had to do with Joseph Brodsky's total conviction about poetry as a force for good—not so much 'for the good of society' as for the health of the individual mind and soul. He was resolutely against any idea that put the social cart before the personal horse, anything that clad original response in a common uniform. 'Herd' for Joseph would have been the opposite of 'heard', but that did not lessen his passion to reinstate poetry as an integral part of the common culture of the United States.

Nor did it mean that he wished to use the sports stadiums for poetry readings. If anyone happened to bring up the huge audiences that attended such events in the Soviet Union, there would be an immediate comeback: 'Think of the garbage they have to listen to.' In other words, Joseph decried the yoking together of politics and poetry ('The only thing they have in common are the letters p and o') not because he had no belief in the transformative power of poetry *per se* but because the political requirement changed the criteria of excellence and was likely to lead to a debasement of the language and hence to a lowering of 'the plane of regard' (a favourite phrase) from which human beings viewed themselves and established their values. And his credentials for such a custodianship of the poet's role were, of course, impeccable, since his arrest and trial by the Soviet authorities in the 1960s and his subsequent banishment to a work camp in Archangel had specifically to do with his embrace of poetic vocation—a socially parasitical vocation, according to the prosecution. This had turned his case into something of an international *cause célèbre* and ensured him an immediate fame when he arrived in the West; but instead of embracing victim status and swimming with the currents of radical chic, Brodsky got down to business right away as a university teacher at the University of Michigan.

Before long, however, his celebrity was based more upon what he was doing in his new homeland than upon what he had done in the old one. To start with, he was an electrifying speaker of his own poems in Russian, and his many appearances at universities all over the country in the 1970s brought a new vitality and seriousness to the business of poetry readings. Far from cajoling the audience with a pose of man-in-the-street low-keyness, Brodsky pitched his performance at a bardic level. His voice was strong, he knew the poems off by heart, and his cadences had the majesty and poignancy of a cantor's, so his performance never failed to induce a great sense of occasion in all who attended. He therefore gradually began to be regarded as the figure of the representative poet, sounding prophetic even though he might demur at the notion of the prophetic role and impressing the academics by the depth of his knowledge of poetic tradition from classical times up through Renaissance and modern European languages, including English.

Still, if Joseph was uneasy about the prophetic, he had no such qualms about the didactic. Nobody enjoyed laying down the law more than he, with the result that his fame as a teacher began to spread and certain aspects of his practice came to be imitated. In particular, his insistence that students should learn and recite several poems by heart had considerable influence in Creative Writing schools all over the United States, and his advocacy of traditional form, his concentration upon matters of metre and rhyme and his high rating of non-modernist poets such as Robert Frost and Thomas Hardy also had the general effect of reawakening an older poetic memory. The climax of all this was to come with his 'Immodest Proposal', made in 1991 when he was acting as Poet

Laureate at the Library of Congress. Why not print poetry in millions of copies, he asked, since a poem 'offers you a sample of complete . . . human intelligence at work' and also tells its readers 'be like me'? Moreover, because poetry employs memory, 'it is of use for the future, not to mention the present'. It can also do something for ignorance and is 'the only insurance available against the vulgarity of the human heart. Therefore it should be available to everyone in this country and at a low cost.'

This mixture of barefaced challenge and passionate belief was typical of him. He was always putting the slug-horn to his lips and blowing a note to call out the opposition—even the opposition within himself. There was passion in everything he did, from the urgency of his need to go into overdrive when rhyming to the incorrigible cheek of his duel with death itself, every time he nicked the filter off a cigarette and bared his teeth to start on it. He burned not with the hard, gemlike flame that Walter Pater proposed as an ideal but rather with a kind of flame-thrower's whoosh and reach, supple and unpredictable, at once a flourish and a menace. When he used the word 'tyrant', for example, I was always glad that he wasn't talking about me.

He was all for single combat. He took on stupidity as eagerly as tyranny (in his understanding, after all, the latter was simply another aspect of the former), and he was as bold in conversation as he was in print. But the print is what we have of him now, and he will survive behind its black lines, in the pace and agility of its poetic metre or its prose arguments, like Rilke's panther pacing behind black bars with an inexorability set to outpace all limit and conclusion. And he will survive too in the memories of his friends, but for them there will be an extra sweetness and poignancy in the pictures they carry. In my own case, these will always include that first sight of him as a young man in a red woollen shirt, scanning his audience and his fellow readers with an eye that was at once as anxious as a hedge creature's and as keen as a hawk's.

On Ted Hughes's 'Littleblood'

O littleblood, hiding from the mountains in the mountains
Wounded by stars and leaking shadow
Eating the medical earth.

O littleblood, little boneless little skinless
Ploughing with a linnet's carcase
Reaping the wind and threshing the stones.

O littleblood, drumming in a cow's skull
Dancing with a gnat's feet
With an elephant's nose with a crocodile's tail.

Grown so wise grown so terrible
Sucking death's mouldy tits.

Sit on my finger, sing in my ear, O littleblood.

Littleblood. The name could belong to oral tradition, to fairy tale, to the world of *A Midsummer Night's Dream*. It could be a cognate of Peaseblossom and Mustardseed, an escapee from the conversation of Peter Quince or Robin Starveling. Like the names of Shakespeare's fairies (and the fact that Littleblood eats 'the medical earth' confirms this impression), it could be the name of an ingredient in folk medicine, the requisite gout or smear from the cut neck of a bird or the pricked thumb of a spinster. It feels as if it might belong to a whole system of story or lore, and it would be easy enough to mistake the poem where it appears for one translated from some collection of material preserved more for its anthropological than its literary interest.

And of course the poem does belong in just such a collection. In the volume named for him, it is the last of the songs Crow sings, and the tenderest, and follows immediately upon the tundra-cheeps of 'Two Eskimo Songs'. Reading it after the 'Bessemer glare' of all the other poems in *Crow* is like being exposed to some kind of healing ray. Like 'eating the medical earth' and finding in it at least a memory of its pre-atomic-age goodness. And this tenderness is probably why Ted always read it with particular delicacy and intensity, articulating the *t* of 'eating' and the *d* and hard *c* of 'medical' so finely and distinctly they were like the small twig-bones of a bird's skeleton, a robin's, say, since it was a robin's breast I glimpsed—and the poem's mention of a linnet has not dislodged the image—when my mind's eye first blinked at the sight and sound of Littleblood, the name.

Littleblood, the name, only the name . . . To echo Edward Thomas is pertinent because this is to some extent a poem like 'Adlestrop', a poem where the lyric tremor of a proper name releases forces well below the surface. And there is another link between the two poets in so far as both are haunted by the shadow of the war in Flanders, and through that preoccupation with the British Expeditionary Force, they are shadowed too by earlier expeditions, such as the one that culminated at Agincourt. In fact, Littleblood could just as well be found among the *dramatis personae* of one of Shakespeare's history plays, although he would probably fit in better with the pathetic flibbertigibbets of Falstaff's 'mortal men, mortal men' in *Henry IV, Part II* than with the blooded soldiers of *Henry V*: he belongs more in the company of Mouldy and Shadow and Wart and Feeble and Bullcalf than of Gower and Fluellen and Macmorris.

But then, how can we be sure that Littleblood is a he? There is an element of androgyny about this 'little boneless little skinless', something pre-pubertal and Ariel-like. Coming at the end of a book dedicated 'In memory of Assia and Shura', this wisp of a ghost dancer could easily be conflated with the shade of the girl-child who in the meantime has 'Grown so wise grown so terrible / Sucking death's mouldy tits'. Certainly the poem is set in the aftermath of traumatic, even cataclysmic events: the reapers of the whirlwind have prayed for the mountains to fall upon them, and now, 'hiding from the mountains in the mountains', something stirs in the eyehole of a cow's skull, a kind of post-nuclear fledgeling, something as frail as the second coming of pity, that 'naked, new-born babe / Striding the blast', an image which Ted reads (in *Shakespeare and the Goddess of Complete Being*) as proleptic of 'a new kind of agonizing transformation'.

This transformation he characterizes as a shift in the plane of understanding from the tragic to the transcendental, and I have always tended to read 'Littleblood' as an instance of just that kind of transition. It is as if, at the last moment, grace has entered into the Crow-cursed universe and a voice that had hitherto been as obsessive and self-flagellating as the Ancient Mariner's suddenly finds that it can pray. More than a quarter of a century before the publication of *Birthday Letters*, before the appearance of the poem 'Freedom of Speech', in which the shift to the transcendental has clearly occurred, Littleblood is granted this little moment of epiphany, sitting on the poet's finger, singing in his ear, singing the song of both omen and amen.

The note of amen is proleptic: 'Littleblood' looks forward to 'Freedom of Speech', where Ted imagines a birthday party in eternity. The shade of Sylvia Plath is being fêted, Ariel perches on her knuckle and there is happy laughter in the land of the dead. 'So be it', the latter poem says, 'let Ariel perch on a knuckle and let the stars not wound but "shake with laughter".' The note of omen, however, acknowledges that the understanding behind all future poems is going to be darkened, and what gives 'Littleblood' its mysterious, votive power is the co-existence of this tragic understanding with other, more transcendent desires and realizations.

Secular and Millennial Milosz

Born in Lithuania in 1911, Czeslaw Milosz is our secular poet not only because he is almost coeval with the *saeculum* itself but because the term 'the century' keeps recurring all through his work. Decade by decade, the story of his life and the story of his times keep in step. In the twenties, he was a student in Vilnius and Paris. In the thirties, a member of the literary avant-garde in Poland. In the forties, involved with the Polish Resistance, a witness to the destruction of the Warsaw Ghetto and the Nazi defeat of the uprising, then attached to the embassy of the People's Republic in Washington. In the fifties, a defector from that regime, an intellectual in exile in France—his equivalent of forty days in the desert. In the sixties, a professor of Slavic languages at the University of California at Berkeley, in the full summer of his poetic powers, a Solomon among the flower-children. In the seventies, still in full creative spate, his status changing from émigré writer to world visionary. In the eighties, the Nobel Prize winner, a moral and political force in the Poland of Solidarity. In the nineties, a marvel of continuing imaginative vitality, a voice somewhere between the Orphic and the Tiresian.

Milosz lived through nine decades of the twentieth century, but culturally he is as old as the millennium. His childhood and youth in the forest lands of the Issa Valley can be seen to mirror the Dark Ages, when the European mind shifted from folk-belief and taboo to the shimmering systems of medieval scholasticism and Renaissance Neoplatonism. His experience of the ideological and military crises induced by Marxism and fascism could stand for the mid-millennial crisis of the Reformation and the Wars of Religion, just as his flight from ideological extremes into a more Voltairean cast of mind in the 1950s could represent the period of the Enlightenment. Romanticism followed, a total embrace of poetry and a trust in his 'prophetic soul', so that he has ended up on a hill above San

Francisco Bay, a sage on the mountain, maintaining the gravity of being even as he inhales the increasingly weightless, late-capitalist, post-modern air of California.

But all this would not necessarily count for a lot had he not been granted what W. B. Yeats called the gift 'to articulate sweet sounds together'. Milosz's poetry, even in translation, fulfils the ancient expectation that poetry will delight as well as instruct. It has a magnificent balance. The needle is constantly atremble between the reality principle and the pleasure principle: Prospero and Ariel keep adding their weight to either side of the argument. Milosz dwells in the middle, at times tragically, at times deliciously, for he will renege neither on his glimpses of heaven upon earth nor on his knowledge that the world is a vale of tears.

There is something Virgilian in this combination of tender-minded susceptibility and melancholy understanding. Indeed, there is something Virgilian about the curve of Milosz's whole destiny, both as man and poet. Like the Latin poet, he is a child of the countryside, starting at eye-level with the ripening grain and the grazing beasts and ending up at the twentieth-century equivalent of the emperor's court. Both poets have left early work that is confidently lyrical and 'gives glory for things just because they are', but then in their maturity both proceeded to give plangent and abundant expression to their sense of *lacrimae rerum*, in longer and more elaborated works. In these, the subject is 'arms and the man', and the intonation of the poetry becomes increasingly grievous.

For example, a relatively early work by Milosz, a sequence of lyrics written during the war and entitled *The World: A Naive Poem*, belongs in the same pastoral mode as Virgil's *Eclogues*. Virgil's goatherds play their reed-pipes and take part in their song contests in a once-upon-a-time that is nevertheless haunted by contemporary reality. The evictions, the land confiscations, the ravage of the wars that followed the assassination of Julius Caesar are the dark backing behind the mirror-glass of his pastorals. His famous 'millennial' Fourth Eclogue, which Christian apologists would later read as a prophecy of the birth of Christ, was almost certainly a celebration of the Pact of Brundisium, concluded in

40 B.C. between Mark Antony and Octavian, and hence the vision it holds out of a return of the golden age is in fact a coded expression of hope for peace to come in the Roman world—although all that the future held in store for the moment was the Battle of Actium.

The World, which is situated in a similar fashion between the idyllic and the political, was originally printed in clandestine conditions on a hand-press in Warsaw. At a time when the Nazis were occupying the city and concentration camps were opening like hell-mouths all over Europe, Milosz lifted up his eyes to the pre-Copernican sunlight of his childhood home, a country where guardian angels hovered in the air and the security of his parents' house felt like a guarantee of harmony and benignity elsewhere and forever. The idiom of the poem is meant to echo the simplified, big-lettered writing in a child's first primer, and the following section, entitled 'The Porch', is the third in a sequence of twenty:

> The porch, its doorway facing westward,
> With large windows, is warmed well by the sun.
> From here, on all sides, you can look outward
> Over woods, water, open fields and the lane.
>
> But when the oaks have covered themselves in green
> And the linden's shadow covers half the flowerbed,
> The world, far off, fades to a blue bark, half seen,
> Carved by the leaves into dappled shade.
>
> Here, at a little table, the sister and brother
> Kneel drawing scenes of the chase, or of battle.
> A pink tongue between lips helps along the careful
> Great shapes of warships, one of which goes under.

What the poet was conjuring was a vision of the land of Arcadia, in the full and ironical awareness that the only line of defence between it and the land of nightmare was the frontier of writing, the line that has to be held between the imagined and the endured. As in the case of Virgil, the felicity of the art was in itself a heartbreaking reminder of the desolation of the times.

There is no point in labouring this Virgilian parallel. At birth, each poet's imagination was like an infant being rocked and cradled in a shield, and for each of them experience of the shield-world gradually darkened his understanding and blocked out much of the light from the cradle-world—although that light did continue to emanate. Suffice it to say that the picture of Virgil enshrined in Hermann Broch's great prose poem about his death, the picture of a man hallucinating at the centre of the world of *Realpolitik*, a man in thrall to memory even as he was turned to for prophecy, a man at work in the mine shafts of language whom others regarded as a guide to the corridors of power, suffice it to say that this picture also fits the figure of the poet that Milosz has created for our century.

Two challenges which W. B. Yeats set for the artist privileged enough 'to articulate sweet sounds together' were to sec to it 'that civilization may not sink' and to do 'the spiritual intellect's great work'. 'Nor can there be work so great', Yeats declared in his poem 'The Man and the Echo', 'As that which cleans man's dirty slate.' Milosz did not shirk this work of vigilance and chastisement, and his prose writings on the moral and political dilemmas of the age are an indispensable backup to his poetry and novels. In a book such as *The Captive Mind*, Milosz rose to the historical occasion with a work which says *j'accuse* to members of his generation in Poland, his intellectual and artistic peers who collapsed because of either ideological ardour or exhaustion into the arms of Marxism. But what gives the book its edge over other cold war polemics is the fact that it is also saying, 'There but for the grace of God—and my own solitude—go I.' It has an Orwellian clarity and rigour about its ratiocinations, but behind the political and intellectual analyses one senses that the author is witnessing a much older drama, the struggle between God and the Devil for the soul of Everyman.

To put it another way, Milosz will be remembered as one who kept alive the idea of individual responsibility in an age of relativism. His poetry concedes the instability of the subject and constantly reveals human consciousness as a site of contending discourses, yet he will not allow these recognitions to negate the immemorial command to hold one's own, spiritually and morally.

That much, at any rate, he makes clear in a poem called 'Ars Poetica?', where the question mark in the title is no trivial gesture
but a way of acknowledging a doubt about the worth of the poetic
vocation—a doubt as serious as any nineteenth-century Christian's
doubt about the literal truth of the Book of Genesis:

> The purpose of poetry is to remind us
> how difficult it is to remain just one person,
> for our house is open, there are no keys in the doors,
> and invisible guests come in and out at will.

Much is at stake from beginning to end in Milosz's poetry. After
all, the tradition of Christian humanism—the tradition he was
born into and that formed the whole basis of his sensibility—was
under assault from the moment he came to consciousness. His
imagination is supplied and made ample by a fundamentally religious vision, the one based on the idea of Incarnation. What this
entails is an assent to the stark, astonishing proposition that
through the incarnation of the Son of God in the figure of Christ,
the eternal has intersected with time, and through that intersection human beings, though creatures of time, have access to a reality out of time. This is the vision, after all, that gave us much that
is glorious in Western architecture and art—Chartres Cathedral
and *The Divine Comedy*, *The Book of Kells* and *Paradise Lost*, Gregorian chant and the Sistine Chapel—and it still inspires this poet
to occasionally symphonic utterance.

'Perhaps we forget too easily', Milosz once said in an interview,
'the centuries-old mutual hostility between reason, science and
science-inspired philosophy on the one hand and poetry on the
other.' The figure of the poet as somebody on a secret errand, with
ancient and vital truths in his keeping, appeals to him. Cultural
memory, Milosz's work implies, is necessary for human dignity and
survival. Many of the great set pieces in his poems are meant to be
heard within the whole acoustic of literary endeavour; they recognize the seeming frailty of the work done by artists and visionar-
ies, yet they continue to oppose it to the work done by armies and
other forms of overbearing force. The following lines—essentially

a paean to poetic composition—constitute one such passage and are placed at the opening of his sequence 'From the Rising of the Sun', written in Berkeley in the early 1970s:

> Whatever I hold in my hand, a stylus, reed, quill or a ballpoint.
> Wherever I may be, on the tiles of an atrium, in a cloister cell,
> > in the hall before the portrait of a king,
> I attend to matters I have been charged with in the provinces.
> And I begin, though nobody can explain why and wherefore.
> Just as I do now, under a dark-blue cloud with a glint of the red
> > horse.
> Retainers are busy, I know, in underground chambers,
> Rustling rolls of parchment, preparing coloured ink and sealing
> > wax . . .

> *

> Vast lands. Flickering of hazy trains.
> Children walk by an open field, all is gray beyond an Estonian
> > village.
> Royza, captain of the cavalry. Mowczan. Angry gales.
> Never again will I kneel in my small country, by a river,
> So that what is stone in me could be dissolved,
> So that nothing would remain but my tears, tears.

Everything that I admire and trust and turn to again and again in Milosz is in these lines. Not only the deep images, but the deep knowledge. The here and everywhere, the now and always of the poetic moment. That which is existentially urgent and necessary, and yet pondered also, and caught up into the lucid order of poetry itself. Every association that the lines call up is a clarification of their unpuzzling mysteriousness. There is an inner inevitability, a sense that we are in the presence of a source of meaning.

'What is poetry', Milosz once asked himself, 'which does not save/Nations or people?' The exorbitance of the question is natural in one who is a survivor from dark times, who was adjacent to the actualities of the Holocaust and many of whose contemporaries died in the face-to-face gun-battles of the Warsaw uprising.

But for all his self-accusation, Milosz is a poet worthy of his century because he never did forget about the terrible reality of those happenings. At the end of a conference I attended in his honour in Los Angeles in 1998, he said, typically, that although many topics had been discussed, not enough attention had been paid to human suffering. Yet within this man who reminded us of suffering, who had seen tanks erase nations and peoples in Europe and seen the body bags arrive daily from Vietnam at the height of the Haight Ashbury drug culture—within this man the boy who had made his first Communion in the age of innocence still survived; and in spite of the evidence of 'human unsuccess' which assailed the adult, the raptures and entrancements of that boy could never be denied.

Milosz is a great poet and occupies his place in the twentieth-century pantheon because his work satisfies the appetite for seriousness and joy which the word 'poetry' awakens in every language. He restores the child's eternity at the water's edge, but expresses equally the adult's dismay that his name is 'writ on water'. He helps the rest of us to keep faith with those moments when we are suddenly alive to the sweetness of living in the body, and yet he won't absolve us of the responsibilities and penalties of being part of the life of our times.

To celebrate his achievement, therefore, and to give one more illustration of how things that seem feeble or useless can be transfigured by poetry into lifelines for the spirit, I'll conclude by quoting the whole of a brief poem written by Milosz more than forty years ago. The title comes from the first line, 'What once was great':

> What once was great, now appeared small.
> Kingdoms were fading like snow-covered bronze.
>
> What once could smite, now smites no more.
> Celestial earths roll on and shine.
>
> Stretched on the grass by the bank of a river,
> As long, long ago, I launch my boats of bark.

ACKNOWLEDGEMENTS

The bulk of the material in this book appeared in four previous volumes: *Preoccupations* (1980), *The Government of the Tongue* (1988) and *The Redress of Poetry* (1995), all published by Farrar, Straus and Giroux, and *The Place of Writing* (1989), published by Scholars Press. Some chapters were published in separately edited books and others are printed here in book form for the first time.

The following list records either the occasion when the original lecture/broadcast was delivered or the periodical/book in which the writing first appeared. I am grateful to the sponsoring institutions, broadcasters and editors who commissioned the work and gave it its first airing.

S.H.

'Mossbawn': 'Omphalos,' BBC Radio 4 (1978). 'Reading,' *Education Times* (April, 1973). 'Rhymes,' *Worlds*, ed. Geoffrey Summerfield. London: Penguin, 1974.

'Feeling into Words.' Lecture. Royal Society of Literature. London, 1974.

'Learning from Eliot.' T. S. Eliot Centenary Lecture. Harvard University, 1988.

'Belfast': 'The Group,' *Honest Ulsterman* (November–December, 1976). 'Christmas, 1971,' *Listener* (December, 1971).

'Cessation 1994.' As 'Light Finally Enters the Black Hole.' *The Sunday Tribune* (Dublin). 4 September 1994.

'Something to Write Home About.' BBC Northern Ireland, 1998. *Princeton Library Chronicle* (Spring, 1998).

'Earning a Rhyme.' *Poetry Ireland Review*. Spring, 1989.

'On Poetry and Professing': Part I, 'On Poetry and Professing,' Inaugural Darcy O'Brien Memorial Lecture, University of Tulsa (2001). Part II, 'Poet as Professor,' *Poetry Ireland Review* (Spring, 1991).

'Englands of the Mind.' Beckman Lecture. University of California at Berkeley, 1976.

'Yeats as an Example?' Lecture. University of Surrey, 1978.

'Place and Displacement: Recent Poetry from Northern Ireland.' Pete Laver Memorial Lecture. Grasmere, England, 1984.

'The Placeless Heaven: Another Look at Kavanagh.' Opening address. Kavanagh's Yearly. Carrickmacross, Ireland, 1985.

'The Main of Light.' *Larkin at Sixty*, ed. Anthony Thwaite. London: Faber and Faber, 1982.

'Atlas of Civilization.' *Parnassus*. September, 1987.

'Envies and Identifications: Dante and the Modern Poet.' *Irish University Review*. Spring, 1985.

'The Government of the Tongue,' 'Sounding Auden,' 'Lowell's Command' and 'The Indefatigable Hoof-Taps: Sylvia Plath.' T. S. Eliot Memorial Lectures Parts I–IV. University of Kent, 1986.

'The Place of Writing': 'W. B. Yeats and Thoor Ballylee' and 'Thomas Kinsella.' Richard Ellmann Lectures in Modern Literature. Emory University, 1988.

'Edwin Muir.' *Verse*. March, 1989.

'The Redress of Poetry,' 'Extending the Alphabet: Christopher Marlowe,' 'John Clare's Prog,' 'A Torchlight Procession of One: Hugh MacDiarmid,' 'Dylan the Durable? On Dylan Thomas,' 'Joy or Night: Last Things in the Poetry of W. B. Yeats and Philip Larkin' and 'Counting to a Hundred: Elizabeth Bishop.' Lectures delivered while Professor of Poetry. University of Oxford, 1989–1992.

'Burns's Art Speech.' *Robert Burns and Cultural Authority*, ed. Robert Crawford. Edinburgh: Edinburgh University Press, 1997.

'Through-Other Places, Through-Other Times: The Irish Poet and Britain.' Lecture. The Research Institute of Irish and Scottish Studies. University of Aberdeen, 2001.

'Stevie Smith's *Collected Poems*.' As 'A Memorable Voice.' *The Irish Times*. 3 April 1976.

'Joyce's Poetry.' As 'Come into the Chamber of Dreams.' *The Sunday Tribune* (Dublin). 2 February 1982.

'Italo Calvino's *Mr Palomar*.' *The New York Times*. 29 September 1985.

'Paul Muldoon's *The Annals of Chile*.' As 'Filling the Cup above the Brim.' *The Sunday Independent* (Dublin). 25 September 1994.

'Norman MacCaig, 1910–1996.' As 'Listening and Writing.' *The Irish Times*. 27 January 1996.

'Joseph Brodsky, 1940–1996.' As 'The Singer of Tales: On Joseph Brodsky.' *The New York Times Book Review*. 3 March 1996.

'Ted Hughes's "Littleblood." ' *The Epic Poise: A Celebration of Ted Hughes*, ed. Nick Gammage. London: Faber and Faber, 1999.

'Secular and Millennial Milosz.' As 'At forblive kun ën.' *Weekendavisen* (Denmark). 29 October–4 November 1999.